FERDINAND I OF AUSTRIA:
THE POLITICS OF DYNASTICISM
IN THE AGE OF THE REFORMATION

PAULA SUTTER FICHTNER

EAST EUROPEAN MONOGRAPHS, BOULDER
DISTRIBUTED BY COLUMBIA UNIVERSITY PRESS
NEW YORK

1982

EAST EUROPEAN MONOGRAPHS, NO. C

Paula Sutter Fichtner is Professor of History at
Brooklyn College of the City University of New York

FOR MY PARENTS

TABLE OF CONTENTS

PREFACE

In dealing with personal first names, I have used English equivalents for figures who appear repeatedly in the text. Where there are no English equivalents, or where the person in question is of minor significance, the native name has been retained. Place names are those in current local usage—Bratislava, not Pressburg or Pozsony, Székesfehérvár rather than Stuhlweissenburg. The only exceptions are those Anglicizations so widely recognized—Prague, Vienna, etc.—that to revert to *Praha, Wien,* would be an affectation.

Archival sources are usually accompanied by folio citations. Where in the case of the Austrian State Archives *Handschrift, Blau,* 587/1, page numbers were available, these were used. In cases where alternative folio numbers existed, the second set appears in parentheses. The Austrian State Archives has been in the process of reorganizing the holdings of the section *Belgien, PA . . .* used for this study. Where new carton and/or fascicle numbers have been assigned, these have been used if available to me. Otherwise, I followed the numbering found in the *Gesamtinventar des Wiener Haus-, Hof- und Staatsarchivs.*

The following abbreviations have been used:

AG = Archivo general de Simancas
AGR = Archives générales du Royaume, Brussels
AöG = *Archiv für österreichische Geschichte*
ARG = *Archiv für Reformationsgeschichte*
Ččh = *Český časopis historický (československý časopis historický)*
DZG = *Deutsche Zeitschrift für Geschichtswissenschaft*
FRA = *Fontes Rerum Austriacarum*
HZ = *Historische Zeitschrift*
MIöG = *Mitteilungen des Instituts für österreichische Geschichtsforschung*
MöSA = *Mitteilungen des österreichischen Staatsarchivs*
QuF = *Quellen und Forschungen aus italienischen Archiven und Bibliotheken*
SA = Haus-, Hof- und Staatsarchiv, Vienna
ZdG = *Zeitschrift für deutsche Geschichtsforschung*

ACKNOWLEDGEMENTS

Like all books long in the making, this one has incurred many obligations which I hope I can in some way repay. The American Philosophical Society, the American Association of University Women, and the City University of New York supported my research travels over the years, and Brooklyn College subsidized its publication from various sources. The holdings of several libraries were made available to me, notably the library of the University of Pennsylvania, Columbia University Library, the New York Public Library, and the *Nationalbibliothek* in Vienna. I have a special debt in the Austrian state archives in Vienna where my queries and problems have never gone unanswered. Dr. Christiane Thomas and Mr. Clemens Höslinger in the archival library have been unfailingly patient and informative.

Chapters one through seven appeared in a somewhat different form as a dissertation directed by the late Otakar Odložilík at the University of Pennsylvania. James C. Davis served as the second reader. David Daniel, Hans Hillerbrand, Béla Király, and John P. Spielman, jr. read one or more of chapters nine through fifteen. Their comments greatly improved the manuscript. Whatever flaws remain are the sole responsibility of the author.

So many people have encouraged me in this project that thanking them singly here is impossible. Two, however, must be mentioned. Edward Fichtner gave unstintingly of expert editorial and linguistic advice and moral support. Ruth Kleinman unflinchingly vetted more drafts of this than she or I would care to remember. Without her concern and understanding, the book would never have been completed.

INTRODUCTION

THE INNER SETTING

Collectively and individually, the modern Habsburgs were a single-minded lot. Though circumstances may have altered the outward form of their policies through the centuries, their purpose stayed the same— the perpetuation of the house of Austria as a sovereign dynasty. Even those among them who seemed to be driven by other ideals were guided by this consideration. A hardheaded awareness of dynastic self-interest tempered the majestic aspirations of Charles V, the Catholic fanaticism of Ferdinand II, the rationalist enthusiasms of Joseph II and Leopold II. Only rarely did the rulers the family produced lack this quality; those of them who did, notably Rudolph II and the nineteenth century Emperor Francis Ferdinand, were, if not deranged, at least dysfunctionally neurotic.

Not surprisingly, these dynastic concerns dominated the first of the Habsburgs to establish his family's permanent control over the east European kingdoms which, with the Austrian hereditary lands, would constitute the core of the empire which endured to 1918. The relentless consistency with which Ferdinand I (1503-1564) attended the interests of his family so stamped his personality as a whole that one searches in vain there for the inner drama so dear to biographers. Despite the ceaseless religious and political chaos which surrounded him throughout his life and conditioned all his goals, his inward self seems to have been little changed by these experiences. Even his physical appearance was remarkably constant. Small and thin in his youth, nothing distinguished him the way ruddy corpulence marked Henry VIII or surface animality stamped Francis I of France. A full suit of Ferdinand's armour made for him as a mature man measures a little less than five and a half feet high. He maintained that stature until the end of his days when he became, if anything, more haggard. The most striking alterations in his face were a wispy mustache he affected around 1530 to which he added a full beard following the death of his wife, Anna of Hungary, in 1547.[1] Until a year or so before his death in 1564, his outward bearing never betrayed the ravages of bad health unlike Charles who was progressively crippled by gout and arthritis. All of this was undoubtedly the reflection of an unusually sunny temperament. Ferdinand experienced more than the normal share of defeats and frustrations, but he rarely yielded to black despair for very long.

Just as consistent was the moderate, indeed ascetic character of his daily habits, strikingly like those of the future descendant, Emperor Franz Joseph, whose emotional life has also tightly resisted the prying of historians. Ferdinand customarily arose at five in the morning, heard mass, then worked through to the evening on affairs of state. After the death of his wife, one meal, albeit a large one, taken at midday, seemed to satisfy him. Such practices contrasted sharply with Charles, whose indiscretions at table were the plague of his doctors, not to mention the gargantuan excesses of some of the German princes with whom Ferdinand spent much of his time.[2] The one passion to which he was in total thrall was hunting. In this, however, he was no different than any other ruler or nobleman of his time. Like all of his traits, this enthusiasm never left him. It diverted him in the midst of his often unpleasant burdens and enlivened the dreary travel from one part of his lands to another which was his constant lot. He attributed his indispositions to being deprived of the sport, and, as infirmities struck him down in the last years of his life, he measured their impact in terms of his inability to hunt either on foot or from a boat.[3]

For all his personal asceticism, however, he took a keen interest in the world around him and approached it with the unselfconscious *bonhommie* that marked his grandfather, the Emperor Maximilian I. Chance callers were sometimes admitted to Ferdinand's bedchambers while he was yet in his nightcap pulling on his boots.[4] Unlike his mercurial ancestor, however, he was usually mindful of his own limitations. When in 1557, Charles was considering a marriage between his brother or one of his sons, and a Portuguese princess, Ferdinand ruled himself out arguing that not only had he fathered more than enough children to maintain his line, but that his endless wars with the Turks precluded his assuming any new responsibiliites.[5] He was characteristically thoughtful of the physical welfare of subordinates, and his generosity to them bordered on profligacy. Even after his Austrian estates forced him, early in his career, to dismiss his trusted Spanish confidant, Gabriel Salamanca, Ferdinand allowed his ex-advisor to import wine free of toll for his castles in Austria and to stock them with gunpowder from Upper Austrian powder magazines. In 1561, three years before his death and with his debts mounting catastrophically, he was willing to borrow 1000 gulden at 8½% interest to pay his court painter, Jakob Seisenegger.[6] His good-naturedness did not, however, mean that he gave up easily on anything. He was capable of carrying on dynastic financial quarrels over two generations, and his lifelong defense against the ever-threatening Turks testified to his awesome stubbornness more than it did to his leadership.

Ferdinand was not only consistently moderate, open-handed, and tenacious, he was consistently conventional as well. His political ideas closely paralleled those of others in his position. Such were his views on the structure and conduct of kingship. In his eyes, good advisors were essential to prudent rule, and he stressed the need to have such men. He sometimes predicted the policies of fellow rulers on what he knew of the policies of their counselors.[8] He frequently described his relationship as a ruler to those around him with the words "natural" and "rational." That which was "natural" was that which was customary, normal, and corroborated by experience or tradition. The term "rational" was applied to behavior which followed these norms. Thus, in 1522, not in full possession of the titles to the Tyrol and Württemberg, Ferdinand asked Charles to give him total control of the territories on the ground that the Habsburg subjects there would be less rebellious if they had a ". . . seigneur naturel." His way of reassuring Charles that he would treat the latter's daughter kindly as his daughter-in-law was to vow that he would always regard the young woman as one of his own and deal with her as "reason" demanded in that situation.[9]

The familiar medieval organic analogy comparing the body politic to the human body shaped his view of the relationship he had with his subjects. As a result, his own causes and those of his people were reflexively seen as one and the same. As the preliminaries to the Schmalkaldic War in the kingdom of Bohemia got underway in 1546, Ferdinand ordered an assembly of troops from Moravia ". . . for our good and /that/ of this kingdom." Attacks against him were attacks against all Bohemians.[10] As a child in Spain he acquired the notion that rule came through divine mandate; he was unshakably convinced throughout his life that kingship and the office of Holy Roman Emperor came from God and in some way implemented His purposes. For this reason alone, the religious pluralism which the Reformation spawned in Germany was abidingly distasteful to him, even though he was forced to compromise with the Protestants many times.[11]

Such a conception of office brought with it responsibilities; Ferdinand felt that it was his specific duty to protect the Christian faithful and those of his lands in which they lived from invasion. A conqueror like the Turkish sultan in such a frame of reference became a destroyer of an order created by God himself as well as by human arrangements. Ferdinand's will to resist the legions of Suleiman the Magnificant was much stiffened by this attitude.[12] But the unquestioned acceptance of duty brought with it the expectation of equally unquestioned obedience. Ferdinand could be petulantly autocratic when his subjects in any way balked him. When the estates of Lower Austria persistently thwarted him in 1521, he snapped that ". . ./er/ wolt es also haben und nicht anders. . . ." Just a few months before his death, he warned the Styrian estates that it did not behoove them to dispute his decisions too long.[13] However, for all the regal fire that smouldered constantly within him, he allowed it to flare up only under extreme provocation. His general approach to the problems of governance in particular and human relations in general was one of moderation, flexibility and reasoned persuasion. He urged compassion and mildness on Charles V in the latter's suppression of the Spanish *communeros* in 1522. Even though he ordered the execution of one Martin Siebenbürger along with others who had led an uprising against his rule in Vienna and Lower Austria in 1521, he interceded for the lives of Siebenbürger's children. Ferdinand would live to see one of the boys become mayor of Vienna in 1560-1561.[14]

Though his endless battles with the Turks gave Ferdinand a good deal of practical experience with the problems of military organization, the world of warfare and diplomacy unfolded in his mind in the quasi-knightly categories of late medieval chivalry. The age which witnessed the spectacle of the Field of the Cloth of Gold quite unsurprisingly gave rise to a man like Ferdinand who argued with his sister, Mary, in 1549 that ". . . honor and reputation were the things that most marked a man in the world. . . . "

"Honor" was more frequently than not the possession of valued things, "reputation," a word Ferdinand used often in his early years, meant to be deemed worthy of an office or to have earned it. It was in such terms that he calibrated his own gains and losses and those of his family.[15] He was very careful of his public ceremonial image. In October 1544, he refused to attend a meeting of the Order of the Golden Fleece, the premier institution of Burgundian chivalry, because he could not put together a large enough retinue on short notice. He scrupulously observed the formalities of war, wishing it to be clear at all times who was the aggressor and who was fighting in defense.[16] This is not to say that he could not be as hard-headed and cynical as any ruler of his day. Though no military strategist, he had a sharp eye for the value of troops. He was able to distinguish the separate worth of Germans, Italians, Spaniards, Poles and Hungarians to the point where he could sometimes put a spot price on their heads. In trying to tame Margrave Albrecht Alcibiades of Brandenburg-Kulmback-Bayreuth, who was marauding through parts of the Empire in 1552, Ferdinand agreed with Charles that the Hohenzollern might be brought into the Habsburg orbit with a life pension. He was poor, and, in the younger Habsburg's view, such men could generally be bought off.[17] But such cynicism was a strategem for Ferdinand, not a consistent principle, even when his courtliness occasionally backfired on him. When one of his commanders, Hans Katzianer, betrayed him in 1537, Ferdinand had him brought to trial with the promise of a three-month safe conduct. Finding Katzianer's defense inadequate, Ferdinand had him clamped in prison, but because the term of the safe-conduct was not up, Ferdinand could not execute him even though he very much wanted to as an example to others. Katzianer took the opportunity thus afforded him to escape. Under far fewer illusions than his ruler, he refused Ferdinand's second offer of a safe-conduct.[18]

Ferdinand's passion for display, like that of other monarchs of his age, spilled over into the area of monumental building and the arts. He was generous to a fault in his patronage of both. Seisenegger, who entered his service in 1530, was ennobled in 1558 and, along with his legitimate heirs, given immunity from taxation.[19] Music was a favored diversion; even in the midst of serious military campaigns Ferdinand looked forward to performances of things which he had not previously heard. The number of musicians at his court grew steadily throughout his lifetime, and he looked for quality performers thoughout Europe. From 1543 until his death, his *Kappellmeister* came from the Netherlands, the home of the most sophisticated vocal composition of the early sixteenth century.[20]

His sense of quality in matters artistic was as consistent as his other traits. Though he would gain his greatest fame at the Prague court of Ferdinand's grandson, Emperor Rudolph II, it was the grandfather's invitation which brought the great mannerist painter Giuseppe Archimboldo from Milan in 1562 to take up residence in the Habsburg domains. Ferdinand's decorative armour was some of the finest of its day, and he would bequeath his taste for it to his sons.[21] His architectural interests left central Europe with at least two of its most noteworthy Renaissance structures. Throughout his lifetime, Ferdinand pressed for completion of the monumental tomb in Innsbruck which Maximilian I had ordered built for himself. He commissioned the so-called Belvedere in Prague, one of the purest Italianate structures north of the Alps for his wife, Anna of Hungary, and he also undertook the rebuilding of the dilapidated *Hofburg* in Vienna.[22]

Perhaps the only area where Ferdinand stood truly apart from the general run of his fellow-monarchs was in the depth of his involvement in the main intellectual currents of his time. Humanism and the Catholic Reformation touched his life early and deeply. He tried repeatedly to coax Erasmus to the University of Vienna, and, failing that, surrounded himself at his court with men whom he thought embodied humanist ideals of learning and piety. As his career wore on, his religious policies increasingly bore the stamp of Erasmian moderation. Many have attributed his flexibility to various practical considerations, chief among them the need to get military support from Protestant estates as well as Catholic ones. While there is a good deal to this, it would nevertheless be a serious mistake to regard Ferdinand's over-all conciliatoriness as no more than another political strategem. He remained convinced throughout his life that a reformed Catholicism was the only means by which the Protestant schismatics would rejoin the Church, and he was equally certain that it was along the lines of Erasmian brotherliness, peace, love, and joy in faith that these reforms should be carried out.[23] So deep was his commitment to this program that it left him with a curious blind spot—the inability to see that the ideas of the Netherlandic humanist and his followers had some attraction for those who plunged into religious heterodoxy.

It would lead to situations where the blamelessly Catholic Ferdinand would find himself harboring Protestant sympathizers at his court, some of whom gained distressingly great influence on members of his own family. But for him there was no inconsistency between piety and good learning—the one was the complement of the other. Murderous fanaticism was not part of his style, though he was exceedingly harsh in his repression of the Anabaptists and the Bohemian Brethren. His most genuine reaction to what he regarded as the heresy all around him was that of incomprehension—a feeling which could only arise in a man so secure in his own faith that he could not understand those who wanted to leave it. He never ceased to believe that with better religious education, all people would see the merits of the Roman church which were so obvious to him. Its precepts comforted him, and its ceremonies relieved some of his most anguished experiences. By the end of his life, he was hearing two masses a day, one for his wife who predeceased him. Deaths of children were stoically reported, as he bowed his head to a power which he accepted as truly supreme, rejoiced for the soul of the infant, and hoped for other offspring to come.[24]

There was a certain practical cast to Ferdinand's humanistic enthusiasms, just as there was a streak of cynicism in his politics. His appointment of the eccentric and perhaps even deranged Guillaume Postel to a chair in oriental languages at the University of Vienna was in some measure due to Ferdinand's hope to use the scholar's formidible linguistic talents to spread the Christian message in the Ottoman Empire, thereby weakening it from within. Though Peter Canisius, the Jesuit who worked closely with Ferdinand in establishing the Counter Reformation in Central Europe took a dim view of Postel and the whole undertaking, the Habsburg himself apparently felt he could let no opportunity slip to reduce the danger from Constantinople.[25] And for all that he was willing to join in the humanist reform of the church, he did not take criticism of his own position very kindly. When Sebastian Franck's *Chronica, Zeitbuch und Geschichtsbibel* was published in 1531, Ferdinand conceded that its goal of presenting a comprehensive history of the world from its beginnings was certainly a worthy one. There were, however, things in it which he ". . . and other prople of understanding. . ." could not accept, namely a discussion of the destruction of all secular authority. He ordered that author, publisher, and others connected with the book be punished.[26]

Some important matters seem to have passed him by altogether. Aside from a few ritualistic mentions of the Habsburg possessions in the New World as a sign of God's approval of his house, Ferdinand seemed to have little understanding of the significance of the American discoveries. In this, however, he differed little from most Europeans who were as tardy, if not more so, in their appreciation of this new addition to their horizons.[27]

His feeling for the new learning, however, was consistent. He himself was an apt student of languages, impressively fluent in Latin and in French, Spanish, and Italian as well. German he learned somewhat late in life and less thoroughly. He conducted his personal correspondence in all these tongues. Greek and Roman history were among his interests, and he sometimes used it to illustrate his arguments. At times he went out of his way to visit sites noted both for their Christian and classical relics as he did when stopping at Trier in 1540.[28] A contemporary catalogue of his coin collection, something to which he was so attached that his will of 1554 ordered that it be kept intact, was organized around the theme of the Roman Empire and its rulers.[29] Humanistically-trained advisors, who more often than not were of non-noble birth, played key roles in his policies.[30]

Thus, as an adult, Ferdinand's traumas were few and his departures from widely-followed conventions equally rare. His story, then, is best told in terms of his one grand preoccupation rather than in the interrelationship of many small ones. In an era when dynastic rivalries kept the continent in a constant state of potential or actual turmoil, he was a man more haunted than most by the fortunes of his house. Concern for his children and concern for his territories and their inhabitants were one and the same for him.[31] He was as attentive to the interests of his family's dead as he was to its living. Early in his career in Austria, he ordered the completion of various literary and artistic undertakings which his grandfather Maximilian had begun. These included the elaborate *Ehrenpforte,* a fanciful genealogy of the Austrian house, and two autobiographical epics, *Weißkunig* and *Theuerdank.* The last-named was to be distributed throughout the Austrian patrimony as Maximilian had commanded.[32]

The outward trappings and setting of Ferdinand's dynastic concerns differed little from those of his royal counterparts elsewhere in Europe. At his court as at others of the day, public and private concerns seamlessly overlapped. All of Ferdinand's children as well as his wife and other relatives had roles to play in consolidating his hold on his territories. Even when the religious and ideological convictions of some members of his house were unacceptable to him, he, as did Charles, chose to use them rather than outsiders to represent him. Native populations always preferred princes of the ruling house to govern them, the Emperor once observed, and in this instance at least, he and his brother did everything possible to fulfill the wishes of their subjects.[33] The family, in Ferdinand's sententious phrasing of it, was born to bear evil and stand by its members in difficult situations. Though he would be disappointed in this belief many times, especially where military aid was involved, he never rejected it.[34] Even servants were regarded as a collective responsibility, as numbers of them were shifted from Spain to Vienna and back again over the years.[35]

Familial images and terms expressed Ferdinand's relations to others, psychologically as well as biologically. As at the court of France so with the Habsburgs—not only were the sisters, children, and wives of kings subordinate to them but their brothers as well.[36] Despite the fact that Ferdinand became a ruler in his own right relatively early in his career, he was the "son" as well as "brother" to Charles who was the "father" and "lord" until the end of their relationship.[37] Injury to himself, Ferdinand said in 1538, would be serious but not crucial for his wife and children, since Charles would remain as their "father." Loss of Charles, on the other hand, would be a devastating blow for himself, his dependents, and all of Christendom. Charles's advice was "paternal counsel," and all the more valued for that reason.[38] Relationships for Ferdinand, and for Charles as well, were thought to be more special and deserving of consideration if they involved brothers.[39] Indeed, the fraternal bond became a kind of explanatory catch-all for him. Ferdinand interpreted Francis I's support of John Zapolya, his rival for the Hungarian crown after 1526, as the result of brotherly love between Charles and himself, rather than as a reaction to the awesome geopolitical vise in which the Habsburgs had clamped the French king. He assumed, with some justice, that others were as moved by the sense of familial responsibility as he was, and tried to turn it to his own political advantage. At the diet of Augsburg in 1555, he sought to dissuade the princes and electors from including the free knights, who were not represented at the gathering, in their proposals by asking those present to imagine how they and their children would feel if someone tried to legislate for them.[40]

None of this was so natural to Ferdinand that he did it without considerable emotional stress. He was a proud and ambitious man, and his constant subordination to his brother frequently became too much for him, especially where his interests and those of the Emperor clashed. He often could bring himself to follow Charles's dictates only by outright self-sacrifice. In the fall of 1546, as Charles waged war against the German Protestants along the Danube, Ferdinand closed his Austrian territories and the Tyrol to all external commerce. The administrations throughout the provinces complained bitterly, fearing that mercantile routes, especially those to Italy, would be transferred to other areas, such as Switzerland. Ferdinand himself was losing income due to the depression in the Tyrolean salt trade which resulted. He resolved to lift the restrictions, but upon hearing that Charles had shut down the same border commerce in the Netherlands, he resolved to do the same in his own lands regardless of the cost.[41] The presence of such tensions goes far to explain the oft-noted lack of affection between the two brothers and their sisters in their correspondence. Expressions of personal concern were usually perfunctory, though Ferdinand was not beyond an occasional outburst of spontaneous sympathy for the condition of the Emperor. Yet, given the high sense of duty to things other than themselves that Ferdinand and all his siblings harbored, not to mention the infrequency with which they were together, it is perhaps remarkable that they had any feelings for one another at all.[42]

But for all the pain it brought him, Ferdinand found many compensations in his dynastic position, secondary though it may have been for many years. It was only through the agreement of his brother that he acquired the Habsburg Austrian patrimony at all. He well knew that a certain amount of the Emperor's lustre was deflected to him. Through marriage between his children and of Charles, he could speak of their having a "common daughter," thereby giving him a status comparable to that of the Emperor. And in his eyes, someone like his older brother who stood in a "fatherly" relation to someone else, was obliged to look out for the latter, in this case, himself.[43] Furthermore, Ferdinand was not wholly defenseless in his efforts to maintain some independence vis-à-vis the head of his house. He was quick to assert the rights that his various titles brought him, undoubtedly one of the reasons he was anxious to acquire them in the first place.[44]

Thus, Charles had a great deal to contribute to the well-being of both himself and his children. And it was his children who became an all-aborbing concern for Ferdinand—that they should be born, that they should be taught and introduced to their roles as rulers or the consorts of rulers, and finally, that they should be appropriately married. He was duly mindful of the need to produce them, as he informed Charles early in his career, and his wife more than satisfied him with fifteen, including three sons.[45] Each of the boys disappointed him in some way, but he tenaciously moulded them to his purposes, especially Maximilian, the eldest. His dealings with other princes of his day were always partially predicated on the assumption that they were as concerned with the fate of their heirs as he was with his.[46]

With so many offspring to work with, Ferdinand was one of the consummate dynastic match-maters of his age. The institution itself performed a number of functions at once. It helped to shore up friendships, to confirm and even enhance political and social status, and to prevent the dispersion of family resources, all concerns which loomed large in Ferdinand's thinking.[47] Yet, for all the instrumental quality of these arrangements, he did not embark on them without some feeling for the individuals involved. If at all possible, he tried to insure that the marriage partners were temperamentally suited to one another. He took the procedure of gaining the consent of his daughters to the unions he contracted for them very seriously, claiming that if they did this before they were old enough to know their own minds, the marriages usually worked out badly.[48] Those of his children who were clearly unsuited to matrimony he preferred to leave single, as was the case with Archduchess Helene whom he described as homely, physically small, hunchbacked, and, as he put it, "flat."[49] Whether he would have been so considerate with fewer than twelve daughters is another question. Where political interests were truly compelling, his fatherly scruples occasionally weakened. Having had one daughter, Elizabeth, badly treated at the court of Poland where she was married to the young Sigismund Augustus, he was loath to commit himself to another match there. Yet, given the importance of that kingdom, where both the French and the Turks were active in anti-Habsburg designs, Ferdinand went ahead with another marriage, which, predictably enough, was disastrous.[50] He himself was very hospitable to daughters-in-law, provided that they were of appropriate rank. The marriage of his son, Archduke Ferdinand to Philippine Welser of the Augsburg banking family, was a notorious misalliance, and was dealt with as an abnormal situation. But he was very fond of his Spanish niece, Maria, Maximilian's wife, and when she lost one of her children in 1552, he found her own pain harder to bear than the death of the infant.[51]

Thus, Ferdinand was never far removed from the pressure of dynastic relations and the goad of dynastic ambitions. His acquisition of Bohemia and Hungary, his endless conflicts with the Turks, and his responses to the Protestant challenge all took place within this personal frame of reference. It is from this standpoint that the story which follows will be told. No full life will be presented here, but only part of a life. It was a part, however, so consuming for the man who lived it, that it all but became a full life, both practically and psychologically. It goes far to enable a historian to fashion a picture not only of an important but neglected European ruler but of the sixteenth-century Habsburg family understaking as a whole.

CHAPTER I

A THRONE FOR A PRINCE

For the Holy Roman Emperor Maximilian I the year 1515 was a particularly satisfying one. Scarcely a throne in Europe, East or West, sacred or secular, had escaped his covetous glances throughout a lifetime of hectic activity. His plans had ended, as do most human endeavours, in a mixture of success and failure. It would have been hard for him to duplicate the brilliance of his first marriage to Mary of Burgundy, which brought the Netherlands into the Habsburg orbit. The king of France, however, had not sat idly by as Habsburg influence grew on his northern border so that the Austrian dynasty's hold on the totality of the Burgundian inheritance was anything but secure. The emperor's second fiancée, Anne of Brittany, had been all but stolen from him by another king of France, and the third, Bianca Sforza of Milan, who actually did become his wife, did not bring him the improvement in his Italian position for which he had hoped.

His children, the issue of his first marriage, gave him far more reason to rejoice. True, his daughter, Margaret, had been widowed three times with no heirs, but his son, Philip, had more than made up for his sister's unproductiveness. The husband of Juana of Spain, a daughter of Ferdinand and Isabella, Philip's offspring, through a series of unexpected deaths, had become the claimants to the Spanish kingdoms. He and his wife had six children, two boys and four girls, and it was two of the latter for whom their Austrian grandfather found queenships in 1515. The eldest granddaughter, Isabella, married King Christian II of Denmark in the summer of that year. More important for Maximilian was the betrothal of another girl, Princess Mary, to the heir of the thrones of Bohemia and Hungary, Prince Louis of the Polish-Lithuanian house of Jagellon, in Vienna during July. Maximilian had been very anxious to

[13]

establish a Habsburg foothold in Hungary; he had gone to war unsuccessfully over the Crown of St. Stephen when it temporarily had fallen vacant in 1490.[1]

Another betrothal was also agreed upon at Vienna—that of Maximilian's second grandson, Ferdinand, and Louis's sister, Princess Anna—but it was not altogether certain that this arrangement would be realized. Indeed, it was Ferdinand who posed the thorniest marital problem of all for his maternal grandfather, Ferdinand of Aragon, the boy's guardian after his father's death in 1506, and the Emperor. The lone nuptial difficulty connected with the eldest brother, Charles, was that he was almost too rich a prize. Heir apparent to Burgundy, the Spanish crowns, the Habsburg Austrian patrimony, and probable Holy Roman Emperor, he could be married off only after the most tortured calibrations of political advantage had been made.[2] Ferdinand's prospects were in no way so dazzling, and he was correspondingly less desirable a partner.

Born in 1503 in the dusty Castilian town of Alcalá de Henares, this fourth child of Philip and Juana was plunged into turmoil and tragedy almost instantly. His grandmother, Isabella of Castile died in 1504, thereby opening up the question of royal succession in that unruly kingdom, at least in the mind of her ambitious husband. Young Ferdinand's father, briefly King Philip I, died prematurely, leaving not only six young children, but a morbidly deranged wife. Her condition led Ferdinand of Aragon to take his young namesake away from his daughter in 1507 with the cold rationalization that the boy should grow up among men.[3]

Young Ferdinand's place of domicile changed frequently. Sometimes he was with the king, sometimes elsewhere, though in general the grandfather was very fond of the boy who impressed him favorably as a child. He impressed others the same way. His tutor left a laudatory account of his charge's precocity which praised his excellent memory and wide interests. None of this should be taken too seriously perhaps, save for the fact that a far more disinterested Venetian ambassador singled Ferdinand out for exactly the same qualities at the end of his life. From the very beginning, his world was that of court ceremonial and the linguistic formulae with which rulers conducted their official lives. It was a training which made both Ferdinand and Charles models of self-control. A few years before his death, Ferdinand would recall that, amidst all the strain and frustration he had experienced, he had broken down publicly only twice in his life—once when his wife died and once when the Vatican had re-established relations with him after a temporary hiatus in the late 1550s.[5]

From about 1513 to 1516, the year Ferdinand of Aragon died, the two grandfathers cagily felt one another out concerning the future of their youngest grandson. There were reports that King Ferdinand was inclined toward his namesake as his heir in the Spanish kingdoms rather than Charles, but he would make no formal provision for this in his will. Maximilian seemed to be toying with the idea of a division of the Habsburg patrimony as early as 1507, but he then appeared to drop it. Both rulers would clearly have been happier if they could have passed on their territories intact. One solution which attracted both men was to have the young Ferdinand marry Renate of Valois, the youngest daughter of Louis XII, who could bring Milan, a bone of contention among Spain, the Empire, and France, with her in her dowry. But this scheme came to naught, leaving king and Emperor more or less agreed that they should do something for Ferdinand in Italy but unwilling to do anything conclusive.[6]

The 1515 Vienna agreement between Maximilian and Vladislav II of Bohemia (Ulászló II of Hungary) called for either Charles or Ferdinand to be the bride of Anna of Hungary. Later that year, after Maximilian had made the informal promise that Ferdinand would have the status of a king, probably in Naples, it was firmly stated that the prince would be the bridegroom of the Jagellonian princess. But Ferdinand of Aragon's death in 1516 put a stop to any Neapolitan succession. Succeeding to the Spanish crowns, Charles signed a treaty on August 13 of that year with Francis I recognizing French claims to the Italian territory. Maximilian protested and even went so far as to have sketches drawn up which revived an old vision of raising the Habsburg Austrian patrimony to a kingdom.[7] This too, got no further than paper.

For his part the young Ferdinand fell ill when he heard that his Spanish grandfather had died. It was not a wholly inappropriate reaction. Ferdinand of Aragon had not been a total partisan of his young grandson's cause, but he did have it firmly in mind. Now the youth was completely at the mercy of the quixotic Emperor and of Charles. The latter, raised at the court of his aunt Margaret in Mechelen, was surrounded by Burgundian advisors whose sole concern was to advance his fortunes and with them, their own.

It was to this group that Maximilian, visiting Brussels in 1517, had proposed the Austrian kingdom with Ferdinand as its ruler. Charles and his counselors had listened politely, but declined to consider the idea seriously.[8] Ferdinand was not completely destitute. Ferdinand of Aragon had left him a yearly income of 60,000 ducats from Naples, and as Charles's formal regent in Spain, he received 50,000 gulden.[9] Charles offered him continual assurances of his good will. But there was much tension between the two youths, or, more accurately put, between their two sets of advisors and partisans. Charles was the heir in Spain, but there were those in the kingdoms who preferred Ferdinand. As discussions went on among the Spanish and Burgundians concerning Charles's journey from the Netherlands for his new realms, it was decided that Ferdinand should not participate in the departure ceremonies since his very presence might "chill" the whole affair.[10]

Thus the two brothers saw one another for the first time in November 1517 at Mojados, a dry, wind-swept village at the confluence of the Eresma and Adaja rivers west of Valladolid. Contemporary portraits show Charles to have been a thick-lipped, heavy-jawed, and sleepy-eyed young man who looks notably unenthusiastic about the burdens he was to assume. From the standpoint of lips and jaws, Ferdinand, could have doubled for his brother. But his eyes were far livelier, though whether this was from a genuine *joie de vivre* or nervous wariness is hard to say. Charles made every effort at this encounter and subsequent ones to show his brotherly feelings for Ferdinand. On November 18, he presented the younger man with the Order of the Golden Fleece. But from the beginning, it was clear that Ferdinand's position was to be the subordinate one. At their first meeting, it was Ferdinand who held a towel for Charles as the latter washed his hands. On February 7, 1518, at the ceremony in which the Spanish nobility and clergy swore their fealty to Charles, Ferdinand was the first to offer his homage to the new king of Spain.[11]

Even harsher changes were in the offing. Charles's Burgundian counselors and many influential Spaniards, chief among whom was Cardinal Francisco Jiménez de Cisneros who had been directing affairs of state since the death of Ferdinand of Aragon, were much concerned that young Ferdinand's Spanish partisans might still put him forward as a king. In September 1517, even before leaving Brussels, Charles ordered that the most important Spanish members of Ferdinand's court be replaced, so that by 1518, he was surrounded almost completely by French-speaking Burgundians. Once in Spain, the new king and his advisors, led by the black-jowled, acquisitive Guillaume de Chiévres, decided to remove Ferdinand from the Iberian peninsula altogether. Much against the will of the Castilian *Cortes,* many of whose members wished Ferdinand to remain in the kingdom until Charles had produced an heir, it was resolved to shift his residence to the court of his aunt in the Netherlands.[12]

Before 1518 was out, he had arrived in his new quarters after an exceedingly rough voyage during which at one point he and his party had taken refuge at Kinsale in Ireland. The change must have been visually disorienting to him, even though efforts had been made to acclimate him to northern ways even before his departure from Spain. While waiting in Santander for sailing preparations to be completed, he found his meat prepared in a Netherlandic fashion, though exactly what this meant was left unsaid.[13] But the palace of his aunt in Mechelen, under construction upon his arrival, has something constrictingly austere about it, especially when compared to the brilliant visual complexities of the Castilian Isabelline Gothic which Ferdinand had left behind. The strangeness of the new environment, however, in no way meant that he broke his links with the old one. Whether in Spain or not, Ferdinand persisted as a rival to his brother, at least in the minds of others.

This problem became acute again in 1519 when Maximilian himself died, thereby opening the question of the election of a new Holy Roman Emperor. There were those, including even Maximilian at one point before his death, who thought Ferdinand a more suitable candidate than Charles. The pope, Leo X, judged Ferdinand to be more intelligent ("più spirito") than his brother, and, from the quarter of the intellectuals, Erasmus opined that Ferdinand would do a great deal more for the cause of learning than would Charles and his intimates. But the king of Spain and his counselors were most troubled by a suggestion from Margaret of Mechelen that Charles remove himself from the imperial election in favor of his brother.[14] Charles, whose grand chancellor, Mercurino de Gattinara, was drumming into his still-impressionable mind visions of universal empire and the reform of Christendom, stiffly refused. He curtly reminded his brother of the latter's powerlessness and argued that a weak Emperor would mean both the sacrifice of the Empire and the annihilation of their house. Promised by Charles that he would be rewarded for his cooperation, Ferdinand submitted with the self-effacing remark that his place was wherever his king said that it was.[15]

Charles's decision to do something for his brother was not a completely free one. Nor was its eventual price solely of his devising. Maximilian's will called for a division of the Habsburg patrimony among the two youths, a practice which had ample precedent in the prior history of the dynasty. The Emperor's motive seems to have been less a concern for Ferdinand, however, than a wish to have both of his grandsons assume responsibility for his debts.[16] The inhabitants of the Austrian lands were so uncertain over the identity of their next prince that in 1519 the cantors of Maximilian's chapel, who had not been paid for some time, addressed their grievance both to King Charles of Spain and "King" Ferdinand.[17] It was to this question of Ferdinand's share in the family inheritance that Charles promised to turn once the imperial election was over.[18] The matter had become all the more urgent since Louis of Hungary, ruler of that country since his father's death in 1516, was pressing the Habsburg to settle Ferdinand's political and territorial status before the consummation of his marriage to Princess Anna, Louis's sister. The king of Hungary and Bohemia had still hoped that Anna would marry the Emperor rather than his younger brother as had his father and his Hungarian advisors before him. But Charles was not keen on the idea, so that on August 11, 1520, his representatives promised the Hungarians that Ferdinand would, in some form or fashion, be the ruler of the Austrian territories.[19]

The two brothers and their advisors worked out a territorial settlement for Ferdinand during 1521 and 1522. The first of these, signed at Worms on April 23, 1521, was only temporary since it did not completely settle the nature of Ferdinand's rights in the Austrian lands. Either party had the right to petition for a change if one or the other felt that he had not been treated satisfactorily. Ferdinand received the five Austrian duchies—Upper and Lower Austria, Styria, Carinthia, and Carniola (modern Slovenia)—with Charles retaining the mineral-rich Tyrol, certain Dalmatian territories as well as the Habsburg possessions in the westernmost reaches of today's Austria and in southwest Germany. It was also agreed that Ferdinand, and not Charles, would marry Anna of Hungary.[20] However, two of Ferdinand's new principalities objected to these arrangements almost immediately. Both Carniola and Carinthia opposed some of Charles's amputations and threatened to withhold aid against the Turks unless their complaints were redressed. Alarmed by the belligerency of the new sultan, Suleiman, Ferdinand journeyed to Brussels in 1522, there to meet with his brother once again. It was this conference that produced a definitive division of the Habsburg holdings. Ferdinand was given the Dalmatian territories as well as the Tyrol and the other western Habsburg lands. In return, he gave up any political claims he had in Naples, and he also promised to keep the Tyrolean arrangements secret. Charles made him his governor (*Statthalter*) in the Empire to act in his name in his absence. Both agreed to divide the debts of their grandfather, though Ferdinand would never be satisfied with Charles's observation of this stipulation.[21]

The Brussels compact left Ferdinand on a fairly independent footing in the Austrian territories. Indeed, it has been claimed that this arrangement marked the split of the house of Austria into a German and Spanish branch, and, in many respects this is true.[22] Charles's multiple responsibilities would bring him to central Europe very seldom in the years of his emperorship, thus allowing Ferdinand and his offspring to gain a dominant role in steering the affairs of the area. But the agreement continued to stress the joint nature of Maximilian's inheritance. Ferdinand explicitly recognized in it that Charles had received the Habsburg territories undivided and that it was only because of Ferdinand's brotherly love and loyalty that he had consented to such a re-structuring of his dynasty's possessions. Charles would not cease to have some proprietary concerns about Austria which Ferdinand would resent, but also exploit.[23]

The investment of Ferdinand with the five Austrian duchies in 1521 had been enough to move Louis of Hungary and Bohemia to allow the celebration of the marriage of the Habsburg to his sister. The ceremonies, which took place in Linz in that year, marked the beginning of one of the more successful dynastic matches of the age. Though the two had never seen one another until their meeting in the Austrian city, they proved to be an ideal couple. What remains of the oval-faced Anna's correspondence reveals her to have been a deeply, though conventionally, pious lady well suited to some of Ferdinand's most basic traits of mind and character. For his part, Ferdinand seems to have had powerful convictions about the sacredness of the marital bond. His later indignation over the treatment Henry VIII gave to his aunt Catherine was as much moral as it was dynastic.[24] He not only came to his marriage apparently without prior sexual experience–something almost unheard of among the princes of his time–but he never strayed beyond the connubial bed for his pleasures. Contemporary commentators remarked upon the tenderness of the relations between husband and wife, and, even at the busiest moments of his life, Ferdinand was mindful of Anna's feelings. He frequently allowed her to join him wherever he happened to be in his travels.[25]

Thus, when compared with the low point to which his prospects had sunk with the death of Ferdinand of Aragon in 1516, Ferdinand had seen a vast improvement in his position by 1522. He had married a woman of status–she was, after all, the sister of a ruling sovereign and the daughter of status–she was, after all, the sister of a ruling sovereign and the daughter of another. And he had been given territories within which he a gift of his brother. Ferdinand had agreed in 1516 that even the choice of his wife was up to Maximilian and Charles.[26] Much still clearly depended upon the good will and support of the new Emperor and king of Spain. In that vein, Ferdinand's nuptial celebrations in Linz sounded an ominous note. The Spaniards in his own entourage had clashed with the natives, openly making fun of them. In the tournament which was part of the festivities, Ferdinand had had to intervene personally to save a Spaniard from having his head hacked off by an Austrian. It was a minor matter, to be sure, but not the sort of thing that should happen when cooperative ventures between the two peoples and their rulers were to be in the offing.[27]

More immediately problematic however, was the question of how valuable a prize the Austrian heritage was for the young Spanish prince. In 1521, when he and Anna arrived in Vienna, the city was racked with plague, hardly an auspicious beginning for any reign.[28] Worse yet, for a ruler with both taste and ambition, was the cloudy financial picture in the Habsburg lands. The fiscal records of Ferdinand's Austrian administration down to 1547 are unfortunately spotty. It can be said with some confidence, however, that the territories were capable of providing adequate revenue, at least in 1521. In that year, total income amounted to 191,680 pounds against 151,391 pounds in expenditures. In 1523, Ferdinand was able to coax 150,000 gulden out of the Tyrolean estates, a sum which even the popular Maximilian had been unable to command. Due to arrangements worked out over previous centuries with Rome, the Austrian archdukes also enjoyed a healthy share in the revenue from church properties in their domains, one of the reasons Ferdinand would always take great pains to stay on good terms with the papacy.[29] But there were significant soft spots in all of this, especially if the system were to be strained in any way.

Most immediately troublesome were Maximilian's debts which not only amounted to 800,000 rhenish florins and far outstripped the capacity of the Austrian territories to repay them, but also encumbered some of the most precious resources in the Habsburg lands. Chief among these were the silver mines of the Tyrol. By the time of Ferdinand's arrival in Austria, these had been so heavily mortgaged to the Fuggers of Augsburg that the new archduke could not mint enough coinage from them for his peoples and himself. The German bankers, on the other hand, drew a yearly income of 200,000 gulden from the mines of Schwatz.[30] One of the first things that Ferdinand did after the death of his brother-in-law, the king of Hungary, in 1526 was to melt down the gold and silver in the latter's household for use of the mint in Vienna.[31] Nor had the Habsburg patrimony, especially in its eastern reaches, participated in the general economic upturn of the second half of the fifteenth century. A good deal of Viennese capital had been dissipated during the sporadic civil war between Ferdinand's great-grandfather, the Emperor Frederick III and his brother, Archduke Albrecht between 1450 and 1470. Moreover, the general patterns of European trade now seemed to favor the merchants of upper Germany rather than those in the east.[32] Maximilian had not troubled himself much with this, nor would Ferdinand, at least consistently. Both turned to the big capital houses of southern Germany for their loans and allowed foreign merchants staple rights in Vienna and elsewhere. Ferdinand, however, would feel this lack of a domestic economic base very acutely since, over-extended or not, the Austrian lands would furnish him with the bulk of his capital, particularly in military ventures.[33]

Ferdinand's new subjects were not only less rich than he would have liked; they were less religiously orthodox as well. The Lutheran Reformation had spread quickly to Austria after 1517, taken up at first by the nobility who had used their traditional rights as advocates and patrons of ecclesiastical foundations to protect Lutheran preachers. Like many of their German counterparts, they could not resist the chance to improve their economic position through the opportunity afforded them by the new confession to add secularized church lands to their holdings. Neither the city council of Vienna nor its bishop gave the university any support in 1521 when the theological faculty tried to argue against the Wittenberg reform. The next year, an evangelical preacher, Paul Speratus, appeared in the cathedral of St. Stephen itself to speak on marriage of the priesthood and justification by faith.[34]

Spurred on by his brother's Edict of Worms, issued at the imperial diet in 1521, which in effect outlawed Lutheranism, Ferdinand moved quickly against the new sect. His successes were trifling. If anything, the measures which he took only heightened the interest of the Austrians in the new teachings. In the Tyrol in 1522 and in Lower Austria in March 1523, he issued mandates forbidding the printing of Lutheran books and toleration of Lutheran and other evangelical preaching. But soon after the latter decree had appeared, multiple editions of Lutheran works came out in Vienna. When Ferdinand ordered the execution of a Lutheran merchant in the city in 1524, such a public outcry arose he feared to leave his capital lest disturbances break out which he could not control.[35] His efforts to make the orthodox confession more persuasive by improving the morals and education of its clergy also failed. During his early years in Austria, he tried to name learned laymen and worthy clergymen to important ecclesiastical positions and committees which sat in judgment over religious deviants. Along with other south German Catholic prices he signed the Regensburg Convention of 1524. While binding all parties to oppose the new religious teachings within the areas of their political authority, the agreement also called for improvements in the education and supervision of Catholic clergy in each territory and correction of financial abuses within local ecclesiastical establishments.[36] But, in fact, despite his self-serving assertion a year later that Lutheranism was no longer spreading in his lands, Ferdinand was clearly mistaken. The ritualisitc mandate against the sect contained in the Regensburg Convention was desecrated in Vienna when the accord was published there.[37]

Two additional factors intensified Ferdinand's opposition to the Lutherans. One was the potential which he felt that movement had for inspiring further sectarianism, such as Anabaptism.[38] The other, and the far more serious one upon his arrival in Austria, was the connection which the reform seemed to have with the explosion of peasant unrest which he found there. This outburst, a complex mixture of political, social, economic, and religious grievances, began in the Tyrol in 1519 and soon had counterparts in other Habsburg territories. For Ferdinand, possibly under the influence of one of his earliest confidants, Johann Heigerlin, an enthusiastic Erasmian known as Faber, distinctions among types of causes were of little meaning. By whatever reasoning it was that the peasants settled on their demands, he was against them, especially when they asserted that it was only they who would decide what they would pay their lords or that they were the equals of princes and kings.[39] He was also badly frightened, especially when even his most trusted advisors, such as the bishop of Trent, Bernhard von Cles, said that the rebellion was directed against higher authority.[40]

The upheavals were especially grave in the Tyrol and the archbishopric of Salzburg, the latter not directly under Habsburg control but of key strategic importance since it fronted on so much of the dynasty's patrimony. The mountainous terrain of both areas made it very difficult to subdue the peasants. Cavalry could not be used there and Ferdinand found his infantry unreliable, drawn, as it was from the very class of people it was supposed to be fighting.[41] The uprisings ended in a series of compromises which Ferdinand did not like since he felt they were much to the advantage of the peasants. To the Tyrolean demand that the bishopric of Brixen be secularized, Ferdinand agreed to take over the management of the see until a general church council was called. He issued a new set of orders easing the financial burdens which the nobility could expect the peasantry to bear. Compulsory services which had not existed for fifty years were abolished, and clergymen were to be subject to the jurisdiction of secular courts. In Salzburg, the peasants and the archbishop came to their own accord. The revised regulation of peasant dues was extended to all the Austrian provinces in 1526 and 1527. Five years later, however, Ferdinand rescinded all the changes.[42]

A further chaotic element which Ferdinand encountered in Austria upon his arrival in 1521 was the near-complete collapse of the legal and administrative structures which his grandfather had established. In 1517, Maximilian had planned that a functioning bureaucracy and a permanent court council would be in place when his grandson appeared, but, if anything, the Emperor's efforts only complicated things for his young heir. For all his unpredictableness, Maximilian had a keen interest in administrative organization, something Ferdinand would inherit from him, and he had spent much of his reign in Austria trying to wrest control of political and legal institutions from local estates and individual feudatories. Among his particular targets had been provincial judicial arrangements which he sought to replace with tribunals representing himself, made up of his own appointees, who were not necessarily residents of the area where they presided. Reaction to this had been bitter. The nobility resented not only their own displacement from judicial seats but the fact that their ruler would not judge them directly even where his own justice was called for, and Maximilian had been hard put to make these innovations permanent.[43]

At the moment of Ferdinand's accession in 1521, the Tyrol and the Habsburg territories in southwest Germany were subordinated to an administration in Innsbruck while Upper and Lower Austria, Styria, Carinthia, and Carniola each had a separate administration representing their ruler. Maximilian had ordered in his will that these bodies were to stay in office after his death, but he never communicated this wish to the individual provinces in writing. To one degree or another, they ignored their ex-prince's command. The lone exception was the Tyrol, and even there the peasants took the absence of a reigning count as a license to plunder his game preserves.[44] Such actions reflected not only general resentment of what was felt to be the usurpation of local authority or of venality and arbitrary procedures which were especially prevalent in the administration of Lower Austria. They also stemmed from a constitutional conviction within the individual estates that rule actually passed to them upon the death of a ruler and could only be transferred to the latter's successor after he had confirmed the privileges of the individual territories and they, in turn, had sworn their fealty to him. The estates of Lower Austria not only erected their own administration, but delegated such princely prerogatives as the coining of money to themselves.[45]

Ferdinand's early relationship to his new lands did little to soothe this restlessness. He was, for one thing, distressingly ignorant of their customs and organization. As late as 1524, for example, his counselors from Lower Austria had to tell him that he need not turn to the pope to request diversion of Austrian ecclesiastical incomes for use against the Turks, these, from time immemorial having been part of the *Kammergut* which the Austrian rulers could use as they wished without asking the permission of the church.[46] Furthermore, from the years 1520 to 1522 he was in Austria only intermittently, preoccupied as he was with the division of the Habsburg territories with Charles. And finally, from the very beginning of his reign, Ferdinand made it clear that he intended to follow his grandfather's model and appoint whom he wished to various administrative, judicial, and advisory bodies, regardless of their territorial origins. That he had to tell this to a committee of the Upper Austrian estates in 1521 with the help of a translator since he could not as yet speak German did not help his cause.[47]

Once, however, the formalities of the oaths of fealty were actually observed, these mutinies seemed to die down of their own accord. Only in Lower Austria did a coalition of the nobility and the Vienna city council led by Dr. Martin Siebenbürger stubbornly refuse to come to terms with their young ruler. Ferdinand initially hesitated to use force against the dissidents, claiming that he had more important things to do. When persuaded by his advisors that to let the matter ride would be to invite future disobedience, he yielded with a laconic, "ergo fiat justicia."[48] In July 1522, he brought the dissident leaders before a court in Wiener Neustadt, made up of Bavarians, Burgundians, and others whose only common denominator was their lack of roots in Lower Austria. In the sentencing that followed, Ferdinand was relatively mild. Two leaders of the aristocratic party were condemned to death along with Siebenbürger and five members of the Vienna city council. The city as a whole lost many of its municipal and juridical privileges. The back of the rebellion was broken, but Ferdinand's relations with his new subjects in the area did not measurably improve as a result. If anything, his actions accelerated the spread of Lutheranism in Lower Austria, the only avenue of protest which remained for the dissatisfied.[49] Ferdinand himself was convinced that mixing clemency and severity was a way of promoting both fear and love among his peoples.[50] What he got was a kind of grudging acquiescence which, while it might have added up to the same thing, was in reality no where near as high-minded as Ferdinand's formulations.

Thus, while Ferdinand certainly had ended up with far more in the division of the Habsburg territories than he had originally had, his situation was far from comfortable. Faced with Lutheranism which he would always equate with sedition, a population hostile to his administrative and judicial techniques, and a not altogether firm financial base, he was in no way a fully independent ruler. To do much of anything, he would need more substantial resources than his Austrian territories were willing or able to provide. His brother, the Emperor, was his most likely supporter. In the heat of his concern for the emperorship, Charles had once promised Ferdinand that they would do great things together, if Ferdinand would only remove himself from the candidacy.[51] But Ferdinand's first few years in Austria saw few indications that Charles intended to live up to this vow.

CHAPTER II

"WE TWO WHO REPRESENT YOURSELF . . ."[1]

The frank mistrust which Charles and his advisors bore Ferdinand which began with the brothers' Spanish days abated only slowly. Well into the 1520s the Emperor kept a watchful eye on the archduke in Austria, at times making it plain that he doubted the younger man's capacity to rule effectively. Nor did Charles appear anxious to promise his brother any wider role in the Empire other than that of a decidely subordinate lieutenant.

As far as the Austrian situation was concerned, Charles had good reason to keep his brother under some supervision. The protests that had resounded throughout the Habsburg patrimony through the first years of Ferdinand's reign had not only been due to general religious and economic unrest; they also arose from a deep popular hostility to some of the people whom Ferdinand had chosen to advise him.

From the beginning of his career to its end, Ferdinand was the willing victim of rapcious intimates. The streak of gregariousness in him meant that he spent vast amounts of time in audiences with people from all backgrounds. As a result, the business of state dragged, despite his enormous personal capacity for work, and he often examined the most important matters only fleetingly. Much, therefore, was left to advisors, many of whom were more than normally venal. Nor, aside from a few, were any of them exceptionally gifted statesmen though Ferdinand clung to them tenaciously.[2] It was one of his major weaknesses as a ruler, explicable in part by his general agreeableness and distaste for open confrontations. He would deal with the failings of his sons in much the same way. In his later years, such counselors were merely burdens on his reputation and on his finances. In his young manhood in Austria however, his

[27]

attachment to such people threatened his authority, and it was for this reason that Charles was disturbed.

Both brothers were more than ordinarily dependent upon advisors. Neither of them had much practical political experience when they came to rule their restive territories, and both needed older men to look out for their interests. Ferdinand, of course, had scant protection save the provisions in Maximilian's will that guaranteed him some share of the Habsburg patrimony. Therefore, he, even more than Charles, could not help but pile up vast debts of gratitude to those who could bargain fruitfully for him with his brother and his counselors. It was in these circumstances that a Spaniard, Gabriel Salamanca, made himself especially helpful to the archduke.

Salamanca's orgins are obscure. The date of his birth in Burgos is unknown as is the avenue by which he came to the Habsburgs. After 1514, however, his name appears in documents which concern both Maximilian and Charles. He went with Ferdinand to Worms in 1521 and again to Brussels in 1522 where he was instrumental in working out the partition agreements between the two brothers. He apparently persuaded Charles's confessor, who in turn persuaded his charge, that a scheme to keep Ferdinand from fathering legitimate heirs by forbidding him to marry was unchristian and punishable by God.[3]

In general, Ferdinand rewarded the Netherlanders and Spaniards who accompanied him to Austria handsomely. His first steward, Claude Bouton, received 700 gulden from the confiscated goods of the Viennese citizenry executed in 1522. When he left Ferdinand's service in 1524, he enjoyed a pension of 800 gulden a year. Bouton's successor, Antoine de Croy, was given a 1000 gulden annual supplement to his income, retroactive to 1520 when he left the Netherlands for Austria. After departing Ferdinand's employ in 1527, he drew a pension of 500 gulden a year. These were generous sums when one considers that in 1522, the diet of Nürnberg estimated that the average wage for a German artisan was six gulden for one month's work.[4] Salamanca was among the chief beneficiaries of the archduke's largesse. By 1524, Ferdinand already owed him 180,000 gold ducats and had granted him large numbers of fiefs and incomes throughout the Austrian lands, especially in the Tyrol.[5] The large number of "foreign" advisors around both Charles and Ferdinand provoked much outrage in Austria, and Salamanca became the focus of this ire.

In 1523, a Tyrolean chronicler, Georg Kirchmair, complained that Salamanca was the true ruler of Austria and that the Tyrol was governed by
a "Spanish count through Spaniards." A jingle scrawled on the castle in
Nürnberg where the diet met in 1524 under Ferdinand's supervision advised that he would be a far greater ruler than he was if he imprisoned
Salamanca and hung Jacob Fugger outright![6]

By 1523, news of this side of Ferdinand's administration had already
displeased Charles. Part of his irritation no doubt stemmed from his
suspicion, or the suspicions of those around him, that Salamanca had
persuaded Ferdinand to delay entering a treaty with the Venetians which
the Emperor was anxious to have in order to separate the republic from
France. Ferdinand had protested that he had no reason to ally himself
with a country which was a ceaseless threat to his own interests, but he
eventually yielded to his brother's wishes.[7] Charles, however, was not to
be placated as far as Salamanca was concerned.

In addition to his regular ambassador at Ferdinand's court, the Emperor
dispatched another, Michael Gilles, to observe his brother and his Spanish
confidant in 1523.[8] The envoy reported that the younger Habsburg was
surrounded by people who ". . . neither spoke nor understood German . . ." and who knew nothing of the customs and different interests
of the Austrians.[9] Still another imperial representative, Jean Hannart,
appeared in 1524 to consult with Ferdinand on the Salamanca issue.
By this time, as the Nürnberg graffiti told, some of the resentment of
Ferdinand's court had begun to spill over into the Empire at large, and
Charles, still regarding the Habsburg lands as ". . . his hereditary patrimony . . . ," instructed Hannart to tell Ferdinand that his Spanish advisor
must go.[10]

Ferdinand's defense of Salamanca, angry though it was, was in terms
of the interests of the two brothers rather than his own. He argued that
those who were maligning the Spaniard to Charles were doing so only to
spread discord among the Habsburgs and that others would try to do so
again in the future.[11] Charles himself was decidedly taken aback at the
vehemence of his brothers' protests. At first he somewhat lamely denied
that he had ever signed Hannart's orders. This was not altogether out
of the question, given the bureaucratic confusions of the day, though it
is hard to believe that Hannart would have presented such harsh instructions to Ferdinand had he not received them from the Emperor himself.

In any case, Ferdinand had made his point. By the end of 1524, Charles had recalled Hannart with assurances to the archduke that the envoy would be punished if necessary.[12] Any information that Ferdinand had to offer on Hannart's presumptuousness would be welcomed. Whether or not Charles signed this precise set of instructions is perhaps less important than his apparent general willingness to believe negative things about his brother's court.[13] But also important was his refusal to interfere too deeply in his brother's affairs, as badly conducted as they were, when the latter defended himself vigorously.

Ferdinand held stubbornly on to Salamanca until the Tyrolean peasant uprising in 1525. At that point, the estates demanded that the administration of the territory be staffed with Tyroleans and that Ferdinand's own counselors be natives of the Austrian hereditary lands. It was plain that the real target of these requests was Salamanca. In the fall of 1525, all of Ferdinand's lands asked that he convoke a general diet where his administrative policies could be discussed. Feeling it would be dangerous not to heed them, he yielded, calling their representatives to meet with him in Augsburg where he was also preparing for a session with the imperial diet.[14] The continued peasant unrest in the Tyrol may have become something of an embarassment to him. The troubles had lasted longer there than in any other German territory, thereby giving the image-conscious Ferdinand the appearance of being the least powerful among the German princes.[15] Charles advised him not to antagonize his subjects at so delicate a time, since Ferdinand was about ready to ask them for aid against the Turks.[16] Reluctantly and somewhat sulkily, he finally gave in, and, in 1526, removed Salamanca from his official position in his treasury. The archduke soothed his wounded *amour propre* with the comment that most of his subjects were sorry for what they had proposed and that the real agitators among them were few in number.[17] But he did not dispense with Salamanca's talents, nor, did he cease to reward him. The Spaniard was entrusted with future diplomatic missions to England and Hungary, and, foreshadowing Wallenstein one hundred years later in the service of Ferdinand II, used the archduke's armies as the outlets for the crops and goods which he produced on his own lands. By 1535, Ferdinand owed him 22,530 florins. As late as 1539, even Charles found him useful.[18]

Charles's limited confidence in his brother in Austria was no more extended when it came to Ferdinand's activities in the Empire. Not that

that sprawling hodge-podge of parochial interests was any more promising a forum of activity for an ambitious young prince than was Austria. Looked at as a totality, the Empire was both rich and populous, but its actual government was in the hands of around 2,500 local and regional authorities. Of these, around 500 were represented in the tricameral diet, which met periodically with the Emperor to bargain with him on taxation and discuss matters of general importance. The rest, the so-called imperial knights, controlled among them less than 250 square miles of territory and were largely concentrated in the southwest of the Empire. At the end of the fifteenth century, Maximilan had tried to strengthen the financial and administrative position of the Emperor, but his efforts had foundered on the not-wholly unjustifiable suspicion of the estates that such moves were far less in the interests of Germany than they were calculated to expand Habsburg *Hausmacht*. Even before Maximilian, his father, Emperor Frederick III, had been accused by Matthias Corvinus, the king of Hungary, of using the Empire for these purposes, and, in truth, the requests for aid which both father and son had made of the diet were constant.[20] If the Habsburgs were not fighting the French they were fighting the Turks, who had been inching their way up the Danube valley throughout the century; given the shaky financial position of several Renaissance German princes, perhaps the wonder is that they attempted to cooperate with their sovereign at all.

Charles had made his first lengthy appearance in the Empire at the diet of Worms in 1521. Anticipating lengthy absences from the territory, he set up an imperial administration (*Reichsregiment*) to replace him during these times with Ferdinand, his *locumtenens,* as his special representative in the body. The imperial estates took no more kindly to the non-German speaking archduke than did the Austrians, and Charles was forced to name Count Frederick of the Palatine to serve in the administration in Ferdinand's place. The government was " . . . ein Teutsch Regiment . . ." as some princes and their counselors complained in 1522; they went on to point out that since only a minority of the diet's membership understood Latin, much business would have to be done through translators. Thus, man to man negotiations with Ferdinand would be impossible, unlike the relationship which the princes had enjoyed with his accessible grandfather. And finally, the Germans did not like the air of proud ambition that Ferdinand, for all his linguistic shortcomings, could not hide.[21]

Looked at instrumentally, the *Reichsregiment* was almost wholly ineffectual. In 1523, it stood by helplessly as the Swabian League, one of the stronger regional defensive organizations in the Empire, waged private war against the Franconian nobles and robber barons who infested the highways. Nor could it do much to control those German noblemen who went into battle of their own accord against a rebellion of the imperial knights which broke out in that same year under the leadership of Franz von Sickingen. When it acted, it invariably angered important members of the estates. An import tax, suggested as a money-making device in 1523, immediately drew fire from the major cities.[22]

But for all their very real weaknesses, the Empire and its institutions offered Ferdinand something that Austria did not—the opportunity to work with his brother on significant matters. The heroic deeds which Charles had promised that he and Ferdinand could do together, especially against the infidel, were possible only if the resources of the Empire could be mobilized. Despite the infrequency of his visits to Germany, a never-ending source of displeasure among the estates, Charles cared very much about affairs there. The spread of Lutheranism disturbed him deeply; although he was to make numerous compromises with the so-called heresy under the compulsion of circumstances, he would never give up on his vow to eradicate it. For all of its stubborn hostility to Habsburg ambition, the Empire was to be an invaluable source of men and money for Charles in his episodic struggles with France over the mastery of Italy and Burgundy which spanned his entire reign. It was Charles, for example, who vetoed the import tax that his *Regiment* was trying to collect for its own support, out of fear that the German cities would deny him the aid he needed in his wars.[23]

Thus the Empire afforded Ferdinand the best way to prove himself in the cooperative activities which his brother had promised to reward. His initial appearances there, however, were anything but impressive. For one thing, he owed 900 gulden from his Austrian lands and 600 from the Habsburg protectorate in Württemberg as his contribution toward the maintenance of the *Regiment,* but was unable to pay it. Furthermore, when the papal nuncio, Chieregati, appeared before the administration in 1522 to ask that the German princes try to halt the spread of Lutheranism in their lands, Ferdinand took the Roman side against the majority of the Germans who refused to do so. In the midst of the heated debate, Ferdinand cried out somewhat squeakily, "I am here as the representative of the Emperor." "Indeed," said Hans von der Planitz, the spokesman of electoral Saxony, "but along with the council and proceeding according to the statutes (*Ordnungen*) of the Empire."[24]

Two diets met during the years 1522-1523 and 1524 at Nürnberg, and Ferdinand acquitted himself especially well at the second. It was at this meeting that the *Reichsregiment*—Ferdinand's sole base of influence in the Empire—came under heavy fire from influential members of the estates. The bishop of Würzburg, for example, asked for exemption from its court, and others demanded its complete abolition though they could not agree on anything to replace it.[25] It was this lack of unity upon which Ferdinand and Hannart, Charles's representative at the diet, capitalized in their rescue of the body. Through a series of concessions, postponements and individual agreements, the two were able to extend the life of the administration for two years and to win agreement to a general tax for its support as well.[26] Their divide-and-conquer technique was particularly effective with the towns. They met with no more than two or three of them at a time, and major urban centers such as Frankfurt, Ulm, and Augsburg were frequently reminded of how much of their prestige was due to their status as imperial free cities, directly subject to the Emperor and the sites of the diets whenever they were held. By March 1524, the municipalities had been broken down into three groups. There were those powerful enough to preserve the *Regiment* or to destroy it and who had agreed to its continuation, those who were not strong enough to affect the situation but who could be counted on for a contribution if some of their objections were satisfied, and those who had already left the meeting but who would probably pay their allotted share. The nobility was assured that if only they promised some financial support to the body, its staffing would be congenial to them. Considerably mollified, they claimed that a change in personnel of the institution was all they had wanted.[27]

Ferdinand also proved at that same diet that he could save his brother much embarrassment in foreign affairs. Weary of supporting his conflict with France and anxious to have a sovereign who lived in Germany, the diet resolved to dispatch two embassies. One was to go to Francis I to open peace negotiations, the other was to appear before Charles to ask him both to bring an end to the hostilities and to shift his residence.[28] Ferdinand's reaction to this was to meet the estates head on with no prior consultation of his brother. Fearing that these emissaries would discuss far more than peace with Francis, the archduke forbade them categorically to see the king. It was all done ". . . a la facon d'Espaigne. . ." as Hannart put it, and the princes had done much muttering among themselves about this kind of treatment. However, when Ferdinand threatened that ". . . he would be forced to do something that he did not want to do. . . ," the estates gave in.[29] Again, he and Hannart had taken advantage of German disunity in gaining their end. The smaller cities, for example, had been much opposed to sending a mission to Spain because of its cost.[30] Just how much of the outcome of these negotiations was due to Hannart and how much to Ferdinand is hard to say. There was much hostility between them in 1524 over the Salamanca affair, and each reported their activities in blatantly self-serving terms. Hannart stressed the archduke's inexperience, and Ferdinand complained that Charles should have sent ". . . quelque grant et notable personnaige. . ." to deal with the Germans whom he depicted as increasingly envious of the house of Habsburg. He did not accuse Hannart of acting against the Emperor's interests. However, the archduke wanted to make it clear that he had been as key to these victories as had been the ambassador. Charles's open gratitude was the reward he sought, and he got it.[31]

As anxious as he was to please his brother, Ferdinand was not without his own concerns at Nürnberg. During the 1522 discussions in Brussels over the division of the Habsburg lands, Charles appears to have made at least a verbal promise to the younger man that he would succeed him in the Empire.[32] Technically, the election of this successor, the King of the Romans of the German Nation, as the full title read, could not take place until the Emperor had been crowned by the pope. However, though Rome was in no hurry to perform this ceremony for fear of seeming pro-Habsburg, Ferdinand saw no reason why he should not start a modest campaign on his own behalf among the seven current electors, whose office had been charged with naming the German ruler since the fourteenth century. He began, properly enough, by working on his brother, urging him that if he could not get to Rome for the imperial coronation, he have it done by papal bull as had been the case with Maximilian. He conjured up the most extravagant prospects of the services he could render his dynasty as a king. He would have far more power to conduct the affairs of the Empire in Charles's absence than he did as a mere *locum-tenens*. He would have more leverage to make necessary changes in the *Reichsregiment*. In general, the house of Austria would see an incremental leap in its grandeur through his elevation to the office. After he attained his majority in 1524, his suasions grew even more relentless.[33]

Though Charles gave him no encouragement, Ferdinand did not hesitate to open talks on the matter at the diet of Nürnberg in 1522-1523. Quiet discussions were continued at the gathering in 1524 where, for the first time, the divisive impact of Ferdinand's ambitions within the house of Habsburg made itself felt in a small way in Germany.[34] Crucial to the archduke's plans was the support of the elector of Saxony, Frederick the Wise. Though Ferdinand took the dimmest view imaginable of Luther and Lutheranism, he resolved to sidestep any airing of the religious issue with the estates even though there was much sentiment for a serious discussion of these matters.[35] Ostensibly his reason was to get the Germans to concentrate on his requests for aid against the Turks, but he also did not want to prejudice the matter of his election in any way.

The archduke opened the diet without having any instructions from his brother on how to deal with the confessional question. The mood of the Lutheran sympathizers was sour from the start due to the appearance of a papal legate, Cardinal Campeggi, who, uninvited either by Ferdinand or Charles, had come with the idea of forming a league among the German princes in support of clerical reform. When Hannart, delayed by floods, finally arrived with his orders from the Emperor in the middle of February, these called for the strict enforcement of the Edict of Worms. It was a far cry from the soft-pedalling of religious matters which the archduke had been promoting, and the Saxons were quick to conclude that Ferdinand did not have the trust of his brother.[36] The soundings which Hannart took among the electors did nothing to increase the Emperor's confidence. The ambassador reported that the seven were generally unenthusiastic about Ferdinand as a prospective king because of his youth and his foreign counselors.[37]

Charles, moreover, did nothing to improve his brother's standing among the Lutherans. The Emperor followed up his harsh instructions with a letter in April in which he urged his brother and Campeggi to do everything in their power to uproot the heresy.[38] But the diet refused to endorse the strict enforcement of the Edict of Worms, so that Ferdinand resorted to issuing a private mandate which ordered this.[39] In order, however, to preserve some sort of position among the evangelicals, the archduke agreed to the calling of a national rather than a general church council which was to meet in Speier the coming November. He begged Charles to go along with the idea though at the same time he encouraged him to promote a more universal gathering with the pope. To Ferdinand's acute embarassment, Charles flatly refused, saying that the local meeting could do nothing but harm to his authority and that of Rome.[40] The archduke fell back to asking his brother to come to Germany to help solve its problems, but here too, preoccupied with arranging his coronation in Italy and his wars with France, Charles could not comply.[41] Ferdinand's attempts to cultivate a more friendly attitude in the Empire toward himself and his house were further frustrated when the Emperor decided to marry two of their sisters, Eleanor and Catherine, to French, Italian, or Portuguese suitors rather than to German electors as Ferdinand had wanted.[42]

Thus, Ferdinand had shown himself fully prepared to act on his own behalf in the Empire, and Charles fully capable of stopping him. But for all the tension that this relationship engendered, neither brother could do without the other. To Ferdinand it was obvious that if he were ever to become king of the Romans it would have to be with Charles's support. And the Emperor, for his part, was not unappreciative of the difficult task the archduke had in dealing with the German estates, and continued to hold out the possibility that he would augment Ferdinand's power within the Empire in some way.[43] In the year that followed, 1525, he was to learn unequivocally how necessary the younger man was to his own ambitions and that he would have to be rewarded accordingly.

Events in Italy prompted the Emperor's new attitude. His wars with Francis I had gone very badly there in 1524 when, late in October, Milan, the prize in the Lombard plain for which both sides were contending, had fallen to the French. The loss was as much a blow to Ferdinand as it was to Charles. In his own quest for power and position, the archduke was as anxious to play a role in the peninsula as he was in Germany.[44] By 1523, he was receiving his own reports on Italian affairs as well as copies of dispatches sent by imperial and papal ambassadors.[45] In 1524, he began to beg his brother to make him duke of Milan for much the same reasons he wished to be German king. His promised services to his house and his dynasty incongruously outpaced his resources, some measure of how much he wanted the title. His precarious finances to the contrary notwithstanding, he argued that the Emperor would be spared the expense of defending Milan if he made him duke. The archduke pointed out that his position in Austria made it possible for him to pour quantities of both infantry and cavalry into the area quickly. He vowed to incorporate Milan into the German Empire, by which he probably meant that he would put tax revenues from the city to imperial use, thereby making Germans more likely to participate in the Habsburg Italian struggle.[46]

Charles's defeat propelled Ferdinand into a frenzy of supportive activity. He requested aid for 10,000 troops from the pope, the Venetians, and Henry VIII and resolved to go to Innsbruck to raise another 10,000 at his own expense. He urged family members to greater effort, asking his aunt Margaret in the Netherlands to give what she could to the cause and to assist in jogging the king of England into action. When the Emperor's viceroy in Naples asked Ferdinand to come to Italy, he resolved to do so.[47] All in all, it looked like the opportunity to do something for his brother which would be richly compensated.

Though German affairs ultimately kept Ferdinand from personally appearing in Italy, his help was decisive. Mortgaging land and people, towns and castles, the archduke contributed more troops to the struggle against Francis I in 1525 than did Charles himself. Nine thousand Spaniards and Italians made up the Emperor's forces; Ferdinand provided an additional 13,000 infantry and 1,200 cavalry.[48] The outcome was a happy one as far as the Habsburgs were concerned. Milan fell to the imperial forces following their great victory over the French at Pavia on February 24, 1525; the king of France was himself seized. Conjuring up the image of the recovery of Rome following its devastating defeat by Hannibal at Cannae, Ferdinand urged Charles to deal with Francis as harshly as possible. He himself hoped to be able to put a stop to what he regarded as French meddling in Germany, and to wring some money out of Francis which would go toward reducing his sizeable debts.[49] But it was the chivalric side of the Renaissance that shaped Charles's thought, not the classical. He freed Francis following the signing of the treaty of Madrid in January 1526, in which the latter gave up French claims to Italy,

Burgundy, Flanders, and Artois and promised on his word of honor to observe these provisions. Five months later, Francis had entered the league of Cognac with the pope and other Italian city-states to counter-act what they regarded as the over-mighty Spanish presence in the peninsula.

Ferdinand continued to try to use his role at Pavia to persuade his brother to give him a larger role in Italy. A month or so after the battle, he even imagined himself as Charles's governor there, though he quickly retreated to his more modest aim of becoming duke of Milan with the right to pass on this claim to his male heirs, who, at that point, were non-existent. With himself installed in the northern duchy and Charles as king of Naples, he envisioned them defending both the peninsula and one another.[50]

Charles would have none of this. But in matters not connected with Italy and his treaty with Francis, he became decidedly expansive with his brother. His correspondence itself took on a less patronizing tone following Pavia; he asked to hear more frequently from the archduke, observing that Ferdinand could give him advice on many things and that they both needed to aid one another as best they could. He asked the younger man his opinion on his prospective marriage with Isabella of Portugal, an arrangement Ferdinand was quick to promote given the need of both of them to father offspring as quickly as possible. The most satisfying outcome of Ferdinand's aid to Charles at Pavia, however, was that it firmed up the Emperor's resolution to do something to improve Ferdinand's position both in Austria and in the Empire.[51]

The compact of Brussels of 1522 had assigned Ferdinand rule in the Tyrol and the Habsburg possessions and protectorates in southwest Germany, but had stipulated that this action be kept secret. Some mention had also been made of Ferdinand receiving control of Pfirt and Hainault in the Burgundian complex, though only for his lifetime. From the beginning, the archduke had been unhappy with these provisions, claiming that since these lands did not know he was their "natural" ruler, they were more difficult to govern. That his aunt Margaret had some claim to Pfirt and Hainault did not disturb him greatly as he proposed that Charles compensate her out of his own hereditary duchy of Burgundy.[52] Even before Pavia, Charles had resolved to publicize Ferdinand's position in the Tyrol and Germany; Pavia moved him to act, although he demurred on Pfirt and Hainault, arguing that disposal of these territories belonged with the county of Burgundy.[53]

But his largest reward to his brother came in the Empire. Charles made it clear that if the *Reichsregiment* collapsed totally, then Ferdinand could act in its place. If the latter were forced to be absent from Germany, he could appoint his own *locumtenens*.[54] And, to Ferdinand's enormous pleasure, he advised him to begin preparing for his coronation as king of the Romans, since he believed his own crowning as Emperor by the pope was near. The archduke was quick to ask Charles to begin making appropriate overtures on his behalf in Germany since the electors would act only after certain financial considerations had been agreed upon. By the middle of 1525, Charles had grown somewhat more cautious, judging the anti-Habsburg mood in the Empire to be so strong that all the gold in Spain could not persuade the electors to vote for Ferdinand until his own imperial coronation was safely passed. Nor did he specify when he would come to Germany to aid his brother in his quest.[55] But having gotten this far with Charles, Ferdinand did not press him unduly on the matter.[56] He promised not to speak of it beyond his confidants. He had won, however, a very important commitment.

Thus, in his somewhat frantic scramble to find himself a place among the ruling princes of the sixteenth century, Ferdinand had been able to use his dependence upon his brother to great advantage. His efforts at Pavia had gone far to overcome Charles's early mistrust of both his motives and his capabilities, and he had manipulated the Emperor into a position where the latter recognized that he owed something to his brother. Francis I had discovered to his grief that the Habsburg system actually had some teeth. But that system, and Ferdinand's ability to extract personal gain from it had been only gently tested. The greatest danger to the position he had so recently won for himself was to emerge on his eastern front and would be thrust upon him in a frightening and sudden way in the summer of 1526 by the Turks. Along with the Lutherans, it was these Asiatic invaders who would try not only Ferdinand's stubborn resourcefulness to the utmost, but the whole structure of dynastic cooperation upon which so much of his career depended. It was a challenge which, at the very beginning, found him a Spanish prince, more than a little displeased at being shut out of the mainstream of activity in Italy, and in the end, would make him into a central European ruler.

CHAPTER III

PRESENT DANGER, FUTURE MISSION

For two centuries, the north-westward expansion of the Ottoman Turks in the Balkans, had set off episodic fits of alarm among the Europeans who watched its progress. Native to Inner Asia, islamicized during a stay in Asia Minor before moving to the continent, these tribesmen and the sultan who ruled them had found territorial conquest in the name of Allah wholly compatible with the plundering from which many of them lived. By the beginning of the sixteenth century, southeast Europe was largely under their control. Though the alleged horrors of their government were more often than not based on isolated anecdote alone, there was something very menacing in their growing might, particularly for Christian rulers who had to face them. The Turks were far from invincible; the Tatars and the Persians frequently forced them to devote their full military energies to their southern and southeastern borders. Yet, for all of this, they had never been decisively halted in Europe itself. The capture of Constantinople in 1453 symbolized the final subjection of much of eastern Christendom to their control and provoked a good deal of fear in the rest of Europe. However, it was the fall of Belgrade in 1521 that sent waves of panic through central Europeans. The Serb stronghold, which had checked the Ottoman advance up the Danube in 1456 following the fall of the Byzantine capital, was the last major Christian fortification in that strategic river valley. Islamic penetration to the heart of the continent now seemed inevitable.

The most dangerous aspect of this situation, from Ferdinand's point of view, was the seeming inability of the peoples of eastern and southeastern Europe to defend themselves. From the beginning of the fifteenth century, the keystone in the struggle against the Turks had been the

kingdoms of Hungary and Croatia-Dalmatia-Slavonia, the latter united
to the Magyar realm in a loose federation since 1102 and ruled not so
much by Hungarian kings but by local regents called *bans*. These officers,
one to each division of the Triune Kingdom, possessed supreme judicial
power in their respective areas, often commanded their armies in place
of their sovereign, could convoke their estates and promulgage laws without royal sanction. By the time Ferdinand appeared in Austria, the Turks
had performed numerous amputations on this south Slav conglomerate;
contemporary documents referred somberly to it as *reliquae reliquiarum
regni Croatiae, Slavoniae, et Dalmatiae.*[1] The Ottomans could frequently
depend on the cooperation of the local underclasses who found the rule
of their conquerors no more oppressive that that of Christian masters.
Indeed, because the Turks were so frequently on the move, they were
preferred to resident landlords. The cost of defense against the invaders
had exhausted Croatia and its associated kingdoms; by the sixteenth
century, local magnates such as Christopher Frankopan who undertook
to raise armies could no longer rely on lesser nobles to help them because
their resources had dwindled too badly. Even if the latter had had the
wherewithal, it is doubtful they would have worked with the likes of
Frankopan since they bitterly resented his ambitions.[2]

   Conditions within the kingdom of Hungary were just as grim. Though
the Turks had not yet seriously violated its territorial integrity, it was no
longer a reliable bulwark against these invaders. Since the fourteenth
century, a procession of non-native dynasties had ruled the Magyars,
some of whose members had been very capable men. None, however, had
been able to generate long lines of succession. The vacuum of power left
each time a house had died out had been filled by a large and vigorous
nobility which had the right to elect their sovereign. Each time a new
dynasty and/or ruler was chosen, it was only after concession upon concession had been made to both the great magnates and the extensive
provincial minor aristocracy. Toward the middle of the fifteenth century a native king, Matthias Corvinus, had brought this nobility under
royal control. He died suddenly in 1490, however, without a legitimate
heir, and Hungary passed to two Jagellonian princes who were kings of
Bohemia as well. Both were equally incompetent. The first, Vladislav,
dubbed "king o.k. (dobrze)" for the good-natured way in which he approved everything put before him, and his son Louis, who succeeded him

in 1516, presided over the destruction of what was left of royal authority in their realms. Figures tell the story most graphically. Whereas Corvinus had realized at least 100,000 gulden a year from his salt mines, Vladislav was drawing only about 25,000 gulden from the same source at his death. Under Louis, the figure dropped to 16,000. Influential magnate families such as the Thurzó held mortgages on many of the richest royal mines. The anarchy which accompanied all this peaked during Louis's reign. Intellectually and emotionally a child when he came to the throne, he was the butt of court jokes and knew no privacy from his surroundings. Both Alexis Thurzó, his chancellor, and Andrea de Burgo, Charles and Ferdinand's ambassador, agreed that age, if anything, made the king less mature.[3]

Louis made little effort to assay precisely the size of royal incomes, something widely known throughout Hungary.[4] Such laxity left people less willing than ever to pay their sovereign his due even when it was a matter of defending the kingdom. Hostility between classes did nothing to strengthen resolve against the Turks either. 1516 had seen a bloody peasant uprising against the landlords who had put it down savagely. Though many magnates had a free hand with Louis, there was much about the conduct of the court they resented, particularly the person and entourage of his wife. This was Mary of Habsburg, Ferdinand's younger sister by two years, who had been betrothed to the Jagellonian in 1515. Intelligent, witty, and strong-willed, Mary was devoted to her infantile husband, possibly because she could manipulate him so easily. He certainly made her wealthy, at least potentially so. His nuptial morning gift to her was an income of approximately 50,000 rhenish florins a year from various lands in the kingdom to cover her household expenses for life.[5] The arrangement left her one of the most powerful landlords in Hungary. She had brought many Germans with her, many of whom were interested in Lutheranism, and it was they whom many Magyars held primarily responsible for the disgraceful conditions in their monarch's household. The financial and administrative mismanagement of the country led to a constantly shifting kaleidoscope of alliances among crown, magnates, and the numerous small nobility as each group tried to fasten its hold on the kingdom. Rumors of uprisings against the king and queen circulated now and again and may have bothered Ferdinand as much as the country's obvious military weaknesses. At least he used this situation as an additional argument in his campaign to be named king of the Romans in 1524. But he did little to dispel the rampant anti-Germanism in the kingdom. When Andrea de Burgo was dispatched on another mission by the Emperor in 1523, Ferdinand chose Johannes Schneidpöck, an Austrian to replace him, who quickly became a faithful advocate of Mary's most personal interests. He also was a confidant of George of Brandenburg, Louis's tutor and a firm partisan of Habsburg interests in Hungary ever since Charles had endowed him with a yearly pension of 3,000 florins in 1519.

Similar conditions were present in Vladislav and Louis's other kingdom, Bohemia, a desirable ally in any protracted struggle with the Turks. An elective kingship like Hungary, Bohemia had lost its native dynasty, the Přermyslids in the fourteenth century almost at the same time its Magyar counterpart, the Árpads had died out. The successors of the Přemyslids, the house of Luxemburg, had some gifted rulers among them, but also some very poor ones. Even the most talented of them—the Emperors Charles IV and Sigismund—were frequently absent from Bohemia due to concerns elsewhere. Religious wars had rent the kingdom asunder in the first third of the fifteenth century, for Bohemia was the home of Utraquism, that first great pre-Reformation heresy which Rome could not quell either through persuasion or force. From 1459 to 1471 a native Hussite, George of Poděbrady had ruled the land, thereby widening its renown as a realm of heretics and giving other European monarchs reason to shun it. George saw that he would have to associate Bohemia with one of the major contemporary dynasties in order to bring the territory back into some kind of community with its neighbors. His choice fell upon the Polish Jagellonians so that he was succeeded by the hapless Vladislav upon his death.

The crown was an enviable prize for any sovereign. It embraced not only Bohemia with its capital at Prague, but four associated territories—Moravia, Silesia, and Upper and Lower Lusatia—all of which rendered fealty to the king. Unlike Hungary, Bohemia had a large middle class which had flourished in mercantile and manufacturing undertakings throughout the later Middle Ages. The royal silver mines at Kutná Hora and Jáchymov were among the richest of their time, producing until the mid-sixteenth century one quarter of all the metal in central Europe. Nor were the estates totally opposed to contributing part of their wealth to the kingdom. In 1522, for example, they voted a 1.66% tax on the total property assessment of each member.[7]

But as in Hungary, social dissension and the political ambitions of large landholders made it hard for any monarch to capitalize on these resources, let alone Vladislav and Louis. The tricameral Bohemian parliament or *sněm*, which had steadily increased its power at the expense of the king, was incapable of acting for the country as a whole. Like all medieval representative bodies it met at irregular intervals and, as a rule, only when it suited the dominant political or religious factions of the kingdom to do so. The gatherings were usually dominated by the first house of the body, the magnates, who controlled the high offices of state and who sent out summonses to the other divisions, the cities and the knights, to attend meetings. The latter two groups, however, often found a stay at the diet to be beyond their means so they habitually left the assembly before it was over or did not come at all.[8] Enmity between burgher and the great landholders was already wide-spread when Vladislav arrived as a sixteen year old in the kingdom, and neither he nor his son did much to close this breach. Both in Bohemia and Moravia, the high nobility tried to restrict the privileges of the townsmen, though in the latter territory, they went no further than to exclude urban residents from provincial courts and administrative offices. In Bohemia, however, the commercial rights of the townsmen were attacked as well. At the end of the fifteenth century, for example, the nobles began to brew beer in their castles and to forbid their peasants to buy the beverage from anyone other than themselves. In 1500, Vladislav agreed that representatives of the cities could come to the diet only when its deliberations directly involved their interests. This provoked an armed response from the towns, and conferences in 1517 and 1518 temporarily smoothed things over. The mutual suspicions between the two groups did not abate, however, and quarreling between them broke out once again in 1520.[9]

Vladislav was as quick to give up his own prerogatives as he was those of his subjects. In 1499, he agreed not to mortgage castles or lands belonging to the crown without the consent of the local representative body within whose jurisdiction the royal holding lay. During his reign, the national estates won the right to have their decrees accepted as legally binding without the approval of the monarch. Vladislav was equally cavalier about his finances. After his death in 1516, the crown debt was

was estimated to be 12,000,000 Bohemian groschen. The major creditors were the highest officials of the country, chief among whom was Zdeněk Lev of Rožmital, the supreme burggrave. Nor was the diet much interested in cooperating with Vladislav or Louis in defense against the Turks. In 1521 the estates postponed discussion of raising a force to go to Belgrade for so long that when they finally did send a contingent of men, they arrived too late to help the beleaguered city.[10] The Bohemians were also open to the blandishments of the French. In 1521, an envoy of Francis I almost persuaded them to pay 20,000 to 30,000 troops whom he could used against the Habsburgs; only a last-minute whirlwind of argument by Andrea de Burgo moved them to back down. The setback did not discourage the French, however, from continuing to keep some of the influential figures in the kingdom in their pay.[11]

From the moment of his arrival in Austria, Ferdinand had deep misgivings about the situation on his eastern and northern borders. For one thing, the dissidence in Bohemia reminded him uncomfortably of the troubles with his own peoples.[12] He kept in close contact with leading Bohemian noblemen such as Rožmital, Vojtěch of Pernštejn, Jindřich Svikovský, Adam of Hradec, all of whom had been present at the Vienna betrothal of 1515, and others as well.[13] Andrea de Burgo, Johannes Schneidpöck, and other informants all corresponded with him regularly on Bohemian and Hungarian affairs.[14]

But it was the Turks who really bothered him. Before departing for the Netherlands and the bargaining on his patrimony in 1521, he ordered the administration he left behind in Austria to stay in touch with King Louis, his brother-in-law and to assure him that he would do everything in his power to drive up help for him in Germany against the Ottomans.[15] Troops from Austria fought in defense of Belgrade in 1521. Even as he discussed his territorial inheritance in Brussels, Ferdinand begged Charles to wring some sort of aid for Louis out of the Empire, pointing out, as he was to do countless times in the future, that assistance to Hungary was assistance to his own lands.[16] If Ferdinand had not seen for himself that he had a key role to play in the conflict with the Turks, he had plenty of people to tell him. A delegation from the diet of Nürnberg visited him in Vienna in 1522 to discuss the Hungarian situation.[17] Reports from Croatia in 1523 warned that Carniola, Styria, and Carinthia were likely targets of Turkish invasion, something he had already tried to ward off with contributions of funds to the south Slavic kingdom.[18] He quickly perceived that he would have to enlist the support of other lands as well. He urged the king of Poland to help, promising that he and Charles would lead some future crusade to restore perpetual peace in the Magyar realm.[19] He turned to Bohemia as well and received what soon developed into a paradigmatic response to such requests. The Bohemians promised aid only if the Turks physcially entered Hungary; Moravia, much nearer to the threatened area, complied.[20]

Thus, from the very beginning of his struggle against the Turks, Ferdinand tried to turn it into a cooperative venture in which his brother played a leading role. He made a sincere effort to get his brother-in-law to help himself as well. Reports from Andrea de Burgo, a timid but fundamentally sensible observer, continued to tell of treachery and disunity among the nobility, financial chaos, and lethargy on the part of the monarch. In the fall of 1523, Ferdinand promoted a meeting between himself, Mary, and Louis in Wiener Neustadt where he attempted to persuade the king to bring some order into his public and private affairs.[21] Though the conference was a festive one with the tournaments and jousting so dear to Ferdinand, it had a sober outcome. Some agreement was reached among all parties on defense measures against the Turks. Ferdinand pledged to raise troops and Louis agreed to undertake reforms which would strengthen his hold on his kingdom. Privately, however, the archduke did not have much hope that Louis would persevere in these efforts; the king's household was so laxly supervised that the reorganization plan called for appointment of one or two chamberlains whose lone duty it would be to instruct those who worked in the royal chambers and make sure that they stole nothing from them. However, Ferdinand sent along two of his own agents when Louis and Mary returned to Hungary who were to do their best to encourage this restructuring of royal administration. Little came of it, however, since the circle which surrounded Louis at his court resisted any of these changes.[22]

The sultan, Suleiman, did not feel his forces sufficiently strong that year, so that east central Europe escaped an invasion. The reprieve did nothing, however, to lessen Ferdinand's anxieties about his own future and that of his family in the face of such a threat. His agent in Hungary, Schneidpöck, made it clear that nothing was improving there. Though Louis tried to enlist the help of the king of Poland, he pursued no line of constructive activity for very long.[23] By 1525, the Hungarian diet was in an uproar, demanding that their king replace the Germans at his court with Magyars and blaming Ferdinand and Mary for the German presence in their kingdom.[24]

With Hungary disorganized, Bohemia undependable, and Austria capable of only limited help, Ferdinand quite naturally looked to the Empire for aid. The princes and the cities were not unconcerned about developments to their southeast as an embassy from the diet made plain to Ferdinand in 1522. But translating those feelings into concrete support was another matter altogether. For those not immediately in line for attack, the Turkish menance was not as urgently troubling as it was for Ferdinand or the archbishop of Salzburg.[25] The domestic chaos in Hungary did little to temper the misgivings which many Germans had about the kingdom. In 1522, a delegation from the Empire which met with Ferdinand to discuss sending aid to Croatia wished to postpone any negotiations with the Hungarians because of their general disunity and their hostility to foreigners, especially Germans. Though the archduke finally managed to persuade the diet to raise somewhere between 2,000 and 4,000 troops to go to the southeast, it was a far cry from the 100,000 which the Hungarians had requested. The diet gave the Magyars until March 1523 to reply, but when they did not do so until July, the *Reichsregiment* withdrew the offer saying they could do nothing about it. The Hungarians protested, not improbably, that they had been waiting to see if a major Turkish offensive materialized before answering.[26] That the Germans were quick to dismiss even so plausible an excuse as this one tells much about their general reluctance to aid King Louis and his subjects. Nor was the imperial diet willing to answer Ferdinand's pleas concerning Hungary without setting a price of its own. At the diet of Nürnberg in 1524, a Hungarian ambassador addressed the gathering on behalf of his homeland in tones which, according to the Habsburg, ". . . could have moved a rock." The Germans responded quite generously, but not out of sympathy to the Magyar cause. Rather they hoped by their compliance to get Charles and Ferdinand to support the calling of a general church council more actively. It was a relatively harmless request from the brothers' point of view since they both endorsed the idea of a conciliar solution to the Lutheran problem in principle. However, the coupling of the German religious question with aid to the Habsburgs against the Turks would make Ferdinand's negotiations for the latter infinitely more complex in the very near future. Nor were his natural confessional allies, the Catholic princes, any more reliable. Though all could agree on certain measures to reform the Church when they met in Regensburg in 1524, they were not especially anxious to help Ferdinand against the Turks.[27]

The richest, and theoretically most dependable, sources of aid for Ferdinand were of course Charles and, to a lesser extent, their aunt Margaret. Aside from the dynastic ties that bound him to his brother, Charles was the Emperor and responsible for the defense of Christendom, and Ferdinand was a man who took the content of titles seriously. Even while haggling over the division of the Habsburg patrimony in 1522, Charles had made it clear that defense of east central Europe was primarily the responsibility of that area's rulers.[28] From the beginning of his career in Austria, however, Ferdinand made it equally plain that he would not accept his brother's view. In 1522, both he and the imperial ambassador, Burgo, told the Emperor that without substantial aid from him, the king of Hungary could not hold out long against Turkish attack. He reminded Charles of the familial ties which bound him to Austria, but he also took the side of the Hungarians, arguing as they were that the funds which the Emperor was dissipating in his conflict with the French could be much more usefully employed in the east.[29] For all of his touchiness concerning his independence in Austria, Ferdinand was quick to assure his brother that the latter was his only hope in getting substantial aid from the Empire. But it was very difficult to make headway with Charles in this matter. While not unsympathetic, he wryly commented that Ferdinand's indebtedness was ". . . a common disease of the day . . ." from which he himself suffered. He could not see himself to aiding his brother in any significant way unless all the rulers of Christendom joined him.[30]

In the late winter of 1526, Ferdinand, on the invitation of the Croatian estates, revived an idea which he had had in 1523—the union of all or part of the southern kingdom with his own lands in order to better defend them all. The plan had foundered on the opposition of Louis' Hungarian counselors the first time; it did so again as Ferdinand refused to make the move without the sanction of the pope who refused to give it because of Hungarian anti-German feeling.[31] But by spring, all of these activities took on a frightening immediacy. On April 23, Suleiman the

Magnificent left Constantinople with an army numbering around 120,000 and began moving in a generally northwest direction. Although confusion over the precise line of Turkish march abounded well into August 1526— it was not certain whether they were headed into Croatia or Hungary proper—both Louis and Ferdinand knew that a dangerous confrontation awaited them.[32] The archduke, however, had other concerns beside the Ottoman forces. Throughout the summer, peasant uprisings in Styria and once again in neighboring Salzburg plagued him, and he continued to feel obligated to assist Charles in Italy, aid which the latter took even though he well realized the threat which the Turks posed for Hungary.[33]

Louis and Ferdinand's main hope for reinforcement lay with the imperial diet which was meeting at Speier during the spring and summer. The king of Hungary had been uncharacteristically active on his own behalf. By the middle of June he had sent out orders for the assembly of troops which met with a gratifyingly patriotic response; by the middle of July, however, Magyar enthusiasm for the venture was beginning to flag. The Hungarian ambassador who appeared before the diet seemed surprisingly vague about Turkish affairs, despite Ferdinand's alarming description of the situation. On August 17, the envoy admitted that he had received no special instructions from Louis who had assumed that the diet would give him the men they had voted him on previous occasions.[34]

The diet also refused to consider Turkish matters until the question of a religious council was settled. To get the former deliberations moving, Charles, who was not present at the meeting agreed to take up the conciliar question with Pope Clement VII. Of far greater significance for the future of Lutheranism in Germany was Ferdinand's acceptance of the formula of Speier which allowed each territorial ruler to exercise the confession he thought proper until the council settled the issue. The decision of the Diet to send aid to Louis only came on August 18, and the details were worked out only five days later.[35] Charles had by that time indicated that he was sending nothing. Affairs with France and England precluded much concern with Hungarian matters, and he was especially anxious not to poison his relations with Clement who, he thought, would see his activities against the Turks as only strengthening the imperial position in Italy.[36]

Thus despite unusually wet weather which slowed their movement considerably, the Turkish forces proceeded forward. Ferdinand, who did not leave Speier until August 27, knew by the thirteenth that Petervarad on the Drava had fallen. Five days later, news reached him that a Hungarian force led by the king was in the neighborhood of the Turkish army somewhere at the mid-point of the river. With only around 4,000 men under him, Louis was encamped at Báta, just slightly north of the plains at Mohács. Despite the urgings of some that he send an advance guard to scout out the Turks and that he await reinforcements coming from Bohemia and Austria, he yielded to the hotheads who called for immediate combat with Suleiman's juggernaut.[37] The Hungarian offensive began on the night of August 26, and the conclusive battle between the two sides lasted from the twenty-eighth to the twenty-ninth. It was a Hungarian catastrophe. Though Louis acquitted himself bravely, he was in the end forced to flee the conflict. Hurrying through the marshy terrain around Mohács, he fell from his horse and drowned.

Ferdinand knew nothing of the disaster for several days. September 7 found him still promising aid to Louis.[38] When he did get word of the fate of his brother-in-law two days later, he reacted quickly. While piously accepting Louis's death as the will of God, he immediately advanced his claims to the Hungarian and Bohemian thrones as the husband of the dead king's only sibling.[39] His swift assertion of what he took to be his rights did not mean that he had hoped to see Louis put out of the way in order to acquire the two kingdoms. He had, however, begun to think in terms of an east central European community in which his own and Habsburg interests were paramount. Once Louis no longer occupied his thrones, Ferdinand had to make certain that not only the Turks stayed far from his Austrian borders but any other potentially hostile ruler as well. There were two figures who were likely to fill the latter category. One was King Sigismund of Poland and the other was John Zapolya, a man who had successively been Sigismund's brother-in-law and son-in-law. Maximilian had been troubled by the implications of the Jagellonian-Zapolya alliance for Habsburg interests in east central Europe, and Ferdinand feared that the Polish king might use the Hungarian magnates to preserve the hold of the dynasty on the Bohemian and Hungarian crowns. Zapolya, the immensely wealthy voivode, or governor, of the easternmost reaches of Hungary called Transylvania, was even more worrisome for the archduke. Since the beginning of the sixteenth century, the magnates had been leading a party in Hungary which had been demanding a native king. Zapolya himself was the chief candidate for the position. He had not been at Mohács which led Ferdinand to suspect that he must have had some sort of prior agreement with the Turks, especially since they did not molest his lands. The Habsburg feared that Zapolya might very well unite with the Ottomans and invade Austria itself.[40] That the voivode had some special relationship with the Turks when they came to Hungary in 1526 has never been proven. However, when Suleiman withdrew from Hungary in September, something which Ferdinand did not anticipate, he promised Zapolya's supporters that he would recognize the magnate as king and offer him protection.[41]

Ferdinand immediately tried to galvanize his family in support of his quest for the two crowns. His widowed sister Mary was still in Hungary, and, promising her all too rashly as it turned out, that she would not suffer because of the transfer of Bohemia and Hungary to him, he sought the help and advice of both her and her royal courtiers. He was especially anxious to staff episcopal sees left vacant by the death of many bishops who had fought at Mohács with Habsburg partisans. He also turned to his aunt in the Netherlands and, of course, to Charles.[42]

But probably mindful of the potential costs of the enterprise neither Margaret nor the Emperor were overjoyed by the prospect of Habsburg territorial acquisitions in the east. Margaret promised to intercede with Charles on behalf of her younger nephew, but she regarded Ferdinand and Mary as equally unfortunate. Charles indeed did believe that one of the causes of Hungary's downfall was the lack of aid from himself; he promised Ferdinand 100,000 ducats as quickly as possible even though he did not have the cash on hand. But neither the Emperor nor the aging archduchess wanted to involve themselves in massive undertakings against the Turks to insure Ferdinand's political safety; they urged him to concentrate on the narrow issues of winning the crowns open to him rather than undertaking any serious offensives.[43]

Thus the disaster which Ferdinand had anticipated almost from the moment of his arrival in Austria in 1521 had come to pass. His efforts to prop up th flaccid regime of his brother-in-law in Hungary and Bohemia and to alert the Empire to the danger on their southern border had all failed. He was now in a position, at least in his own eyes, where he had to acquire two royal crowns in order to keep the archducal one he had so recently been awarded intact. Austria, Bohemia, Hungary—they had so many common borders that it was natural for him to see them as a unity in considering the Turkish problem. The difficult thing was to get his hands on them and, once having done that, to organize their resources. It was a new goal which he would pursue, not always successfully but with the same single-minded intensity and alert opportunism that he applied to the division of the Habsburg lands and the imperial succession.

CHAPTER IV

FROM ARCHDUKE TO KING

Though Ferdinand was quick to insist that he had hereditary claims to Bohemia, the estates of the realm felt quite otherwise. For them, or at least for the vast majority among them, the vacancies on the two thrones were the occasion to begin electoral bargaining with whatever candidates for the offices there were. It was this process which in the past couple of centuries had weakened monarchs in both kingdoms to the point where they possessed their titles but few of the powers and prerogatives that went with them. Other contenders besides Ferdinand appeared almost immediately. In Bohemia it was the elector of Saxony and his son; Sigismund of Poland; and most seriously, the dukes of Bavaria. It was in all likelihood to discourage the competition and to avoid compromising negotiations with the estates that Ferdinand strained himself mightly, although vainly, to prove that the kingdom rightfully was his through his wife.

History supplied him with contradictory precedents, from which he understandably chose the ones most congenial to his cause. Though both George of Poděbrady in 1458 and Vladislav in 1478 had been named to the Bohemian throne in free elections, Ferdinand could and did cite a number of instances in which Bohemian kings had laid claim to their position through their consorts. These were, most recently, John of Luxembourg in 1310 and a Habsburg, Albrecht, in 1437. He pointed out that by Charles IV's order in 1348, elections were to take place when a ruler had neither male nor female descendants. The Habsburgs had also concluded a mutual inheritance pact with the Luxembourgs in 1346, but, since the latter had long since died out, Ferdinand's position here was especially shaky. More significant was Vladislav's expressed provision

[53]

that Anna, his daughter, could inherit the kingdom, though he had qualified this by agreeing that she could not be married without the consent of
the Bohemian estates. Representatives of that body had attended the
Vienna congress of 1515, but they had never formally approved of Ferdinand's union with Anna, thereby leaving open to question the Habsburg's
contention that he had any right to the throne through his wife. Despite
the general uncertainty that enveloped all of these claims, Ferdinand's
first spokesman in Bohemia carefully avoided all mention of the term
election in his discussions with representatives of the estates, and stuck
doggedly to his master's hereditary arguments.[2]

For the moment, however, these debates were little more than aca-
demic quibblings as Ferdinand quickly saw that he would have to buttress
his claims with more than inconclusive legalisms. By October 9, 1526,
he was ordering his emissaries to downplay the notion of hereditary
succession and to deal with the actual concerns about his policies that
the estates had. He promised that he had every intention of confirming
the rights and privileges of the latter and that he would staff his administration with native Bohemians, a matter of great concern in the kingdom
since Salamanca's reputation had drifted eastward.[3] But two arguments
for a Habsburg succession in Bohemia dominated the presentations made
by Ferdinand's spokesmen. One was that since Austria and Bohemia
were geographically so close, he would not be an absentee king, a worry
to those who feared that Hungarian matters might overwhelm him. The
other was that he was of royal blood and stood in " . . . brotherly unity
and understanding. . . " with the Holy Roman Emperor himself. This
relationship would, or so he argued, insure that he could aid the kingdom
more than any other prince.[4] Indeed, Ferdinand had already tried to get
Charles to invest him with the kingdom on the basis of the loose feudal
relationship it had had with the Empire since the Middle Ages. Charles
himself, however, was not really certain what the ties, if any, between
the two polities were, and his very cautious response to his brother's
request apparently discouraged Ferdinand. While he continued to insist
that Bohemia was a part of the Empire, he did not press the issue.[5]

Through such arguments and through the ritual distribution of money,
offices, and other aids, Ferdinand managed to build up an influential
body of supporters within the estates relatively soon. One group, led by
the Rožmberk family, had for some time believed that the kingdom

needed a stronger monarch and joined Ferdinand's camp for that reason. Others were more forthrightly mercenary—Lev Zdeněk Rožmital for one was enlisted by Ferdinand's promise to pay his debts of 50,000 florins. Count Hans Pflug and the Šlik family were won over when Ferdinand vowed not to touch incomes which they drew from the royal mines at Kutná Hora.[6] Though there were those like the Polish ambassador to Spain who believed that all Charles could do for Ferdinand was summed up in the five letters "NIHIL" many Bohemians believed otherwise.[7] It was widely felt that Ferdinand was the lone candidate for the throne whose connections and resources would allow him to assume the debts of the previous two kings. Then too, by comparison with the dukes of Bavaria who were his only serious rivals, Ferdinand appeared to the Bohemians to be relatively moderate on religious matters. More conservative elements in the Utraquist church were no more friendly toward Lutheranism than the Catholics, thereby giving them some common ground with their sovereign-to-be. In general, however, the confessional debate played a minor role in discussions between the archduke and the estates. A sixteenth century chronicler remarked that when Ferdinand finally agreed to uphold the *Compactata* of 1438, the argeement between the Bohemian estates and King Sigismund which had established the liberties of Utraquism, the majority of Bohemians with whom he had been discussing the matter had only a vague notion of what the document was.[8]

Ferdinand was duly named to the Crown of St. Václav on October 23, 1526. While election had been unavoidable, he had done the next best thing by persuading the estates to defer most substantive discussion about their liberties and limitations on the monarch until after his formal selection had taken place. Meetings on thse issues only got underway the following month, and, true to form the estates' demands were sweeping—not only did they want Ferdinand to confirm privileges and rights they had exacted from former rulers but they wanted his promise that he would accept their advice as binding on appointment of all provincial, court, and ecclesiastical officials. To meet this challenge, he employed a negotiating strategy that he was to turn to with great success many times in the future. This involved an apparent willingness to compromise, especially where the issue seemed to be lost to begin with, but a steadfast refusal to yield points which Ferdinand felt were key to his real purposes.

In this case he immediately agreed to the Bohemian demand that he declare himself to have been chosen king in a free election. On the surface of things, this would seem to have been a major concession on his part, given his initial insistence that he had hereditary claims to the kingdom. However, since the dukes of Bavaria had actually renewed their quest for the crown after his election, Ferdinand feared that his prize might be snatched from him at the last moment. He therefore agreed to the estate's demand, distasteful though it might be. On other matters, he simply delayed their discussion so long that the estates threatened to break off the talks altogether. Then, in a document issued on December 13, 1526, he agreed to uphold certain articles of the Bohemian constitution which his predecessors had supported. These included, besides the recognition of the *Compactata* and a promise to work for papal recognition of them, protection of the rights and freedoms of the Bohemian nobility and the vow not to use foreigners in church or administrative positions.[9] Again it would seem that a truly damaging constraint on his powers had been granted, but Ferdinand was making a demand of his own which went a long way toward minimizing his defeat on the election question. He asked the estates to permit the crowning of his heir during his lifetime.

The request was not an innovation inasmuch as both the Hungarian and Bohemian estates had permitted Vladislav to do this with Louis. And Ferdinand certainly knew from his own experience that an accepted order of succession was as vital to the interests of his dynasty as the principle of inheritance. One of the reasons for the chaos which he had found in Austria had been Maximilian's failure to exact an oath of fealty from the estates to Charles or Ferdinand before his death.[10] His public argument in Bohemia, while nowhere near so self-interested, was obviously honed by Austrian circumstances. In the event of illness or extreme old age, he contended, he would have to turn the kingdom over to a regency, something which would not be in Bohemia's best interests. He also held out stubbornly on the question of royal control of appointments. Even though he agreed not to name foreigners to offices in the realm, he continued to insist the he might not be able to find natives who were competent for the jobs, especially where finance was concerned. He pointed out that just as regencies were to the disadvantage of the kingdom, so were unfit civil servants who could not be fired.[11]

His delaying tactics enabled him to be crowned even before a compromise had been struck. The coronation took place amidst great celebration on February 24 and was in itself a great source of satisfaction to him. The new king thoroughly enjoyed the massive festivities which accompanied the event and personally participated in the jousting. There he acquitted himself with a skill and vigor that much impressed his subjects, or, at least the nobility "... and consequently everyone in the country..." as Ferdinand somewhat complacently put it after it was all over.[12] Nor did he have reason to be discouraged at the arrangements concerning his successor and his bureaucracy which he and the estates accepted in a document issued on March 2. The latter agreed that a son who had achieved his majority could be crowned in his father's lifetime and that the king could use foreigners in his administration in areas such as finance and mine management. For his part, Ferdinand promised to listen to the advice of the estates and Louis's former officials on the matter of appointments, but continued to insist that he was not bound to take it.[13]

His accession in the lands associated with the Bohemian crown was far easier. Here he enjoyed the advantage that Moravia, Silesia, and the two Lusatias did regard Anna as having hereditary rights in these territories and through this connection recognized Ferdinand as their ruler. His prompt request for their allegiance which contrasted favorably with the slow approaches of the other Bohemian aspirants also flattered them, and their response to Ferdinand was all the more positive. But above all, they wanted to beat off the candidacy of John Zapolya, one of the claimants to the Hungarian throne, who was threatening to incorporate the areas into that kingdom on the basis of a 1478 treaty signed by Matthias Corvinus and Vladislav at Olomouc. Ferdinand successfully capitalized on these fears by promising to protect these lands from Hungarian incursions.[14] The succession agreement which he won in Moravia was especially favorable. In return for his consent not to elevate anyone to the office of margrave during his lifetime, the estates promised that if he had children of his own they would succeed to the position. They had, however, to have attained their majority and won their mother's consent if she were still living. As in Bohemia, he balked at any restrictions on his power to appoint whom he wished to his bureaucracy.[15] Smooth relations between Ferdinand and the Moravians, who perceived many of their interests to be altogether independent of Bohemian ones, were to be very important for the Habsburg in the future. Due to its proximity to Hungary, the margravate would be especially cooperative in furnishing him with large amounts of men and money in the Turkish wars. 1300 troops from Moravia had fought at Mohács, and immediately after that debacle, their estates had agreed in Brno that each member should raise ten men to be used in any future combat.[16]

Upon hearing of his brother's election in Bohemia, Charles expressed the hope that he would soon have the same news from Hungary. Ferdinand felt much the same, but that goal was far harder to reach. He was prompt to send commissioners to both that kingdom and to Croatia-Dalmatia-Slavonia following Mohács, announcing him as a candidate for their thrones and pledging in the most extravagant terms imaginable his intention not only to protect these lands but to enlarge them as well. The latter was to be done with aid from the Empire. The magnates of both kingdoms were assured of money, land, and positions in return for their support.[17] These were the kinds of offers that Ferdinand's predecessors had successfully used; his position, however, was considerably more complex than theirs had been. There is no question that the presence of the Turks in the area helped him in his pursuit of the Magyar and south Slav crowns, even though he was appallingly ignorant of even the names of the peoples who lived in these areas. The estates of all these territories were genuinely worried about the integrity of their lands. But once it became apparent that the Turks had substantially withdrawn after their victory at Mohács, all of these representative bodies became more cagey in dealing with the archduke.[18]

The reason for their coyness was the presence of a strong Hungarian national counter-candidate, John Zapolya. As noted before, he enjoyed the sympathies not only of many influential Hungarians, but of the king of Poland as well who was, at that moment, his father-in-law. Not that Ferdinand was without Hungarian sympathizers of his own. Among these were Stephen Báthory, the palatine and chief official of the realm after the king, who had the very important power to call diets; the Hungarian treasurer, Alexis Thurzó; and Thomas Szalaházy, the bishop of Veszprém. The high clergy of Hungary was especially opposed to Zapolya's ambitions, but since many of these had died fighting at Mohács, the good will of this group was perhaps less decisive than it might otherwise have been.[19] Those Hungarian mining towns which had been part of Anna's dowry to her husband also remained notably loyal to him. In Croatia, Ferdinand at least initally enjoyed the support of the ban, Francis Batthyány, though, as he was to find out, it would be only temporary. A major asset for Ferdinand in keeping this heterogeneous band together, especially after Mohács, was the presence of his sister Mary in Hungary. Unlike the Bohemian nobles, many of whom were intensely suspicious of her, important Hungarians had clustered around her from the beginning of her years there, eventually leading to the nucleus of the pro-Habsburg party.[20] Privy to their views and to those of her brother, the widowed queen was a unique go-between for both sides.

Ferdinand made the same efforts to claim the Hungarian throne through succession and inter-dynastic agreement that he did in Bohemia. He met with equally little success. If anything, his constitutional law was worse here than it was in Bohemia. As in the latter kingdom, precedent had been set for the transmission of the crown through female succession. However, the treaties on which he was basing his claims as well, signed by the Habsburgs and Hungarian rulers in 1461 and 1491, made no provision for such an eventuality. Unlike in Bohemia, however, he was more vague in making these demands, rarely citing documents in which his supposed rights were guaranteed, leading one to wonder whether he took the argument seriously at all. Briefly, he even thought of applying the right of conquest to the kingdom but gave it up when he found that it would not allow him to duck his obligation to guarantee the rights and privileges of the Hungarian nobility.[21]

But from the beginning, Ferdinand knew that empty legalisms would neither isolate Zapolya nor defeat him. He did what he could to discredit the magnate. While he did not accuse him of outright collaboration with the Turks, Ferdinand pressed the point of his absence at Mohács hard with the papacy, Venice, and France, all of whom were potential supporters of the voivode from abroad.[22] Within Hungary itself, he scattered money, lands, and promises of more to anyone who would join his side. Fittingly, the first post-Mohács document in the registers containing the communications of his chancery in Vienna to Hungary is a promise to the castellan of Bratislava, John Bornemisza, assuring him of his privileges and rights should Ferdinand become king of Hungary.[23] In the late fall of 1526, on Mary's advice, Ferdinand signed a contract assuring the palatine Báthory of 2,000 rhenish gulden and the city of Kőszeg and

Batthyány, the Croatian *ban* 6,000 gulden in six weeks. Other important figures were promised smaller sums. In return, he was supposed to receive both moral and military support in his quest for the Hungarian crown. In other dealings in Croatia he promised Christopher Frankopan extensive lands in Croatia and Slovenia along with the post of commander-in-chief of the Hungarian armies for life and a salary to match. Ferdinand also agreed to pay his debts of 2,000 gulden. The drawback of winning one's friends in such a fashion was pointedly illustrated in the Habsburg's dickering with Simon Erdödy, the bishop of Zagreb who wanted to be named bishop of Esztergom as well. Since Ferdinand had already nominated someone else to the post, he had to offer Erdödy the less prestigious see of Eger. The bishop decided to switch his allegiance to Zapolya. In all of this, Ferdinand was on the thinnest of financial ice. At the beginning of November, he had sent Mary 4,000 gulden, and it was on this flimsy basis that most of the Habsburg financial guarantees had been made.[24]

The price of keeping this band together grew even higher when on November 10, 1526, a splinter group of the Hungarian estates, meeting in their ancient coronation city of Székesfehérvár, elected Zapolya as their king. Important defections from Ferdinand's party came at once. Bishop Erdödy convinced Christopher Frankopan that the Austrian would be unable to fulfill his financial commitments to him, thereby swinging the Croatian magnate to Zapolya's side. Ferdinand tried to take some comfort in the small numbers who had participated in the Transylvanian leader's election and continued his efforts to blacken his reputation by associating him with the Turks. For his part, Zapolya, with his hold on the Hungarian crown at least partially legitimized, tried both to undercut Ferdinand's sources of foreign support and to come to some sort of *modus vivendi* with the archduke in which the latter would recognize his sovereignty. He urged the Bavarian dukes not to aid the Austrian against him, but congratulated Ferdinand on his election in Bohemia and offered to cooperate with him against the Turks. In 1527, Zapolya went so far as to offer to renounce his claims to Silesia and Moravia and to marry Mary if only Ferdinand would accept him as a monarch.[25]

But firmly resolved to have the crown for himself, Ferdinand responded coldly to all of this, refusing to give an audience to Zapolya's initial embassy to him. Now in the role of a counter-claimant, the Habsburg redoubled his efforts to get his own supporters within the estates to elect

him king. Doling out bribes on the spot, Mary managed to assemble the
Habsburg party in Bratislava by the end of November 1526. Ferdinand's
financial assurances grew more lavish. Promising the Hungarians aid from
both Austria and the Empire, he vowed that within two years he would
be able to use royal incomes to compensate anyone whose possessions
and livings had been damaged because he had joined the Habsburg side.
Tolls, taxes, revenues from ecclesiastical establishments and other royal
incomes—all were to be used to pay off his adherents. Any lands which
could be confiscated from Zapolya and his partisans were also to go to
this purpose, though given the ease with which the Hungarian magnates
jumped from one side to the other, this reward was not as significant
as it might seem at first glance. Remarkable little was set aside for Ferdinand and his immediate family. Those who suffered no losses would
receive appropriate gifts and favors. He also swore to protect Hungarian
freedoms, laws, and institutions and to keep foreigners from his court
bureaucracy, though, as in Bohemia, he was quick to reneg on that promise once he received the royal title.[26] Given Zapolya's willingness to
accept the electoral principle, Ferdinand could not do otherwise, so that
he did not press this issue. The group named him their sovereign on
December 17. A few weeks later, Croatia-Dalmatia-Slavonia also chose
him their king on the promise that he would undertake to defend them.[27]

Thus by the beginning of 1527, Ferdinand had a grip of sorts on both
Hungary and the south Slavic kingdom associated with it. Neither situation,
however, was settled. No mention had been made in Croatia that the
Habsburg's election there had in any way been conditional on his election
in Hungary, and Magyars anxious to maintain their influence in that
realm, wished to have this relationship clarified. When Ferdinand tried
to explain the difficulty away by claiming that the estates of the Triune
realm had not elected him but merely offered him their fealty (*Erbhuldi-
gung*), they, in turn, were offended.[28] His most immediate problem,
however, was that Zapolya's election in Hungary had taken place before
his own. To nullify this, he drew on a number of strategems. In Croatia,
he argued that the Transylvanian magnate could not defend his kingdoms as adequately as could he, the brother of the Emperor, a not wholly
imaginary boast. In November 1526, Charles had issued a mandate in
Granada in which he had pledged his determination to aid Hungary and
to defend the possessions of his sister and brother in the kingdom.[29] He

also attacked the validity of Zapolya's selection. With considerable precedent on his side, Ferdinand asserted that only diets summoned by the
palatine could legally elect a sovereign. Zapolya, therefore, was simply
in rebellion. He hammered away at this point not only within his own
family, but in Europe at large; Salamanca carried the message as far as
England in 1527. To Charles he pointed out that the absolute number
of those among the estates who had been present and voting for him at
Bratislava was larger than those who had chosen Zapolya, but he did not
press this view very far.[30]

But the other side was also ready with precedents, observing that no
palatine had ever summoned the diets which had elected Matthias Corvinus and Vladislav. And while Ferdinand dismissed these arguments
as sophisms, he knew full well that his cause would never be won on
constitutional grounds.[31] He did his best to swell the number of his
partisans through the dispensation of even more funds and incomes. Mary
received plenipotentiary powers to dispense aid and properties, though
Ferdinand did make the cautious request that she do so in moderation.
He was now in the unpleasant position of having to make good on all
the promises he had made prior to his election, and the Hungarians were
not men to let him forget them. For her part, Mary had little in the way
of advice or money to help her brother out of the financial noose that
was tightening around him. She did little other than to urge him to meet
Hungarian and Croatian demands and to hope that the prompt response
to these might save him greater outlays in the future.[32] Though he supplied her with additional funds, these were not enough, and, as desperate
as he was to be the lawful and only king of Hungary, Ferdinand began
to complain that all too much was being asked of him. He was especially
vexed by Batthány, the ban of Croatia, and he began urging his sister
to string him and others like him along with promises. Indeed, Mary herself had emerged as something of an economic burden. Since she had
been unable to recover any of her Hungarian incomes which had been
lost to Zapolya and his followers after Mohács, Ferdinand was supporting
her and her counselors.[33]

But even as he rummaged in his treasuries to meet his sister's stream
of requests for money, another idea was taking shape in him mind. Not
surprisingly, he had concluded that the funds which he was shipping
to Hungary might be better spent in outfitting an army to drive Zapolya

from the kingdom by force.[34] Unlike Charles, Ferdinand was no military leader, but he was certainly not averse to military action when he felt that it could accomplish something. Through the fall of 1526 and the early part of 1527, he had simply felt himself too ill-equipped for such ventures, and he had therefore accepted Sigismund of Poland's offer to act as mediator in arranging a treaty between the sides in Hungary.[35] Being poorly prepared for anything, however, never stopped Ferdinand from thinking about it; in that very same fall of 1526, he had broached the idea of an armed offensive against the voivode with Mary and had even felt out the imperial diet on the matter. The princes, however, resolved not to assist any overt Habsburg aggression in Hungary, an attitude which would harden with time and make their response to Ferdinand's pleas for aid more unpredictable. Nor was Charles especially encouraging. As far as he was concerned, Ferdinand had a valid claim to the Crown of St. Stephen, an achievement which the Emperor thought quite sufficient under the circumstances. An antagonized Zapolya, he felt, might very well ally himself overtly with the Turks and together they might destroy Ferdinand's Austrian patrimony in revenge. Though late in the winter of 1527 Charles did send his brother 100,000 ducats to aid him in Hungary, he begged Ferdinand not to undertake war there or in any other place equally dangerous to him. "Time," the Emperor suggested, not "fortune" would bring the younger man what he wanted.[36]

But though he did not openly disagree with Charles, Ferdinand refused to turn his back on his hope to win what he regarded as "justly" his through armed victory. The solidity of his purchased support seemed more doubtful than even when in May 1527, Batthyány, the Croatian ban, defected to Zapolya. Mary herself, physically indisposed and in despair over the prospects of her house in Hungary, called for her brother to come to the kingdom personally and do what he could to patch together his band of partisans.[37]

For the moment, however, Ferdinand had had enough of bribes and counter-bribes. Rather than go to Hungary in May he went to Bohemia, asking the estates there to help him in his military undertaking. Despite all of Charles's cautionary advice, he also asked him for aid. Neither source greeted his requests enthusiastically—the Bohemians were reluctant to do anything that would unduly increase Habsburg power and Charles persisted in trying to dissuade Ferdinand from war long after he had begun—but they sent some assistance anyway.[38] At the end of July, Ferdinand began an offensive in Hungary. In a lifetime filled with indecisive battles and outright defeat, this campaign was a true exception. As he moved through the kingdom in August, he reassembled not only his own party but won over some of Zapolya's adherents as well. By August 20 he was in camp at Buda where he heard that one of his most capable commanders, Nicholas von Salm, defeated Zapolya at Tokaj, about a hundred miles to the north and west. Though his power base in Transylvania remained, the voivode was now on the defensive in Hungary itself. He fled back to his home in the eastern part of the kingdom and, from there, to the court of his Polish father-in-law. For his part, Ferdinand triumphantly looked forward to the arrival of his wife in his camp since, as he put it, ". . . good husbands never willingly lose time when the opportunity presents itself. . . ."[39]

Ferdinand had not seen the last of Zapolya; Charles's warning that the magnate might join with other powers against Ferdinand was soon realized. Having been defeated by one German prince and not aided by any of those whom he had asked for help, he was now squarely in the hands of the Turks who would soon make use of him.[40] But Ferdinand had bought himself a little time to make some rudimentary administrative changes in the kingdom. And his hold on the realm was certainly better than it had been at any time since Louis's death. His commitment to central Europe was not yet complete. At the end of May, following the plundering of Rome by Charles's imperial troops, he once again asked to be made duke of Milan. And when the Bohemian estates had expressed some reluctance to make him their sovereign because they feared he might leave the kingdom to rule in Spain should Charles die, he did not flatly deny it.[41]

But the territorial logic derived from the interconnected borders of Hungary, Austria, and the kingdom of Bohemia was sufficiently compelling to make him see that he had deep interests in the area. That Zapolya was still alive meant that he would have to stay armed, despite his brother's pleas, even after Tokaj, to avoid military engagements.[42] In winning at least a claim to the Hungarian crown, Ferdinand could no longer be counted on to subordinate himself automatically to Charles's western policies. In September 1527, the Emperor, assuring his brother of their common aims, urged him to send as many men as he could to Italy. To do so, Ferdinand would have had to leave the Magyar realm to canvass Austria and in all likelihood, the Empire as well. He refused, pleading that Hungarian conditions did not permit him to depart.[43] It was not the sort of answer that Charles liked to hear nor Ferdinand especially liked to give. But, as Mary had put it in another connection, he now had a "few kingdoms" (*etlich kunigreich*) rather than simply a "principality" (*furstenthumb*) in Austria, and these brought with them imperatives of their own.[44]

CHAPTER V

THE PATTERN OF CONSOLIDATION

The acquisition of Bohemia and Hungary widened Ferdinand's opportunities to exercise the organizational bent which he had inherited from Maximilian. Indeed, he had been seriously restructuring his administration almost from the time of his arrival in Austria. Ferdinand was not especially innovative. Much of what he adopted had already been worked out by his grandfather and other Habsburgs before him, but it was Ferdinand who put these arrangements on a permanent footing.[1]

As soon as he had come to the Habsburg patrimony, the archduke set up a Court Council for Lower Austria which was to run the administrative and judicial apparatus of his government while he was absent from the area. After his brother turned over the Habsburg possessions in southwestern Germany along with the Tyrol, he empowered this Court Council to perform a similar function for all of these territories. In 1522, a so-called *Raitkammer,* a financial chamber charged with the collection of *regalia,* was also organized in Lower Austria. The city of Vienna itself did not escape his ambition to bring his lands under much tighter control.[2] Since the fourteenth century, the archdukes of Austria had been permitted to change the privileges of their capital, something Maximilian had restated as recently as 1517.[3] Ferdinand reserved for himself the right of final selection of the candidates for the two city councils which operated in the municipality. In one of those bodies, the so-called Inner Council, he had the right to name twelve of its twenty-four members. He also began to name a council which in effect oversaw the office of the chief city magistrate.[4]

But it was in bureaucratic reorganization that Ferdinand's desire to gain effective control over his holdings was most clearly expressed. The general diet of his Austrian lands which met with im in Augsburg in 1525-1526 urged him to establish a permanent Court Council. They also requested however, that it be staffed by reputable persons, by which they presumably meant native Austrians. Under the pressure of the Salamanca affair, Ferdinand carried through on this in 1526 and named officials to the offices of chancellor and treasurer as well. The results of all this activity were summarized in his *Hofstaatsordnung* of 1527 which ordered the establishment of a Court Council and a Court Treasury; a Court Chancellory was added in 1528. A Privy Council also appeared at this time, though there is no written evidence of its founding. There is a good deal of contemporary testimony to its existence, however, and to the central role which it played in advising Ferdinand on foreign affairs and legal and financial matters. Members of the Court Council, the Court Treasury, and, much later, the War Council sent their reports to this body. Staffed with secretaries for all domestic concerns, the Chancellory was responsible for developing documents for both the Court Council and the Privy Council. Only the Treasury had its own chancellory, a measure no doubt both of the importance which Ferdinand assigned to this body and the volume of business it had. In 1531 he created a War Council to supervise the raising and maintaining of army and naval personnel, artillery, bridges, and land and marine fortifications. In 1556, this was expanded into a *Hofkriegsrat* which oversaw all military matters. This body would also have its own chancellory and cabinet. Since, however, the funds which it had at its disposal to spend independently were very small, its field of action was limited.[5]

None of these institutions were more than functional aspects of the ruler, and they therefore could do little without his consent or that of his representative. The resolutions of the Privy Council had the force of law only through archducal sanction. In all probability, Ferdinand frequently presided over this body since only one person—Bishop Bernhard of Trent—is mentioned as president of the group and then only between 1535 and 1537. The intermediate administrative organizations throughout the Austrian lands were closely bound to instructions from the court. While having some leeway in judicial questions, they nevertheless could make no important decisions without first ascertaining Ferdinand's wishes. Throughout his life, he reaffirmed his right to control their membership. Despite frequent local protest, he continued to appoint non-Austrians to these positions. Nor did he allow his provincial nobility to monopolize these places. While they were certainly represented in these councils, the petty knights and university educated bourgeoisie also appeared. Ferdinand repeatedly would refer to them as his advisors and explicitly reject the view that they were simply envoys of his different possessions.[6]

No part of Ferdinand's bureaucracy more sharply registered the personal focus of his administration than did his financial apparatus. The resources of the polity were the resources of the ruler and vice-versa. All revenues from the Austrian lands, regardless of whether they were domainal income, taxes voted by the estates, or tolls and tariffs, flowed into one archducal repository. Thus, the Court Treasury had to meet the needs of the Austrian territories at large, the prince, and his family at once. The *Hofkammerordnung* of 1537, declaring as it does that extra-ordinary income from the estates was to be sought only after those from the *Kammergut* were exhausted, implies that the former were to be treated as a normal supplement of the latter. The Austrian lands were perhaps more inclined to accept such arrangements than their other German counterparts. Whereas in the latter, the territorial ruler's treasury could operate locally only to oversee regalian holdings, the estates in the Habsburg patrimony did not have tax treasuries which received, then dispensed monies which they granted to their ruler. Rather these funds went directly to subsidiary archducal treasuries in the various provinces. Again, Ferdinand's supervision of these structures and their personnel was tight. His involvement with the activities of the central Court Treasury were even closer. All important fiscal affairs had to have his consideration before any decisions were taken. The 1537 decree ordered that payments of more than ten gulden had to have the ruler's signature as well as those of the treasury superintendent and of a treasury councilor. Following the model set in other areas of Ferdinand's bureaucracy, the Court Treasury could dispatch only minor matters independently. If even these became difficult, the councilors had to consult Ferdinand who would then participate with them in the resolution. All financial complaints went directly to him. Subsidiary chambers in Vienna and Innsbruck, and later in Bratislava and Prague actually conducted most of the day-to-day business, but Ferdinand and his Court Treasury closely controlled them, even requiring them to adhere to the collegial organization of the parent body.[7]

The centralizing thrust of his Austrian administration carried over into Ferdinand's restructuring of his Bohemian and Hungarian bureaucracies. He initially planned to use the Vienna Court Council, Privy Council, and

Treasury as the highest royal offices in both realms. The idea behind this scheme was to free these structures from the influence of local estates, but it soon proved unworkable. Ferdinand then named vice-chancellors for Bohemia and a little later for Hungary, who had their own staffs. Finance, however stayed under the supervision of the Vienna Treasury. Taxes and aids as well as royal income from both kingdoms were sent to that chamber which was now responsible for directing most of the fiscal matters of all Habsburg possessions both new and old. Moravia, Silesia, and the two Lusatias were subordinated to the direction of Ferdinand's subsidiary treasury in Prague. While Ferdinand was willing to compromise with the Bohemians and to leave Chancellory and Court Council positions in the hands of natives, he relentlessly defended his right to appoint whom he wished to administer his monies. In Moravia too, fiscal matters were the one area where he was unwilling to accommodate the staffing suggestions of the estates. To shore up his uncertain control of Hungary, he simply did not fill the more powerful offices of the kingdom when vacancies occurred in them. After 1531, there was no palatine in the realm until the beginning of the seventeenth century.[8]

Wherever possible, Ferdinand tried to minimize provincial differences. Until 1542, he periodically attempted to call general meetings of the estates from all his territories to discuss matters common to the entire area and their single ruler. Twice in 1528, he summoned gatherings to air possibilities for establishing a common coinage in all his possessions; at other times Turkish defense problems were central in their agenda. Once this pressure to shoulder these burdens were placed on all of them, Ferdinand's estates themselves saw some value in cooperation. In 1537, for example, the Hungarians were very anxious for him to promote such a general meeting to aid them in warding off the sultan. In 1540, the estates of Upper Austria repeated the demand in the hope that the support for the Turkish wars could be spread more equitably among all the Habsburg possessions. In 1541-1542 such a session took place in Prague. For the first time Bohemian and Austrian representatives appeared together, though with meagre outcome. In 1544 and again in 1547, committees from the lands met in common, but no general diet was ever held again. In part the difficulty lay with the estates themselves who, while willing to call upon one another's resources, resisted incorporation into a true communality and the loss of individual influence with their ruler that went along with it.[9] Nor did such organizations meet Ferdinand's deepest needs. His military obligations required him to raise aid quickly and regularly; general meetings of estates conducted their deliberations no more swiftly than did local ones, and the time it took to assemble representatives from such far-flung possessions slowed down the proceedings even more.[10] But for all of these mechanical snags, Ferdinand conceived of his lands as an administrative unity very early in his career. In his first testament of 1532, later superseded, he ordered that if he should die with his male heirs in their minority and Charles unable to assume their guardianship, a regency drawn from all his possessions should be formed. This was to reside one year in Hungary, one year in Bohemia, and one year in Vienna, repeating the cycle until his sons could rule in their own right. A Hungarian would preside one year, someone from a joint Bohemian-Moravian-Silesian delegation another, and someone from the Austrian lands a third. Dynastic continuity was to be maintained by the presence in the body of Queen Anna if she were still alive and still widowed.[11]

But the results of Ferdinand's organizational measures were in no way commensurate to the attention he lavished on them. His administration continued to suffer from the confusions and oversights which bedevil most institutions when their responsibilities are growing. The peripatetic nature of his rule and the vast distances which separated his major cities, made it extremly difficult to centralize papers, registers, accounts and all the other by-products of bureaucracy.[12] Originals of testaments were often lost or mislaid, as were treaties and copies of them.[13] And surprising gaps showed up in his personnel at crucial moments. As Suleiman got underway to attack Vienna in 1529, Ferdinand had to admit that no one in his administration could translate the sultan's letters. It was only after his forces captured a Turk in 1530 who was apparently fluent in some western languages that Ferdinand had access to someone who could perform this task.[14]

And no mere bureaucratic reshuffling was going to solve his most pressing problem—the regularization and augmentation of his monies from all his lands. His Austrian territories were faced with ever rising levels of taxation. At the beginning of his reign, Ferdinand's estates paid taxes based on .5% of the total income of property. This figure quickly grew to 1, 1.5, 2 and 2.5% of these revenues. By 1525 they were paying the archduke 2 million gulden.[15] The pressure on Austria became even more intense after Mohács. Not only did Ferdinand incur heavy expenses in winning the Hungarian and Bohemian crowns, but his need to maintain a standing army in Hungary meant that he was always returning to his patrimonial lands for help.

Sporadic efforts were made to develop independent sources of funds. In 1527, hearing that the price of quicksilver in Portugal was high, Ferdinand tried to establish a monopoly in the trade with that kingdom. 1529 saw him raise the duties on good exported from Hungary and Lower Austria to Italy, an act which indeed guaranteed him an important supply of future revenues. Regardless of their political allegiance, Ferdinand encouraged merchants to conduct at least part of their trade in or through his lands.[16]

But none of this was viewed as more than a supplement to the traditional incomes which came from estates and *regalia,* and it was on these that Ferdinand focussed his attention in his new kingdoms. From the beginning of his rule in Bohemia, he obviously hoped to extract as much as he could from the kingdom by taxation; as early as 1529, he expected it and Moravia to pay 148,000 out of the 349,000 gulden he had requested as aid from all his possessions that year.[17] Louis and Vladislav had both mortgaged vast sums which were due the crown, and Ferdinand was most anxious to bring these under royal control once again. His chief problem was a nobility which held stubbornly on to these mortgages and made whatever concessions they made to their king with the utmost reluctance. One of the most important sources of crown income was the right to mint silver coinage from Kutná Hora and Jáchymov. The mortgage to the latter was held by the Šlik family; before his coronation Ferdinand had agreed to let this continue. Once he came to rule, however, he began to try and break the contract, claiming that it allowed him to do so if it became prejudicial to the kingdom.[18] In this he was successful, but it did little to solve his long-range difficulties. He himself continued to mortgage royal possessions and to accept loans on the basis of future revenues in Bohemia; the Jáchymov mines themselves would eventually be inadequate to cover the demands of those who had extended credit to Ferdinand on the basis of their projected output.[19] While Ferdinand's orders for an exact accounting of his revenues represented a great improvement over Louis's conduct of the royal office, they led to no immediate bettering of the Habsburg financial position in Bohemia. The

Venetian ambassador who reported in 1543 that the only regular incomes left the king in Bohemia were the tolls at the gates of Prague was perhaps exaggerating, but not completely. As far as extraordinary revenues went, the Bohemian diets rarely refused their sovereign's requests altogether.[20] However, bargaining with them was a tedious undertaking; the amounts they granted were given for only short periods of time and seemed to be fixed by convention rather than the king's needs.[21]

Ferdinand's situation in Hungary was different, though the results, as far as royal income went, were no better for him than in Bohemia. The Magyars were not especially enthusiastic at the way the Habsburg incorporated the financial administration of the kingdom into his Vienna bureaucracy. However, after he argued at a diet in Nagy Szombat in 1545 that he had the right to organize finances as he saw fit without the interference of the estates, they seemed to have agreed.[22] His great problem was getting his hands on the revenues in the first place.

Mohács had been not only a military disaster but a financial one as well. Upon hearing of the battle's outcome, Mary had fled Buda by ship up the Danube, taking with her a collection of church silver from the town, freshly minted coins, and some of the treasures of the Corvina, Matthias Hunyadi's great Renaissance library. On the way to Bratislava, her announced destination, the boats were plundered and many of the valuables simply sank. Of what remained, part was immediately carted off to Vienna and the rest fell temporarily into the hands of John Bornemisza, the burgrave of Bratislava who refused to release it from his castle on the ground that he had not made up his mind to vote for Ferdinand or Zapolya as king.[23]

Bornemisza's indecision symbolized the plight of all royal finance in the kingdom. The only part of the realm that was firmly under Ferdinand's control was the stretch between the Danube and his Austrian borders. Zapolya's influence, even after his defeat at Tokaj, was paramount from the Danube east. From a strategic point of view, this was no great disadvantage to Ferdinand. His territory was compact and relatively easy to defend. Because it was small, however, the revenue to be drawn from it was limited. But territorial allegiances were far more complex than that and so were the financial problems. Many counties in the kingdom were half for Ferdinand, half for Zapolya. Fortresses frequently swore loyalty to one man, then to the other. A victory of Charles V in the west or some sign from him that he planned a major thrust against the Turks brought more supporters and aid for Ferdinand. A success of the French or the Turks or a failure of imperial troops in Hungary, and Ferdinand's partisans would once again fade away.[24]

None of this encouraged the steady production of revenue. In 1528, Ferdinand was able to realize only about 7,000 gulden from all of his Hungarian territories, an almost laughable sum when one realizes that he owed the army he was supporting in Hungary that year 90,000 florins by May.[25] Nor were the Hungarian estates especially cooperative in paying for their own defense. Recently freed by the Jagellonians from the need to support a standing military force, something which had been imposed on them under Matthias Corvinus, they were doubly grudging in their grants to their king. The split of their country between Ferdinand and Zapolya adversely affected their incomes as well. In 1527, part of the 277,000 gulden which the estates gathered for defense purposes came from loans. Ferdinand, furthermore, could no more eschew the bad habits of previous monarchs in Hungary than he could in Bohemia. Royal income went regularly to pacify his followers. Between 1527 and 1536, he gave up thirty-six royal castles to various Hungarian landowners.[26]

In all of his early endeavours to strengthen his hold on his new realms, Ferdinand discovered that his family was of only limited utility to him. Charles did not ignore him—in 1528 he sent along 100,000 ducats to outfit his brother's Hungarian force—but his response to Ferdinand's pleas for aid were never predictable. His aunt Margaret reported that the estates of the Netherlands were unwilling to participate in the Habsburg recapture of Hungary from the Turks and pressed them no further.[27] And, as time went on, Mary's presence in Bohemia and Hungary as a dowager queen, proved to have a very dark side indeed.

Mary was a clever woman, and her partisans in both kingdoms were important and widely connected. In Bohemia, she and Adam of Hradec, Ferdinand's chancellor, had earlier been allies in trying to dislodge Zdeněk Lev of Rožmital from his position as high burgrave of Prague, the governor of the realm in the absence of the king. Through this tie, she was able to win Hradec to Ferdinand's cause, though Rožmital's supporters continued to resent her. Her Hungarian circle was much wider, and since she had become one of the richest landlords of the territory, her influence there was much stronger than in Bohemia.[28]

But Mary had her own mind and her own person to look out for, factors which became positive liabilities to Ferdinand as he tried to tighten his control over his new possessions. For one thing, her religious views became something of an embarassment to him. No matter how strongly Ferdinand felt about the need for church reform, he could ill-afford a break with Rome. Once the formalities of papal approval were gone through, never a difficult matter in emergencies, Ferdinand could summarily seize the jewels and gold and silver objects in ecclesiastical establishments. When estates demurred at paying him subsidies, as the Upper Austrians did in 1526 and 1527, he inventoried the religious valuables in the territory and confiscated them. In 1529 alone, one quarter of his military budget for that year came from church possessions.[29]

In all his official publications, Ferdinand closely followed the lead set by his brother in the Edict of Worms of 1521. The younger Habsburg issued a mandate from Buda in 1527 which made Lutheranism, Zwinglianism, and Anabaptism civil offenses and sharply limited the economic and political freedoms of those who belonged to these sects. In 1528, he ordered that all persons who dealt in heretical books be drowned.[30] His attitude toward the Anabaptists was especially harsh, undoubtedly because many of them argued for common property and against civil authority. Charles's mandate against them in 1528 was followed by an even more stringent one of Ferdinand's in 1529. Whereas the Emperor's document allowed the possibility of recantation, the new king's limited this chance only to a period just after the accused had embraced his or her new faith.[31] The measures carried beyond the Austrian patrimony. Burnings and executions of Anabaptists began in Moravia in 1528.[32]

In Hungary, neither Ferdinand nor Zapolya could afford to have too many scruples about the confessional leanings of their supports. But what the Habsburg did out of sheer necessity and what he regarded as correct religious belief were two quite different matters. He was therefore aghast to discover in 1527 that his sister in Hungary had not only gone to hear an Anabaptist preacher who was evangelizing in the neighborhood where he was staying, but, having decided that the man's ideas should be opposed, hit upon a Lutheran to do so!

Mary's religious attitudes were very similar to Ferdinand's. Much inclined toward Erasmian reform, she was as anxious as her brother to see

abuses removed from the church. At her court, she had been surrounded
by humanists who were sharp critics of contemporary religious institutions; many of these transferred their allegiance from Erasmus to Luther
following the Leipzig Debates of 1519.[33] Unlike Ferdinand, however, she
may have given Lutheranism serious thought. To the former's great annoyance, Luther dedicated an edition of four psalms of consolation to her
following Louis's death.[34] Her observation that if Charles and Ferdinand
could not stop the Wittenberg reformer from writing what he pleased,
neither could she, set the tone for future discussions with both her brothers
on religious matters.[35] Having read a book by Luther on baptism and the
sacraments and having found that it made great sense, she saw no reason
not to turn Lutherans loose on Anabaptists. She was so impressed by the
tract that she forwarded it to Ferdinand.[36]

Ferdinand himself well knew that both Luther and Zwingli were opponents of Anabaptism.[37] The political implications of his sister's gesture
for his own position and that of his house frightened him, however, and
his response to Mary was prompt and vigorous. His job was a delicate
one—to persuade her of her mistakes without offending her—no easy
task when dealing with so head-strong a person as the widowed queen.
He apologized for sounding like a confessor, but then embarked upon
a powerful defense of orthodoxy which he tried to couch in terms of
dynastic self-interest. The Emperor and the pope had both condemned
the Lutherans as heretics, he argued, and he invited her to imagine what
supporters of the Habsburgs would do if they discovered that one of the
family was harboring such people at her court. Mary, however, was an
intelligent woman, and Ferdinand appealed to that side of her as well.
He pointed out that the Roman church had also written on subjects such
as baptism and communion, so that there was no need for her to consult
Lutherans and Anabaptists on these questions. Along with his letter he
enclosed a Lutheran New Testament, annotated to show where in Ferdinand's opinion, the reformer had twisted the text.[38] The lecture was at
least moderately successful—by August 1528 Mary sounded as grim about
the spread of Protestantism in Hungary as did Ferdinand, but her identification with the movement remained. At the Diet of Augsburg in 1530,
attended by both of her brothers, herself, and Ferdinand's wife Anna,
the Lutherans attempted to win her support. It was only after intensive
discussions with Charles that she appears to have renounced her flirtation
with their cause.[39]

But the greatest problem which Mary posed for her brother in his efforts to pull together the tattered Magyar realm was financial. He soon learned to suspect her judgment in such matters, particularly when she was dealing with the Hungarians. While Ferdinand was not adverse to subsidizing her favorites such as Alexis Thurzó who were also faithful supporters of the Habsburg cause, he could not allow her to be as generous as her impulses sometimes led her to be with her courtiers. Put bluntly, he simply could not afford it. The costs of the Bohemian election and the 1527 campaign against Zapolya even made it impossible for him to hold to the vow which he had given Mary that he would cover the expenses she incurred in meeting his obligations to his Hungarian partisans. In 1527, he grew so anxious about his sister's fiscal irresponsibility that he dispatched his own agents to the kingdom to counter the influence of the Magyars on her.[40]

More vexing than anything else to Ferdinand, however, were the fiscal conditions that came with Mary's status as an ex-royal consort. As Louis's self-proclaimed heir, the Habsburg had guaranteed that he would fulfill the terms of the Habsburg-Jagellonian marriage contract of 1515. It brought, as Ferdinand was later to observe, great pain to himself.[41] For one thing, he was now responsible for payment of the Jagellonian counter-gift, the groom's counterpart of the bride's dowry in their marriage contract, and Mary's widow maintenance, to which she had a right so long as she did not re-marry. The former sum amounted to around 200,000 ducats; according to the agreement between Vladislav and Maximilian in 1515 if the widow's portion did not come to 25,000 ducats annually, the reigning king of Hungary had to make up the difference from his own treasury.[42]

If Mary had controlled outright all the lands, cities, and mines that were to guarantee these monies, she would have had a strangle-hold on almost all the royal income of Hungary. As it was, however, much of this fell into the hands of Zapolya and the Turks. At the end of 1526, Ferdinand had promised to defend these possessions and to win them back; where that could not be done, he had to compensate her in some way. At first he promised a pension of 1500 florins a month which he quickly raised to 2000. Her debts continued to rise, however, and the Lower Austrian treasury, to which the new king had first turned for these funds, refused to pay them, especially after 1529.[43]

Beginning in 1528, Ferdinand tried to persuade her to turn some of her incomes, particularly from the royal mines back to the Hungarian treasury. But despite all his pleas about the dangers to the house of Habsburg that his financial plight in Hungary brought with it, and his moderation of his request to one-third of these revenues rather than all of them, Mary refused to listen. She did promise to inventory her incomes more carefully, a tactic she quite appropriately urged her brother to adopt, but she pointed out that she herself owed a great deal and had a position to maintain.[44]

The middle of that year saw Ferdinand on a different tack—that of persuading her to marry. The prospective husband, at least as far as he was concerned, was James V of Scotland. Charles had been trying to head off a French-Scottish alliance, and James, as the nephew of Henry VIII looked like a possible heir to the English crown, since, according to Ferdinand's speculations, the Tudor might no longer produce any heirs. All of these considerations aside, he tried to persuade his ambitious sister of the happiness which a true queenly estate would bring her once again. Though he did not say it openly, Ferdinand was also well aware that her remarriage would bring the resources of her widow's pension in Hungary finally under his control. But Mary thwarted him once again, claiming that no love could make up for her first one.[45] He continued to dangle the Scottist marriage before her, but he did not press her closely.[46] Even when she became Charles's regent in the Netherlands and was out of the kingdom altogether, she did not give up her rights in it. Much to Ferdinand's disappointment and her own, Charles refused to contribute more than 47,000 florins a year to the upkeep of the Habsburg court in Brussels. Mary had to make up the difference herself, and for this reason, her Hungarian resources were still important.[47] Between the years 1527 and 1544, she drew altogether 258,368 florins from the Magyar kingdom, enough by the price level of 1527 to have paid a mixed cavalry-infantry force of 7000 for seven and one-half months service.[48] Though some settlement of the issue between Ferdinand and Mary finally did come in 1548, which returned the Hungarian royal incomes to the kingdom, the former continued to receive yearly compensation for it from her brother. By her death in 1558, Ferdinand had paid her almost 26,000,000 florins on her Hungarian claims.[49]

Thus, despite herculean efforts to bring some organization into the administrative structure of his lands, Ferdinand was far from solving his main problem—an increase in revenue which would permit him to complete the task of meeting the Ottoman challenge to which his promises and circumstances had commited him. His own profligacy did nothing to help his situation of course, but neither did the stubborn parochialism of his estates and the highly individual concerns of other members of his family. His most important ally in Hungary, his sister, was as concerned with her own interests as she was with his. By 1529 it was readily apparent that these were to be chronically problematic issues for Ferdinand. The following four years—1529 to 1532—would show how unpleasant they could be in a crisis.

CHAPTER VI

A PARTIAL VICTORY BREEDS ANOTHER

Judged in terms of political formalities, much in Ferdinand's life had been settled by 1528. The Austrian patrimony was clearly his as were the titles in the several lands of the Bohemian crown. His status in Hungary, while still seriously contested by Zapolya, had acquired at least a partial legitimacy especially after his victory over the magnate in 1527.

Much, however, remained undecided. His acquisition of the Bohemian crown and a solid claim to the Hungarian one had in no way dampened his ambition to succeed his brother in the Empire. Even though Charles, after initially supporting the election of his brother as King of the Romans in 1525, postponed serious discussion of the matter until he himself had been crowned by the pope, Ferdinand's aspirations to the title had never flagged. Acting through Count Frederick of the Palatine in September 1525, he contacted the Fuggers about financial backing for his candidacy. At the same time, he took up the question with the elector of Trier during the diet of Augsburg. Two years later, anticipating his own coronation, Charles finally sanctioned these feelers and encouraged Ferdinand to put them out to all the electors.[1]

Most problematic of all, however, were the Turks, always poised, it seemed, to seize for themselves or their puppets the territories which Ferdinand had so painstakingly acquired. So many of his troops in Hungary had been deployed against Zapolya since 1527 that his remaining forces were too few to resist occasional Ottoman marauders on his borders, let alone the entire Turkish army.[2] To make things worse, Charles V's gloomy prediction that military offensives against Zapolya might provoke more trouble than his brother could comfortably handle had become a reality. On January 27, 1528, the Sultan had announced that

[79]

Zapolya was now under his protection and that the two of them had concluded an alliance against Ferdinand. Zapolya's father-in-law, Sigismund of Poland, had signed an armistice with the Turks, so that when Ferdinand asked that he at least keep Polish troops out of the magnate's army, he coldly replied that he could no more do that than Charles could keep Germans out of French ranks.[3]

A serious anti-Habsburg coalition was therefore in the making in the east, and Ferdinand went on the diplomatic offensive against it. In 1528, he dispatched a mission to Constantinople to arrange a peace with Suleiman. However, his clumsily extravagant demands that the Turks give up the areas of Hungary which they occupied only moved the Grand Vizir, Ibrahim, to wonder that the Habsburg did not ask for the Ottoman capital itself. Whether the Turks had even received the embassy in good faith is a matter of speculation. At the beginning of 1529, Ferdinand was warned that a major invasion from Constantinople was almost certain, since large-scale preparations were underway.[4]

Ferdinand had begun asking for aid even before that, both abroad and at home. About the only thing which he gained in foreign quarters was some understanding of how deep anti-Habsburg feeling was running among the other European dynasties and their supporters. Locked in battle with the papacy over his wish to divorce Catherine of Aragon, Ferdinand's aunt, Henry VIII remained impassive to the pleas of Ferdinand's envoy, Johannes Faber, even as the latter forecast that, unchecked, the Turks might eventually be watering their horses on the Thames. The Polish diet regarded Ferdinand's difficulties in Hungary as punishment for having taken that land and Bohemia out of the Jagellonian orbit, so that they too refused to help even when Sigismund, frightened by the possibility of a direct Ottoman attack, asked them to do so. That the French were hurrying aid to Zapolya, a member since 1526 of the League of Cognac, made up of Francis I, the pope, Venice, and Milan, was to be expected.[5]

His more likely sources of aid—his own lands and his family—were more responsive. After listening to his arguments about their interdependency, Moravia and Bohemia together promised 9,000 infantry and 800 cavalry, and the various Austrian provinces were very generous.[6] In the Netherlands, Margaret discouraged her nephew from any efforts to raise funds there, an attitude which did not prevent him from at least trying once the Turks actually did appear before Vienna.[7] Charles was more encouraging. He promised his brother money and urged others such as the pope and the king of Portugal to help as well. He also indicated that a peace between him and Francis I was in the offing, a condition which Ferdinand viewed as a key not only to checking the Turks but German religious unrest as well.[8]

But Charles was in no hurry to follow through on any of this. Ferdinand regarded his position in Hungary as far more central to Habsburg anti-Turkish strategy than did his brother. For Charles, Ferdinand's predicament in the kingdom was an unwelcome diversion from what he increasingly treated as his main theater of activity, the west and the Mediterranean. Ferdinand's antagonizing of Zapolya had handed Francis I yet another ally, thereby adding even more to the already crushing weight of the Emperor's military and diplomatic concerns. Ferdinand, on the other hand, felt that his undisputed control of the Hungarian crown was the only way to block further Ottoman advances into Christendom. The lack of immediacy felt by Charles in the situation was readily apparent in April 1529 when he asked his hard-pressed brother to raise more troops for him in Italy. Under protest Ferdinand complied, somewhat ruefully commenting that he knew his duty.[9]

One major source of support remained untapped—the Empire itself. A diet was to meet in Speier during the first part of 1529; Ferdinand arrived there in March prepared to argue his cause as vigorously as he could. He hoped that the deliberations would be brief and that the Emperor would add his presence and prestige to it, but in both instances he was disappointed.[10] As the meeting began, Ferdinand delivered a ringingly militant oration in German in which he outlined the consequences for all of Christian Europe which an Ottoman invasion of the Empire would hold. Stressing that it was far more advantageous to counter such aggression on foreign rather than native soil, he argued that the sultan be hunted down whether he attacked with all his forces or not. He begged the diet to put whatever aid they might give him into effect at once rather than waiting for the actual Turkish onslaught.[11]

However, all of this aroused only the deepest mistrust among the estates, a reaction which bode ill for anyone who planned to be German Emperor as Ferdinand did. When it became apparent that the Turks really were on the way, the diet did vote to give Ferdinand 16,000 men, but only in the form of temporary aid. There were those who muttered that any funds the king received would only go toward paying off his debts. Some resented the power which they felt Salamanca and Faber continued to have in his government. A lavish banquet which he gave near what he hoped would be the end of his stay in Speier left many of the cities grumbling that such monies could be more wisely used elsewhere.[12]

But his chief problem was the high level of antagonism between Protestant and Catholic that had been reached. Both Ferdinand and the Catholic estates, a majority of the diet, resented what they felt were Lutheran abuses of the concessions made to them in 1526. When Ferdinand spoke of the "cuius regio eius religio" formula of that diet, he very much sounded as if he wanted to nullify it. His public behavior certainly confirmed this. Because members of his own retinue and household staff streamed to Lutheran services during the Easter celebration which occurred during the diet, he tried to put a stop to Protestant preaching and breaking of the fast. Nothing, however, came of it. He made a great show of his own orthodoxy throughout the holiday, publicly feeding, clothing, and washing the feet of twelve poor men in the rites of Holy Thursday. On Easter Sunday, he appeared in the choir where Elector Albrecht of Mainz performed the mass.[13] More concrete political action also bespoke his loyalty to the Roman faith. Since 1528, Ferdinand had been exploring the formation of some sort of Catholic league, a move which the ever-suspicious princes viewed as just another way of expanding Habsburg power in Germany. While at the diet, Ferdinand continued negotiations on this matter which ended with the establishment of such an organization on April 22, 1529.[14]

The true peak of the Lutheran-Catholic hostility at the gathering, however, had been reached two days before. In a hurry to leave Speier because of the Turks and because of the impatience of his wife who was bitterly lamenting his absence, Ferdinand approved the recess of the diet which had the support of the overwhelming majority of the Catholic members. Calling for an end to the 1526 concessions, it provoked an explosion of wrath from the Lutherans who summarized their objections in the famous Protest of Speier of April 20. The way it was presented to Ferdinand angered him almost as much as its contents. Brought to him by representatives of the princes and cities, the king insisted that it was the rulers themselves who should have brought it and sent the document back with its bearers. Ferdinand himself resolved to ignore the Protest and advised others to do so as well, arguing that no minority had the right to overturn a recess supported by a majority of the diet. He took his own counsel seriously. At three times he made appointments with the Lutherans to discuss the problem with them, and before each of these, he broke the engagement.[15] Yet, despite this and the Protestant decision to withhold their promised military aid as a sign of their displeasure, Ferdinand was not altogether downcast as he left Speier. He had gotten at least some troops for defense, although attacking either Zapolya or the Turks was out of the question as far as all the estates, including the Catholics, were concerned. And he continued to hope that the elector of Saxony and Landgrave Philip of Hesse, chief among those to withdraw their assistance, might have second thoughts about their action.[16]

Circumstances alone did not allow him the luxury of yielding to passive despair. As the diet had wrangled, the Turks were moving up the Danube valley. Despite dreadful weather, they reached Belgrade toward the end of July and about a month later they were approaching Buda.[17] By the beginning of September, they were in that city. Mary had reminded Ferdinand that the birth of his second son, also named Ferdinand, made it all the more necessary for him to defend his territories; the pace of his efforts to drive up more support for himself against the invaders became correspondingly frantic. At the end of July, he tried to buy Suleiman off with a "pension"—the word "tribute" was carefully avoided—but the sultan remained unshaken in his course. From Linz Ferdinand issued a manifesto to all of Christendom, begging for help and vowing in the grandiose language of most such documents to liberate Jerusalem if possible. Special pleas were sent to the pope.[19]

Once again, he turned to his family. As worried about her Hungarian possessions as her brother, Mary asked him to send a contingent of men to protect her holdings rather than sending any aid of her own. Ferdinand refused, claiming that he could not split his forces in the kingdom; they had enough to do there as it was.[20] With Charles, he was somewhat more successful. True the Emperor had no personal funds to put at his disposal, and his promise to do more for his brother once his affairs with Clement VII and Francis I were in order, included no timetable for the accomplishment of this. But he sent embassies to several corners of Europe to beg aid for Ferdinand, and most important of all, he brought the Lutherans back into the contributing ranks of Germany's defenders. The latter had sent a delegation to the Emperor with their protest only to be told in very threatening terms that their sovereign expected them to meet their military obligations to his brother. Charles made it clear that as soon as he came to peace with Francis, he intended to return to the Empire. Seeing the risk in their position, the Protestants complied so that at the siege of Vienna in September 1529, their troops were among the forces which held the city.[21] If nothing else, Ferdinand's lifelong belief in the ability of his brother to bend the German situation a bit more to Habsburg liking was vindicated.

The Turks arrived before Vienna on September 27. Twenty thousand motley defenders, drawn from all over Europe, awaited them. Ferdinand himself was in Prague, drumming up last minute aid from the Bohemian diet. Despite the lateness of the season, Suleiman decided to settle down for a siege, but in doing so, he made a grave miscalculation. Fodder for his army's horses grew short and many of his troops, accustomed to somewhat milder climates, found the biting dampness of a Viennese autumn debilitating. Far from his sources of supply, the sultan ordered a retreat. On October 14, he broke camp.

It took a while for the news to reach Ferdinand in Bohemia. On October 15, he had not yet heard that the Turks were at the walls of his capital, let alone that they had left. But by the nineteenth he knew. He also knew that sheer luck—he called it divine providence—had saved him and that he had not seen the last of the Turks. The decisive defeat that he felt he needed to remove them permanently as a threat to his lands had not been administered; indeed, he expected Suleiman to return in the spring.[22] With the troops that he had, he decided to take advantage of the Ottoman withdrawal and try to recover some of the Danube forts which had been in their hands, as well as hwat he could of Hungary east to Buda. By the middle of November, Ferdinand discovered that his enemy's armies had evacuated Hungary far more thoroughly than he had imagined, and prospects seemed brighter than ever for the recapture of all the fortresses which had fallen to Zapolya and the Turks. The total reconquest of the kingdom itself did not seem to be impossible. But to do this, he had to pay his troops who had already mutinied once at the end of October. Ferdinand therefore renewed his efforts to raise subsidies where he could.[23]

Unpaid or not, the forces which he had assembled in Vienna were startlingly successful through November. They won both Győr and Pécs; Ferdinand hoped to go on to Buda. The ever-ambitious bishop of Zagreb, Erdödy, abandoned Zapolya and tried with about 350 men to make himself ban of Slavonia, but Ferdinand's troops defeated him as well. Zapolya's followers defected to Ferdinand in increasing numbers, and the Habsburg joyously saw Hungary to be at last within his grasp. His elation, however, was short-lived. Charles, who had raised some money for his brother in Spain which he himself described as "inadequate," had no more to spare and recommended a three-year truce with Suleiman. Ferdinand, however, was not quite ready to give up. He called general diets of his Austrian territories in Linz and of the Bohemian lands in České Budějovice to plea for emergency aid from them once again. Since he could not be in both places at once, he asked his sister and wife to be his representatives in Austria while he lent his person to the Bohemian meeting. To save time at the latter gathering he asked that all delegates from the various lands come with plenipotentiary powers from their parent diets so that they would not have to ask these to authorize any actions which they took at the general conclave.[24]

But little came of all these activities. Mary spent a good deal of her time at the Austrian meeting trying to dispel the suspicions of the delegates that Ferdinand was avoiding them because he did not wish to face their criticism. The king's experiences with the Bohemian deliberations were even more frustrating. The Moravian and Silesian representatives had come to the diet with the powers which their sovereign had requested, but the Bohemians did not. Though the first two groups did not oppose granting Ferdinand long-term assistance, the Bohemians did. Much against his will, he decided to follow the latter back to Prague to meet separately with them there. Not only did he want money from them, but he wished to head off negotiations which he heard were taking place between Zapolya and several members of the Bohemian estates. After a month of fierce bargaining, with Ferdinand not in good health, the Bohemians granted him 125,000 florins for a period of two years.[25]

But it was already too late. After their first successes in Hungary, Ferdinand's troops were beset with difficulties by the middle of January 1530. With no money and poorer provisions, the men foraged wherever they could. A large number of them had simply deserted, many of them for Zapolya's camp. Still in the middle of negotiations for soldiers and funds, Ferdinand reluctantly saw the need for a quick truce with the sultan. But in any case, he did not regard such an agreement as anything more than a temporary expedient which would allow him to gather strength for the future confrontation which he felt must come in order to settle satisfactorily his central European position.[26]

Even though Ferdinand had to back away from his long-range objectives against the Turks in 1529 and 1530, his conduct against his enemy had much enhanced his stature both in the eyes of his family and other contemporaries. Commemorative medals struck after the siege of Vienna was lifted showed him with unmistakable Habsburg facial characteristics—the undershot jaw and half-open mouth—but with a lively confidence in his eyes that registered clearly even in a metallic medium. His feeling was not misplaced. Even Mary began to refer to him as a great prince. Within the Empire, his warnings about the Turkish threat increasingly came to be understood as something more than a cynical cover for his territorial ambitions. This plus his now-established status as a king in his own right made some of the princes more willing to fulfill his other unrealized goal —his election as King of the Romans and imperial heir-apparent.[27]

Most of all, Charles, too, indicated that he would actively promote this move. Early in January 1530, the Emperor disclosed that he planned to come to Germany and that one of his reasons was to see that his brother was raised to this new title.[28] Ferdinand, who had not lost the opportunity to air the question at Speier in 1529, even in the midst of his military and religious concerns, was delighted to hear the news. He was quick to reinforce his brother's intentions by pointing out that if anyone other than a member of their house were to be elected to the office, his own position vis-à-vis the Turks would be doubly dangerous. Nor, he commented, would a hostile Germany be much help to Charles in Italy.[29] But the Emperor apparently nneded little additional convincing. Italian diplomats were astounded that he did not want the title for his son, the future Philip II, but the lad was only three years old, and Charles seemed to recognize that he could not personally spend enough time in Germany to give it the direction it needed. Though he left no direct statement on the issue, an anonymous document drawn up in the Burgundian chancellory in 1532 claims that this is what he thought, and his actions certainly confirm it. The arrangement in which Ferdinand served as his *locumtenens* and the head of the *Reichsregiment* had been far from satisfactory.[30]

Charles and Clement VII had already removed the most serious impediment to Ferdinand's election. Technically no King of the Romans could be chosen until the reigning Emperor was crowned by the pope, a ritual which had been completed in Bologna in 1530. However, there were other barriers to be surmounted, thrown up by those who chose to find or to construct them. For example, the Golden Bull of 1356, which had regularized election procedures, made no provisions for the crowning of the brother of an Emperor as Roman King. Liberal applications of bribes could induce even the most stubborn of constitutionalists to forget his scruples, at least for a while, so long as these did not serve as a mask for other and more important issues. It is this sort of delaying action that Ferdinand encountered. Growing maturity had not altogether eradicated the negative impression which he had made on the estates when he first met them. A few influential princes still regarded him as too energetic and ambitious to be trusted completely.[31] The Lutheran rulers—Elector John Frederick of Saxony, Lardgrave Philip of Hesse, Duke Ernst of Lüneburg, and others—were the most predictable sources of opposition. It was they who argued most forcefully the point about the Golden Bull's silence on the role of the Emperor's brother.[32] A serious rival for the position also existed—Duke William of Bavaria— who had strong support form the king of France and earlier from Pope Clement VII. The Wittelsbachs had already shown their fear of Habsburg encirclement in the vigorous contest which they put up in the Bohemian election; the two families would find a bond in their common Catholicism only as the Reformation progressed. The elector of Trier also had some reservations about Ferdinand.[33]

Just as he had done the year before in forcing the Protestants back into Ferdinand's army, Charles once again proved how central he was to his brother's goals. Upon arriving at the diet meeting in Augsburg in 1530, he described Ferdinand's talents in glowing phrases. Money and other favors were also distributed among the electors, and, with the very important exception of the Lutheran elector of Saxony, all came over to the Habsburg camp by the end of the year. On January 5, 1531, Ferdinand received the votes of five electors minus Saxony and himself, who, as elector of Bohemia did not participate. A few days later, he was crowned.[34] The price of all of this for Ferdinand alone was 356,845 gulden which he had coaxed out of the Fuggers. A month after the banking house had agreed to cover the sum, they and their descendants were raised to the status of imperial *Freiherren.*[35]

Thus another title was added to Ferdinand's growing collection. His crowning as his brother's successor fulfilled an ambition held for many years. In theory, the new office would give him a degree of freedom in the Empire which he had not heretofore enjoyed. But much still depended on what others were ready to allow him to do. Almost immediately after his coronation in Aachen, the reservations held about him and his family began to surface. For one thing, Charles, who still harbored some doubts that the Germans would obey his brother, was not ready to turn all his rights as Emperor over to Ferdinand quite yet. A secret document, appended to the public one in which the Emperor granted plenipotentiary powers to the new King of the Romans, was sent to the latter in March 1531. In it, Ferdinand's competence to grant titles and to impose the imperial ban was sharply limited, prerogatives with which he had hoped to discipline the recalcitrant elector of Saxony and his ally, Philip of Hesse. The Emperor also reserved for himself the privilege to review and alter foreign treaties which his brother signed in the name of the Empire.[36]

Charles was genuinely worried about growing Protestant hostility to the Habsburg position in the Empire; the impact of Ferdinand's election gave him more reason for concern.[37] John Frederick of Saxony complained bitterly at now having to obey two rulers.[38] On February 27, 1531, the Protestant princes formally joined with one another in the so-called Schmalkaldic League. Bavarian militancy also grew. In 1531, a document circulated among the estates there accusing the Emperor and his brother of wanting to control the Empire for themselves, thereby crushing German freedoms. Their fears were translated into formal protective measures. By October 1531, the Wittelsbachs entered into the religiously improbable but politically sound alliance of Saalfeld with the Schmalkaldians. Cooperation among this coalition, France, and Zapolya was the next logical move.[39] Other South German Catholic rulers were equally suspicious of Ferdinand. Meeting in Ueberlingen in September 1531 to discuss ways of protecting their faith, they at first refused him admission to their gathering.[40]

Ferdinand was quick to admit that he was too weak to deal with these problems himself, title or no. As early as the spring of 1531, he began to urge Charles to return to the Empire and bring the estates into line. He did not want to go to war against the Germans—the Turks were threatening to move again—but he did not have the money to bribe the dissidents either, so that a meeting of the Emperor with the princes "beard to beard" as he put it in Spanish seemed to be the only way to persuade them to accept him in his new offices. Charles was sympathetic and agreed to return again. However, he was anxious not to push the Lutherans too far for fear that they might assist the Zwingliites who were then at war with the Catholic cantons in Switzerland. Charles instructed his agents who were to begin preliminary negotiations with the elector of Saxony to reassure John Frederick that his electoral powers were in no way prejudiced by Ferdinand's elevation. Nor did Ferdinand's accession to the office in any way determine who his successors might be. The groundwork of a devastating future quarrel between the brothers had already been laid.

By the time the Emperor got to Germany himself, however, it was 1532, and the recognition of Ferdinand's election had become tied to still other issues. The Turks were threatening central Europe again, and Charles was terribly anxious to have the military support of the Protestants. The latter agreed, at least temporarily, to accept his brother as King of the Romans in an agreement hammered out in Nürnberg, but at a price. In return for this gesture and the troops, Charles promised to observe the religious *status quo* until a general council settled the matter. Worried though they might have been over the growing might of the Habsburgs, at least in a formal sense, the German estates were not without their defenses.

Thus Ferdinand's enhanced political and military stature had brought him few of the advantages which he had expected. Neither he nor Charles seem to have considered that it was their policies which had aroused so much hostility in Germany; their exalted notions of themselves and their prerogatives seemingly immunized them from the self-doubt and second thoughts which plague ordinary men. But Ferdinand was no stranger to incomplete holds on titles—the Austrian lands had come to him only gradually and his claim to Hungary was still hotly contested. Some sort of possession of office was better than none, and both he and the Emperor knew it. Equally important for him was that Charles had apparently kept the promise made after Pavia in 1525. The German election simply could not have taken place as it did without the

Emperor's support. However, Charles's decision to back Ferdinand had been based not so much on the latter's interests as they had been on his own. His indifferent response to the younger man's military difficulties in 1529 in part stemmed from his determination that these problems were exclusively Ferdinand's. Whether he could or would assist his brother in matters of primary concern only to the latter remained to be proven.

CHAPTER VII

STALEMATE

Ferdinand was always racked with alarm whenever news of Ottoman militancy reached him. At the same time, he never thought that the sultan's armies nor those of his protegé Zapolya were unbeatable, provided that there were adequate forces to counter them. Given the alternative which Turkish expansion posed for him, he could hardly think otherwise. However, practical experience reinforced his conviction. For example, a campaign which he ordered against his rival in Hungary late in 1530 brought gratifying results. Ferdinand's troops were able to take both Esztergom and Visegrád, although Zapolya was able to get enough men to Buda, the primary target, to defend the city successfully.[1] The Turks themselves were decidedly intimidated by the idea of a grand Habsburg coalition, the instrument in which Ferdinand vested all his military hopes. In 1531, the sultan, who was toying with the idea of an Italian invasion, promised not to molest Ferdinand if only he would not interfere on the peninsula. He refused, saying that he could not abandon the Emperor if the latter were in need.[2]

But putting together such a force was not easy, especially in the early 1530s. Neither Charles nor Mary wanted war in east central Europe and the Balkans, and they pressed Ferdinand to undertake peace talks with his Hungarian rival and with the Porte. Separate sessions with the Turks and Zapolya began in 1530; Charles was sufficiently concerned that they be fruitful to send envoys to both sets of discussions. The talks with Zapolya begain in Poznań in January under the personal mediation of King Sigismund. Little progress took place, although Ferdinand did win the Polish ruler over to a marriage between his eldest daughter, Archduchess Elizabeth, then four, and the ten-year old Polish heir apparent, the fugure Sigismund Augustus. Ferdinand's uncompromising demand that Zapolya recognize him and his heirs as the rightful rulers of Hungary was the chief issue between the parties. The Transylvanian magnate offered to assure the Habsburg and his heirs the Hungarian succession if he died without legitimate male issue of his own; he was also willing to allow Ferdinand the right to carry personally the title king of Hungary during the latter's lifetime. Whatever compensation Ferdinand promised for all of this was to come from the Emperor, a proposition which Zapolya and his advisors rightly deemed suspect. They had even better reason to doubt his good will when he began a short campaign against the voivode in the latter half of the year, as previously mentioned. A one-year truce was eventually agreed upon in December 1530; in May 1531, both sides decided to prolong it for another year. A final settlement between the rivals, however, seemed very far off indeed.[3]

The problem of the Hungarian succession dominated Ferdinand's talks with the Porte as well. Perhaps unrealistically, he believed that total possession of the kingdom could be wrested from the Turks through diplomacy; perhaps, given the attitude of his brother, he accepted such procedures as his only alternative. He volunteered to pay up to 100,000 ducats for a longer period of peace in the kingdom where he would be allowed to rule alone. The size of the tribute would depend on just how much of the realm the Turks were willing to cede to him. More flexible in this case than he was with Zapolya, Ferdinand authorized his representatives in Constantinople to sanction yielding Hungary to the magnate provided that after the latter's death, the Hungarian throne went to the Habsburgs in perpetuity. But claiming that all of the kingdom belonged to him, Suleiman adamantly rebuffed these gestures.[4] The major thing which Ferdinand gained throughout the entire negotiating process was the trust of his brother. On the whole, he conveyed the impression that his wishes for peace were sincere, so that Charles, by the beginning of 1532 was to admit that if war with the Turks came again, it was no fault of Ferdinand's.[5]

Neither brother believed that he was financially ready for such a conflict. Each vied with the other in protestations of fiscal hardship. Charles had harbored genuine religious scruples about dealing with the non-Christian Turks, but he overcame them when he estimated his resources to combat them. Ferdinand admitted to the Bohemian diet in 1531 that he could not bear these costs either.[6] Viewed within this light, his dilemma was real. In all likelihood, the effect of the repeated Turkish invasions was not only to raise Ferdinand's expenses but to limit the potential extraordinary revenues he would need to parry them. Evidence for the precise impact of Turkish expansion on the economy of central Europe is spotty; however, the records of one firm in Wiener Neustadt clearly show that the Ottoman invasion of Hungary substantially depressed trade with that land.[7] Ferdinand's revenues were not even adequate to cover his grandfather's debts, let alone the costs of a war. In 1531, he was reduced to selling part of the Neapolitan income which had been Ferdinand of Aragon's legacy to him.[8]

However, though both his brother and his finances called for peace, his Hungarian position dictated otherwise. Suspicion, not to say resentment, among the Magyars of Ferdinand's seeming passivity toward the Turk ran high. In general, he was not unresponsive to what he viewed as Hungarian need. For example, to aid areas in the western part of the country which Turkish marauding had hit badly, he allowed residents to trade wines freely in Moravia, Silesia, Bohemia, and Poland for a few years. And anti-Habsburg Hungarians saw their most heartfelt wish realized when Mary, at Ferdinand's urging, took up the post of Charles's resident in the Netherlands which the death of their aunt Margaret in 1530 left vacant.[9]

But the Magyars still had cause to be displeased with him. The troops which he garrisoned in their kingdom were at times little more than looting bands, pillaging both peasant and royal property alike. Even Mary's holdings were not exempt. For his part, Ferdinand seemed little inclined to do anything about such conditions, other than to beg for more money.[10] Not surprisingly, groups in Hungary began to organize themselves to demand an end to such practices and more effective action against the Turks. In the beginning of 1531, one nobleman, Peter Perényi, began exploring the idea of forming a party of dissidents from both Ferdinand and Zapolya's camps and approaching the Turks with the proposition that he be made Hungarian regent. After preliminary consultations, the diet was supposed to meet on the issue in May. However, both Ferdinand and his rival forbate attendance at the gathering, so that it had to be dissolved for lack of participants. Nevertheless, it was symptomatic of a dangerous mood in the kingdom.[11] In November 1531, another group of magnates indicated that they wished either the Habsburg or Zapolya to be king of Hungary. A delegation they dispatched to Ferdinand was to ascertain if indeed he was capable of defending the country "... not only in words and writings, but in deeds and results."[12]

But words and writings were about all he could give. In 1532, a former Habsburg supporter, Thomas Nádasdy proposed calling a diet in which both Ferdinand and Zapolya would be asked if they truly thought they could defend the kingdom. Whichever man could prove he could do so would be named king. If neither could honestly do so, Nádasdy and his followers were resolved to turn Hungary over to the Turks. To head off this challenge Ferdinand called a counter-diet at Esztergom, an apparently effective tactic since once again both this gathering and Nádasdy's were too poorly attended for business to be conducted. Nor were Nádasdy and his party happy at Ferdinand's lengthy and frequent absences from the country, petitioning him at one point for his return. All that he could say in his reply was that he was doing his best and that he would punish the misdeeds of his troops.[13] Mistrust of him ran so deep that in 1532, when it was amply clear that the Turks were preparing a major offensive once again, the Hungarians sent their own representatives to the German diet in Regensburg on the theory that by doing so they could get subsidies more quickly. Their presentation before the estates was full of complaints about him. His travels outside the kingdom were given as the reason for the constant plundering of his armies, his taxes were too heavy, and, in general, he had done little that was positive for the realm since his coronation. In their opinion, that he was a "gentle prince" by nature had done little to improve their situation.[14]

Ferdinand's normal strategm for soothing such restiveness was to promise the Hungarians that outside aid to the kingdom was imminent. In 1530 he went so far as to claim that unspecified ". . . Christian kings and rulers. . . " were prepared to back him. But there was little to support such avowals. In May 1531, Mary disabused him of any hopes that foreign rulers had the slightest interest in helping him.[15] His contention that Charles stood behind him—a relationship that had enhanced his initial candidacy in the estates—had a bit more to it. The diet of Augsburg in 1530, with the Emperor presiding, had been unusually generous in appropriating aid for the Magyars, though most of it had been given for defense of the realm rather than a crusade to reunite it as the Hungarians had wished. At least one of the several ambassadors whom Charles sent to meetings of the estates or their committees argued that compared to Ferdinand, who had the potential power of the Emperor and his own lands behind him, Zapolya looked very weak indeed. And the imperial presence had a perceptible calming effect on the Hungarians. For example, in 1531, Charles's representative Cornelius Scepperus, was able to defuse the Magyar contention that neither Ferdinand nor Zapolya was able to rule the land.[16]

The impact of the Emperor's person in Germany impressed Ferdinand as much as it did the Magyars in 1530. The younger Habsburg had always placed great weight on Charles's attendance at the diet as a means through which big problems such as the religious issue and Turkish aid could be resolved. Recent experience bore him out. For all the weakness of his office, there was a certain fear of Charles in the Empire as already seen in the Protestant response to his demand that they aid his brother in 1529. The princes themselves had told Ferdinand that it was only some move from their sovereign that could bring the religious division to some settlement.[17] It was the imperial promise at Augsburg in 1530 to work with the pope and the king of France to arrange a church council that had lured the German estates into giving Ferdinand that very liberal aid against the Turks—40,000 infantry and 8,000 cavalry.[18]

Therefore, when the Turks began to sound menacing in 1531, Ferdinand was anxious to have Charles preside at at diet in the Empire once again. However, the complex responsibilities of the Emperor neve kept his interests close to those of his brother for very long. His efforts to arouse some enthusiasm for a church council in the pope and Francis I had failed, and Charles had decided to return to Spain to put his affairs there in order. On religious matters, he advised Ferdinand to temporize with the Germans with whatever means were at his disposal, just so long as the essentials of the Catholic faith were not breached. Recognizing that the threat from Constantinople was real, he urged Ferdinand to ask the princes for support and to point out to them that Christendom itself was at stake. He himself promised some sort of aid, but gave no specifics. In any case, from Ferdinand's point of view, it was all very unsatisfactory since Charles in no way indicated that he would return to the Empire to warn the estates of the danger they were facing. He did his best to convince the Emperor that the concerns of both of them were not that far apart, pointing out the hazards to Charles's security in Italy that Ottoman conquest of Hungary brought with it. With sects multiplying in Germany, Ferdinand felt that the Emperor's back was all the more vulnerable to assault from the Turks. For these reaons, the latter's presence at a diet was essential; when Charles reported that his attempts to get a council under-way had been fruitless, his brother urged him to return to Germany and give an accounting of his efforts in Rome. The Emperor, however, was not won over, and held to his resolve to return to Spain and Italy.[19]

By the middle of the summer, he had changed his mind; he ordered Ferdinand to prepare for a diet in Speier to be held the same year. Once again, however, his myriad undertakings and connections kept him from turning his attention to German affairs immediately. It was illness in August that set back his time of departure until September, but he then decided to confer with the king of France with whom he was engaged in peace negotiations.[20] In Stuttgart, Ferdinand could not hide his rage. While peace with France had always been high on his list of priorities, the moment hardly seemed appropriate. He himself had abruptly broken off discussions with the diets in his own lands about the aid he had re-quested in order to get to Speier. Mindful that much of his own position and reputation rested in the Emperor's support, he feared that Charles's cavalier postponements of his departure might be read as signs of dis-agreement between the two.[21]

The Emperor however, was not to be hurried. His meetings with Francis were further put off due to the illness of the latter's mother, Louise of Savoy. Ferdinand despaired of his coming to the Empire at all, a feeling which only grew as Charles now decided to stay in the Netherlands for an even longer period.[22] He did not have the funds to outfit himself with men and equipment for the trip, and furthermore, the king of Denmark, Christian II, had put in a most unwelcome appearance on the scene. The latter was an erstwhile Habsburg brother-in-law who had been married to Charles and Ferdinand's sister, Isabella. He had come to the Lowlands for ships and ammunition which he claimed to be part of the dowry which the king of Spain still owed him. Charles also feared that he was conspiring with the duke of Gelders to assist the spread of Protestantism in the area. The Emperor told Ferdinand to return to his own lands for a time as he wished and promised to send a letter to the German princes accounting for his delay.[23] Ferdinand had little choice but to consent; however, he asked his brother to move the diet to Regensburg which was somewhat closer to his own territories. Charles complied; the diet was set for its new location at the beginning of 1532.[24] But by this time, Ferdinand had begun to doubt his brother's word altogether, especially when discussions with the king of France continued well into November. Charles had told him that he was coming to Speier and "...the rest of the world the opposite..." as he bitterly observed; nevertheless, he himself was so weak that he had little choice but to wait. The winter of 1532 had almost passed, before Charles, held back at the end by bad weather, finally got underway.[25]

The diet was only opened in April 1532. Ferdinand was himself not present, but in Bohemia and Hungary trying to raise funds. His estimate that he could by himself have done very little with the princes was probably correct. Aside from the continued objections which John Frederick of Saxony and Philip of Hesse were raising to his election as King of the Romans, a considerable amount of tension had developed between the Protestant princes and himself over the Habsburg occupation of Württemberg. The original duke of the territory, Ulrich, had been ousted in 1519 for trying to seize the free city of Reutlingen by the Swabian League, a union of the south German territories. His lands were first administered by Charles and later by Ferdinand; his repeated demands for their restoration were backed by several princes. At the diet of Speier in 1529, Ferdinand had accepted mediation of the dispute; when, however, the decision was in Ulrich's favor, he flatly refused to comply.[26]

Charles's appearance at the diet in 1532 did not mean that he was altogether of one mind with his brother on anti-Turkish strategy. As far as direct involvement in the east went, he saw his role there as defensive at the most. His ambassadors in Venice had told him that the Turkish attack might be concentrated in Italy, rather than Hungary, and it was this prospect, as much as the threat to the Magyars, that moved him to ask the Germans for troops. His own tactics in central Europe would depend on Suleiman's. If the latter appeared at the head of his army in Hungary, then Charles planned to be at the head of his. If the sultan did not accompany his troops, then the Emperor would take appropriate defensive precautions and depart. His reluctance to involve himself in any war for the reconquest of Hungary, Ferdinand's real goal, became even firmer when he saw how strongly the Germans opposed the idea. Led by Philip of Hesse, both Catholic and Protestant princes steadfastly argued that the Habsburgs wanted German money for the subjugation of Hungary and dynastic aggrandizement rather than simply for defense against the Turks. The pressures at the diet and elsewhere were many for Ferdinand to renounce the Hungarian crown. Clement VII advised the Emperor to promote a compromise with Zapolya in which Ferdinand would yield all his claims in Hungary in return for a few border areas taken from Venice. Ferdinand briefly toyed with the proposal, but finally concluded that the responsibilities he had incurred in the kingdom did not allow him to consider the idea seriously.[27]

However, the Germans became more willing to contribute to the defense effort as they saw that the Turkish threat was no false alarm. Charles's chances of winning some aid from the Lutherans as well as the Catholics grew even better when he pledged to conclude a religious truce with the former. Holding forth promises of at least a territorial *status quo* on the religious question, he also swore that all actions of the imperial court against the Protestants would cease, a measure which had actually been introduced in the recess of the diet of Augsburg in 1530. By the end of April, Ferdinand could travel to Prague, confident that his brother could muster the German support that he needed.[28]

In Bohemia, the Habsburgs were faced with opposition from the old pro-Bavarian party which had been aroused by the Wittelsbach chancellor, Leonhard von Eck. This wily diplomat had tried to persuade the estates that no matter what they gave Ferdinand, his reserves were so low that he could do nothing. Eck urged the Bohemians to deny their king any money and to demand that he make a peace with Zapolya. This position, was of course, not without support in Germany and from the Emperor himself.[29] By the beginning of June, however, Ferdinand was assured of some aid from Prague and the other Bohemian crownlands. For all their "customary complaints," as he put it, Bohemia, Moravia, and Silesia had promised him between 35,000 and 40,000 men. At this point, the Turks had just passed Belgrade, but Ferdinand was confident that his armies would be larger than those of his enemy, provided that they assembled punctually. His vision of what he and his brother could win in the coming campaign grew increasingly extravagant. To the consternation of his wife who was as worried about the Emperor's safety as that of her husband, he proposed that he and Charles lead their armies personally. This was to prove that the brothers were far better servants of Christendom than either the kings of France or England.[30] But German objections that he was not sufficiently neutral forced Ferdinand to drop the idea, and a further illness of Charles ruled out any active campaigning on his part.[31]

At the beginning of September, the force which the Habsburg had drawn from all over Europe began to arrive somewhat haphazardly in Vienna. The German diet had granted 40,000 men, and the Emperor brought an equal number from Spain and Italy. Even the Hungarian estates which had been pressing Ferdinand to take a more aggressive posture against the Turks, were awed by the backing which Charles was giving his brother. Clement VII finally produced 100,000 gulden for recruiting in Hungary. After being forced to relent somewhat in his measures against the Reformation in his Austrian lands, Ferdinand had also received promises of help from them. All in all, the army gathered to meet the Turks numbered well over 100,000 men. Charles himself was impressed with his situation.[32]

But just as it seemed that the conclusive battle which Ferdinand had hoped for against the Turks might take place, Suleiman met with an unexpected show of resistance in Hungary. With a small number of men in the fortress of Köszeg, Nicholas Jurisić had held down the sultan's army for about thirty days. This delay, plus the news that Charles's navy had launched an attack on the coast of the Morea, were enough to convince Suleiman not to dare another fall campaign in central Europe. He turned back toward the Balkans without even encountering the imperial forces. It was an unparalleled opportunity for Ferdinand to begin a triumphal march through Hungary, but he was not to be able to utilize it. The Emperor appeared in Vienna on September 23 and, having discovered that the Ottoman threat had vanished, at least for a time, decided almost immediately to remove himself to Italy along with a good part of the army. The German troops had come on the condition that they were to fight only in a defensive capacity, so they too were determined to leave. For his bitterly disappointed brother, Charles left only a few regiments of Italian mercenaries which he himself admitted were inadequate. Plague swept through Vienna, and Ferdinand lost a number of members of his household. Even his sturdy health suffered as he complained of digestive upsets. Of all the troops he had personally assembled, only those from the Tyrol and *Vorderösterreich* were willing to go on to Hungary.[33]

Both strategically and politically, military activity in the kingdom seemed advisable. Zapolya felt himself so threatened that he withdrew from Buda. The Habsburg party in the kingdom expected their king to act forcefully. Alexis Thurzó refused to serve as Ferdinand's chancellor unless he did something more decisive about capturing Buda and suppressing the "rebels." During the middle of October, Ferdinand's supporters declared that if he could send them only seven or eight thousand men, Transylvania could be entered and taken.[34] But by the end of the month, the troops whom the Emperor had left for his brother had begun to mutiny in a way which Ferdinand himself called "indescribable." Wretchedly, he observed that the army on which he had set such high hopes was now promoting nothing other than destruction. Yet, even without a full complement, his general, Hans Katzianer, could proceed some distance in the kingdom. The commander was reportedly anxious to invade Transylvania, and Ferdinand begged the Emperor for more men.[35]

But Charles was silent, and there was nothing left for Ferdinand to do but to recommence negotiations with Zapolya and the sultan. In this Charles was willing once again to cooperate, instructing his envoy to the discussions with the voivode to observe Ferdinand's wishes closely. The reports which the king received from his realm spoke of a desolation and exhaustion and the need for him to subject the area once and for all, but he now thought only of peace. On December 30, Katzianer concluded a four-month truce with Zapolya while armistice negotiations were being readied. Ferdinand remained convinced that he could have wrested much of Hungary from his rival, but now all he could do was ask for money from his sister to hold those positions which were legitimately his.[36] The next year, he and Suleiman also entered a truce which the latter was anxious to have since he was faced with the prospect of a Persian campaign. The sultan agreed to recognize the *status quo* in Hungary and to permit Ferdinand and Zapolya to continue their talks about the division of the kingdom.[37]

However, though Ferdinand had no way of knowing it, 1532 marked an important milestone in his relations with the Porte. The Ottoman offensive of that year was the last massive threat to be mounted against the Habsburg Austrian patrimony during Ferdinand's lifetime. Though many armed conflicts between the mortal enemies flared up between 1532 and his death in 1564, these centered on Hungary alone rather than on his family lands. Francis I, too, unsuccessful in persuading the Germans that the Turkish advance of 1532 was the fault of the Habsburg brothers, turned his efforts to using the Ottomans in the Mediterranean against the Emperor rather than against Ferdinand in central Europe.[38]

Yet for all that, the total victory so deeply desired by himself and his Hungarian subjects and once again eluded them. That most restless and uncertain of his holdings still remained questionable. And perhaps his grandest dream of all—the subjugation of the Turks through the joint efforts of the Emperor and himself—had been shattered. His disappointment was all the more sharp since the dream had come so very near to realization. From the year of his arrival in Austria, Ferdinand had viewed Charles and himself as one another's most dependable supporters in their battles for the greater good of Christendom and the advancement of their family undertakings. Though these policies usually were to advance his own fortunes, they were not calculated to undermine those of his brother, and Ferdinand expected the Emperor to reciprocate. When the westward thrust of Ottoman aggression left the younger Habsburg with little choice but to occupy the vacant thrones of the two kingdoms to the east of the Austrian lands, his financial resources as well as his dynastic loyalties dictated that these new possessions were the concern of all Habsburgs. Resistance to the Turks, as Charles himslef would admit, was the only way to assure the safety of the house's possessions throughout Europe.

But the two brothers differed sharply in their estimates of the importance of central and eastern Europe in this scheme of things. For the Emperor, it was sufficient to have a foothold in the area without solid occupation of it. For Ferdinand, the complete destruction of Ottoman power and equally complete control of Hungary were basic to Habsburg security. By 1532, the division between the two men on this issue was clear. The future would make it even clearer.

CHAPTER VIII

WAITING, 1532-1540

The absence of major Turkish offensives against his lands in the next years after 1532 left Ferdinand none the less watchful of every move in Constantinople. He fully expected Suleiman to return to central Europe at almost any time, a situation which drove him to mobilize whatever means and resources he had to strengthen his influence in the area.

The most intimate members of his family quickly became a part of his designs. After the birth of his first child, Elizabeth in 1526 and his first son, Maximilian in 1527, came a procession of daughters and two more boys, Ferdinand and Charles. The children grew up in a relaxed, yet austere environment, thoroughly consistent with the character of their father. All blonde, they were said by Cardinal Aleander, with perhaps some pastoral hyperbole, to look like a chorus of angels when he saw them together in 1538.[1] There was a considerable show of open affection between parents and children; the tiny Archduchess Anna was dubbed the "little monkey" by her father. But they were also made to understand at a very early age that they were of royal estate with very special tasks to perform with very special attitudes that they had to bring with them. Self-abnegation was a value taught even in their eating habits. Queen Anna often ordered that her daughters satisfy their hunger with black bread and thin beer, sour wine, or water to wash it down. The boys were schooled in the same habits of deference to their father that the latter followed with Charles. Ferdinand exacted the formalities of the Spanish court ceremonial from his sons, expecting them in his presence to stand before him with their barettas in their hands. Only after a sign from him could they don them and sit down.[2]

Ferdinand was equally quick to introduce them to state occasions. At the marriage of his first daughter to the future king of Poland in 1538, Archdukes Maximilian and Ferdinand were present along with Archduchesses

Anna, Maria, Magdalena, Leonora and Margaret. During the accompanying festivities, the youthful Maximilian and Ferdinand appeared on richly ornamented horses, and the former also gave a public Latin address which pleased the Polish ambassador immensely.[3] Archduke Charles, the youngest brother of that very same Elizabeth, served as the chief male representative of his family at her funeral in 1545 when he was barely five years old.[4]

The appearance of a family allowed him to introduce a marital component to his diplomacy, but, for all his disappointment with his brother in 1532, he was generally willing to follow Charles's directions in these questions closely.[5] In part this was undoubtedly because as head of his house, Charles did have the right to supervise the marriages of all its members. However, the Emperor was also a potential source of financial help for these children, especially since he had so few of his own. In 1535, for example, Charles had hinted that he might be willing to invest one of Ferdinand's sons with Milan, though he never followed through on the idea.[6] Elizabeth was married to the king of Poland as Ferdinand had wished, but the fate of his next two daughters, Anna and Maria, was tossed back and forth between the brothers throughout the 1530s. The dukes of Orléans, Lorraine, Bavaria, and Saxony were all possibilities, but Ferdinand left the final decision in these questions up to Charles, even though he had his own preferences. The only constraint which he placed upon the Emperor was when he thought that his daughters were too young to enter into such relationships.[7]

Ferdinand exercised far more personal control over the education of his children. Their early lives were spent largely in Innsbruck, but even in his ceaseless travels, he apparently took an interest in the minutiae of their daily lives. Their measles, their purgations, the places where they played were reported to him, and he gave orders on these matters himself.[8] The education of his sons was of particular concern to him, and he sought out some of the leading humanists of central Europe to supervise their intellectual development. Languages both ancient and modern were the core of their studies; both Maximilian and the young Ferdinand were expected to master German, French, Italian, and, as a sign of their father's commitment to a lasting Habsburg presence in east central Europe, Polish and Czech. Young noblemen from throughout Ferdinand's lands were brought to Innsbruck to study with the archdukes so that these future rulers could practice their tongues on their subjects and, by so doing, begin the creation of the supranational aristocracy on which future Habsburg control of their realms would depend so heavily.[9] Ferdinand's determination to give his children a place in the affairs of east central Europe was reflected in his first testament and that of his wife as well. Drawn up in 1532, as he awaited the Turks who never came, and subsequently modified, the document provided that the Austrian lands would fall to Charles and his male heirs should Ferdinand's sons die childless. In Hungary and Bohemia however, he strained to uphold the fiction of hereditary Habsburg rule of the kingdoms in his line. A few days prior to his own will, Anna had issued a separate one in which she named her sons, Maximilian and Ferdinand, as her heirs in the two realms. She also reserved for herself the right to continue ruling them should Ferdinand predecease her.[10]

Charles once again, as head of the house was called upon to ratify these arrangements, but the dependence of both Ferdinand and his children upon him was more than formal. Even after his deep disappointment with the Emperor's behavior in 1532, Ferdinand continued to refer to him as his "... bon seigneur pere frere et protecteur ..." if for no other reason than the state of his finances.[11] These did not improve at all during the 1530s, despite a rise in both direct and indirect taxes in areas such as Lower Austria. There, between 1527 and 1537, the so-called *Leibpfenning* which hit the common man the hardest, was increased from one to two pfennings during the period as was the somewhat less uniformly applied beverage tax. In 1537, Ferdinand issued a *Hofkammer-ordnung* which was designed both to order and to increase his revenues. The document frankly confessed that the possibilities for new resources were limited; thrift was strongly recommended. All salary increments among Ferdinand's court employees which could be shown not to have his approval were withdrawn, and the hiring of new personnel was to be done sparingly. Orders to the four provincial chambers in Prague, Bratislava, Vienna, and Innsbruck directed these bodies to find savings where they could. Future enfiefments were not to be hereditary; none, in any case, were to come out of princely domains of those lands. The central court chamber was to review all mortgages and other incomes alienated during the reigns of both Frederick III and Maximilian as well as in Ferdinand's early years in Austria. Where any irregularities turned up in these arrangements, the councilors were to find ways to reacquire the lands or other possessions on which they were based.[12] But none of these gestures came anywhere near to enlarging Ferdinand's income to the point where it met his needs. His strictures on his subordinates to the contrary notwithstanding, Ferdinand remained as cavalier as ever about money. Taxes in 1539, for example, drawn from "several" unspecified imperial cities, went to pension off two of his servants, the count of Nassau and a certain Maximilian Transylvan, whom he called "special."[13] Perhaps it was because he observed no meaningful distinction between private ambition and the public weal, perhaps it was his sense that as a ruler his relationship to the exigencies of finance differed from that of other men, but for whatever reason, Ferdinand never seemed to recognize that changes in his own fiscal behavior might improve the condition of his treasury.[14]

Charles had it within his power to be very helpful in such matters. Not only was he a valuable financial ally in military undertakings, but as Emperor he could assign lucrative trading concessions within Germany. Thus, in 1537, he temporarily gave Ferdinand the right to distribute salt from Milan there, an activity which brought in between 12,000 and 13,000 ducats a year.[15] With so much to gain from continued cooperation with Charles, it it hardly surprising that Ferdinand persisted in trying to work with him even where it was inconvenient or downright disadvantageous.[16] Occasionally, narrow self-interest did get the upper hand with him. Charles's military demands on his resources were as incessant as his own on the Emperor, and he sometimes either had to refuse the latter's requests outright or alter them significantly. In 1535, Ferdinand begged his brother not to use the Tyrol as a mustering place for troops to be sent on to Italy since, in his opinion, their presence in his territory only fueled the inflation there and made its natives unwilling to serve him when he needed them. In 1537, he flatly asked Charles to cease recruiting there. Although Ferdinand promised the Emperor 1,000 light cavalry for use against Francis I in 1536, it was only with the reminder that he could not wholly denude his own lands of troops because of the ever-present threat of Zapolya and the Turks. When he did finally send the men along, he subtracted 200 from their number for use in his own defenses.[17]

But self-sacrifice before the Emperor's goals was still far more typical of him. Ferdinand knew well that the resources which the Emperor mobilized in a naval expedition against the Barbary pirates in 1535 could have

been equally useful to him; he was, however, full of admiration for the size
of the fleet which his brother assembled and hoped that the venture would
give many, the king of France included, second thoughts about Habsburg
power. He promised to do all that he could to live in peace with the bothersome Venetians, given their importance for Charles's Italian policies. And
even though he had withdrawn the 200 men from the contingent he sent
to the Emperor in Italy in 1537, it was due to circumstances and not to
policy. Indeed, in 1536, he had volunteered to negotiate with his Austrian
subjects about establishing a permanent armed force there which Charles
could use whenever he needed it. In Ferdinand's view, such an arrangement would be far more trustworthy than having to turn to the Empire
each time Charles needed German military support.[18]

But if Charles had occasional difficulties with the princes, Ferdinand
had them constantly, leaving him as vulnerable as ever to attack from the
east. The abiding hostility of leading Protestants and the Bavarians to his
election as King of the Romans and the stubborn resilience of Lutheranism
frequently left him with little choice but to accept compromises that ran
contrary to his better judgment. Such was the case with the running controversy surrounding Württemberg. The exiled Duke Ulrich had developed
strong Lutheran sympathies, and the Schmalkaldians, particularly Philip
of Hesse, had taken up the cause of his restoration.[19] The landgrave calculated, with good reason, that Ferdinand might be willing to sacrifice
the duchy in return for recognition from the elector of Saxony of him as
King of the Romans and support for defense of Hungary. By April 1534,
Ferdinand was aware that Philip was plotting something in Württemberg
against him and that the king of France was backing the venture both
morally and financially.[20] When Philip and Ulrich invaded the territory
late in the month, Ferdinand was in Hungary, and his Württemberg forces
put up only a token defense. The Habsburg ritually protested the illegality
of the occupation and sent out a familiar call for aid to Catholic Europe.
But the pope decided that this was a private war with which he would
have nothing to do, and by the time Charles authorized his brother to
raise 100,000 florins in Augsburg for the resistance, the actual fighting
had ended.[21] On June 29, the belligerents signed a peace at Kadan in
Bohemia. Duke Ulrich was awarded Württemberg as a sub-fief from the
Habsburgs, but agreed to protect those Swabian prelates, counts, and
lords who wished to remain in their Catholic faith. Of greatest importance

to Ferdinand was the consent of the elector of Saxony, at least temporarily, to the Habsburg's election as King of the Romans. John Frederick also promised that those in the Empire who had supported the Saxon stance would join him. For his part, Ferdinand vowed to uphold the religious peace of 1532 and to renew his efforts to persuade the *Reichskammergericht* to halt their proceedings against the Lutherans. The Saxon recognition was to last until 1535, and hung on other conditions as well. John Frederick still wanted the Emperor to amend the Golden Bull of 1356 to allow the electors to decide whether or not a Roman King should be elected during the lifetime of an Emperor. The electors wre also to be given the power to decide whether their sovereign should speak German in order to rule them and whether two or three kings could be of the same house.[22]

Ferdinand was anxious to have the clauses in which Saxony recognized his election approved by the Emperor and was genuinely pleased at the latter's generally favorable reaction to the treaty. However, the younger Habsburg was far from happy with the total agreement, understandably so in view of all the restrictions it placed on his dynasty's ambitions. Indeed, he claimed that if the position of his forces had not been so weak or if he had received more support, he would never have consented to it. In any case, he felt that he merited some compensation from Charles for his territorial loss and once again raised the possibility of being invested with Milan. Perhaps worst of all with regard to his long-term interests, he did not think that the treaty did much to resolve Germany's most serious problems.[23] In all dealings with the electors, he resolved to use the greatest caution. Toward the middle of the spring of 1535, he began to suspect that John Frederick and the landgrave were once again planning to augment membership in the Schmalkaldic League and urged Charles to give serious thought to establishing a standing army in the Empire.[24]

But Charles was not interested in pushing the issue, and given his signature to the Peace of Kadan, Ferdinand had little choice but to be conciliatory to the Protestant leadership. Philip of Hesse and Ulrich of Württemberg were given very friendly receptions in Vienna during the summer of 1535 as was John Frederick in November. Ferdinand was favorably surprised by the elector's flexibility, prompting him to remark that if he had gotten to know the latter at the diet in 1530, negotiations over the

German election might not have gotten so far out of hand. All parties
to the negotiations, including the Emperor, came away from the meeting
with something. John Frederick, anxious to win even greater security for
his religious cohorts, once again got Ferdinand's promise that the *Reichskammergericht* would cease its legal harassment of Protestants. He also
left the elector with the impression that he would not forbid new addi-
tions to the Schmalkaldic League. Ulrich of Württemberg's increasingly
aggressive support of Lutheranism, a matter of great concern to Ferdin-
and, was not mentioned. For his part, John Frederick agreed to prolong
his recognition of Ferdinand's election, and, in a concession to Charles,
to remove men and matériel which he had sent to Christian III of Denmark who was now a fellow Schmalkaldian. But for all that he had tried
to keep his concessions to the Protestants to a minimum, Ferdinand un-
happily knew that he had solved very little with this new compact. Even
as the elector was withdrawing his troops from Christian's territories, the
younger Habsburg deemed John Frederick to be still a dangerous opponent.[25]

There were times when compromise and willingness to look beyond
his immediate needs did lead to positive gains for him in the Empire.
Such was the Habsburg rapprochement with the Wittelsbachs of Bavaria
which took place in the 1530s.

Territorial rivalries in east central Europe had made enemies out of the
two dynasties whom confessional affinity should otherwise have held
together. However, as early as 1531, Charles began to urge upon his
brother the value of more cordial relations with the two Bavarian dukes,
Ludwig and William, who ruled their lands jointly. Anxious to lighten
his load in Germany, the Emperor argued that the Wittelsbachs could be
of great help to Ferdinand against the Turks and in his quest for permanent
recognition of his election. Ferdinand too appreciated his need for trustworthy support in the Empire, and by 1534, negotiations for an alliance
between the two houses were underway in earnest. Ferdinand's emissaries
placed heavy stress on getting the Wittelsbachs to accept his election, and
Charles emphasized the issue as well. By September, both parties had
hammered out an agreement signed in Linz which resolved major points
of conflict between them. Most important for Ferdinand was the provision in which Ludwig and William recognized his election. A marriage was
also arranged between one of Ferdinand's daughters—it would eventually

be Anna, the "little monkey"—and Prince Albrecht the son of Duke William and future Bavarian ruler.[26]

Though Ferdinand characterized the agreement as a matter of Charles's wishes to which he gladly conformed, he knew that it ultimately was to his own advantage as well, even when Bavarian purposes and his own remained seriously at odds.[27] As early as 1529, the dukes had held talks with Zapolya in which division of Ferdinand's lands had been among the things discussed.[28] Despite the Compact of Linz, the Wittelsbach chancellor, Leonhard von Eck, continued to interfere in Hungarian affairs behind Ferdinand's back. At times the dukes themselves did not support Eck as in 1535 when he suggested that Zapolya attack the Habsburg.[29] But Ferdinand still had frequent cause to find Bavarian behavior toward the kingdom suspect. In 1535, he discovered that the dukes had dispatched an ambassador to Zapolya for unknown reasons, and in the fall of the same year, he was startled to learn that William and Ludwig had secretly kept one of their secretaries, Georg Ubenmaister, with his Hungarian rival. Indeed, Ubenmaister was actually managing Zapolya's affairs. A year later, one of Ferdinand's most trusted diplomats, Sigismund von Herberstein, reported that a Bavarian envoy on the way to Zapolya had been intercepted in Poland.[30]

From the point of view of relations with other princes in the Empire, particularly the Protestants, Ferdinand's new found friendship with the Bavarians was not altogether advantageous either. His own wish, indeed need, to stay on reasonably good terms with the Schmalkaldians clashed repeatedly with the Wittelsbach concern over Ulrich of Württemberg's support of Lutheranism so close to their own borders. The dukes had originally wanted to restore Ulrich's son, Christoph, who had remained a Catholic to the duchy, and, in 1535, they approached Ferdinand and proposed that Ulrich be removed from power once again. Ferdinand was reluctant to embroil himself in such a venture since, in his opinion, Ulrich had not really broken the Peace of Kadan. He was, however, so anxious to perserve his recent alliance with the Bavarians that he suggested to Duke Ludwig that he marry the widow of Francesco Sforza, the duke of Milan, and receive the duchy as a fief of the Empire. Ludwig did actually approach the Emperor with the proposition, but nothing came of it. A year later, the dukes threatened Ulrich with armed attack; the latter appealed to Ferdinand who could do nothing other than describe the Wittelsbach, as breakers of public peace. At this point, Charles's intervention at Ferdinand's request was both crucial and successful—his lack of enthusiasm for the Bavarian designs saved his brother any lasting embarassment with the German Protestants.[31]

Yet, for all these provocations and difficulties, Habsburg-Wittelsbach cooperation grew, and Ferdinand had resolved to foster it. His ability to rise above the irritation of the moment where the Bavarians were concerned eventually brought him important rewards. When he undertook a serious military expedition against the Turks in Hungary in 1542, the Wittelsbachs alone sent him 1000 wagons (*charrotz*) of flour.[32] And Albrecht, his eventual Bavarian son-in-law, proved to be one of this most trustworthy lieutenants in the Empire during his later years.

Ferdinand's military and political weaknesses in the Empire would of course, have been much less pronounced had he been able to effect some kind of solution to the Catholic-Lutheran split. The heresy cropped up even in his own household. In 1537, he discovered that one of Maximilian's tutors, Wolfgang August Schiefer, was a Protestant sympathizer. Sometime between then and 1539, he dismissed Schiefer; in October 1538, he called together the other teachers of his children, court officials, Maximilian, the young Ferdinand, his oldest daughter, and Bernhard of Cles, his chief confidant at this time. They heard an order which promised beheading to anyone who spoke to the archdukes and archduchesses of the new religious teachings. If his sons failed to inform him that they had been approached with these doctrines, they could expect corporal punishment from him. All of this was greeted with great satisfaction in Rome; a year later, when both his sons and two of his daughters were confirmed, .Aleander officiated at the ceremony, and Giovanni Morone, the papal nuncio, served as witness for Maximilian. Ferdinand's decrees and actions aimed at stemming the Reformation in his lands during the 1530s had a similarly draconian quality. Closely following his brother's Edict of Worms in 1521, he continued to order the seizure of Protestant pastors, to forbid Bohemians to study in Wittenberg, and to attempt to ban Lutherans from his territories altogether.[34]

But none of these gestures were more than marginally effective, even at his own court. Here his problems were in part of his own making. There is no greater measure of Ferdinand's deep and sincere advocacy of the Erasmian reform program than his lifelong inability to believe that it had connection with religious heterodoxy. In any case, the dismissed Schiefer was followed by a certain Collatinus, a close friend of Joachim Camerarius who in turn had strong ties with Melanchthon. The impact of these men had on their young charges is difficult to assess. Their connection with the boys was short-lived, but so was that of Caspar Ursinus Velius, a strong defender of the old church and the best-known of the humanists to tutor them.[35] But Protestant sympathizers were never absent from his entourage. Johannes Hofmann, the president of his Court Council during the 1530s had such well-known Lutheran interests that the archbishop of Salzburg and the Bavarians would have nothing to do with him.[36] Much later the presence of such people in his midst would upset Ferdinand's relations with Rome and nurture Protestant sympathies in Maximilian. One can only speculate about the source of this blind spot. In 1529, he blamed the spread of the Reformation on the irreligiosity of his fellow rulers, thereby implying that the religious attitude of the prince was central to the posture of all those below him.[37] Such a premise quite logically could lead him to conclude that as long as his own orthodoxy remained unaffected by his commitment to the Erasmian reform, the beliefs of others around him who thought as he did would stay sound as well.

It was, however, strategy as much as conviction that led Ferdinand to adopt a more conciliatory, indeed experimental, policy with the Protestants in the 1530s as he tried to firm up his personal position in central Europe. He himself admitted to the diet of Upper Austria in 1536 that his decrees calling for observation of the Edict of Worms and forbidding the circulation of evangelical writings had not worked. The frequency with which he issued such documents confirms his judgment.[38] Throughout the 1530s, a gradual shift in his methods of dealing with the Protestants began to appear. Even more stress was placed upon removing abuses in ecclesiastical institutions and improving the religious understanding of the general populace. In no area can the general easing of his approach toward heterodoxy be seen more clearly than in his treatment of the Anabaptists who had been the object of some of his most remorseless mandates early in his career. After 1534, his pronouncements on them emphasized the need to reincorporate them into the church through training and persuasion. In a mandate issued in the Tyrol in 1536, he ordered that the property confiscated from them be given to their children and other heirs so that no one would think that these seizures had been made out of raw greed. By 1545 and 1546, he was attributing the Anabaptists heresy like all the others to their ignorance and that of the priests who had taught them.[39]

But reasoned persuasion was as ineffectual as force. Communion in both kinds was celebrated at St. Stephen's and elsewhere in Vienna and Ferdinand's lands throughout the 1530s.[40] Nor did he get very far with such methods in the Empire. Given, on the one hand, his own political and military problems and, on the other, the large number of variables he had to deal with, Ferdinand's conciliatory approach to the estates was near-inevitable. The religious peace of 1532 and the Peace of Kadan had aroused Protestant expectations of leniency from both Ferdinand and Charles. At the same time, the ever-dwindling number of Catholic princes, the most obvious allies of the Habsburgs, believed that both brothers should support their faith actively. Ferdinand was obliged to make gestures toward both sides and to be mindful of Charles and the pope, as well, who themselves settled on no clear line of policy during the period. For example, as part of his agreement with John Frederick of Saxony in Vienna in 1535, he ordered the Catholic-dominated *Kammergericht* to cease its legal suits against Protestants mentioned in that compact as well as the one drawn up at Kadan. Aware, however, of the implications of such an action for his own faith, he limited his prohibition to suits which had been opened before the Vienna meeting. This, quite naturally, sparked more Protestant objections. Moreover, the court, arguing that its proceedings only dealt with secular matters, continued its activities, thereby poisoning Ferdinand's relationships with the Lutherans during the decade and long afterward.[41]

Ferdinand was well aware the the only way of reducing the *Kammergericht* to his wishes would have been to withdraw Habsburg support of it. However, calculations of his brother's interest, and, implicitly, his own, argued against such an action. The disappearance of the *Kammergericht*, as Ferdinand saw it, would weaken Charles's authority in the Empire as well as the position of Catholicism. He did not hestitate to ask the Emperor to support the body, nor did Charles hesitate to pay.[42]

Ferdinand's efforts to stay on good terms with all sides on the religious dispute was even more understandable given the international efforts to bring together a general church council during the 1530s. Ferdinand was predisposed toward such a measure intellectually and committed to it diplomatically, since the religious peace of 1532 had called for such a meeting. Indeed, he was so concerned to promote the council that when Clement VII's health suddenly worsened in 1534, Ferdinand began to push the papal candidacy of his closest advisor, Bishop Bernhard of Cles as someone who both knew the German situation intimately and would continue to press for a council.[43] Though that effort collapsed—Charles never seriously urged anyone's case after the Medici pope's death in September 1534—Ferdinand continued to believe that only a council could bring Christendom out of its agony and to hope for its calling several years afterward.[44]

However, his overriding concern was that such a gathering solve the German religious dispute. By 1537, he began to realize that the drawn-out procedures of any council conflicted sharply with his own need for an immediate solution to the discord in the Empire. Moreover, it became ever more apparent to him that the princes were not interested in participating, and that to force them to do so would only exacerbate his problems with them.[45] Therefore, when the new pope, Paul III, started to talk of postponing the meeting which had been set for Mantua, Ferdinand did not argue strongly to the contrary, and when the actual announcement that the council had been called off was made, Ferdinand reacted positively. He did not, however, give up on the idea of a reform of the church from within. This the popes could implement themselves, though Ferdinand had doubts which he did not hesitate to tell Paul's nuncio, that the worldly Farnese would do so.[46]

Though hopes for a general religious solution had faded, pressures for a local counterpart in the Empire did not. For Ferdinand, the need was doubly urgent since the Turks once again prepared for a major offensive in the late 1530s. His hereditary lands were complaining bitterly of the financial burdens which the wars had brought them. At one point, rumors circulated that some of them were willing to become tributaries of the sultan unless the Empire as a whole participated more fully in these conflicts.[47] For a time in 1538, Ferdinand believed that negotiating separately with the German princes on Turkish aid might enable him to avoid the religious bitterness that meetings of the diet always brought with them. But this tactic too, brought little fruit, and confessional hostility and suspicion appeared even in discussions between individuals. He saw no way of getting the help he needed except through the calling of a diet.[48]

This brought with it the need for a religious settlement, or, at the very least additional religious compromise. Charles saw this as well; in December and January of 1536 and 1537, Ferdinand and the Emperor's vice-chancellor, Matthias Held, discussed the idea of a council minus the participation of either the pope or the French. If this did not please the German Protestants, they were resolved to work out some further agreement with them so long as imperial authority was not impaired. Though depressed by the advances of Lutheranism and the increasing age of Habsburg supporters such as Duke George of Saxony, Ferdinand remained convinced that he could win the support of the Protestants if only he could assure them of Habsburg good will.[49] He went so far as to argue with the papal nuncio, Morone, for papal concessions on communion in both kinds and marriage of priests as well as moral abuses within the church. When he began discussions with the German Protestants in 1538, Ferdinand was outraged when Paul dispatched Cardinal Aleander, one of the moving figures behind the Edict of Worms, to participate in the talks. Even when a new papal representative, Fabio Mignanelli, appeared in October 1538, voicing considerable worry over making concessions to the Protestants, Ferdinand retorted that it was better to give up a finger than an arm, and an arm rather than the whole body.[50] When approached in 1538 with the request for extension of the religious peace of 1532 to all those who had converted to Lutheranism after that year and suspension of the *Reichskammergericht* action against them, he offered relatively little resistance. He asked Charles to consider the proposals sympathetically, and on his own, he promised to rid the court of some members whom the Lutherans found offensive. He also vowed to promote a stricter division between temporal and spiritual cases in that body.[51]

But none of these maneuvers implied that Ferdinand was willing to put Protestants on a permanent footing. He privately found the sect intolerable for both confessional and political reasons. When he had the opportunity to restrict his concession to them, he took it. The outcome of the 1538 discussions was the so-called Frankfurt Interim of 1539. The Turkish threat which had made Ferdinand so anxious to get the princes together had abated, so that even though he agreed to a prolongation of the 1532 religious peace, he also was able to add stipulations which ordered a fifteen-month freeze on new membership in the Schmalkaldic League and a cessation to Protestant secularization of church lands.[52]

Nor did he shrink from appearing more forceful if he thought that something was to be gained from doing so, as can be seen through his participation in the Catholic League of Nürnberg, formed in 1537. As discussions about a church council had become serious in 1535 and 1536, Lutheran rulers and theologians met in Schmalkalden to decide whether or not to accept an invitation to the gathering. Charles sent vice-chancellor Held to the discussions who was both to persuade the Protestants to attend the council as well as to ask them to aid Ferdinand against the Turks.

The Schmalkaldians, however, were anything but receptive to Held, and the vice-chancellor himself, whose confused instructions left him considerable leeway for action, was not inclined to be patient with them.[53] He and Ferdinand had already explored the idea of a Catholic counterpart to the Protestant alliance. The Habsburg, well aware that his conciliatory policies toward the Lutherans were antagonizing the Catholic stalwarts in the Empire, was not unfavorably inclined toward the idea, though he was unwilling to give up on the idea of peace with the Protestants either. Without much consultation with Ferdinand at all, Held left the gathering in Schmalkalden and turned his energies wholeheartedly to putting together the Catholic alliance.[54] Though distressed at the cavalier way in which the vice-chancellor had by passed him, Ferdinand realized that he could ill-afford to antagonize the Catholic princes and decided to participate in their negotiations. As these went on, Ferdinand warmed to the idea of the league and never was so perturbed by Held's behavior that he wished him removed from the scene. By July 1537, he began to believe that the threat of Catholic unity would bring the Protestants to a diet. In any case, his membership in the group gave him the appearance of being less in the thrall of the Schmalkaldians, which was important in maintaining good relations with his fellow Catholics. He also harbored the fear that the latter might undertake negotiations with the Protestants on their own and felt that his and the Emperor's participation in the organization would enable them to direct such a move. The fear of a armed Lutheran uprising with large popular participation was never far from his mind either.[55]

Though the league enjoyed financial support from Charles, it came to very little. Important figures such as the Elector Palatine distanced themselves from it, encouraging others to do so as well.[56] And Charles's fiscal underwriting of the organization was not followed up by his close attention to its actual problems. When Duke George of Saxony, who held the funds of the league, died in 1539, these fell into the hands of his Protestant brother and heir, Duke Henry. The Catholic princes petitioned Charles to do something about this, but the Emperor dallied for almost a year. The Catholics grumbled that Charles was only trying to incite them to war against the Protestants so that he could eventually be master of both sides. Ferdinand too reminded the Emperor that technically Duke Henry's actions were punishable by force, and that Charles would be the natural leader of such an expedition. The latter had little taste for such ventures at that point, however, and did his best to pacify his religious cohorts by other means.[57]

Lack of Catholic confidence in the Habsburgs spilled over into other political endeavors in Germany as well. Ferdinand was still convinced in 1539 that a diet was necessary, under the Emperor's personal direction, for the solution of basic German difficulties. Charles agreed, but also, with his brother's concurrence, felt that some preliminary discussions of religious issues between Catholic and Protestant would have to be held.[58] The first of these was scheduled for Nürnberg in Ausgust 1539, but never got underway. Charles set another round to take place in Speier the following year, but an epidemic forced the transfer of the talks almost immediately to Hagenau. Ferdinand soon discovered that local religious discussions were as trouble-ridden as general ones. His Catholic allies gave him almost as much difficulty as did the Lutherans. Wishing to consult with them before the appearance of their confessional rivals, Ferdinand complained that they did not even come on time. The dukes of Bavaria did not think that the discussions were important, and when he finally persuaded them otherwise, he still had to work on the electors of Trier and Cologne. Nor did he trust the sincerity of a papal promise to concede anything to the Protestants which was "reasonable" and "feasible."[59] He suspected Rome of still wanting to solve the German problem by force, and he knew very well that the Bavarians were anxious to do so. For his own part, he wanted to proceed far more pacifically, resorting to force only if the Lutherans proved to be totally unreasonable. It was not only the need for aid against the Turks which made him so peaceable. He was still interested in getting final recognition of this title of King of the Romans from the elector of Saxony and hoped to air the matter with John Frederick at Hagenau. Though the latter neither showed up at the meeting nor sent a representative,

Ferdinand continued to hope that he would, so that he could not afford
to abandon his conciliatory appearance.[60]

By July 10, Ferdinand had concluded that the Hagenau meeting would
get nowhere. Disease struck the city, killing among others, the archbishop
of Trier. He still wished to have a diet with Charles in attendance, however;
the Emperor still agreed, but urged once again that a preliminary theological discussion be held, this time in Worms.[61] Ferdinand again went along,
calling upon such notables as Faber, Friedrich Nausea, Johannes Cochlaeus,
and Johannes Eck to represent him.[62] But when the conclave opened in
July 1540, Ferdinand had to hurry back to his own lands because of an
abrupt change in his affairs there. On the 21st of that month, John Zapolya
died, and Ferdinand, whose efforts to resolve the German religious situation
had been conditioned by his expectation that the Turks would once again
invade Hungary, had now to shift the bulk of his attention to the southeast.

CHAPTER IX

"BELLA GERANT ALII...?"

Instability had been the only constant in the relations between Ferdinand and Zapolya from the latter's defeat at Tokaj in 1527 to his death in 1540. The truces and treaties to which they agreed during the period served only as breathing spaces in which each side gathered military strength to fight its way to undisputed hold on the Hungarian crown. Pretexts could always be found in broken promises, or invented out of whole cloth, to renew hostilities if it was advantageous to do so. Nor could Ferdinand and the voivode of Transylvania carry on their struggle oblivious to the interests of others. The Turks had a mighty concern in the outcome of the contest between the two men. Zapolya's claim to legitimacy did not rest solely on his somewhat questionable election in Székesféhervár. A vassal of the sultan since 1529, who maintained that all of Hungary was really his, the voivode had received the Crown of St. Stephen from his new overlord as well as a diploma which named him the genuine king. Suleiman had also installed him in Buda, the royal capital.

All of these factors complicated Ferdinand's efforts to win exclusive control of the kingdom for himself and his heirs. Failing any immediate improvement in his military resources, he pressed his case through diplomatic channels both in Constantinople and wherever Zapolya happened to be. Any progress which might have been made was initially blocked by the machinations of Ludovico Gritti, Suleiman's resident ambassador in the Transylvanian camp. Urging Zapolya to make no concessions to Ferdinand, he tried to persuade the Habsburg's supporters to desert him. Suspected of wanting the crown for himself, Gritti was killed by the Hungarians, an act which all camps seem to have greeted with relief. Publicly, however, Suleiman found it in his interest to act the injured party. Fearing his overlord's wrath, Zapolya therefore was more anxious to negotiate with Ferdinand than he otherwise might have been, so that serious talks between the two once again got underway in 1535.[1] These foundered almost immediately once again on the question of the royal title to Hungary.

Zapolya at first demanded control over the entire kingdom, including the areas loyal to Ferdinand. He offered, however, to allow all of the realm to pass to Ferdinand's oldest son, once he himself had died. But calling such terms "shameless and marvelous," Ferdinand stubbornly maintained that all of Hungary belonged to him and rejected the proposal. He also would have nothing to do with Zapolya's suggestion that he marry one of Ferdinand's daughters, even though the voivode promised to disinherit any offspring of the union. In return for full sovereignty in the kingdom, Ferdinand was willing to endow Zapolya with a part of it during the latter's lifetime as well as an income of 80,000 ducats from such territory. He also toyed with the idea of marrying Zapolya to Francesco Sforza's widow in Milan—the same device he suggested to the Wittelsbachs—but did not pursue it. Beyond that, he was unwilling to go.[2]

His Hungarian rival had good reason to find such propositions suspect since Ferdinand did not have ultimate control over Milan and his finances were notoriously shaky. But the Habsburg had equal cause to mistrust Zapolya whose every military move might bring with it Turkish support. In 1534, Ferdinand believed that the latter was organizing some military enterprise against him in Transylvania. Recourse to arms was never far from Ferdinand's thinking; given the opportunity to send troops into Hungary at least to make Zapolya think twice, he considered undertaking a more serious offensive in the winter. The season, he felt, would keep the Turks away. Zapolya's negotiators offered to abstain from war, however, and he decided to agree to another truce.[3] But in 1536, the voivode laid siege to two of Ferdinand's fortified castles in the kingdom, thus breaking the agreement. One of Ferdinand's continued fears was that such acts would demonstrate his weakness to his own partisans. At the same time, the Turks had begun to enter Hungary again. When Ferdinand learned that Zapolya had been in contact with them, he suspected all the more strongly that his protagonist was using the negotiations only as a way of gaining time for himself. Furthermore, even though the Hungarian's commissioners had privately confessed to Ferdinand that their master did not have the

wherewithall to defend their homeland, he had not given up his prose-
tytizing among Ferdinand's partisans.[4]

The truce which Ferdinand had come to with Suleiman in 1532 had
been equally unsatisfactory. The Turks had not ceased to harass his borders; depending upon Charles's policy toward the Porte, he swung between
the hope of meeting the sultan in decisive combat and the need to negotiate
with him to keep his borders at peace. In April 1535, he formed an alliance with the voivode of Moldavia, Peter Rares, in the full expectation
that he would be at war with the Turks. However, when Charles won a
major victory over their common Islamic foe at Tunis during that same
year, Ferdinand was far more willing to use peaceful means to realize his
goals. He even volunteered to serve as a mediator between Charles and
Suleiman to gain the latter's good will.[5] The threat of a full Turkish
invasion of Hungary in 1536, however, brought him face to face with
even starker realities than those to which he had become accustomed.
Not the least of these was the way he saw such a move complicating his
relationship with Zapolya. Open aggression against him in the kingdom
from Constantinople would make it doubly imperative for him to come
to terms with his rival. Yet, as he saw it, such a gesture would tempt his
ever volatile partisans to switch their allegiance. In such circumstances,
he felt that he had little choice but to seize the opportunity to rid himself
of Zapolya altogether. By the end of 1536, he had assembled the estates
of all his lands to request military aid from them.[6]

As had been true of all of Ferdinand's military undertakings in Hungary,
the Emperor was something less than supportive. Important figures in the
kingdom still saw Charles as the solution to their struggle against the Turks
and to ending Ferdinand's rivalry with Zapolya. In 1534, they hinted that
if Charles were to take an active role in Hungary, some of the magnate's
supporters would desert him for Ferdinand.[7] Even Charles's advisors
agreed that with little hope of outside support, Ferdinand's position in
Hungary looked bleak. But they also continued to press a pacific policy
toward Zapolya and the Turks, urging Ferdinand above all not to violate
the integrity of either of his enemies' possessions. In theory they supported Ferdinand's right to the Hungarian title, but he appeared so weak that
they suggested he make minor border adjustments in favor of the Porte
to make his position as secure as he could. Above all, no military aid was
to be expected from the Emperor, even though Ferdinand strained himself

in 1537 to explain his moves simply as a way of forcing Zapolya to reason and protecting his subjects from repeated Ottoman harassment. Even his argument that Zapolya's advisors themselves had urged such action upon him had little resonance with Charles.[8] Out of his wish to appear in compliance with his brother's wishes, however, Ferdinand continued negotiating with Zapolya even as he was gathering troops to attack him.[9]

At the beginning of August, the Habsburg armies entered Hungary against Zapolya and Slovenia against the Turks. Military disasters and near-disasters dogged Ferdinand's career; this campaign was one of the very worst he sponsored. By October, his forces had been crushingly defeated. Hans Katzianer, Ferdinand's chief captain and the leader of the Slovenian contingent, deserted and took part of the cavalry with him.[10] The papal nuncio at Ferdinand's court estimated the loss as more catastrophic than Mohács, and Ferdinand himself was more painfully aware than ever of the dangers to which he was exposed. Though he continued to hope for aid from Charles, if only he could bring his hostilities with France to an end, he saw that he would have to arrange some more permanent peace with Zapolya. The Turks, too, were willing to call a halt temporarily to their activities in central eastern Europe since they were besieging Venice which both Charles and the pope were aiding.[11]

Zapolya too, was not unhappy at the idea of peace, since he judged his position between Habsburg and Turk to be precarious in the extreme. Two of his chief partisans, Francis Frankopan and Stephen Brodarics were threatening to switch their allegiance unless the magnate came to some agreement with his rival. All too much blood, in their opinion, had been shed both domestically and against the Turks.[12] The treaty concluded at Nagyvárad in 1538, allowed Zapolya to keep his possessions in Transylvania and Hungary proper and to call himself king of Hungary during his lifetime. Ferdinand vowed to protect him and his holdings. In return, the Hungarian crown was to pass to Ferdinand and his line, or, failing that, to Charles and his heirs. If Zapolya were to father a son— something which up to that point he had not done—the lad would have ducal rank and his father's territories in Zips. Only if all three lines were to die out could the Hungarian estates assert their elective prerogatives, a victory for Ferdinand in itself. Such a stipulation expressly shifted Habsburg claims to the Crown of St. Stephen from the Jagellonian Anna, Ferdinand's wife, to the males of his own line, a development quickly incorporated into his testament of 1543 and its 1547 codicil.[13] Ferdinand disliked the secrecy which surrounded the treaty, for Zapolya and his chief minister, a wily Croatian monk named George Martinuzzi who soon became Ferdinand's main antagonist in the struggle for Hungary, feared offending the Turks with the succession arrangements. Nor did Ferdinand trust his cosignatory completely. He promised to uphold the compact, however, and when in August 1538, Zapolya asked both Charles and Ferdinand for aid against an anticipated Turkish thrust at Buda, Ferdinand was willing to help because the Nagyvárad agreement required him to do so. He urged Charles to do the same.[14]

But the treaty could not erase the misunderstanding and suspicion between the two men. Ferdinand and his advisors chafed at Zapolya's refusal to publicize the succession provisions. They suspected that he was only waiting to see the outcome of Charles's undertakings in the Mediterranean before making other moves; worse yet, they feared that he still might father a son by his new wife, Isabella, the daughter of Bona Sforza and Sigismund I of Poland.[15] For his part, Zapolya accused Ferdinand of reneging on the aid promised in 1538 against the Turks, a delinquency which the Habsburg acknowledged but excused on the ground that the attack had never materialized. In 1539 he was willing to gather a force for Zapolya to use against the Turks once more. When the latter decided to concentrate their fury on Moldavia rather than Buda, several German princes withdrew their contingents, something which Ferdinand could not help but which once again angered his Hungarian rival. Zapolya's intimates began spreading the rumor that the treaty had turned their kingdom over to their master and that, if he had children, they would succeed to the realm. Ferdinand correctly insisted that this was a violation of the agreement and proposed that they renegotiate this point once again. But Zapolya continued his evasive ways, made doubly provocative by his occasional skirmishing raids on Ferdinand's subjects.[16] In 1539, when he learned that Zapolya had opened some sort of negotiations, presumably about Hungary with the sultan, Ferdinand resolved to send his own ambassador to Constantinople to begin talks there as well.[17]

Zapolya's death in 1540 hardened Ferdinand all the more in his pursuit of the Hungarian crown. However, a new factor had appeared in the situation. Though Zapolya had passed from the scene, his line had not, for he left behind him a two-week old son, John Sigismund. Martinuzzi who had been Zapolya's treasurer and now assumed responsibility for his entire house, was convinced that Ferdinand had neither the diplomatic nor military clout to ward off the complete subjugation of Hungary by the sultan. As soon as his master died, the monk asked Suleiman to recognize the child as the legitimate heir to the kingdom. Martinuzzi was to act as regent until the boy came of age. For his part, Ferdinand hoped to win control of Buda, the prestigious royal seat and Transylvania, where he believed potential new revenues awaited him. He therefore sent emissaries to the king of Poland, to the widowed Isabella, and the Hungarian estates urging them to observe the treaty of Nagyvárad. He also asked Charles to send similar missions.

The Habsburg position in Hungary was not as weak as Martinuzzi painted it. Zapolya family partisans made up only one of the three identifiable faction in the kingdom. Relatively neutral observors agreed that Ferdinand had the support of the bulk of the Hungarians. They were, however, divided. One group favored recognizing the treaty of Nagyvárad without further ado; the other, while willing to accept Ferdinand as their ruler, would do so only if he and Charles attacked the Turks immediately and freed all of Hungary. Though Ferdinand had lost some important supporters to Martinuzzi and his charge, he had also picked up some from among Zapolya's former adherents.[19]

But major complications offset many of these advantages. Zapolya's testament had dictated that his followers observe the Nagyvárad compact only when Ferdinand had shown that he would live up to his part of the agreement. Since however, he had already distributed some of the territories reserved in the treaty for Zapolya's male heirs among his own followers, he had unwittingly given Martinuzzi a defensible reason to delay any moves to resolve the succession question. This impasse simply perpetuated the status quo of the monk's regency. Furthermore in Poland, Queen Bona had a long-standing quarrel with the Habsburgs over claims which she had in Milan. She therefore felt even more inclined than usual to keep a watchful eye on her daughter, who was called a virtual prisoner of Martinuzzi in Buda, and did everything in her power to frustrate Ferdinand's designs in Hungary.[20]

As soon as Ferdinand heard that Martinuzzi was negotiating with the Porte, he dispatched one of his most skillful diplomats, Jerome Lasky, to Constantinople to argue his own case. One of his most reliable military commanders, Nicholas von Salm, was delegated to open talks face-to-face with Isabella Zapolya. This move began a ten-year verbal cat-and-mouse game at which the Polish princess was to become an adept. Her comment for the moment, however, was that Martinuzzi was the true master of her situation.[21] But, as he had done so many times before, even as he was negotiating, Ferdinand was toying with military alternatives as well. Such thinking violated all vows he had made to Charles that he would seek his ends in Hungary through peaceful means; Ferdinand felt, however, that such action would make an especially deep impression on the Transylvanians with whom he was holding discussions.[22] The debacle of 1537 was seemingly forgotten.

In the early autumn of 1540, he sent an army under Leonhard von Fels to capture Buda and Pest, across the Danube. They actually succeeded in taking the latter, but while laying siege to the ancient city on the other side of the river, the men had mutinied over their bad provisioning. German troops had turned the artillery on the very Hungarians they were supposedly assisting; von Fels himself died of a wound he suffered while quieting the fracass.[23] By the first of November, Ferdinand had resumed his talks with Martinuzzi who insisted once again that John Sigismund be given his patrimony before Ferdinand entered Buda. This the Habsburg was simply unable to do, given the number of his own partisans who already were using these lands; his offer to recommend a cardinal's baretta for the Croatian was of no avail. His suggestion that the monk, Isabella, and her son remain in Buda if they swore loyalty to him and that the city be guarded by troops of both sides was also turned down as was the proposal that Martinuzzi become a hostage of Ferdinand with Isabella and her son remaining in the royal residence. To the sultan Ferdinand offered himself as a tributary if only Suleiman would recognize him as the legitimate king of Hungary.[24]

Few aspects of Ferdinand's career display his gritty tenacity more clearly than does his quest for the Magyar kingdom. Despite his defeat in 1540, he began plans for a military undertaking once again in 1541. In part, he was responding to real necessity. Reports which told of a sizable Turkish force wintering in the neighborhood of Vác, worried him since he had never heard of such a large Ottoman contingent staying in the field during that season. He suspected that Martinuzzi and his adherents might use them to seize Pest. Indeed, Ferdinand believed that Suleiman himself might show up.

But he also had been given important encouragement in resorting to arms once again. Peter Perényi, Ferdinand's Hungarian chancellor, had reported that Isabella was anxious to rid herself of Martinuzzi. She promised to leave a gate of Buda open for Ferdinand's troops, still in Pest, to enter, an arrangement Ferdinand gladly accepted. From Constantinople, Jerome Lasky declared that any armistice agreeable to the Turks would never allow Ferdinand to have Buda. The ambassador argued that the only Habsburg alternative was to strike a military blow there which would move Suleiman to greater flexibility. The Moldavians had recently risen up against the Turks and were offering to subject themselves to Ferdinand, though he worried that this could not be done without heavy cost to himself. Charles too, though he did not deem the Hungarian situation that grave, agreed to support his brother by stationing his own forces in Italy and the Mediterranean. Scheduled to meet with the German diet in Regensburg that year, he also promised to allow a German religious council in return for the princes' assistance to Ferdinand. With all this in mind, Ferdinand resolved to fortify Pest as best he could and take Buda as well.[25]

Contemporary commentators thought his position to be relatively favorable. The Turks had apparently been drained by the long stay in winter camp, and their nearness in any case had made the citizens of Buda increasingly wary. And, indeed, the 20,000 or so troops which Ferdinand sent off in the spring of 1541, were gratifyingly successful, at least at the outset.[26] But on the second of June, the defenders of Pest handed them a stunning defeat, and, worse yet, news that a large army had left Constantinople to meet the Habsburg challenge in Hungary had drifted to the diet in Regensburg.[27] Undaunted, Ferdinand's men turned their attention to Buda where sheer tactical incompetence ruined whatever chances they might have had. True to Isabella Zapolya's offer, a gate of the city was opened for thirty of Ferdinand's men and their captain. When the reinforcements who were supposed to enter behind them did not show up, however, all withdrew.[28] On June 25, Ferdinand appeared before the German estates to beg for some kind of emergency aid against the now-approaching Suleiman. The Catholic estates voted him 10,000 men and 3,000 horses; the Protestants agreed to nothing until the end of July. Charles was little help since he rushed off late in that month to begin what would be a disastrous campaign against the Barbary pirates in Algeria.[29]

As at Mohács, the full fury of the Turkish attack came late in August. By the twenty-six, Buda and Pest had fallen to the Turks, and, perhaps the greatest blow of all to Ferdinand, Suleiman declared John Sigismund as rightful king of Hungary. Until the boy came of age, the sultan himself would act as regent. He also announced that from that time forward, the entire region between the Danube and the Tisza rivers were under his direct control so as to secure them more effectively against Habsburg attack. But the damage to Ferdinand was not only political. The retreat of his forces from Pest had been wildly disordered; his troops had overloaded the ships at their disposal to the point where they simply sank. Huge stores of artillery, provisions, and munitions worth thousands of florins fell into Ottoman hands when they captured the city. Finally, the Turks were now more advantageously situated than ever for a thrust into his Austrian lands.[30]

Though unhappy at this turn of events, Ferdinand lost neither his equanimity nor his determination to recoup his losses in Hungary. Despite the Turks' request that he cease arming, he began laying plans for attacking the royal residence once again. To bolster Hungarian confidence in him, to keep Martinuzzi from striking further deals with Suleiman, and to halt any further westward march of the Turks, he wanted to move as quickly as possible. An outbreak of plague in both Buda and Pest temporarily blocked his moves, however, so that he returned to negotiating with Isabella and her advisor.[31]

Many Hungarians had been shocked by Suleiman's actions in August, especially his occupation of Buda and Pest. Almost as soon as they had taken the two cities, the Turks began to add to the fortifications already there. For all of his military fumbling, Ferdinand seemed the best hope for freeing the kingdom. A diet which he called in 1542 was attended by representatives from counties which up to that time had stood behind the Zapolya cause. Ferdinand found Isabella and Martinuzzi more easy to deal with than ever before. By December 29, they had worked out an agreement in which the latter vowed to be loyal to Ferdinand and to enter his service. All of the kingdom was to be under Habsburg control with the exception of Zips which would go to John Sigismund when he reached his majority. Ferdinand promised Isabella 12,000 ducats a year; there was to be a financial settlement with Martinuzzi as well. General pardons were offered to the monk's cohorts who were to continue in their offices, dignities, and benefices as well.[32]

Central Europe as a whole also wished to regain Buda. The dukes of Bavaria, who, after Ferdinand, had the most cause for anxiety with the Turks in their neighborhood, called for a meeting of the German diet to discuss the issue as soon as possible. Elector John Frederick and Philip of Hesse were also genuinely worried. Upon hearing Hungarian emissaries explain the desparate plight of their homeland, the Bohemians and Moravians voted in February 1542 to draw up tax and conscription plans to come to the aid of the Magyar royal residence.[33] For Ferdinand, however, the crucial question was his brother's reaction to his scheme.

The feeling at Ferdinand's court was that the Emperor should play a more active role in the defense of Hungary. There had been some grumbling there following the defeat of 1541 at Charles's seeming willingness to do so much against the Barbary pirates and so little in east central Europe.[34] Ferdinand's reasons for wanting to draw his brother more closely into his plans were far more specific. His military disasters of the past few years had increased his dissatisfaction with the quality of the troops raised by his patrimonial estates and the imperial diet. Both were tiresomely slow actually to send the men whom they promised, and Ferdinand was anxious to have an army with which he had greater flexibility. Then too, the German *Landsknecht* and armed cavalry were easily provoked to mutiny, desertion, and plunder, all of which Ferdinand had seen in Hungary where the natives had worked up a hearty dislike of their supposed allies.[35] Nor were the Hungarians much more reliable. Both Ferdinand and contemporary observers agreed that he needed Spanish and Italian mercenaries both of whom had excellent records in assaulting fortifications, a basic problem with Buda. The Spanish also had experience in combined naval and military maneuvers, something which the placement of the royal residence on the Danube made desirable. The troops whom the papacy hired were especially renowned for their over-all dependability.[36]

But it was not only money that Ferdinand wanted from Charles for all of this. It was his person as well. He believed another of his problems to be the quality of his leadership, a flaw he was sure Charles could remedy.[37] The Emperor's record of cooperation with Ferdinand from 1532 on had been mixed. While consistently urging the ways of diplomacy on his brother in the contest with Zapolya and the Turks, he had sometimes failed to tell Ferdinand of steps he had taken which might have a bearing on the latter's own dealings. The Venetians heard before Ferdinand that the

Emperor had concluded a peace of sorts with Francis I in 1538, prompting the younger Habsburg to remind Charles angrily that it was as necessary for his interests in the east as it was for Ferdinand's own to inform him first of such arrangements. One of Ferdinand's main problems in Hungary in 1538 had been that he had too few men to cover all the territory which he had to defend against the Turks. He was both shocked and infuriated to learn that Charles and the pope were jointly recruiting that year in Friuli, one of his own territories, for their own anti-Turkish expeditions. Charles eventually sent him 2,000 Spanish troops in 1538, but insisted that his brother pay for them.[38] In a face to face meeting between the two in Ghent in 1540, Charles did grant Ferdinand 50,000 florins to be used in Hungary, but only on the latter's promise that he would sell some of his Neapolitan income to reimburse him.[39]

His attitude had undergone some change after the fall of Buda in 1541. When the news reached Charles in Lucca, he dispatched his vice-chancellor, the Luxemburger Jean de Naves, to Germany immediately. There he encountered the same resentment found at Ferdinand's court of Charles's apparent willingness to abandon the Empire to the Turks. In November, Naves had made a highly qualified promise that the Emperor would participate personally in an expedition against the enemy, provided that the pope and the imperial diet shared appropriately in it. Ferdinand was convinced that the campaign could succeed only if Charles led it and contributed to it; he began to press him to specify the number of troops he would provide.[40] Not only Ferdinand and the Germans felt this way. After the diet, meeting at Speier early in 1542 authorized a force of about 40,000 infantry and 8,000 cavalry, Mary agreed that only the Emperor could keep order in such an army. Paul III, too, obviously felt that Charles's direction of the undertaking would enhance its chances for success. Morone, his legate in Germany, held out the hope to the diet that the pope would fund 5,000 troops for the campaign if the Emperor actively participated in it. Otherwise, only 2,500 men could be expected from Rome.[41]

Paul and the Germans, therefore, had lived up to their side of Naves's formula. But though Charles endorsed it—in writing according to Ferdinand—he did so only half-heartedly.[42] Late in December 1541, even as he was offering his person to the expedition, he was balking at sending any more men to it other than his contingents from the Empire and

Austria. Only if all Christian princes contributed to the offensive—a clear impossibility—would he give anything for his other lands or support Italian mercenaries. The French and the Mediterranean theatre all had greater claims on his armies and his captains. Pushing him to change his mind was his chancellor, Granvella, with whom such Spanish-oriented concerns weighed very heavily. For him, Ferdinand's trials in central and eastern Europe had little bearing on the fate of the Iberian peninsula, and Charles needed little persuasion. In March 1542, he told his brother that the Cortes of Castile would not back any expedition to Hungary and that since Francis I seemed once again to be arming for war, he would have to remove himself from any imperial endeavors. He begged Ferdinand to excuse him as best he could before the diet.[43]

Ferdinand did all that he could to compensate for his brother's withdrawal. Indeed, if Buda and Pest could have been won through sheer expenditure of energy, the cities would have been his. Knowing that earlier expeditions had failed in part because of inadequate supplies for his men, he personally supervised the collection of victuals and payment for them. From a strategic point of view, the campaign was perhaps more comprehensively planned than any other Ferdinand commissioned. Elaborate arrangements were made for munitions and equipment; around 180 ships to block Turkish supply lines up the Danube were also assembled. Charles, whom Ferdinand continued to beg for aid even if he would not appear, actually warned him that too large an army could be dangerous. In his opinion, so many men were not needed to take Buda; boredom, disease and disorder might rapidly spread in so vast a force.[44]

But Ferdinand had little choice but to keep at Charles for more assistance. While the diet of Speier had agreed in 1542 to raise men for the campaign and to support them, another diet, scheduled for the summer in Nürnberg, was to work out details for the funding. It was expected that a "common penny" would be levied, but until the way to assess this had been settled, the princes and cities were to pay their contingents separately.[45] To avoid delay in discussing these matters and widespread dissatisfaction among the estates, Ferdinand continued to ask Charles for substantial aid as a sign of good will and concern. The Germans were especially anxious that Charles tax his Netherlandic territories, nominally part of the Empire, something they had been demanding of the Habsburgs since the beginning of the sixteenth century and something which the dynasty and its subjects in those lands had been vigorously resisting.[46]

The problem of moving the diet to act grew more acute for Ferdinand by June as the army which he had recruited began to assemble around Vienna. Some of the troops, most notably those from the spiritual electors who were under heavy financial pressure in their own territories, had been paid for only a month. This period had long since run out, and general disorder and indiscipline now reigned among the men.[47] In July Ferdinand went to Nürnberg to hurry the diet along with its financial deliberations, but, as was its wont, the body was not to be rushed. Local conflicts preoccupied its attentions: the Schmalkaldic League had attacked the Catholic Duke Henry of Braunschweig who had ben trying to get control of Goslar, and the perennial problem of the role of German cities were to play in the gathering's deliberations had arisen once again. Ferdinand, too, had upped his demands, for he was now asking that the estates supplement the support to which they had originally agreed at Speier.[48] Finally, just as he had feared, the Germans continued to lament Charles's absence and refusal to send aid, especially from the Netherlands. Ferdinand dutifully protested that his brother was in no position to help him at this time, but he did turn to Mary for assistance in quieting resentment in the Empire over lack of Netherlandic financial support. As Charles's regent, however, she was simply the executor of his policies in that quarter and was no more responsive to Ferdinand than the Emperor. Indeed, he did not hear from her for the five weeks that he was in Nürnberg, a slight to which he reacted bitterly.[49] By the end of August, Ferdinand was reduced to begging the estates simply to maintain their original contingents. He also promised to call upon only some among them for reinforcements and then only in emergencies. The meeting closed on August 26. Ferdinand had hoped to appear personally in Hungary in September. He went instead to Bothemia where the crown lands had not come up with 2,000 florins they had promised him and on which he had been counting.[50]

Charles's withdrawal from the campaign had also opened anew the question of who would lead it. One candidate for the post—Elector Joachim of Brandenburg—had asked for it even before Charles had removed himself. Until the Emperor's intentions were clear, Ferdinand had answered the elector evasively. Once his brother had declared himself, he decided to go along with the Hohenzollern, especially since the dukes of Bavaria, his closest allies, also supported his bid. Joachim's appeal was not his military talents—he had never held a command and was thoroughly inexperienced—but rather as a mediator between the religious factions in Germany. Though a convert to Lutheranism, he had worked very hard in 1538 to arrange some sort of a compromise between Ferdinand and the Schmalkaldians which guaranteed religious freedoms for the latter and aid against the Turks for the Habsburg.[51]

At the same time in July that Ferdinand left for Nürnberg, it was decided to send Joachim on to Hungary with the men who had assembled in Vienna to join with the main body of the Hungarian force. Even though the army was not yet at full strength—at most, it had reached between 30,000 and 40,000 men—discipline in the camp was so bad that getting them moving seemed the best thing to do.[52] Germans, papal mercenaries, and Hungarians began an agonizingly slow and insect-tormented march down the Danube, gradually picking up other contingents from Hungary and Bohemia along the way. By the beginning of September there were around 60,000 of them as well as 200 ships.[53]

On September 28, with neither the leadership or type of troops from the Emperor Ferdinand had wanted, his forces laid siege to Pest. His worst fears were quickly confirmed. Harmonizing the multinational army was difficult. The various Hungarian commanders fell to quarreling with one another over the apportionment of provisions and men. Joachim complained that they gave him no assistance, hardly surprising given the rampant mistrust among them. The German diet which had drawn up an order to regulate the camp conduct of its troops had specifically warned them against drinking Hungarian wines because of their allegedly lethal properties.[54] Joachim himself was unable to coordinate his chief officers; his own decisions were actually the product of a majority vote of his German sub-commanders, an arrangement probably intended to compensate for the elector's scanty military experience. Indeed, it was this body, along with some Hungarians which decided to attack Pest rather than Buda as Ferdinand had ordered, probably because they felt it was an easier target. And in any case, by the time the siege had begun, large parts of the army were in shambles. Many of the Germans had been completely abandoned by their princes; the weather was already turning chilly and many men were poorly clothed. Foraging brought them little since almost everywhere they looked, others who had fought there before had already despoiled and depopulated the land.[55]

Italian artillery opened a breach in the wall of the city large enough to enter on October 5. Mercenaries, also Italian, who had lived up to their reputation for skill and dependability, were the first to go through. However, they were stopped short by a moat which had been dug around the inside of the wall. The Germans and Hungarians who were to follow them in retreated immediately when they saw that their advance guard was stymied. The defenders of the city were quick to take advantage of this and reigned arrows down on the helpless Italians who lost somewhere between 700 and 1000 men, about one-third of their total number. There was some talk of resuming the assault, but the German leaders who claimed that they had been inadequately informed of the attack to begin with, said that their troops were in no shape to go on. A retreat was called.[56]

The withdrawal was chaotic. Joachim returned to Austria by the end of October, a "half-fugitive" from soldiers who were clamoring for their wages.[57] Embarrassed as he was, Ferdinand's first concern was to persuade the elector to leave behind 7,000 to 8,000 men to maintain Habsburg garrisons in Hungary. Despite the ignominious end of the undertaking, both men were remarkably temperate in their criticisms of one another. Joachim had no complaint about the size of the force or the provisions and weapons which Ferdinand had supplied. While Ferdinand initially blamed the elector's leadership for his latest disaster, he quickly came to see that its root lay in the long delay of his forces in Vienna who had waited in vain during the spring for their pay from Germany. The Turks themselves admitted that had the army moved quickly, it could probably have taken Pest and even threatened Buda.[58]

The Hungarians had been especially anxious to have Ferdinand at the head of the army. Whether this would have materially altered the outcome of the campaign is, of course, impossible to say. In any case, his role in raising funds behind the lines for his forces may very well have outweighed any impact his personal command might have had.[59] The effect which the Emperor in such a position might have had was another matter. Ferdinand was now more sure than ever that if such expeditions were to prosper in the future, Charles would have to back them substantially. He was not the only person who believed this. Many Hungarians also felt that without the Emperor's personal appearance in their homeland along with Spanish and Italian troops, they were as good as lost to the Turks.[60]

Thus, even though Charles thought that such military ventures had little chance of success, Ferdinand did not give up trying to change his mind.

When in 1543, he re-entered the field to improve his position in Hungary, he once more pressed his brother for aid, even though he knew that Charles's widespread commitments all but precluded this. The venture was as fruitless as Ferdinand's other tries.[61] Again leading his army himself, Suleiman captured Esztergom and Székesfehérvár, both of which were central in Ferdinand's plans to secure a line of defense all the way from Transylvania to Vienna.[62] But he still continued to regard the Turks as merely fightening, not invincible. For all the advances they had made in 1543, they did not get quite as far as he had feared they would, and the weather had weakened them so badly that he thought he could have won back Esztergom with proper help.[63]

But though he hinted that he might undertake an anti-Turkish crusade in 1544, Charles never did so. He sent an advisor to Vienna in 1545 to help Ferdinand with the fortifications of the city, but what the latter really wanted was troops and the money to pay them. His Austrian and Bohemian subjects were increasingly reluctant to meet his demands for extraordinary outlays for his wars; the Bohemians and Moravians in Hungary in 1543 had simply refused to move forward when he asked them.[64] Fueled both by inflation and need, his indebtedness had surged dramatically. In 1540, Anton Fugger had loaned him 25,000 gulden at 10% interest, the going rate in Augsburg. The next year, Ferdinand asked for 184,975 gulden and between 1542 and 1547, he borrowed close to 1,000,000 gulden, that is, roughly 200,000 gulden a year.[65] Charles did send him 3,000 Spanish soldiers to use in Hungary in 1544, but the brothers argued for two years over who was to pay them. Supported only sporadically, the men vandalized the kingdom to such an extent, that they were more loathed than welcomed by the local population. Even Mary's holdings were not spared. The Spanish troops plus fortification costs left Ferdinand out of pocket 180,000 florins by 1546. His only recourse was to try to impose a beer tax in the Bohemian crown lands, something he frankly confessed was illegal.[66]

Financial exhaustion, his exposed position in Austria and what little of Hungary was left to him, plus Charles's apparent lack of interest in his fate all left Ferdinand with little choice but to negotiate a more advantageous position for himself. As always Charles seconded such policies. Both brothers sent ambassadors to Constantinople, and Ferdinand was very pleased by the work of Gerard Veltwyck, the Emperor's representative. Discussions moved slowly, but by 1547, a truce had been arranged. In return for a yearly tribute of 30,000 ducats, Suleiman, who was facing a major campaign in Persia, granted his Habsburg rival a five-year respite.[67]

But within Hungary itself, Ferdinand could ill-afford to abandon his efforts to extend the territories under his control. The collapse of the offensive against Buda and Pest in 1542 had unleashed a kind of anarchy among his supporters who now scrambled to rescue something for themselves in what they felt was a deteriorating situation. Perhaps most alarming were the actions of Peter Perényi, his chancellor and the captain of the Hungarian forces in the 1542 campaign. Late in that same year, he seized the territories belonging to the cathedral of Györ and two properties of the cathedral of Eger. He then occupied the castle and town of the latter, contending that the Turks were about to take it anyway. He was also suspected of secret dealings with the enemy after the Pest disaster to win Ottoman support for a governorship of Hungary. Ferdinand had little choice but to capture and imprison him, a move which provoked even more hostility among the Magyar nobles. George Karlowitz, a close advisor of Duke Maurice of Saxony, believed that the only way Habsburg control over the strip of Hungary still left to them could be maintained was for Ferdinand to install one of his sons as king. The latter would rule that country and no other, thereby, at least in theory minimizing Hungarian hostility to foreign rulers.[68] Ferdinand did what he could to defuse the disappointment and mistrust he had aroused, even though at times his credibility must have suffered. In 1545, a diet meeting in T'rnava demanded that Mary return all royal incomes from mints and tolls for defense purposes. Ensnared in his financial embarrassment, his need to retain Hungarian loyalty, and his scrupulous deference to dynastic agreements, Ferdinand pointed out that his sister had received these rights from her husband and father-in-law and that he could not forcibly strip her of them. At the same time, through his Hungarian counselors and other surrogates, he issued memoranda which disputed Mary's claims and promised that he would do all he could to put an end to them. When in 1548, the Hungarians urged him to press Charles on resuming a general church council, he complied even though a papal nuncio assured him that the pope would not cooperate. Much against his will, he finally named a palatine for the kingdom in 1554, but in choosing his old supporter, Thomas Nádasdy for the post, he obviously hoped that his new official would not abuse his powers.[69]

The most obvious place for Ferdinand to strengthen his hand territorially, however, was in Transylvania which had briefly recognized him as ruler after his agreement with Isabella and Martinuzzi in 1541. The estates had been more than willing to swear obedience to him provided that he aided them in recovering certain places that Zapolya, his wife, and Martinuzzi had taken over. For his part, Ferdinand had begun talks almost immediately with local merchants about a loan to support a force in the territory.[70] But after taking Buda in 1541, Suleiman had reinstalled Isabella, John Sigismund, and Martinuzzi in the province, thus making Ferdinand's presence there far more problematic. He tried to win the monk to his side by incorporating him into his service. At the end of 1542, Martinuzzi was appointed Ferdinand's commissioner in Transylvanian along with a co-commissioner, Andreas Báthory who, because of ill-health, never took the position. But the monk was not to be lured by such wiles. Suleiman had returned him, his mistress and her young son to the territory not in any Habsburg name but in Zapolya's, and Martinuzzi, in any case, refused to turn Transylvania over to Ferdinand out of the well-grounded fear that the Habsburg could not defend it. The Transylvanian estates also saw that their position had changed. Now recognizing John Sigismund as their ruler, they began collecting taxes to support a tribute to the Turks.[71]

But Ferdinand was as stubborn a negotiator as he was a military organizer. Despite all that had passed in Transylvania and Martinuzzi's continued molesting of his Hungarian possessions, he continued to press him and Isabella to observe their 1541 agreement with him. Working in his favor was the utter lability of political relations in the province. The estates did not like Martinuzzi and Isabella's close dependence on the sultan's good will, and, more important, mistress and advisor had become ever more suspicious of one another's ambitions. Martinuzzi, in particular, felt that Isabella, who was increasingly anxious to have some independence, was putting his position in jeopardy.[72] Taking advantage of these divisions, Ferdinand had won both around to where they were ready to begin talks with him once again in 1547.

By 1551, the split between Isabella and Martinuzzi had grown so wide that Ferdinand was able to win her agreement to recognize the compact made between them ten years earlier. In return, he promised her the incomes and territory of Opole, then a fief of the Bohemian crown. But the story was far from over. If anything, it passed from the realm of the merely complex into that of the bizarre and even ugly. Martinuzzi, who quickly became Ferdinand's partisan once Isabella turned against him, was rewarded with a cardinalship and the title of voivode of Transylvania. He continued to deal with the Turks, however, arousing doubts about his loyalty in Ferdinand and the open hostility of the Marquis de Castaldo who commanded the Habsburg forces in the province. Ferdinand gave the general plenipotentiary powers to treat Martinuzzi as he saw fit in such circumstances. Though there is no conclusive evidence that the monk was engaged in open treachery, Castaldo apparently thought otherwise and on December 17, 1551, ordered that he be murdered. He was duly stabbed and bludgeoned to death, a procedure which Ferdinand defended rather clumsily to a distressed pope in 1552.[73]

And in Isabella's instinct for self-preservation, Ferdinand had found a match for his own. She did not even wait to arrive in Opole with her son before asking even more from him than their agreement had specified. Though he did his best to satisfy her, some of her demands were impossible to meet. Among other things that she wanted were complete freedom for John Sigismund from military obligations and exemption of his subjects in his new land from any taxes due the Bohemian crown. Ferdinand would hear nothing of this, claiming that such conditions would not only be generally prejudicial to the interests of Bohemia and Silesia, but that they would have to have the approval of the Bohemian estates. By 1554 she had demanded flatly that John Sigismund be fully sovereign in the duchy and that the Bohemian estates recognize his full independence from the suzerainty of the Crown of St. Václav.[74]

But those were not the only problems which the Polish princess presented to Ferdinand. Whether deliberately or not, he had handed Isabella a shabby retreat in Opole which triggered her ire immediately. Wooden poles were propping up the castle which was to be her residence when she arrived, and basic furnishings such as tables, beds, and chairs all had to be purchased. Incomes from the lands were irregular, and the ponds and woodlands had been emptied of game and fish. Ferdinand protested that the previous holder of the territory, a Hohenzollern, had left it in this condition, but such disclaimers in no way met Isabella's basic objections to her treatment. Worse yet, the Habsburg really did not have the money to meet his commitments to her. As part of his betrothal contract, Zapolya had promised his wife 140,000 Hungarian gold gulden as a *contradote,* the incomes to be drawn from castles in his possession in Hungary and Transylvania. Through the transfer of the Hungarian crown to him, Ferdinand had now assumed these obligations. He sent 40,000 of this to her in 1551 out of funds which he drew from other territories. Of the remaining 100,000 gulden, Ferdinand promised to pay one-half by Christmas of that year and the remainder, with 5% interest attached, at regular intervals until 1554. This he never did, so that by the end of 1554, he owed Isabella 122,000 gulden in accumulated interest and principal.[75]

Whether the Jagellonian princess ever seriously intended to observe the treaty is arguable. But Ferdinand's inability to fulfill his side of the bargain gave her the excuse to open negotiations with the Turks and anti-Habsburg Transylvanians to return her and her son to her late husband's province. Both the kings of Poland and France were interested in John Sigismund's fate, and in 1553, she asked Sigismund Augustus's assistance as well. The Turks were now making it known that they would like to see the German ruler out of Transylvania and a native prince installed as voivode. Though he knew such discussions were underway, Ferdinand desperately hoped to put a stop to them by finding the money to pay Isabella and by convincing the king of Poland to intervene on his behalf. Charles sent him letters he could forward to the princess, Sigismund Augustus, and Bona Sforza if he thought these could be helpful. But all of this was empty posturing. The marauding of Ferdinand's forces in Transylvania did little to increase Habsburg stature, and Charles's position in the west had deteriorated so badly that word from him was of little value.[76]

Isabella continued to plot her return to Transylvania, and, as Ferdinand's time to meet his obligations to her grew near, he desperately promised her incomes from other Bohemian lands. He also offered to exempt John Sigismund from taxes and other obligations in Opole so long as he, Ferdinand lived.[77] But Isabella was no longer seriously interested. By January 6, 1555, when the stipulated monies had not come, she established residence in Poland, right on the Hungarian border. The next year, the Transylvanian estates recognized John Sigismund as their prince; on October 22, 1556, she and her son, now a youth of sixteen, entered Kluj, thus ending effective Habsburg rule of the province until the beginning of the eighteenth century. The Turkish presence loomed large both in the action of the estates and Ferdinand's passive reaction to it. There were those such as his son, Maximilian, and some Hungarians who felt that he could have done more against the Turks who were tied down through 1554 in Persia.[78] Once he made peace with the Shah, however, Suleiman threatened the Transylvanians with invasion if they did not take John Sigismund as their prince. Ferdinand also wished peace, and the sultan insisted that he would come to no terms with him unless John Sigismund was restored to his inheritance and position. It was a condition that Ferdinand had rejected earlier; now, he stoically accepted it.[79] He continued to think of Hungary as his last line of defense for Austria, to plan campaigns against the Turks, and to negotiate with Isabella. But little came of it. From his quarter, Suleiman gave some thought to expeditions against the Habsburg rival, but fear of renewed Persian attack, quarrels within his dynasty and army unrest, all crippled his military effectiveness in the last years of his reign. Individual positions, fortresses and cities were lost, then sometimes regained, by both sides as well as by John Sigismund who proved to be a restless figure, but the effective lines of demarcation which separated all of them remained much the same.[80]

Thus what was left to Ferdinand in Hungary was essentially what Charles had recommended many years earlier—undisputed possession of the crown of St. Stephen and the westernmost part of the kingdom. Through his treaty with Isabella, that crown was also hereditary in the Habsburg male line, though the Hungarian estates had not officially accepted such procedures. But he had failed to reunite the kingdom as the Magyars had hoped; indeed, his ill-executed military ventures had, if anything fixed the divisions between the Habsburg west, the Ottoman central region, and Transylvania. It was an unhappy arrangement for him in many ways, not the least of which was economic. Even though endless warfare had left vast areas of the kingdom bare both of people and crops, pockets of considerable mercantile and agricultural prosperity continued in central Hungary and Transylvania.[81] Customs records from 1542 show significant domestic capital still present in Hungary; the export of cattle and hides to Italy from the Hungarian plain occupied by the Turks continued to expand until the end of the sixteenth century. Ferdinand would probably not have been able to maximize the potential export duties from such a trade, since the Magyar noblemen, who were the chief cattle raisers, and customs guards had turned evasion of such taxes into an art form. But the Turkish presence in the mid-section of the kingdom and the essential independence of Transylvania made it impossible for him to even begin to realize any income from these areas.[82]

But his great failure had been his inability to gain the upper hand in the kingdom militarily. While constitutional and diplomatic maneuvers undoubtedly helped, they usually exacerbated tensions between ruler and estates and were easily interrupted by external events. Only through effective armed offensives against the Turks would the Hungarian nobility as a whole have accepted their German ruler more or less wholeheartedly and pulled together with him in long-term action against their common enemy from Constantinople. A Venetian observer commented that it need not have been done with a large force, but it had to be well-disciplined and well-led. What he really meant was that Suleiman's success was as much due to the poor quality of Ferdinand's armies as it was to Turkish prowess.[83]

All this Ferdinand knew, but he was also convinced, as were his Hungarian supporters, that it was only the Emperor who could have given him what he needed. There had been substantial agreement from all sides on this in 1541 and 1542; ten years later, Piotr Kmita, the voivode of Kraków, was still saying the same thing to Ferdinand's ambassadors who had approached him for aid.[84] But Charles had demonstrated over and over that he would commit neither himself nor much of his resources to such undertakings. Ferdinand, who had struggled from his youth for recognition as a ruler in his own right, was that if nothing else in what he controlled of Hungary. The results were not, however, quite what he had expected.

CHAPTER X

THE VICTORY OF BOHEMIA

In its own way, the kingdom of Bohemia was as much a challenge to Ferdinand's ambitions as was Hungary. Though the territories of the Crown of St. Václav were not divided among mortal enemies, the realm was far from at peace with itself. Provincial antagonisms abounded, especially between Bohemia and Moravia. The estates of the kingdom, which included a stronger urban contingent than in Hungary, were jealous of their very substantial rights and privileges. Finally, the people were deeply split religiously, a situation which had both advantages and drawbacks for Ferdinand. An influential minority of Catholics, who would be among his strongest supporters, was present. Their power, however, was tempered by the several types of Protestantism which had captured the loyalties of the rest of their countrymen. Many splits had taken place within the ranks of Utraquism since its formal establishment in the fifteenth century. A conservative faction, which dominated the governing consistory of the church and in theory still hoped for reunification with Rome, was frequently inclined to cooperate with the new Habsburg ruler. This was especially true when Ferdinand moved against other sects in the realm to which the Hussite persuasion had given birth, most notably the *Unitas Fratrum.* No longer as resolute in their other-worldliness as their predecessors, the Brethren were still very well organized, and Ferdinand regarded them as very dangerous. There was also a sizable group of Utraquists who, after the 95 Theses began circulating throughout Europe, grew increasingly sympathetic to Lutheran doctrines. These were perhaps even more problematic for the king because they were likely allies of the German Protestants. To add to the confessional disarray in the kingdom, the Anabaptists had also made an appearance, coming, in many instances, from Ferdinand's own Austrian lands.

The initial reservations about Ferdinand in the kingdom centered on his ignorance of Czech and his reputation for absolutism. There was also some fear that Mary would be involved in his administration. With this in mind, Ferdinand moved cautiously for several years following his coronation in 1527 as he worked to consolidate his authority in Prague and beyond. Traditions both large and small were observed. In 1539, when the powerful nobleman Jošt of Rožmberk died, Ferdinand appointed his brother Peter to the provincial court of Bohemia, thereby continuing the practice that one member of the family always sat in that body.[1] Indeed, he promised that if Peter could not hold the position because of ill-health, his place would be open for yet some other member of the house. To his favorites, such as the Pernštejn family, he was generosity itself in turning over incomes to them.[2] But when he, or his representatives, served as mediators in the countless family squabbles which arose in the kingdom, he proceeded with great even-handedness, even where his supporters suffered. Thus Vojtěch Pernštejn, who became Ferdinand's Lord High Steward in 1528, was fined in 1529 for damage he had done the subjects of another nobleman.[3]

Where, early in his reign he did introduce major changes, he acted only if substantial support for such measures existed. A case in point was his redivision of Prague in 1528 into two municipalities, each with its own chief magistrate. The merger of the Old and New Towns as they were known, had taken place only in 1517, largely due to the machinations of an ally of Zdeněk Lev of Rožmitál, Jan Pašek, who then became mayor of the new entity. From this vantage point, he had begun a drive against the Lutheran elements in the Utraquist church. With the support of the head of the consistory, Gallus Cahera, a Lutheran apostate, he had banished citizens from the capital for their religious and political opposition to him. In 1528, Ferdinand, reviving an old prerogative of the kings of Bohemia, which permitted them to name the magisterial councils in Prague, separated the city again and installed a new set of magistrates in each division. This was happily received in Prague where the union of the Old and New Towns had never been popular. In some quarters, Ferdinand was hailed another Charles IV, the fourteenth century king under whom the Bohemians had flourished. Though Pašek made some effort to reingratiate himself with his ruler, in 1530 Ferdinand ordered him and Cahera from the realm. Those whom Pašek had driven out were allowed to return.[4]

He was equally circumspect in religious matters. Ferdinand's Catholicism troubled conservative Utraquists far less than did the inroads which

Lutheranism was making into their church. They begged their king to forbid the marriage of priests and attacks against the Virgin. Indeed, they came to look upon Ferdinand as a kind of ally in protecting what they saw as the national faith. For his part, Ferdinand had assured the estates at the time of his election that he would uphold the fifteenth-century *Compactata* which had established Utraquism in Bohemia and Moravia. He also promised to ask that the pope formally endorese the arrangement, step Rome had never taken. On the other hand, Catholics were pleased to hear of his determination to have an archbishop once again in Prague, the see having been vacant since the Hussite wars. To the Silesians, Ferdinand vowed that he would do everything to promote a well-ordered and Christian life. His most delicate problem was in Moravia where sectarianism was especially wide-spread. The estates of the margravate had presented him with a request for virtual religious toleration in 1526. He avoided committing himself to that concession, though he did promise to observe the territory's "liberties, regulations, and good and old customs," a formula which the diet mistakenly believed covered confessional freedom.[5]

It may be, as has been said, that Ferdinand's extra-Bohemina preoccupations in the early years of his reign gave him little time to deal with religious radicalism in the kingdom, and that he therefore did not press the matter. Nor could he afford to offend any potential sources of help against the Turks. But, looked at in the light of his desire to restore the supremacy of Catholicism in all his lands, the strictures placed upon him in Bohemia were not wholly disadvantageous as he himself admitted.[6] In the *Compactata* and the St. James Ordinance of 1508, the latter issued by Vladislav against the Bohemian Brethren, he had two widely supported legal instruments which gave him a good deal of room to manuever against the Protestants. Through a literal construction of the *Compactata,* Ferdinand hoped to rally the timid and moderates around him. This policy generally succeeded, at least insofar as its goal was to foster good relations between the monarch and the two established religions in the kingdom. By maintaining the support of those Utraquists opposed to Lutheranism, Ferdinand could sway Hussite ecclesiastical affairs somewhat in the way he could Catholic ones. In 1530, the king and the consistory reached an agreement regarding the role of the Hussite church in the kingdom, the legal jurisdiction of its ruling body, and the

elimination of heresy. But for all the good will he enjoyed among the
Utraquist conservatives, control over the sects, particularly over the
Brethren and Anabaptists eluded him during these years. Both had powerful noble sponsors in Bohemia and Moravia, and, despite sporadic arrests
of these men for harboring the forbidden confessions, Ferdinand and his
backers had too little force at their disposal to wipe them out. Persecuted
as they were, the Brethren nevertheless presented an outraged king with
their articles of faith in 1535 and asked that they be tolerated.[7]

Aside from the challenge which confessional heterogeneity mounted to
his religious views, Ferdinand wanted Bohemia under his control for the
revenues it offered. Even after it underwent massive political upheaval
in the 1540s, the kingdom was a source of considerable wealth. Foreign
imports, a key indicator of domestic prosperity, rose through the end of
the century. Between 1552 and 1555, a Venetian ambassador reported
Ferdinand's income from his domains, mines and other *regalia* to be
500,000 thalers. However, almost all of it was obligated. The Tyrol
was next, with 400,000 thalers, but the Tyrol did not have Bohemia's
depth of wealth and therefore was a less reliable source of extraordinary
income.[8] Rare was the Turkish campaign, therefore, that did not bring
Ferdinand to Bohemia, and while the kingdom had no great love for its
Hungarian neighbors, influential Bohemians such as Zdeněk Lev of Rožmitál felt that it was better to have the Magyar " . . . er sey, wie er sey . . . "
than the Turks on their borders.[9] But for all this, the Bohemians could
be extremely lukewarm in supporting their elected ruler, and some of
them continued to dicker with Zapolya through the 1530s.[10]

Ferdinand's economic interest in Bohemia was an obvious response to
his own deteriorating financial position. Incomplete records hint that
while revenues did come in from his Austrian and Hungarian domains,
they did so unpredictably. Some years the Austrian holdings turned a
profit, some years they did not.[11] The problem in part stemmed from his
personal outlays. As far as domestic expenses were concerned, equally
scant documentation during this period indicates that the daily cost of
his court and those of his sons may not have been his major expenditure.
Until 1544, when separate households were established for Archdukes
Maximilian and Ferdinand, undue sums seem not to have been squandered
in this area. Between 1543 and 1546, his personal staff encompassed
between 275 and 300 persons, considerably fewer than the 472 whom

Maximilian I employed at his death in 1519. While the figure for Maximilian includes gentlemen-at-arms and members of the imperial horse guard and the one for Ferdinand does not, when we come to a number for the latter in 1554 that does take such personnel into account, it is 451, still smaller than Maximilian's household.[12] Even if one argued that Maximilian, as Emperor, merited a far larger staff than his grandson, who was only heir-apparent, there are other reasons to believe that Ferdinand was not unduly lavish where his household was concerned. As late as 1554, while the number of his employees had increased, their salaries had not. And Ferdinand had a streak of austerity in him, at least where his own person was concerned. In 1549, his expenses came to 1,754 florins 58 kreuzer, about three times the salary of his Lord High Steward. In 1530, he and Queen Anna required approximately 204 yards of velvet for their personal use, a quantity which the representational duties of monarchy and the full-draped costumes of the period easily accounted for.[13]

His habitual extraordinary extravagances may have been more serious. Anna herself seems to have gone heavily for gold decoration on the velvet and taffeta she favored as fabrics. The total value of the metal she ordered for such purposes in 1534, 1536-1538 was 929 florins, 25 kreuzer, of which only about a third had been covered by 1538. In 1539, Ferdinand promised to pay the Augsburg merchant Leonhard Weiß 1,750 gulden in principal and interest—a sum which almost matched his *total* outlay for personal needs ten years later—for a cross of diamonds with a ruby center and pearl decorations. Some of these bursts of expenditure were probably unavoidable, such as the almost 2,328 gulden which went to outfit his court in mourning clothes after the death of Charles's wife, Isabella, in 1539. The relatively stable salaries of his personnel belie the numerous underground benefits which their positions conferred and to which Ferdinand undoubtedly contributed. For example, in 1524, he obligated himself to pay a 4,000 gulden dowry (*Heiratssteuer*) and 200 gulden in annual interest until the principal was delivered in full to Barbara von Weisproch, one of Anna's ladies-in-waiting.[14]

But his chief problem was that from Mohács to the middle of the 1540s, his military expenses far outstripped his normal income. To cover his costs in Hungary alone in 1541, he had to arrange a loan of 184,975 florins, more than twice his total income from the Hungarian royal domains from 1537 to that year. After borrowing approximately 200,000 gulden a year through much of the 1540s, he asked for and received 311,000 in 1548 and a staggering 519,499 in 1549.[15] Foreign merchants were his biggest creditors; by 1530, he already owed 989,400 florins to the Fuggers. Compared to the German bankers, his family all but neglected him. Of the 218,018 florins which he borrowed from the Turkish campaign of 1537, the Fuggers loaned him 83,278 and his sister Mary, 6,000. In 1540, Charles V advanced his brother 50,000 florins, but the Fuggers and Leonhard Weiß topped this with 60,000. The Emperor loaned him nothing, however, in 1541, nor between 1547 and 1551 did any of his family appear among his chief creditors.[16]

Thus, Bohemia was a very attractive source of additional revenue, and Ferdinand attempted to better his yields there from the very beginning of his reign. He tried to revive an old mandate of Charles IV which ordered that all goods imported into the kingdom had to be brought to Prague where all the regalian tolls and taxes on them were to be levied before they could be sold at large in the kingdom. In 1541, the Bohemian estates agreed to a general property tax to support him in Hungary, and throughout the sixteenth century, the Moravian diet voted imposts on beer sales in the royal cities, import and export of wines, and various types of property. Such measures were neither adequate nor, in all instances, acceptable. Both native and foreign merchants objected to the Prague waystation for imported goods, and they began selling right at the edge of the kingdom. When customs officials were deliberately placed in border towns, traders simply sought out less traveled roads to ply their commerce. In 1538, Ferdinand's Bohemian treasury formally protested the practice, and he allowed the duty to be collected in any of the twenty-eight royal towns in the kingdom. Nor were the taxes which the estates voted him meeting his needs. In 1546, he complained bitterly that his treasury was receiving very little from the kingdom, particularly in view of his heavy military outlays. Other princes, he grumbled, with far fewer responsibilities, were treated far more generously by their subjects.[17]

Ferdinand's complaints about Bohemian tight-fistedness were echoed by the estates of his other territories. The Styrians, through an elected committee, asked the Bohemians in 1536 and 1537 to do more in the effort against the Turks, a request which Ferdinand seconded enthusiastically. In 1541, the Styrian governor, Hans Ungnad, speaking not only for his own duchy, but for all the other lands of the Habsburg Austrian patrimony, urged the same thing of the Bohemians once again. This time, however, they proposed a scheme in which Bohemian and the lands of the Crown of St. Václav would pay two-thirds of an annual three million florin tax, the Austrian territories to make up the balance. Ferdinand was actually able to implement something like this at a general diet of his lands in 1542 though the total yearly contribution was lowered to 1,146, 000 florins. The ratio of Bohemian to Austrian revenues remained the same however.[18]

But Bohemian participation in Ferdinand's designs was usually grudging at best. Resentment persisted at the flow of their tax monies abroad.[19] His religious and political policies disturbed them increasingly as well. Anabaptist settlements multiplied, especially in Moravia where they had come from Switzerland, southern Germany, and Ferdinand's Tyrol among other places. Ferdinand voiced his hostility to their persuasion frequently and vigorously. His efforts to rid the margravate of the sects, however, only succeeded in arousing the enmity of the landed magnates in the area. Having discovered that these new immigrants made excellent agricultural workers and artisans, the lords were not about to lose them to the whims of any king. They implacably opposed Ferdinand's persecution of them which began in earnest after 1535; a decree which he issued against the Anabaptists in Moravia in 1545 was pointedly ignored by the local political establishment.[20]

Perhaps more serious was the way in which Ferdinand's anti-Lutheran measures unavoidably offended more and more Czechs as the Wittenberg reform spread among the ranks of the Utraquists. In 1543, a year in which Ferdinand assured Rome that he would punish all manifestations of Lutheranism in his territories unmercifully, an open clash broke out between the king and the administrator of the Utraquist consistory, Jan Mystopol. Impressed by Luther's teachings, the clergyman had tried to introduce some of them into Bohemia. Ferdinand flatly forbade Mystopol and his supporters to preach, though Turkish pressures in Hungary and a fear of civil revolt in Prague forced him to relent temporarily. But he resumed his anti-Lutheran campaign the year afterward when he ordered the Bohemian nobility not to tolerate married priests on their holdings. He also commanded that all priests not ordained in the Roman rite, a practice of both Catholics and Utraquists, be expelled from the kingdom.[21]

Mistrust of his political ambitions also grew among the estates during the late 1530s and the years that followed. Ferdinand had never inwardly forsaken his wish to make the Bohemian kingship a hereditary Habsburg preserve. At his election, he had been forced to acknowledge that the estates had chosen him as their ruler, but in winning their assent the next year to the crowning of his adult, male heir in his father's lifetime, he had already moved one step closer to his goal. The disasters of Ferdinand's career were to a certain extent counterbalanced by sheer luck, and, in 1541, just such a break came his way. As usual, he was quick to exploit it. By accident, a fire destroyed the Bohemian Land Tables in the Hrad-čany, the royal castle in Prague, in which were recorded all solemn acts of state. When new ones were reconstituted, Ferdinand managed to have his recognition of the elective principle left out.[22] In 1544, he came to a diet in the Bohemian capital which, as he said to the Emperor " . . . grandement me touche . . . . " Here he won the assent of the estates to his claim that the Bohemian crown was hereditary in his house. They also accepted his right to staff all offices of the kingdom, though only with natives, and to call diets. He alone was to give out important fiefs.[23]

But it was disunity and inattentiveness among the estates, not a spirit of cooperation, that caused them to yield to this erosion of their privileges. None of it happened without much grumbling, as a letter of Jan Pern-štejn to Ferdinand in 1539 discloses. Loyal monarchist though he was, the magnate accused the king of provoking dissatisfaction among his Bohemian subjects with his endless tax requests, his bent toward absolutism, and what Pernštejn delicately called his excessive seriousness and concern for religion. Ferdinand's reply had all the eloquence of a man truly on the defensive. The heavy imposts were attributed to the Turkish burden which ultimately was a problem for the kingdom and Christendom as a whole. As for those who found him too earnest and remote, he pointed out that in Bohemia, where subject and monarch had become one another's familiars, a reference to the Jagellonians, subjects ruled far more than the king. It was a relationship that Ferdinand refused to encourage. As to confessional matters, he swore he had harmed no one of the Utraquist faith, nor would he do so in the future. As for the others, they believed neither in God, the sacraments, nor the resurrection. They were therefore, as far as he was concerned, like animals and unworthy of toleration. Their errors, as he saw them, arose not out of misunderstanding but out of evil. His vigilance in defending his faith, he contended, was only a way of thanking the divinity for all the blessings that it had bestowed on him—good health, a devoted wife, sturdy children, a brother who treated him as a father rather than as a brother, and a great inheritance which was expanding without a great deal of open conquest.[24]

Such protestations did little to soothe touchy Bohemian sensibilities in the years that followed. In the 1540s, a loose anti-Habsburg coalition of both nobility and townsmen began to take shape in the kingdom. The relentless spread of Protestantism also put added pressure on the king. At a time when his financial needs were growing exponentially, dissidence and disobedience due to religious differences were mounting in all his hereditary lands. He dreaded the general diet of his territories in 1542, anticipating that it would demand from him such things as communion in both kinds, marriage of priests, and other practices which had become the common coin of Protestantism. To his great relief, religious questions did not bulk as heavily at the gathering as he thought they would, but his fears and gloom did not abate as what he believed to be heresy continued to gather force in his lands.[25]

The common frontier of Bohemia and the Empire made it almost impossible for either Charles or Ferdinand to take action against Lutheranism in one area without affecting the other. Conversely, their inability to roll back the spread of the new persuasion in Germany encouraged it to leap over territorial boundaries. Throughout the early 1540s, it was clear that whatever conciliatory gestures the Habsburgs had made toward the Lutherans had only emboldened the latter. At the diet of Regensburg in 1541, Charles had promised to leave the Protestants unmolested, provided that they did not try to extend their influence by force, and to allow them access to the imperial *Kammergericht*.[26] Diets in Speier, Nürnberg, and Worms from 1542 to 1545 saw them pressing Ferdinand to continue these concessions and to incorporate them into a formal recess of the body. For his part, the Habsburg evaded such steps as best he could without alienating his religious opponents to the point where they would deny him military aid. The short-lived opening of the Council of Trent in 1545 abetted his strategy insofar as it gave him a plausible reason to urge that such questions be forwarded to that gathering rather than settled locally. But his motives were altogether too transparent to the Protestants who well knew that he wanted to get help from them against the Turks and defer religious matters indefinitely. Rather than contribute to the common defense, many Lutheran princes apparently preferred to recruit their own forces.[27]

Ferdinand did not completely abandon hope that the religious issue in the Empire could be resolved peacefully. Nor did he rule out altogether the possibility that some decisions in this area might be taken by a national council if a general one refused to act. But as in Bohemia, his impatience with the Protestants and the inconvenience which they brought him intensified throughout the early 1540s. The reluctance of even his Catholic allies to help him probably increased his rancour.[28] At a diet in Nürnberg in 1543, the Saxon chancellor, Burkhardt, had scarcely begun his address announcing the refusal of Protestant support against the Turks when Ferdinand arose and stormed from the room. The following year he privately swore that he would sign no more agreements with the heretics. He also swore to avenge himself on them.[29]

Added Lutheran militancy throughout the 1540s gave him additional reasons to adopt a more militant posture toward them. Henry of Braunschweig's territories fell to the Schmalkaldic League in 1545, a victory which Ferdinand feared would make the confederates more bold than ever. The size of their army seemed to have grown. Though he felt that they could not keep such a force together for too long, it still bothered him. He had underestimated the staying power of the League when they began their campaign against Braunschweig in 1543, and the error probably added to his unease. Worse yet, John Frederick of Saxony had already declared that he could operate both militarily and politically in the lands associated with the Bohemian crown. In 1541, he asked the Silesian diet to aid him if either Charles or Ferdinand attacked his holdings. That same year, the elector recaptured the abbey of Dobrilugk, a fief which he held in Lower Lusatia, after it had been taken from him by a relative of the governor of the area.[30]

Armed expeditions in the Empire were something that Charles had to initiate. By 1544, the idea had become more attractive to him. A temporary respite in the hostilities with France had come about with the Peace of Crépy, and the Emperor had begun thinking seriously about forcibly crushing the Lutherans. He discussed such a plan with Ferdinand at Worms in 1545; rumors that he was about to go to war against the new faith swept Germany that year. Ferdinand steadfastly denied it before the estates. He remained tightly secretive on the matter, speaking of it neither to councilors or servants. The truth, however, was that both brothers had been willing to open an offensive following their meeting at Worms; only the lateness of the year had persuaded them against it.[31] Ferdinand's hope was that the Lutherans would be defeated so badly that they would be thrown upon the Emperor for clemency and thus reduced to his complete obedience. Yet, he did not want the undertaking to look like an attack on Lutheranism as such. Rather, he wished to use what he called the aggression of Philip of Hesse and John Frederick of Saxony against other secular and spiritual princes as the pretext for going to war against them. At the diet of Regensburg in 1546, Ferdinand still tried to keep a civil tone in his relations with the Protestants. Only after the abrupt departure of the Schmalkaldic leaders from the gathering did he drop his mask of politeness, accusing both Philip of Hesse and the Saxon elector of disobedience in the guise of defending religious belief.[32]

In carrying out so complex and, in many way dangerous a campaign—his potential front stretched from the Rhine through Saxony—Charles had allotted to Bohemia two key roles in his strategy.[33] He did not wish to tip his hand too broadly in Germany by actually buying gunpowder there. Ferdinand assured him that part of the rich saltpeter reserves of Moravia and Silesia would be his.[34] Even more important for the Emperor was the way the Bohemians were geographically situated to harass John Frederick on his eastern front. Even though Charles as a much younger man had doubted that the Empire had any real jurisdictional power in the kingdom, he behaved quite differently once his immediate interests were at stake. He had published and posted there his decree of August 1546, which outlawed John Frederick and Philip and orderd the Bohemians to observe it. Indeed, he hoped that they would attack the elector's territories immediately.[35]

Ferdinand had two key responsibilities in this undertaking. It obviously would fall upon him to raise troops in Bohemia. Meeting with the estates in July and August 1546, he asked them for a commitment of men, though he presented the request in the most disarming terms possible. He reassured them that the conflict now underway in the west had nothing to do with religious differences, an important consideration in winning the confidence of many Bohemians and one which explains Ferdinand's insistence on it with his brother earlier. He also argued that the levée was for the protection of Bohemia's borders against attack. By this he meant a preemptive strike, but the estates chose to interpret the condition far more narrowly. While they granted him 4,000 cavalry and 20,000 infantry and supporting funds, they specified that they were to be used only for defensive purposes, a far cry from Charles's intentions. Furthermore, the length of service for each contingent was not uniform—some had support for one month, others for more or less. Ferdinand decided to prolong the negotiations.[36]

The outcome of his efforts in the kingdom also depended heavily on how well he performed another task. Convinced that he would need more than Ferdinand's Bohemians to worry John Frederick on his eastern flank, Charles wished to draw the elector's cousin, Maurice, who ruled the ducal part of the Wettin inheritance, to the Habsburg side. Cleverer by far than most of his princely counterparts and more ambitious as well, the duke had first come to Ferdinand's attention during the Hungarian campaign of 1542. There he acquitted himself with distinction; the following summer, he had aided Ferdinand in the kingdom once again. That fall, Maurice met with the Emperor, leading Ferdinand to remark somewhat cryptically that ". . . he could be useful if he were employed."[37] When it came to negotiating with the Saxon, however, Ferdinand found him to be exasperatingly slippery. The duke's ultimate goal was the electoral as well as the ducal title in Saxony, something that only the Emperor could sanction. He was understandably reluctant to invade the territory of a blood relative without important outside assistance. This he defined, among other things as Bohemian aid. But the reluctance of the estates there to deploy their forces outside the kingdom forced Ferdinand to try, on the one hand, to persuade his subjects that the duke would seize Bohemian as well as imperial fiefs in electoral Saxony if they did not assist him and to convince Maurice that the Bohemians might do the same in his lands if he did not join them.[38]

He was more successful with Maurice. Agreement between the two of them was reached on October 14, 1546, though the actual transfer of the electoral title and provision for lines through which it was to be inherited remained to be ironed out.[39] But it was clear that Maurice would get in John Frederick's lands and the imperial fiefs as well as those held by various bishoprics; those which the elector had held from the Bohemian crown were to fall to Ferdinand. Each man was to help the other if either were

attacked in their newly conquered territories. No one consulted the Bohemian estates during the negotiations, though they were later asked to
sanction the outcome. Both Maurice and Ferdinand bound themselves to
go on the attack against John Frederick almost immediately.[40]

Though Ferdinand had promised Maurice that he would be able to
raise an offensive force in Bohemia, he was less than sure that the estates
would accept his designs. His uncertainty was well-founded. Many in the
body did not feel that their king's diplomacy had committed them to anything; indeed, in the summer of 1546, Ferdinand had already had a fore-
taste of open resistance which was to become increasingly stubborn.[41] An
early part of his dealings with Maurice had been the renewal of a so-called
Erbeinigung which the kingdom had made both with ducal and electoral
Saxony in the fifteenth century. Among the stipulations of the compact
were guarantees of territorial integrity for all signatories. Led by Prague,
the large Bohemian cities refused to recognize any agreement with Maurice
alone, as did the Bohemian knights, though they were later won over.[42]
But the kingdom could not remain aloof from Habsburg imperial politics
indefinitely. In August, the estates received a letter from John Frederick
in which he warned them, Ferdinand to the contrary notwithstanding,
that once Charles defeated the German Protestants, the Bohemians were
the next in line. Saxon spies in the kingdom reported on the level of
support which Ferdinand could expect there.[43]

In spite of the opposition of the estates, Ferdinand did get enough men
from them and from his other lands to cobble together an army that invaded electoral Saxony at the end of October. Rag-tag a force though it was,
it enjoyed considerable success, giving Charles much reason to be
pleased. Campaigning along the Danube, his armies were riddled with
desertions, but John Frederick was so disturbed by the invasion of his
territories that he withdrew from the west altogether.[44] Charles's tactic
had apparently worked.

Ferdinand's initial conception of the offensive against the Schmalkaldians had had a basically imperial focus, even where his own interests were
involved. He was delighted to have his brother encamped in Germany,
since he believed that the Emperor's presence there would make Suleiman
more cautious. He wished to see Charles's position in the Empire enhanced
in such a way that in the latter's absence, not too much responsibility would
fall on Ferdinand and his children. He also hoped, as he saw opposition in

Bohemia to Habsburg schemes surfacing, that he would be able to punish disloyalty in the kingdom without any intervention from his brother.[45] However, as soon as he learned that the elector was returning to defend his territories, he began to beg Charles for aid. The force which he had sent into Saxony was beginning to fall apart as colder weather took its toll. Maurice's loyalties also looked shakier. Not only was the duke facing armed conflict with his cousin; he was Philip of Hesse's son-in-law![46]

But for Ferdinand, the gravest situation had become Bohemia itself. where Charles had badly misread local feeling. For all of Ferdinand's denials, the estates still believed that the Habsburgs had embarked on an anti-Protestant crusade rather than a punitive expedition against mutinous vassals. As early as September 1546, both John Frederick and Philip of Hesse had written their estates that Charles did indeed intend to exterminate their confession, pointing to the aid he had received from the pope for war to confirm their case.[47] Charles had also realized that Ferdinand's relationship with Maurice might disturb the Bohemians, but hoped to avoid it. It was, however, this very alliance which provided a major spark to the oppostion in the kingdom.[48] Prague, which had been especially reluctant to go along with the renewal of the *Erbeinigung* with Maurice alone, withdrew its troops from Saxony earlier in November. By December, Ferdinand had begun to enforce a harsh discipline on some of his subjects. One provincial leader who had resisted his orders that troops leave the kingdom for Saxony was decapitated on December 31, and but for the personal intervention of Queen Anna, the king would probably have dealt out the same treatment to others.[49] With future retaliation in mind, he made a preliminary search of persons and towns in Bohemia to seek out those among them who were allied with the German heretics. He asked Charles, who was dealing with recently subdued Protestant cities to find out who had contacted them from Bohemia. All this was to provide " . . . a perpetual obedience [and] security for me and my heirs and successors in this realm and other lands."[50] The Bohemian resistance had given their king a somewhat different program than the one with which he had intially entered the campaign against the Schmalkaldians. As with his rewriting of the Land Ordinances after the fire of 1541, however, he was not a man to let the opportunities of the moment slide.

But before he could capitalize on at least some of them, he lived through some of the blackest days of his life. By the beginning of January

1547, John Frederick was rallying his forces in Thuringia and Saxony, close to those Bohemian crownlands where Lutheranism was most widely spread. Around the tenth of the month, the elector entered Lower Lusatia, a prosperous area where Ferdinand feared local wealth would be used to finance further Saxon aggression.[51] However, personal calamity dwarfed even these troubles, at least for the moment. Toward the end of January, Anna was delivered of another girl, the couple's fifteenth child in twenty-six years of marriage. The queen was unable to expel the afterbirth; her body remained so large that it was not generally known that a child had actually been born. Complications followed immediately and then, death. Ferdinand was inconsolable. His tender fidelity to his wife had set him apart from almost all the rulers of his day; as a sign of permanent mourning, he began to grow a full beard which he kept until his death. The court saw him only at mass or at the funeral itself.[52]

For the first and last time in his life, public and private man seemed locked in conflict. Immediately following the Saxon invasion of Lower Lusatia, he had ordered Prague to arm immediately and to appear before him in Litoměřice in the near future. Anna's death left him unable to decide whether to meet with the Praguers himself or to send one of his sons; in the end, he chose to go himself.[53] The military situation was certainly precarious enough to warrant his personal supervision. Once John Frederick became a real threat to Maurice, the latter immediately called upon Frederick to assist him under the terms of the *Erbeinigung.* Bohemian balkiness forced Ferdinand to turn to Margrave Albrecht of Branden-burg-Bayreuth and the bishops of Würzburg and Bamberg for temporary aid. However, John Frederick also had sympathizers in the Empire who were willing to help. When the Hanseatic cities sent assistance to the elector, Ferdinand became even more alarmed about Maurice's position.[54] The Bohemians and Charles had to be mobilized.

A two-hour harangue on Bohemian duties which Ferdinand delivered to those who showed up at Litoměřice availed him nothing. Prague, which he had specifically called upon for military aid in January, said it could given him nothing without another diet, and the estates as a whole took up the cry. To Ferdinand's argument that John Frederick's offensive in Lower Lusatia was a breach of the *Erbeinigung,* they replied that the original agreement had been with the entire Saxon house. In any case, they had not consented to Maurice's attack on the elector.[55] They were convinced that Ferdinand intended to destroy their traditional freedoms; on February 15, 1547, a confederation numbering about 1,738 knights and nobles along with Prague and the other royal cities formally issued a manifesto to that effect. They asked Ferdinand to air these matters in a full diet; in the secret hope that Charles would have cleaned up his affairs with the elector of Saxony by that time, he suggested that it be held around April 18 in Prague. Until then, he forbade any diets or local conferences within the administrative districts into which the kingdom was divided.[56]

But at this point, the Bohemians were not to be cowed by their kings's orders. Encouraged by John Frederick's promises of protection, they called a diet which met in Prague around the middle of March. Once assembled, they issued 57 Articles, some of which preemptorily overturned much of Ferdinand's prior work to enhance his position and that of the crown. On the advice of the district captains, the estates declared that they too could summon a diet if the king would not do so or was out of the kingdom. If Ferdinand was to have his own treasury, Bohemians were to oversee it, along with Kutná Hora and other royal mines. A tax on beer passed by the estate in 1546 which was yielding roughly 200,000 gulden was to be abolished. Most serious of all, Ferdinand's insertion in the new Land Ordinances of 1545 that his wife had a hereditary right to the kingdom and that his son could be crowned there during his father's lifetime was to be excised. Finally, the gathering voted to raise a substantial military force which they put under the direction of Kašpar Pluh, a longtime foe of the king. Aside from the military threat which this step represented, it was, in Ferdinand's opinion, clearly illegal since neither he nor his representatives had called the gathering to begin with.[57] He felt that he was in the eye of a full-scale rebellion. Broadsides mocking both him and the Emperor began to appear in the streets and taverns of Prague, some of which fell into the king's hands.[58]

But by the middle of February, the Emperor had resolved to assist his brother in view of the importance of the Bohemian-Saxon front for his German enterprise as a whole. His determination was quickened when John Frederick defeated Albrecht of Brandenburg; Ferdinand's news that the elector had moved into Kutná Hora, giving him the opportunity to coin money almost at will, could not have been very heartening either.[59]

The appearance of Charles in the east was the one move that the Bohemain insurgents dreaded. John Frederick himself had warned that the

Emperor would almost certainly turn on the kingdom once the latter had dealt with him in Saxony, and the Praguers were especially mindful of the way Charles had quelled an uprising in Ghent against him in 1539. Then he had not only levied heavy fines on the town, but abolished the privileges of the guilds as well. Though he claimed that he meant the estates no harm and that in helping him, they would be helping themselves, many grew uneasy. Those meeting in Prague through March asked the kingdom as a whole for more substantial support.[60] But they continued to provoke him. When they refused to supply him with provisions for his troops in Germany and persisted in their mutinous ways at home, he promised to send Ferdinand Spanish troops under the Duke of Alva.[61] The rebels branded the Spaniards as "sodomites" and said that Ferdinand intended to wipe out the Czech language. The core of the opposition actually hardened. Led by the city of Prague and a group of noblemen around Vilém Křinecký, an alliance drawn from members of the diet in Prague joined together on April 22 explicitly against Ferdinand, vowing to defend rights and freedoms which they said had been theirs before the destruction of the old Land Ordinances.[62]

But two days later the Emperor, with Ferdinand in his camp, won one of the great victories of his career at Mühlberg in Saxony, capturing John Frederick in the process. The dissidents in Prague reacted quickly. Some scattered to their homes; others vowed to continue their opposition.[63] By May 3, however, a mission from the estates had reached Charles to persuade him that the force they had assembled had been only for protection of their privileges, crown, and land. They offered to send the Emperor any victuals he needed and to assist him to the utmost against the Turks, though, as one of Mary's observors on the scene observed drily, no immediate threat from that quarter existed. Charles and Ferdinand demanded that the Bohemians abandon their league; the Emperor, furthermore, made it clear that if this were not done, he would support his brother in any way necessary.[64]

Ferdinand had four major grievances to settle with the rebels: that they had called a diet without his permission, that they had continued to aid John Frederick, that they had formed a league against their king and encouraged their peers to enter it, and that they had impeded the passage of imperial forces through Bohemian territory. By the middle of May, he was ready to leave Charles in Wittenberg and return to the kingdom to begin his charges.[65] The brothers differed somewhat over how vigorously Ferdinand could proceed in Bohemia without provoking further upheaval—Charles seems to have argued for far harsher measures than the king. The Emperor was fully aware, however, how important his victory was for the Habsburg position in Bohemia, and he seems to have accepted Ferdinand's more cautious strategy for turning it to full advantage.[66] At the beginning of June, Ferdinand reentered his realm to meet with members of the estates whom he had called to Litoměřice, reminding them as he did so, that he had the full trust of the Emperor who was "pressing" on all borders of the kingdom.[67]

He began his dealings with the estates on a deliberately magnanimous note. Declaring that he would consider pardons for all who had joined against him, except those who had injured his honor and prerogatives too grossly, he denied that he was out to destroy Czech freedoms as such. His calculated generosity got him at least part of what he wanted. Around two hundred noblemen accepted his invitation to Litoměřice, as well as representatives from several cities.[68] However, with Prague still at the heart of the opposition, the rebel league held stubbornly on; Ferdinand urged his brother to indicate his displeasure to the Bohemian representatives who were still with him. He also asked that Charles keep them there until the arrival of the captured Philip of Hesse, presumably to intimidate them with a naked display of imperial power. It was assumed that they would report all that they witnessed back to Bohemia.[69]

Charles willingly followed his brother's instructions.[70] But the Prague rebellion continued, and Ferdinand saw that he could not break the back of it by conciliation. For this he needed a larger army which only Maurice and the Emperor could provide. In a rare burst of self-sacrifice, he volunteered to pay for whatever troops Charles sent. By the end of June, Charles had dispatched a contingent of men under the Marquis of Marignano who assembled on Ferdinand's orders before Prague on July 6. This appearance, coupled with a setback for the dissidents at the hands of Ferdinand's own force that had been skirmishing nearby, shattered the uprising.[71]

Both Ferdinand and his contemporaries were quick to see that the Emperor's contribution had meant much for his Bohemian triumph. Characteristically, he gave all due thanks to the deity for his victory, but he regarded his brother's aid as almost as helpful.[72] He moved swiftly to deal with the miscreants. A diet summoned for August was preceded by the execution of four of them, upon which Ferdinand assured his subjects that he was not limiting their freedoms but protecting the rights of the crown. Quite clearly, however, he was reading those "rights" rather one-sidedly. He forced the estates to rescind most of the 57 Articles of the previous March, and they promised to allow the crowning of an heir to the throne during Ferdinand's lifetime.[73]

Where he did substantially restrict freedoms, it was usually in the cities. Throughout the 1540s he had been increasingly angered by their slow response to his pleas for aid against the Turks; almost the entire third estate, including many of the royal towns, had sympathized with the Schmalkaldians.[74] Ferdinand singled out Prague for punishment, because of its eminence throughout the kingdom, but his wrath fell on many other municipalities as well. Royal justiciars were to be sent to the royal cities and to Prague, which had to accept an additional *hejtman* as well. All were ordered to look out for the king's interests; the justiciars were to hear the deliberations of civil and religious bodies and defend the rights of the king before them. Signs of conspiracy against Ferdinad and his family were to be rooted out. Somewhat later, a royal appellate court was created which could decide cases not only involving the cities but any area throughout the realm. The towns also saw their right to vote in the diet temporarily removed.[75]

Of equal importance were his financial gains in the kingdom. The Schmalkaldic venture had been costly—by Ferdinand's own calculation it had forced him to muster 73,972 florins and 40 kreuzer a month.[76] But his profits from outright confiscation or revenues voted him by the estates substantially made up for this. Again, his main target was the cities rather than the nobility. This is not to say that individual members of the latter group went unscathed—Václav of Vartemberk was stripped of one holding that contained 161 villages and some tin mines and Count Šlik lost his control over an entire administrative district. Bohus Kostka of Postupice had to give up the city of Litomyšl, the chief seat of the Bohemian Brethren against whom Ferdinand renewed his persecution. Other noblemen simply had to pay fines. But the king had many loyal allies among the powerful families such as the Rožmberks and the Pernštejns, and he may have feared wounding whatever class loyalties these men had too deeply. He was later ¹to return some of the lands he had confiscated as fiefs.[76]

What his reasons, the total fine exacted from the twenty-five royal towns was around 80,000 *kop* Bohemian groschen. Almost three months of war expenses, therefore, were paid by the cities alone. They also had to submit to a perpetual beer tax—two groschen in the royal towns, one in the rest—something later extended to the entire realm. This proved to be immensely profitable, averaging 28,018 *kop* in the years between 1553 and 1564 and only falling below 25,097 *kop* in 1554 and 1564. Confiscated lands brought Ferdinand 500,000 *kop* groschen. On the advice of his chief financial counselor, Florian Griespeck von Griespach, he did not put all these properties on the market at once for fear of driving down the price. Their sale, therefore, continued during the Bohemian reigns of Maximilian and his son, Rudolph realizing a nice sum for them as well. Though the estates requested that the confiscated property remain part of the crown, Ferdinand paid them little heed.[77]

In general the estates became far warier of provoking their king. From 1548 on, yearly allowances to him of men and money became the rule, though committees and officers of the diet were sure to see that these were used for the purposes which their ruler had specified. And Ferdinand still, on occasion had to spend a good deal of time with the body such as a particularly vexing meeting in 1556 where negotiations over Turkish aid and settlement of a land dispute between the house of Rožmberk and the princes of Plauen cost him a great deal of time and effort.[78] But more and more Bohemian revenue flowed out of the country, and the estates could do little to prevent this.[79] Ferdinand also took the opportunity to resolve a long-standing dispute between himself and the Bohemian chancellor over the latter's right to interfere in the supervision of the state treasury. Inspecting the Bohemian crown lands now became the duty of the head of the treasury, a royal appointee. Administration of court and state revenues were brought much closer together, a further incursion of the Austrian model into the kingdom. Royal gifts (*milostivé dary*) from court funds were now entered into the accounts of the state treasurer.[80]

Ferdinand was confident enough of Bohemia in 1548 to leave it in the hands of his second son, Ferdinand, who became its governor. It was a wisely popular move; the young man was politically deft as well as pleasant and accomodating. His tastes were, if anything, more lavish than those of his father who soon had to raise his allowance for the kingdom from 80,000 to 120,00 gulden a year. The archduke and his secretaries organized hunting parties, banquets, and theatrical spectacles with the same attention they gave to matters of state. When he came to Prague in 1558 as Emperor, Ferdinand was greeted by the sight of 5,000 horses massed in his honor! But the young man tempered his extravagance with generosity where the needy were concerned, and many noblemen far preferred his light-heartedness to the earnest ways of his father that Jan of Pernštejn had deplored so many years ago. Some continued to visit the archduke long after he left the realm to reside in the Tyrol.[81]

Residual resentment of Ferdinand's harshness lingered—by the middle 1550s there was still much unhappiness at his curtailment of municipal freedoms and at his continued confinement of some noblemen who had joined the 1547 uprising against him to their castles. Nor, despite the reestablishment of an archbishop in Prague in 1562 and truly vicious measures against the Bohemian Brethren was he able to check the spread of this sect or of any other throughout the kingdom. Anabaptism continued to flourish while Lutheranism and later Reformed ideas gained increased acceptance among sympathetic Utraquists.[82] But he knew, and others did as well, that 1547 had been an important turning point in his career. He had been able to call a halt to the troublesome legal and political independence of the Czech towns, especially Prague, though in any case at a moment when their economic importance had begun a decline that would accelerate in the centuries to come.[83] In at least one of his kingdoms, he had been able to realize a degree of control that he wished to have in all his lands. The promise that Charles had made to him that some day they would accomplish great things together had, somewhat accidentally perhaps, come to fruition. A contemporary epitaph in Prague read:

> The prince elector of Saxony is conquered by the Emperor
> The royal city of Prague is overwhelmed by terrible evils.

It bespoke a kind of flawless coordination of Charles and Ferdinand's purposes for which the latter had always hoped. But, though neither brother knew it in 1547, that kind of relationship was not to last for very long.

CHAPTER XI

A MATTER OF TRUST

In 1538, Charles had given some thought to marrying one of Ferdinand's daughters to the Duke of Orléans. Part of the young lady's dowry was to be Milan, but until the French prince was old enough to rule it, Ferdinand was to act as a kind of trustee for him in the territory. The king's long-standing designs on the Lombard metropolis were known to many, moving someone to ask the Emperor if such confidence in his brother were not misplaced. Charles's reply was unequivocal. Ferdinand's promise was not to be doubted, for, as he put it, " . . . he was a good man who respected his word and honor more than he loved his brother."[1]

For all the disagreements which had arisen between them, Charles was not overly idealizing his brother's character. Few long-term relationships are even consistently smooth, especially when they were almost exclusively political, as was the case with Charles and Ferdinand, and conducted via the hit-and-miss communications of the sixteenth century. Up through the Schmalkaldic Wars, diverse territorial and hence military concerns had created what divisions there were between the two men—Charles's preoccupation with the French and Turks in the Mediterranean, Ferdinand's with the Islamic threat in the central and eastern parts of the continent. But no major break had developed between them, if only because of mutual dependency. For Ferdinand, the relationship was obvious. His brother was his greatest potential source of help. Charles's needs were not as obvious but were nonetheless real. His Italian-Spanish interests left little time for systematic attention to German affairs so that a trusted lieutenant was essential for guiding these. While Ferdinand had often differed with his brother over the details of imperial policy as well as its general direction, his loyalty to Charles and the interests of his family had never come into question. Charles's comparative neglect of the Empire had perhaps made Ferdinand's subordinate role there somewhat easier to bear since, to all practical purposes, he was its ruler. At the very least, he could console himself with the thought that he was developing the political skills and contacts with the princes he would need as their future sovereign. Certainly his secondary status never led him to believe that his affairs were any less important or complicated than those of his brother. To his way of thinking, the Bohemian estates were every bit as troublesome as those of Aragon because their deliberations took even longer than did those of the latter. He offered his own experiences in the form of advice to the Emperor as the latter did to him. When Granvella began raising an army in Germany in 1543 for Charles to use against the duke of Cleves, Ferdinand was quick to call upon his Hungarian disasters to remind him of the dangers of using imperial troops unreinforced by Spaniards or Italians.[2] But symptomatic of Ferdinand's burgeoning political individuality though such gestures might be, they in no way foretold any open break with the Emperor. Disagreements, however deep they may have been at the time they appeared, were but temporary disturbances in an overall pattern of cooperation, or at least attempted cooperation.

This pattern seemed to continue throughout much of the 1540s. Infrequent and imprecise communications from the Emperor to his brother continued to vex the latter.[3] Charles, in Ferdinand's eyes, could be needlessly arrogant with the German estates, postponing his arrival at diets without formal excuse from either himself or his representatives. His financial support for the Catholic League did not always come promptly. And a joint policy in Hungary was out of the question. Charles continued to regard his brother as little more than his lieutenant in central Europe, a role that Ferdinand sometimes flatly refused because of the press of business in the Magyar kingdom.

But on the whole the brothers attempted to coordinate their policies, especially in the Empire. The results of the Schmalkaldic War were unusual, as far as the Habsburgs were concerned, not because a novel policy of cooperation between them had come into being, but because their long-stated desire to work together had paid higher dividends than at any time since Pavia. Ferdinand steadfastly clung to his belief that only Charles could deal with German religious, administrative, and social policies definitively and repeatedly urged him to come to the Empire. And the Turks did not always divide them. The conciliatory Declaration of

Regensburg which Charles issued in 1541, effectively allowing Lutheranism to spread provided that it did so peacefully, grew out of his feeling that both Ferdinand as well as he needed aid in the face of a joint French-Ottoman attack. The Emperor reminded the Rhenish electors in 1543 of their duty to help the king against Suleiman.[5] In purely tactical questions, Charles took his brother's advice on German affairs seriously. When he could not get to the diet of Speier for its opening in 1544, he followed Ferdinand's counsel and sent ahead commissioners to deal with important matters first. Ferdinand did his best not to allow his private interests to interfere with his brother's wishes. For all his protests late in 1544 and at the beginning of 1545 that Hungarian and Bohemian affairs kept him from opening the diet of Worms, Ferdinand actually got there quite quickly.[6] At the diet itself, the brothers were instrumental in engineering the election of Otto von Truchsess, the cardinal of Augsburg, to the recently vacated archbishopric of Mainz.[7]

However, Ferdinand was still clearly the junior of the two and rarely failed to observe the niceties of deference due his brother. Before sending prelates from his lands to Trent at the pope's request in 1549, he did not move until he heard from Charles on the matter. His two eldest sons, Maximilian and Ferdinand, were in residence with their uncle in 1547. When Ferdinand resolved in September of that year to name one of them his regent in Bohemia, it was apparently left to the Emperor to chose which of the two boys to send.[8] When the marriage of his daughter Elizabeth to Sigismund Augustus of Poland proved to be unhappy, Ferdinand not only sent his own representatives to the Jagellonian kingdom to straighten the situation out, but also asked Charles to intervene.[9] Despite his lukewarm reaction to Sigismund Augustus's attempt to resuscitate a treaty of friendship which Maximilian I had once had with his kingdom, Ferdinand was nevertheless willing to listen to Charles's counsel in the matter. Though he pursued an increasingly independent line in Hungary, he continued to solicit Charles's advice on Turkish and Hungarian matters, especially since both Martinuzzi and the estates of the kingdom kept up their own channels of communication with the Emperor. Charles's opinion was sought (and given) on a five-year truce which Ferdinand signed with the Turks in 1547. When, in 1548, the Hungarian diet asked Ferdinand to promote in Rome the consecration of bishops without payment of annates on the ground that the war-wracked ecclesiastical lands in the country could no longer afford the outlays, Ferdinand begged the Emperor to intercede with Paul III on the issue.[10]

Some irritations could not be soothed. Ferdinand had hoped to use Charles's victory in the Schmalkaldic War to clean up certain German problems which displeased him. Chief among these was Württemberg, which he described as "...the heart of Germany..." and where he wished to regain the foothold lost to Duke Ulrich and his Protestant supporters in 1534. He urged Charles to return it to neither father nor son after the Emperor captured it in 1546, but Charles could not bring himself to depose an entire German princely family. He installed an occupying force of sorts in selected fortifications throughout the duchy, but pardoned Ulrich himself. Though Ferdinand was duly grateful for whatever provisions were made for him in the act of clemency, his brother never could act decisively enough for him in the area.[11] Even after Charles had found the occupation to hound him on what he felt were his rights in the territory, leading Mary to chide him sharply for being far too concerned with his own interests in the matter.[12]

And Charles rarely hesitated more than briefly to sacrifice his brother's hopes to political expediency. The 1540s brought many of Ferdinand's children and two of the Emperor's to marriageable ages. Ferdinand almost automatically looked to Charles, "...his father and the father of his children...", as the final arbiter of marital matters for both their families. This did not mean, however, that he was without ideas of his own to advance to his brother. One that he seems to have held most dearly was that of marrying directly into his brother's line, thereby beginning a pattern of alliances which would endure down to the extinction of the house in Spain at the beginning of the eighteenth century.[13]

When the duke of Orléans, the fiancé of Ferdinand's second daughter, Anna, died in September 1545, the king clearly hoped to marry her to his nephew, the future Philip II. Indeed, he had contacted Charles about the possibility of the union almost as soon as the latter's first wife, Maria of Portugal, had died.[14] Charles, however, found no diplomatic utility in such a marriage; in 1547 he decided to try pairing his son with Marguerite, the daughter of Francis I, as part of a general peace to be struck with France. Ferdinand bravely commented that he could hardly prefer "...the welfare of his children to that of the public...", but his every word betrayed his disappointment.[15]

With the plan to marry Archduke Maximilian and Charles's daughter, Maria, Ferdinand's interests and those of his brother coincided more closely. It was not out of the question, given the fact that Charles had only one legitimate male heir, that the Castilian succession might pass to Maria herself. The kingdom itself was no stranger to female rule—indeed, it had very recently experienced it.[16] Charles's motives were less transparent. Lack of more than the bare minimum of male progeny may have spurred him to look to his brother's family for marriage partners for his daughter; he was, however, in no way as categorically determined to see through the union of Maria and Maximilian as was Ferdinand. He regarded the arrangement as one best suited to the young lady in question and as a way of building up Ferdinand's good will toward his son, but he most certainly would have embarked on another union if the diplomatic situation had compelled him to do so.[17] The marriage did take place, however, even though one of the Emperor's conditions put Ferdinand to a great deal of trouble in Bohemia, namely that Maximilian be assured that he would be a reigning sovereign some day in the kingdom. This the estates still found difficult to bear since it smacked of hereditary monarchy, and it was only by a considerable amount of arguing that Ferdinand won them over.[18]

Still, there was very little in the record of interdynastic contacts between the two men to hint that disagreements could arise which would substantially alter not only their feelings about one another but their policies and in the end, their roles. Perhaps it was the very fact that relations between the brothers were so normal and, in the case of the cooperation in the Schmalkaldic War, exemplary, that Charles's plans for the imperial succession as they emerged in the late 1540s shocked Ferdinand so deeply.

The Emperor's promise that Ferdinand would follow him in the office dated back to 1522 and the Brussels territorial agreement betwen them. This was confirmed by Charles's support of the younger man's election as King of the Romans in 1531, though just which line would succeed Ferdinand seems not to have surfaced at the time.[19] By 1546, the king may have been giving serious thought to this question through a scheme which would have had the effect of strengthening the hold of his line on the imperial crown. In a proposal which he advanced that November to his brother on German finance, he suggested that the Emperor establish

a permanent tax for improving the organs of justice in the Empire. He
went on to note that such recurring revenues might make the emperorship more attractive, thereby moving some of the more powerful princes
to challenge the Habsburgs for office. His solution was to urge Charles
to coax promises from the electors that in the next two or three elections,
they choose only members of the house of Austria. Such an arrangement
would have given the *Kurfürsten* a free choice among Charles or Ferdin-
and's heirs, though, as has been observed, with Ferdinand in line to succeed Charles, he would be in an advantageous position to favor his own
children over any other candidate, including his brother's own son. Just
how seriously he meant all this, however, is open to question.[20] In 1545,
he had been a model of avuncular concern to his nephew in consoling
him over the death of the latter's wife of only two years.[21]

Gathered for a diet in Augsburg in 1547 and 1548, however, the estates
heard the startling rumor that the Emperor intended to displace his
brother as his successor altogether in favor of the young Philip. Although
none of the Germans present were happy about the arrangement, they
raised no vigorous objections to it either.[22] Just what Charles was planning
is difficult to say. He and Ferdinand broached the succession question at
the diet; it is equally clear that at that point, the possibility that someone
other than Ferdinand might follow him in office had crossed the Emperor's
mind. He wished to postpone any discussion of the matter until the arrival
of Philip in Germany which was scheduled in 1549. But in his testament
to his son, done at Augsburg in 1548, he unambiguously counseled the
young prince to respect his uncle's "imperial authority" and spoke of his
own prior efforts in bringing about Ferdinand's election as King of the
Romans.[23] By the same token, however, Ferdinand's behavior at the
diet bespoke a man who had suddenly become very anxious about his
future position. In sharp contrast to the aloof Emperor, he was rarely
without a guest from the princes' courts or from the ranks of the princes
themselves. These he lavishly wined, dined and entertained both with
professional musicians and his own conversation. His mouth, as one
observor put it, was never at rest.[24]

At some point before 1549, the brothers appear to have discussed the
matter between themselves again. Charles spoke of a prior agreement between them that Ferdinand would not take up the question of succession
with the electors until they had settled it within the dynasty.[25] But this did

not keep the latter from talking about it with other Habsburgs. In July 1549, Ferdinand sent a letter to Mary in which he characterized the rumors circulating that his brother intended to bypass him in the imperial succession as costing him heavily in terms of lessened honor and reputation, " . . . that thing that more than anything else marks a man in this world . . . ."[26] The intensity of his reaction could only mean that he took such stories seriously; both Charles and Mary grasped this quickly. Even before Ferdinand put pen to paper on the subject, the Emperor had dispatched a representative to him with assurances that he could never do anything so "unfraternal." Mary sent the same denials. In November, the Emperor said that the issue between them was that of deciding between Philip and Maximilian as Ferdinand's successor, thus temporarily putting an end to any doubt about the king's personal position.[27] Charles's ministers, however, continued to question it. Charles, obviously, was promoting Philip. Throughout 1549 and 1550, the young prince toured the Empire to meet its princes first hand. It was not a brilliant appearance. German dislike for Spaniards and things Spanish was growing by the middle of the sixteenth century, and the polite, but shy and taciturn, Philip was ill-suited to the earthy ways of some members of the estates, even though on one occasion he manfully allowed himself to get drunk.[28]

In the summer of 1550, Charles and Ferdinand met in Augsburg to hammer the matter out. In return for accepting Philip as his successor, the latter was promised that his daughter, Margaret, would be married to her Spanish cousin. Ferdinand himself was to be consoled with territorial increases and more aid from the Empire for Hungary. The Emperor had begun gently enough, but he reminded his brother that if he did not follow his wishes, he would deal with him in such a way as to show him the error of his position.[29] But Ferdinand would not be moved, even though the Emperor's offer would have fulfilled some of his long-standing goals for both himself and his children. Perhaps he was still inwardly bristling over the way his brother had allowed the rumors of his being passed over in the succession to fly around the Empire for two years before putting an end to them. More likely, he was planning to steer the imperial succession into his own line once he achieved the dignity himself and was feeling thoroughly thwarted by Charles's designs now that these had become clarified. As early as 1545, he had placed an order in Nürnberg for identical suits of armor for Maximilian and himself, a practice that Charles and Philip were already following.[30] He was certainly

under some pressure from young Maximilian himself, whose volatile de-
fensiveness and mercurial character was to become a major burden for
his father from this time on. The archduke was acting as Charles's regent
in Spain at the very same time his cousin was testing the mood of the
electors in Germany, a broad hint of the Emperor's plans for the imperial succession. In any event, Ferdinand immediately demanded that
Maximilian return from Spain to participate in the discussions, even
though he admitted that the gulf between the young men would only grow
wider. Charles argued that Spain needed a regent, to which Ferdinand
rejoined that if this were so, Philip should return to his native land. In
September, Charles, who had lost his trusted chancellor, Granvella, in the
interim, yielded on his nephew and ordered him to come to Augsburg
from the Iberian peninsula. The archduke appeared in December and
this, coupled with Mary's arrival at the beginning of 1551 allowed real
negotiations to get underway. Distressed at the dissension which she
saw arising in her family, she had volunteered her services as mediator
as early as August.[31]

Her job was formidable. The bitterness between the brothers, especially on Ferdinand's side had grown so great that they could not communicate face-to-face. In considerable anguish, Charles reported that
the king of France had never employed the terms with him that his brother was now using, nor did he seem to regret that he was doing so.[32] The
real breakdown between them, however, was precipitated not by the succession question, although it was clearly poisoning the atmosphere between them, but over Ferdinand's renewed requests for aid in Hungary.
On the night of November 22, they had been speaking of it with the
Emperor angrily interrupting Ferdinand several times.[33] With that, the
younger man had decided simply to terminate all discussions with the
Emperor, suggesting that they think about such matters alone. On December 14, Ferdinand wrote Charles, pleading again for help in Hungary,
especially in Transylvania. He suspected the Turks of plotting to seize
the area from Isabella Zapolya and pointed out the material and strategic
advantages that the principality would bring him if it were in his hands.
He reminded his brother that it was his duty, as head of Christendom,
to protect Christians, and that he, Ferdinand, regarded it as a matter
of conscience and protection of his own soul to bring anti-Turkish aid
up with the estates. To Charles's previous complaint that he made matters

of conscience out of anything he wished, he protested that he did not do this sort of thing lightly where the Emperor was involved, but since it was a matter of both Christians and commodities, the Transylvanian situation was unique.

Charles was correct to observe that he had heard much of this before —the strength of Ferdinand's arguments rarely lay in their subtlety but in the stubbornness with which he held to them. He was also quick to guess that it was the succession issue which was really at the heart of his brother's intransigence. But to understand his brother's resentment was not to excuse it or the actions which flowed from it. The pacification of Germany was far more important to the Emperor than Hungarian affairs which, he pointed out with some justice, Ferdinand had stirred up himself. As far as honor and conscience went, Charles claimed to know very well their meaning and accused his brother of having no sense of "public affairs."

He suspected that Ferdinand refused to bend on German aid against the Turks to strengthen his bargaining position on the succession quesion, but he had been able to get very little out of him or of Maximilian on the matter. When he had thanked the latter for his services as regent in Spain, the archduke had changed the subject abruptly. To the Emperor's annoyance, the young man had already begun lining up electoral votes for himself, thereby openly flouting Charles and Ferdinand's agreement to confine discussion of the matter to members of the dynasty. Charles claimed that he and Philip had observed this stricture closely though the latter's recent grand tour of the Empire could legitimately be taken as an exception to that. The Emperor had finally turned to Granvella's son, the bishop of Arras who was Mary's observor on the scene before her arrival, to see if the clergyman-counselor could coax something more out of Ferdinand on the succession issue. The bishop duly pointed out that disharmony between the Emperor and his brother could spell disaster for both of them. At this, Ferdinand had sighed and rather weakly replied that he knew this to be so; Maximilian, he claimed, would willingly accomodate himself to any arrangement that could be struck. But, according to Arras, while saying this he blushed visibly, then swore he had not discussed it with Maximilian. He contended not once but many times that his only concern was the well-being of his subjects, but ended by asking the bishop to make his apologies to the Emperor for his angry display. For his part, Charles was willing to yield a bit on getting aid from Germany for Hungary. Negotiations reopened, though the Emperor was not completely mollified.

With Mary acting as mediator, discussions went on for weeks at a time, five to seven hours at a stretch. While Ferdinand and Maximilian at least outwardly resumed their deferential attitudes toward the Emperor, the German princes and others knew well that serious trouble was afoot in the house of Habsburg.[34] Charles, who was rapidly succumbing to a variety of bodily ills, believed that the irritation he was suffering might kill him. At one point he did indeed fall into a fever of nervous exhaustion. As talks continued, he refused to even see Maximilian.

Instrumental in producing a final settlement were Mary and Arras, who conferred with the Emperor daily, regardless of his infirmities. Their underlying concern was to preserve Habsburg control of the Empire, and, equally important, selling whatever arrangement they worked out among themselves to that polity. For this reason, they proposed that Philip rather than Maximilian succeed Ferdinand because the Spaniard had far greater resources than his Austrian cousin, a line of reasoning identical to the one used against Ferdinand's imperial candidacy in 1519. In truth, Maximilian, at least on paper, did not look as powerful as his father. Ferdinand's testament of 1543 had assigned Bohemia and Hungary to his eldest son, but ordered that the Habsburg Austrian patrimony be divided among all three of his male heirs. To pacify the king, Mary and Arras again suggested a marriage between Philip and one of Ferdinand's daughters. A match between his second son, Ferdinand, and another Spanish cousin, along with a substantial dowry, additional aid in Hungary, and Württemberg were also offered. But these sweeteners were more than offset by another of Arras's ideas. Wishing to give the house as great an appearance of unity as possible, he proposed that the election of a new King of the Romans take place as soon as possible. This would have left the Empire not only with a reigning Emperor but two German kings as well, a snag which the bishop thought to circumvent by having Philip treated as Ferdinand's coadjutor, following the model of episcopal administration.[35]

Ferdinand's reaction to this was predictably negative. Calling upon both tradition and analogy, he argued that there was no precedent in the empire since it had come into the hands of the Germans for such an arrangement.

Where such divisions of power existed, such as that between Emperor and pope, these arose from the nature of their separate responsibilities. Many customs in both Charles's territories and his, he observed, were neither useful nor reasonable and were sometimes downright prejudical to the realms concerned, but one observed them simply because one had vowed to uphold them. While he granted that bishops took on coadjutors, he felt that he was already playing such a role vis-à-vis Charles. No coadjutor needed another one, which would be the case with himself and Philip. Nor did he think that the plan was politically wise. If the electors did not consent to it, their prestige and authority would be that much more diminished; after the death of both him and Charles, they could conceivably void the entire arrangement and look for an Emperor from outside Germany. Such a thing would be incalculably dangerous for their house. He finished, however, by assuring Mary of his desire and that of his children to maintain close contact between themselves and Charles and Philip.[36]

Ferdinand's protests won the day. Mary and Arras dropped the idea promptly though it continued to circulate among other members of the Spanish camp. With its removal from an official agenda, Ferdinand seemed to soften a bit. He was somewhat more discreet with his sons, preferring at one point to talk things out with Mary alone rather than in the boys' presence as she herself suggested. He agreed that Philip should succeed him, provided that certain conditions were met. The included a discussion of Maximilian's eventual succession after Philip's so that the Germans would know they were to be governed by someone who knew their language, customs, and people. He wanted assurances as well that neither Philip nor the archduke would interfere in his conduct of the Empire once it fell into his hands. He pressed for the marriage of his nephew to one of his daughters, again on the ground that it would please the Germans and asked for guarantees of Philip's assistance in the Empire if rebellion broke out there. He also asked for aid in Hungary and in Transylvania.[37]

Charles was willing to meet all of these requests, or at least to treat them seriously. He accepted Maximilian's eventual succession and Ferdinand's independence in the Empire. But now he had a qualification of his own. In view of what he described as the constant turmoil in Italy, he asked that Philip be allowed to function as Ferdinand's vicar in his absence there, just as Charles had allowed Ferdinand to do this in the Empire.[38] Ferdinand dug in his heels again, arguing that to do so would dismember the Empire and turn the government of the peninsula over to the Spaniards, even though Charles had promised that such a role for Philip would not prejudice imperial feudatory rights in Mantua, Montferrat, and Ferrara. Two heads in Italy would create confusion which would weaken the respect the Emperor drew from his Italian position and enflame the resentment of the Germans who would blame him for the arrangement. To lure Charles away from this idea, he offered to leave the marriage of one of his daughters to Philip completely up to Charles and to drop the question of Turkish aid altogether.[39]

By March 9, Ferdinand had been worn down to the point where he would accept Philip's vicarate in Italy when he himself was not there, something that would occur frequently because of his heavy German commitments. Retaining his reversion rights in the aforementioned duchies and Florence, he asked only that his nephew communicate with him fully on Italian matters and that he be allowed to call upon those areas of Italy in which the Empire had residual claims for aid against the Turks. His flexibility here paved the way for conclusion of the final agreement. Ferdinand promised to work for the election of Philip as his successor in the Empire; his nephew vowed his cooperation in securing Marximilian's election after his own. Whenever Ferdinand was absent from Italy, Philip would have governing and administrative rights there although he could not use Italian monies, even for their own defense, without his uncle's consent. Ferdinand, however, could get similar funds without asking Philip. These provisions were to stand only as long as Ferdinand lived. If he did not carry out his part of the bargain to seek Philip's election, the marriage clause between the latter and one of Ferdinand's daughters would be nullified.[40]

Beyond the Italian provisions, which he accepted only under protest, the agreement was not all that disadvantageous for Ferdinand. He had promises of aid against the Turks and in the Empire if trouble should occur there, something he had never had so specifically in writing before.[41] But trouble over the arrangement both in the Empire and within his own household began almost as soon as it was signed. The Germans in general did not like the idea of Philip as a potential emperor.[42] Maximilian and those among his intimates who were trying to strengthen the hold of the

Austrian Habsburgs on the imperial succession read the arrangement as an open insult. While the twenty-four year old archduke seemed momentarily reconciled, at least according to his aunt Mary, he was not nearly so circumspect with the German princes before whom he freely vented his displeasure over his cousin's primacy in the imperial succession. It was an attitude which did him no harm in those quarters, if French observers are to be believed.[43] The Venetian ambassador Giovanni Michele had suggested to him on his return from Spain that his father was all too dependent on the Emperor to ever thwart the latter's designs seriously. Maximilian had agreed with the envoy then, and his resentment over this situation grew along with his ambitions.[44]

Ferdinand had his own reservations about his brother's sincerity, as well he might have. Rumors already reappeared in 1551 that Charles intended to skip over him and work for Philip's succession directly after his own. While he was delighted to hear from Mary that Maximilian was behaving in a properly respectful way toward his uncle and cousin and assured her that both the archduke and he would continue to do so, he did not rule out abandoning this posture for just cause.[45] Even as the marriage clauses of the Augsburg agreement were being hammered out, Charles had begun putting out feelers in England concerning a match for Philip there.[46]

But Ferdinand was trapped between his still immediate dependence on his brother and the hostility of his son and the latter's German supporters. What he felt in his innermost being once the agreement was concluded remains hidden. He never backed away from his promise to arrange Philip's succession, nor did he use the troubles which were to visit the Emperor in the near future to extort any changes in their compact.[47] Many have suggested and Ferdinand himself said that his ultimate concern was the preservation of a Habsburg emperorship. If nothing else, the 1551 arrangement did that.[48] But unity on this most elementary of goals could not mask the depth of difference between the brothers that the succession crisis brought with it. It was not merely, as some have said, that Charles was looking at affairs from his more universalistic perspective and Ferdinand from his central European one. True, during the discussions as well as their preliminaries, it was Ferdinand who time and time again had brought German attitudes up as crucial to the success of any agreement that they might make.[49] But more important, from the standpoint of Ferdinand's own development, were the changes which the succession crisis wrought on his position in the dynasty. Up to this point, he had done little more than try to accomodate his very lively ambitions to the general direction of his brother's plans. While he had often disagreed with the latter, and even on occasion departed from them, he had never totally disavowed them either. The challenge which he threw down to Charles in 1550 and 1551 and its results, both in the Emperor's household and his own, cast upon him a heavy responsibility to repair the internal unity of his house so that it could continue to occupy the imperial office and cooperate effectively on the international front. It was not only the preservation of the emperorship for the Habsburgs but the Habsburgs for the emperorship that he had to insure. This, in turn, had to be coordinated with his more narrowly personal interests.

Signs of good will toward the Emperor and his son quickly appeared. In the same spring as the succession agreement was signed, Ferdinand opened discussions of Philip's election with the electors of Saxony and Brandenburg. He suggested to Charles that they both send representatives to such talks because his brother had commissioners negotiating wit the other four electors and Ferdinand did not want Saxony and Brandenburg to feel slighted. He made it plain that Maximilian's future in the Empire was to be an integral part of the agreement with the seven princes, but he also hoped that nothing agreed upon would give Charles any reason to doubt his sincerity.[50] He was routinely solicitous of his brother's feelings and prerogatives. After consenting that one of his daughters marry John Sigismund Zapolya as part of the agreement signed with Isabella, Ferdinand begged Charles's forgiveness for taking this step without getting his permission, excusing himself with his wish to move the negotiations along as quickly as possible. When Charles did accept the arrangement, Ferdinand thanked him humbly.[51] The old formulas of deference remained in their correspondence. In 1552, Ferdinand called Charles " . . . lord, father, and brother. . . " in speaking of the latter's relationship to himself and his children. For his part, Charles continued to describe his bond to Ferdinand as "fraternal" with all the positive connotations carried in that usage. As late as 1555, following a long period of stress connected with negotiations leading to the Peace of Augsburg, Ferdinand would still ask for his brother's "paternal counsel."[52] At a moment in 1552 when he could not find time to write Charles, he had his secretary send an apology.[53]

But through all of this, Ferdinand's diplomatic talents and capacity for self-control were strained to the utmost. Ferdinand was certainly not prepared to betray his house to see the succession agreement worked out to his total satisfaction. When in 1554, the French appeared to be trying to use the succession issue as a way of separating him and Maximilian from Spain, Ferdinand refused to allow their representatives access to Austrian territory, to his eldest son's great distress.[54] This he did even in the face of rumors that persisted in Spain through that year that Philip should directly succeed his father in Germany. These tales seem to have come from Charles's court rather than from the Emperor, one of the reasons perhaps that Ferdinand himself did not become unduly upset, but the hostility that they provoked in the Empire made it plain that its princes wanted nothing to do with a Spanish succession and/or its advocates.[55]

But Ferdinand himself was not entirely innocent in these matters either. An anti-Spanish party existed at his own court which happily fanned the flames of opposition to Philip in the Empire.[56] Leader of the group, whose avowed purpose was to build a pro-Ferdinand party in Germany was Ulrich Zasius, the son of a major humanist and a member of the Habsburg's Privy Council. Philip, who was anxious to see the agreement between his uncle and father carried out, was usually the target of his attacks along with the bishop of Arras.[57] Now Charles's new chancellor, he did indeed have spies in the Empire and was described by Zasius as the source of much Spanish treachery.[58]

Zasius was perhaps even more attached to Maximilian, in whom he found a willing listener. Despite Mary's pleas, Charles had done little to regain the affections of his nephew. Even when Maximilian had requested an honorable position in his service, the Emperor had refused him. The slowness with which the latter paid his daughter's dowry did little to increase the archduke's good will toward his uncle.[59] At any rate, through 1553 and 1554, Zasius openly campaigned among the princes for Maximilian as Ferdinand's immediate successor, thus bypassing Philip altogether. He also did his best to arouse the archduke's hatred of things Spanish on the domestic level. In October 1553, for example, Maximilian heard that there were those in the imperial court who wanted to use his wife to oppose his becoming King of the Romans.[60] In the Empire, at least, Zasius's program met with considerable success. A recitation of Philip's qualifications to rule Germany to the Elector Palatine and his officials in 1553 was greeted with open disbelief. Zasius described Land-grave William of Hesse as totally committed to the archduke.[61]

Ferdinand and Charles could have put a stop to these maneuvers if they had so wished. Zasius himself knew that he was in a most dangerous position between two powerful and closely related heads of state, imply-ing that either or both of them could have called a halt to his activities any time they wished.[62] Yet, for all the trouble that Maximilian and his party gave him, there were certain advantages for Ferdinand in allowing their machinations to go forward. It gave him the air of having German interests at heart, something very important for his own future succession which he was still quick to defend whenever it came under challenge.[63] The fact that the differences between the two branches of the house, once the 1551 agreement had come into being, were expressed through surrogates, such as Maximilian and Philip or Arras and Zasius, gave the two senior members of the dynasty a way of controlling their quarrel as well. Hopelessly divisive propositions could always be written off as rumors by either Charles or Ferdinand provided that they had not openly made them themselves. At the same time, they could see just how viable such suggestions were. And finally, in comparison with Maximilian who became even more difficult as time went on, Ferdinand looked like the soul of moderation to the Spanish. He frequently denied that his son had any serious anti-Spanish feeling and worked hard to convince that court that the archduke bore them no ill-will.[64]

Ultimately, events played into Ferdinand's hands. Given the depth of anti-Habsburg feeling in the Empire, it was unrealistic of Charles to have believed that the electors could have been manipulated as easily as the Augsburg *Hausvertrag* seemed to assume. Ferdinand had warned of this, though he may simply have been dragging his feet yet another way in order to block an arrangement to which he was hostile. By 1555, German resentment had mounted to a point where Philip himself had begun to doubt that he could ever succeed his uncle. His 1554 marriage to Mary Tudor had also dampened his ambitions in Germany. In August, a Spanish representative appeared both in Vienna and Augsburg where the diet was meeting to announce the prince's renunciation of the succession provisions in the 1551 agreement. Possibly hoping to firm up his uncle's commitments in Italy to him, Philip promised to support his cousin's imperial candidacy.[65] Whatever his motives, Philip had officially ended the question of a Spanish succession in Germany though the issue would continue to trouble Habsburg dynastic relations until Ferdinand's death.

Yet, having once challenged his brother so gravely on dynastic policy and aroused the anger of his own son, Ferdinand was no longer willing or able to resume his secondary role in the house. This became immediately apparent in 1553 and 1554 as the family undertook highly delicate marriage negotiations for the hand of Mary Tudor, now queen of England. One of the most scrupulously observed of all of Charles's prerogatives as head of his dynasty was his direciton of its marital alliances. This did not keep Ferdinand from having ideas of his own on these matters—he was one of the more imaginative nuptial politicians of his age—but it did mean that Charles could veto any arrangement which looked disadvantageous and substitute one which offered greater rewards. Thus, though Ferdinand had once hoped to see his daughters Anna and Maria paired respectively with Philip II and Duke Albrecht of Bavaria, the reality was that Anna went to Bavaria and Maria to the duke of Cleves as part of a treaty which Charles made with the latter prior to his assault on the Schmalkaldic League.

As in other aspects of his career, Ferdinand unquestionably hoped to have a kind of parity with his brother in marital arrangements. When in 1545, Charles was exploring a match between Marguerite, the daughter of Francis I, and Philip, Ferdinand wished to have a French union for one of his children as well, the duke of Orléans, who had been affianced to one of daughters, having died.[66] But overt competition between the two brothers for the same quarry had never appeared.

Thus, when Ferdinand began pursuing Mary Tudor for his second son, Archduke Ferdinand, at the same time Charles was proposing Philip as a candidate, another intradynastic upheaval was in the making. Not only were Charles's privileges at stake, but his policies as well. Not without some bitterness he had come to see by 1553 that Philip had little future in the Empire; the young man had, however, thereby become all the more useful for his father's English diplomacy.[67] The Emperor did not fully discuss his plans with his brother, probably because he did not want to publicize his growing misgivings about Philip's appeal in the Empire. He was also reluctant to excite the English with prospects of a foreign consort for their new ruler until she was more firmly entrenched in her realms. Nor, finally, was it altogether clear that Philip would end up in an English rather than a Portuguese marriage until September 1553.[68] In any case, poor communication between Ferdinand and Charles even on matters of great importance was nothing new—it was one of Ferdinand's repeated complaints. But there was something novel indeed in Ferdinand's striking out in England, an area heretofore almost solely within the domain of Spanish-Burgundian rather than Austrian interests, without prior consultation with his brother. And though he never explicitly rejected the young Ferdinand as a possible marriage partner for Mary, Charles, along with his advisors, was thoroughly irritated at his brother's choice. Not only England was at stake, but Burgundy as well. Mary had made it known that she wished to resign her regency in the latter territory. Philip, Maximilian, and Ferdinand were all at least formally under consideration for the position. The gregarious Ferdinand was already a popular figure in the Lowlands, something which bothered Charles very much. If he were to become king of England, the Emperor and his counselors feared that Philip would be all but out of the running in the territory. With the archduke ensconced on both sides of the Channel, the balance of power within the dynasty would shift dangerously from the Spanish point of view.[69]

In July 1553, King Ferdinand set an ambassador, Martin Guzmán, to England with a portrait of his son. He also went to Brussels to clear his plans with his brother and to ascertain that the latter had not irrevocably staked out Mary for Philip, something not sure until much later, though Ferdinand and the rest of diplomatic Europe were privately convinced that they knew in what direction the Emperor would go. Guzmán was allowed to continue his journey to England on the condition that he did nothing but convey Ferdinand's good wishes to the queen. To insure that he did so, he was followed like a spy by the Spanish ambassador, Simon Renard, on orders from Arras. Whenever Guzmán was in Mary's presence, so was Renard. If Guzmán went so far as to propose marriage, Renard was to interject immediately that it was not "convenient."[70] Guzmán's instructions were most circumspect—he was to suggest archduke Ferdinand only in case Charles had not advanced Philip before Mary—but the presence of ambassadors from both brothers promoting the same suit was more than a little bizarre.[71] That Ferdinand also sent a second mission after Guzmán's, this time under Alonso de Gamez, did nothing to dampen suspicions in Spain of his intentions.

Gamez met with the Emperor in the fall of 1553 before proceeding to England and apparently assured him that Ferdinand did not wish to preempt an English marriage for his son, a point which the king personally seconded. Charles observed that any division between him and his brother on this matter could have disastrous consequences for their house and spoke of men around Ferdinand, left unnamed, who were promoting such a split to advance their own interests.[72] And indeed, the same figures most opposed to Philip's succession in the Empire were also pushing Archduke Ferdinand in England—Maximilian and Zasius. Maximilian was much disappointed that his brother was running behind in the competition in London and deplored what he felt was the shabby treatment his uncle had meted out to his father. Even after Charles had made it plain to all that Mary and Philip were to be matched, Zasius continued to speak of the admiration which the archduke enjoyed in England because of his mild treatment of religious sects in Prague—a very limited truth if there ever was one—and to urge that Ferdinand keep his second son available should the arrangement with Philip fall through.[73] It was young Ferdinand himself who seems to have called a halt to all these schemes, insisting to his brother early in 1554 that he was not interested in marrying at this time, even though Maximilian pressed him to do so.[74]

Maximilian harshly scored what he called his father's lack of courage with the Emperor in pursuing the project, and it is true that throughout the fall of 1553, Ferdinand's position on the marriage grew markedly more guarded as he manuevered between Spain and Vienna. Late in the year, he wrote Mary Tudor a letter in which he voiced his preference for Philip over his own son, the gesture which prompted Maximilian's accusation of weakness. All of this found great favor with the Emperor though he continued to resent what he felt had been Ferdinand's lack of candor in the negotiations. A continued flow of rumors out of the latter's court from English ambassadors that there was some kind of discord between the brothers also plagued him.[75] Down to the very conclusion of the alliance of Philip and Mary, however, Ferdinand kept in contact with the latter and her advisors. This he justified by claiming that Charles had never totally ruled the archduke out as a suitable partner for the English queen and that since such close blood ties existed between him and Mary, there was no reason for him to break off relations with her altogether. For his part, Charles said that he was being guided by his estimate of English affairs.[75]

The French, of course, had the most to gain from a genuine split between the brothers. The apparent disagreement over the English match had tempted agents of Henry II to ingratiate themselves with Ferdinand. Such dynastic treason was beyond him; by the beginning of 1554, the French envoys had begun to sense that their undertaking was hopeless. Almost to the day that Archduke Ferdinand protested that he wanted nothing of the English match, his father assured the Emperor of his complete loyalty.[77] Maximilian was unhappy, yet in the long run, there were possible advantages for Ferdinand in allowing the marriage of Philip and Mary to go ahead. The joining of Spain and England could conceivably persuade France not to go to war against the former. This, in turn, would permit the Emperor to be of more help in eastern Europe. While the German estates might aid the Austrian Habsburgs a bit more readily than the Spanish, given Ferdinand's increasingly central European orientation, he could not afford to dispense with all assistance from his brother.[78] Maximilian's intransigence was to give Ferdinand some terrible moments in the future, but as far as Spain was concerned, he was the archduke's father and in a position to compel a certain amount of obedience from him. Charles, and for that matter Philip, were both in positions in which they could be very helpful or very dangerous to his most immediate ambitions; Maximilian could do very little. Reconciliation with Spain, therefore, was his highest priority. From almost every point of view, Ferdinand had done rather well in these two crises which were in part of his own making. He had blunted any designs there may have been to remove him the succession altogether, and, by 1555 it was all but assured that Maximilian rather than Philip would follow him. Despite this and his English adventure, he had not permanently alienated either his brother or his nephew.

Yet, something in the relationship of Charles and Ferdinand had changed. The years 1551-1555 saw ever bitterer quarrels between the two, indicative perhaps of no more than the toll which age and stress were taking on their capacity to tolerate frustration. Their grandfather Maximilian had undergone much the same development.[79] There is widespread agreement however, that it was the succession struggle which brought about a kind of inner divorce of Ferdinand from Charles.[80] The degree of such conditions is very hard to calibrate, especially in someone like Ferdinand whose mode of expression was characteristically ritualistic and reportorial. But the very stylistic monotony of a correspondence makes whatever small differences do appear in it all the more noteworthy. Just after the succession agreement was signed in 1551, Ferdinand referred to what he called " . . . our houses of Austria and Burgundy . . . ." It was not the first time he had done so and he would not repeat the phrase in quite that form, but it was an exceedingly unusual locution for him and one loaded with meaning in the circumstances in which it appeared.[81] What better way could a man, for whom dynastic ambition was second nature, say that the reflexive subordination which he had shown his brother was no longer there?

CHAPTER XII

THE GULF WIDENS

Whatever subtlety there was in Ferdinand's German policy lay usually in its execution, not in its purpose. He never ceased to view the Empire as an important source of help in his eastern struggles even though he frequently despaired at the slowness of the estates to aid him and the quality of what they sent when it finally arrived. He was furthermore acutely sensitive to the prestige and power inherent in political structures and therefore deeply respected the imperial office. To lose that support altogether, and worse yet, to have another European dynasty installed in the emperorship would have been an outright disaster for him and his heirs in Austria, Bohemia, and Hungary, and he knew it. Thus, as in his Austrian patrimony, he saw little distinction between the welfare of the Empire and its institutions and the private affairs of the house of Habsburg. Whether it was a question of remedying religious hostilities, getting the estates to issue a general declaration of war against France, dealing with Württemberg and other defeated territories in the Schmalkalic wars, the timing of a diet, or the structure of imperial administration, Ferdinand defined the issues in terms of the enhancement of the prestige of his house and the offices which it occupied.[1]

To his way of thinking, the confessional problem posed the greatest potential for opposition and rebellion in Germany; his solution to it was, in ideal circumstances, a general church council.[2] But the prospects for that approach were not bright. Protestants did not even attend the first meeting of the Council of Trent in 1545, and Paul III, along with Charles and the other sovereigns of Europe did not support the conclave unequivocally either. During the 1540s, Ferdinand himself was not on the best of terms with Rome, and the following decade brought little improvement.[3]

Thus, given his defense needs and his concerns for the position of his house, Ferdinand had little choice but to strive toward at least some temporary religious agreement in the imperial diet. Here again, as in his relations with Charles and Maximilian on the succession question, he found himself to be a man-in-the-middle—in this case an especially unhappy station for him since he privately was altogether hostile to those whom he deemed heretics. One of his most heartfelt wishes was that they be destroyed; he cheered any small sign that this process was underway.[4] His natural allies were the Catholic members of the estates, the Rhenish archbishops and Salzburg, the bishops of Bamberg and Würzburg, and especially the Bavarians who aided him in Bohemia in 1547. He was keenly aware that loss of their support would make his position in the diet untenable; on the other hand, neither he nor Charles could afford to offend the Protestants too greatly either.[5] In the first place, divisions within the ranks of the latter were such that Ferdinand could occasionally call upon the more moderate among them to carry out important missions for him. Joachim of Brandenburg, the ill-fated imperial commander in Hungary in 1542, also volunteered in that year to be Ferdinand's go-between with the more militant Protestants at the diet of Speier, an offer the Habsburg accepted with alacrity. The Schmalkaldic League had powerful allies in the kings of France, and the Saxon territories were, as we already know, central to Ferdinand's territorial security in the east. And finally, one of the few things that confessional allegiance could not taint was money; Charles and Ferdinand accepted whatever revenues they thought due them regardless of whether these came from Protestant or Catholic.[6]

Thus, Ferdinand had to balance the goal of preserving the good will of the Protestant princes and cities with his equally important wish to stay true to his Catholic allies, not to mention to his own deepseated orthodox loyalties. From 1540 down to the outbreak of the Schmalkaldic War, both he and his brother did their best to master this art, and more often than not, they did get the financial aid they wanted. In the end, however, as in the 1530s, their compromises satisfied no one, least of all themselves.

The controversial Declaration of Regensburg of 1541, for example, which called for a temporary suspension of imperial court activity against Lutherans, left everyone hanging. At the end of November of that year, Ferdinand found that the most influential Protestant princes—the Saxon cousins, Joachim of Brandenburg, and Philip of Hesse—wanted a two-year surcease to the court's prosecutions, and vowed to press for it at the next diet to be held in Speier the following year. Ferdinand feared that the Catholics would be put off by such a procedure, and so they were. When the estates gathered, the Lutherans demanded a formal guarantee of the Regensburg concessions and admission to the imperial court. After some initial truculence, Ferdinand made them an informal promise of religious peace, though this was not to be included in the official recess of the diet— in effect, revalidating the Declaration of Regensburg pending resolution of the religious issue by a council. Already resentful of Charles's approval of the 1541 formula, the Catholics now demanded a statement from Ferdinand to the effect that a permanent solution to the German problem could only come from Rome. This had actually been in the Regensburg resolution, and Ferdinand duly repeated it.[7] He urged his brother to send along reassurances to the Catholics, especially in Bavaria and the archbishop of Mainz, that nothing had been done which prejudiced either their interests or beliefs. Nevertheless, Ferdinand remained mindful of Protestant sensibilities. At another diet in Nürnberg that same year, he begged Charles, for the sake of Protestant cooperation against the Turks, not to allow any of the dukes of Bavaria to serve as imperial commissioners since the Lutherans were so terribly suspicious of them. He also advised the Emperor to call off any visitations of the imperial court at least until he personally appeared in Germany. When in 1543, negotiations concerning the coming council in Trent failed to satisfy either Protestants or Catholics, Ferdinand urged Charles to ask Paul III to send legates and commissioners who could intercept and avert the complaints of both sides.[8]

As tiresome and ultimately futile as all of these maneuvers were, they had one positive side for Ferdinand. Though Charles played a major role in fashioning these policies, it was the younger Habsburg who largely carried them out. In so doing, he developed a far surer grasp than his brother of the realities of German politics and the individuals behind them. He firmly believed in the power of personal contacts, once advising the taciturn Emperor that the value of holding dinners with each of the princes was ". . . not in order that they get . . . to know your intentions but you theirs. . . ."[9] He could be both flexible and persuasive and sometimes, through one-on-one diplomacy, could coax funds out of single territories in the most unpromising situations. For example, in 1545, the imperial *Kammergericht* judged in favor of Hamburg and against the Emperor in a suit brought by the latter. The city had reneged on pledges to send help against the Turks with the claim that it was not immediately subject to the Empire. Ferdinand met with its representatives privately. The result was that they agreed to give 8,000 florins in aid if they could be exempted from any subsidies voted by the estates as a whole, an arrangement which the king felt the best possible under the circumstances. Above all, he was close to the tactical conditions in which he and his brother had to function, able to see, as he did in 1543, how the very meeting place of a diet could weight the Protestant-Catholic balance in that body to the advantage of the former.[10]

There were even occasions when he was willing to sacrifice the interests of his brother for those of the Germans. Charles had maintained for years that the Empire had no legal and fiscal competence in that part of the Netherlands called the Burgundian Circle in imperial terminology. When he won control of Ghelders and Utrecht in the 1540s, he tried to incorporate them into the Burgundian territories, leading Ferdinand to oppose him strongly because of the resentment such a move would arouse in the Empire.[11] In this, as in other such episodes, Ferdinand spoke not as a disinterested friend of German constitutionalists. Every difficulty he had with the estates meant delays in Turkish assistance or time spent away from his own territories, often at great inconvenience. But as imperial concerns increasingly shaped his own plans, he found himself speaking if not for Germany as a whole then as a German Habsburg.

For all his feelings that his brother was best able to defend German interests as well as those of their house, Ferdinand grew markedly less willing to follow Charles's lead if he caught him in acts of bad judgment in Germany which would eventually effect his own emperorship.[12] The succession crisis had been one such miscalculation on the Emperor's part; his treatment of John Frederick, the ex-elector of Saxony, and Philip of Hesse was another. Both had been a long-standing plague to the Habsburgs not only because they had spearheaded Lutheran intransigence in Germany but because they were potential allies for France. Ferdinand once suggested sending them to the Netherlands to head Mary's forces against an attack of Francis I, presumably as a way of blocking the Valois king's recruiting in Hesse and the Electorate.[13] Following the defeat of the Schmalkaldians, Ferdinand remained implacably hostile to John

Frederick. The capitulation which Charles forced upon the hapless elector required him to surrender his territories around Wittenberg to which his office and title were attached, leaving him only with some holdings in Thuringia—Weimar, Gotha, Eisenach, and Coburg. Ferdinand's hatred of John Frederick was so great that even after Mühlberg he angrily accused him to his face of trying to hound him and his children out of their lands. He was anxious to have the Saxon as far from Germany as possible, suggesting the Tyrol as a possible place for his imprisonment and worried that he might escape by some trick.[14]

His attitude toward the landgrave was much different. This was not because Ferdinand liked or trusted him more, although in 1545 he briefly seemed to think that he might be able to use Philip to coax some aid for him from the Protestants. Rather it was because Philip was the father-in-law of Maurice, now elector of Saxony, who had specifically set as a condition of his alliance with the Habsburgs that he not be asked to do anything against the landgrave.[15] His pressure for the release of Philip and Charles's utter hostility to the idea, at least for the forseeable future, left Ferdinand once again in the middle of a very uncomfortable situation.

Even though the landgrave had made peace overtures to the Emperor in the fall of 1546 following Charles's triumphant Danubian campaign, the Habsburg would hear nothing of it. Both Philip and John Frederick were his mortal enemies whom he was determined to "exterminate," to use his word. His keen sense of honor had been deeply wounded when in August 1546, a Hessian page had appeard in the imperial camp bearing a letter from the Schmalkaldic leaders demanding his abdication. As if he had already done so, he was repeatedly referred to as "Charles of Ghent" in the document. In Charles's mind, the removal of John Frederick and Philip from the scene was a basic precondition for what he called the pacification of Germany.[16]

Though he readily admitted that both princes had committed serious offenses against the Emperor, Ferdinand was exceedingly evasive when Charles asked him to capture Philip in 1546 if he should visit his son-in-law. While he did not flatly refuse, he only promised to do whatever was in the brothers' common interests.[17] Under the elector's suasions his attitude softened even more. By the end of December of that year, he pointed out to Charles that Philip could do really very little if John Frederick were destroyed and Ferdinand and Maurice's alliance remained firm. Maurice made a particularly strong plea before Ferdinand in February 1547 for a reconciliation of his father-in-law with the Emperor. The Habsburg did his best to defend his brother's position, at least according to his report, telling Maurice that the least the landgrave could do was hand over his principal fortified places to Charles as the duke of Württemberg had done. Maurice had tried to convince Philip to do this, but to no avail. Ferdinand still granted that Philip had been been gravely derelict. But he also tried to persuade the Emperor to treat their foe more generously.[18]

When Philip and John Frederick were brought to Charles's camp in Wittenberg after the collapse of the Schmalkaldic forces, Ferdinand advised his brother to strike some sort of agreement with the landgrave if he seemed at all reasonable. Charles had it very much in mind to create some league of princes to assist in keeping the peace; the king suggested that an arrangement with Philip might make Charles's plans more palatable in the Empire.[19] In their negotiations with the Emperor, the two Protestant leaders asked that they not be harmed in their bodies or personal possessions, conditions which Charles accepted. He also foreswore any life imprisonment for either man. But he did not feel that Maurice could object too strongly to the incarceration of Philip for a short time, which he duly ordered. Ferdinand supported certain parts of the capitulation which called for such things as the demolition of Schmalkaldic fortifications, handing over of firearms, monetary fines, and rendering oaths of fealty to the Emperor. He was unalterably opposed to Philip's imprisonment, saying that it would be enough that he be closely guarded until he gave up his fortified places and arms. He warned Charles against stirring up any hostilities among the electors. Although he used the plural, his real concern was Maurice.[20]

And the new elector of Saxony was truly distressed by the Emperor's treatment of his father-in-law. Both he and the imperial councilors had left the landgrave with the false impression that Charles had given him a safe-conduct to come to Wittenberg which removed all threats of imprisonment. Philip's sons held Maurice responsible for securing the release of their father. They pressed him constantly on the subject, and the elector, ruthless though he was, placed some value on the reliability of his word which the Emperor's actions had seriously undermined. Ferdinand begged his brother to rethink the whole matter in light of German feelings about the need for more clement treatment of Philip, especially after he was visited by two electors—probably Maurice and the Elector Palatine—in July 1547. These asked that Maximilian serve as their spokesman before the Emperor, an early hint that the archduke was identified with specifically German interests. Ferdinand did not refuse.[21]

Thus, by the fall of 1547, Charles had already earned the political enmity even of his most effective non-Habsburg ally in the Schmalkaldic War. His efforts to solve the religious problem at the diet which followed the conflict, held in Augsburg in 1547-1548, won him few friends either. He summoned the gathering—dubbed the "geharnischter Reichstag" because many of the participants appeared in the battle dress they had worn in the recent conflict—with several purposes.[22] One was to fashion yet another temporary solution to confessional discord, another was to establish the aforementioned peacekeeping force based on the model of the old Swabian League. He also wished to take up the problem of administrative reform once again.

Ferdinand was very doubtful at first about the usefulness of any leagues. Closely following the recommendations of his own advisors who urged a conciliatory policy on the part of the Habsburgs and on Ferdinand in particular, he advised Charles to confine such an organization to relatively dependable allies. He was far more enthusiastic about an interim religious arrangement. Early in 1547, hard upon the collapse of the first session of the Council of Trent, Ferdinand, along with scholars and theologians in his own entourage had come up with what he termed a "Christian Reformation" which he passed along to Charles who was not unreceptive. This called for the creation of a body sanctioned by both pope and council to discuss the German religious problem. Not apparently to have been granted any decisionmaking power, its chief function was to have been to report its deliberations to Rome and the diets. Ferdinand nevertheless felt that it might dampen what he called Protestant "conspiracies."[23]

The idea of a league never got off the ground, and what Charles proposed as a temporary religious solution aggravated the problem even more, if such a thing was possible. This was the so-called Augsburg Interim which removed all legal guarantees that Lutherans had won up to that time, though it also recognized a *status quo de facto*. Some concessions were made to the Protestants on clerical marriage and communion in both kinds, though they would have to petition Rome if they wished to take advantage of the marital provisions. Justification by faith was half-heartedly sanctioned, but reference was also made to the treasury of merits. The seven sacraments, transsubstantiation, recourse to the intervention of saints and the Virgin, fasting, and elaborate ceremony were all left intact. Though all at the diet save a few Lutheran die-hards accepted it, practically no one, regardless of confession, was satisfied. The result was as massive noncomplicance which in Ferdinand's eyes was less the fault of the Empire's political leaders than of bishops who refused to ordain married priests and to tolerate communion in both kinds. He himself seemed to view the Interim as a test of Habsburg good faith in Germany which, if found wanting, would preclude any future religious settlements.[24]

His attitude toward religious dissidence, as toward Philip of Hesse, grew increasingly cautious following the Schmalkaldic War. In 1549, he urged Charles to come to terms with Magdeburg, which had held out in a long rebellion against its archbishop, since military victory did not seem likely and the city could fall into the hands of secular rulers. And he was especially careful in dealing with Maurice on the introduction of the Interim into the Saxon electorate. From the beginning, Maurice had difficulties with the agreement, being reluctant to arouse the hostility of his new subjects by forcing more religious innovations upon them. Nevertheless, he initially offered to follow the Interim, an act which Ferdinand termed "generous" but at the same time advised his ally not to move too precipitately for fear of stirring up trouble throughout Germany again. When Maurice grew increasingly wary about the impact which the arrangement would have on his peoples, Ferdinand reminded him that his disobedience would tempt others to do the same, but he urged Charles to deal with the elector and his representatives generously. Maurice was volatile and could easily enter into alliance with ". . . cities or [the] estates of his neighbors." A threat from John Frederick's sons to move against him brought a promise from Maurice once again that he would comply with the Interim. However, Ferdinand's counsel led him to consult with the Emperor and asked Charles to send commissioners to deal with the question as quickly as possible so as to avoid future difficulties.[25]

But for all Ferdinand's elaborate concern for Maurice's welfare, his dissatisfaction with the Habsburg grew. The canker of Philip of Hesse continued to fester. At the beginning of November in 1551, Ferdinand warned

Charles that, with French support, leagues and confederations of cities and princes were being discussed in Germany. At the center of this sedition was Maurice, along with Margrave Albrecht Alcibiades of Bayreuth whose financial straits made him a ready ally of anyone who promised to better his circumstances. In Ferdinand's opinion, the only way to avert a very dangerous situation was to release Philip, thereby pacifying Maurice, and to draw him and Albrecht into Habsburg service. He repeated his misgivings thoughout December along with his plea that Philip be freed, claiming that the landgrave had, on the whole, behaved honorably.[26]

What the treatment of Philip had done to alienate Maurice, the succession agreement of 1551 had done to increase the resentment among almost all of the estates against the Emperor. On top of what was generally taken to be a Habsburg plot to turn the emperorship into a permanent family possession, came Charles's heavy-handed machinations to secure his son's election as King of the Romans. In 1551, he threatened to release John Frederick and restore him to the Wettin electoral lands unless Maurice promised his vote for Philip.[27] The apparent division between the brothers that had become general knowledge during the succession discussions also tempted the princes, particularly the opportunistic Maurice, to think that there was something to be gained from having Ferdinand as the chief negotiator for the dynasty in the Empire rather than the increasingly mulish Charles. In 1550, the Saxon had assured Maximilian in Augsburg of his support in the talks going on between the latter's uncle and father. To Ferdinand, he offered help in Hungary, once again a problem in the winter of 1551-1552.[28]

Charles reacted to these danger signals with a detached indifference which baffled even his closest advisors. Arras speculated that perhaps his means did not allow him to do anything. But whether it was his spirit or his purse that was strained, he refused to understand why Maurice attached such significance to Philip's release. As for Margrave Albrecht, he had already been drawing a pension from Charles which he had voluntarily abandoned.[29]

Political, religious, and personal discontent all came to a head on January 15, 1552, when Maurice and Philip of Hesse's oldest son, William, signed an alliance with Henry II of France at Chambord. A previous agreement with Margrave Hans of Küstrin, one of the Protestants most bitterly opposed to the Augsburg Interim, had spoken of attacking Charles while remaining neutral toward Ferdinand, but the French compact was in no way so selective. Hostilities were declared on both the Emperor and his adherents, and the confederates promised to make no peace with either "the Emperor or his heirs or supporters" without the express permission of one another. The treatment of Philip of Hesse and Charles's alleged wish to destroy German freedoms were cited as the reasons for the uprising.[30] In March 1552, a combination of German and French forces began to move upon various areas of the Empire. With the south German cities and Bavaria, his most likely allies, avowedly neutral and Henry II blocking him from the Netherlands, the poorly-protected Emperor established headquarters in Innsbruck.

One of the thoughts that had haunted Charles was that Ferdinand and Maximilian had stirred up the princely sedition against him. Ferdinand's communications on the German situation had been, in his opinion, so vague and empty of offers of assistance against the conspirators that the Emperor suspected his brother to have had some sort of assurances from them. He believed his nephew to have met directly with Maurice and refused to send him to the Netherlands to serve as chief of Mary's military operations there, delicately giving as his reason " . . . the conditions that prevail . . ." between him and the archduke.[31] Maximilian vehemently denied this, but he did not help his case any by badgering his uncle for 300,000 ducats due from his wife's dowry just as Charles began to realize he would have to do something to defend himself. This, too, Charles believed had been done with Ferdinand's knowledge.[32]

Charles's finances were so strained that he could find no merchant, in Augsburg or elsewhere, who would substantially underwrite a campaign against the German-French coalition. It was here that he had his greatest reason to suspect his brother's loyalty. Viewing Ottoman penetration into Transylvania in 1551 as deeply significant for his Bohemian, Moravian, Silesian, and Austrian possessions, Ferdinand had not wanted to have a war in the Empire at his back.[33] When it came, he steadfastly refused more than token assistance to Charles on the ground that Turkish defense was more important. Even as he admitted that the princely uprising affected him and his family, the few troops he ordered mustered against Maurice were for the protection of the Austrian borders only. Charles threatened that Ferdinand's denial of help to him now would foreclose any future aid, but to no avail. The contrast between his attitude toward his desperate brother now and almost thirty years before at Pavia, when he had scoured Austria and the Empire for men even as he was faced with serious peasant uprisings in his own lands, is truly striking. The wounds opened during the succession dispute at Augsburg had not fully healed. When Mary chided Ferdinand for assigning Hungary a higher priority than the Empire, he shot back that he had warned Charles the previous year of the impact which the succession compact would have on the political sensibilities of the Germans and asserted that if his brother had taken these to heart, they would not be in their present predicament.[34]

But his eastern concerns aside, there was little reason to doubt Ferdinand's loyalties. With her familiar caustic insight, Mary had observed early in February of 1552 that should Charles be driven from Germany, the Empire would be lost to the family, thus removing once and for all the need to fight over anyone's succession.[35] Ferdinand's thinking, while taking more variables into account, ran much in the same vein. Even before the Treaty of Chambord made it plain, he saw that his interests were still intertwined with those of Charles and that the uprising would affect them both.[36] Nor did his treatment of the princes betray any favoring of them. For all that he wanted Maurice's aid in Hungary, his letters to the elector were hardly friendly, stressing as they did the sacrilegious nature of the latter's sedition, the possibility that the Turks and the French could injure the Saxon's lands, and finally, recalling the fate of those who had challenged Charles before, such as John Frederick.[37] At the very least, practical considerations on both sides argued against Ferdinand as a co-conspirator. It is highly unlikely that all of the princes would have admitted him to their innermost circles; many of them saw no difference between the concerns and attitudes of the brothers anyway. Charles's humiliation would have inevitably weakened Ferdinand's own emperorship, not to mention his effectiveness in Hungary. Limitless religious concessions forced out of a captured sovereign would have done the same thing.[38]

Ferdinand's repeated urging that Charles free Philip of Hesse and simply buy off Albrecht Alcibiades meant that he felt that some sort of negotiated settlement with the dissidents was still possible. By March 1552, Charles also saw this to be his only alternative. His respect for Ferdinand's knowledge of German affairs and the tone of the latter's correspondence with Maurice overcame his suspicions. He asked his brother to conduct the talks for him, but insisted that he be consulted. The princes were not to think that any agreement was strictly Ferdinand's concern.[39]

Ferdinand, then, was an improbable member of any conspiracy against his brother. Yet, the discussions which he began with the princes in Linz in April and continued on through the summer in Passau showed how great the distance had become between him and Charles. That they saw eye to eye on the need for some peaceable solution with the dissident Germans did not mean that they were at one on its details. From the very beginning, Charles indicated that while he had never wholly opposed releasing Philip, but rather, with Ferdinand's concurrence, was awaiting an opportune moment to do so, he saw little hope for any religious arrangement which would please him. Claiming that he had followed closely the imperial recesses which called for such devices as a council to solve the Lutheran controversy, he refused to challenge the authority of that body. He spoke of preferring death to concluding anything contrary to the Catholic faith. At the same time, he allowed for a certain amount of flexibility in the provision of any settlement. Throughout the Linz meeting, he stuck unwavering to this position, which Ferdinand, with good reason, found vague and "contradictory." However, he dutifully vowed to adhere to the recesses and the Emperor's confessional scruples.[40]

In a narrow sense, Ferdinand accepted nothing at Linz that grossly violated his brother's wishes. There were heavy pressures on him to do otherwise; his closest advisors were pushing him to separate himself from Charles if the latter did not support him in his dealings with the princes and to take military matters into his own hands. Yet, he assured Charles that his oath of fealty to him superseded any other obligations he might have, and he asked for instructions on what to say to Maurice and the other electors. His general goal was not to conclude a peace in his brother's name, but, through personal conversations with the Saxon, to find the basis upon which a later settlement might be reached.[41] At the beginning of their meetings on April 19, he was able to say, with the Emperor's backing, that Philip of Hesse would be released and that the Augsburg Interim would be lifted. At the same time, he argued that neither he nor Charles had taken any steps in religious matters which had not been authorized by the imperial recesses. He did promise, however, that the diet would have an opportunity to air the decisions of the Council of Trent before these became policy in Germany. The concluding resolutions

of the Linz conference called for a mutual cease-fire and another gathering
to discuss religious affairs at Passau beginning May 26.[42]

The Emperor was not at all pleased by the prospect of the Passau meeting since it would mean a discussion of the confessional problem outside
of a formal meeting of the diet. He was, however, in no position to do
anything about it. Ferdinand had finally convinced Charles that he should
begin arming himself; by early April the latter had resolved to leave the
Tyrol, observing mildly as he took this decision that the defense resources
of Ferdinand's lands were meagre indeed. The king only asked that he
withdraw gradually and gracefully; he did not want to hurry the Linz
talks unduly and Charles's presence nearby made him a more acceptable
mediator with the German electors. Too hasty a retreat might impair the
Emperor's prestige in Italy and the Netherlands as well.[43]

Thus Charles remained in Innsbruck well into the spring. The armistice
called for at Linz supposedly went into effect on May 11, but a little over
a week later, troops under Duke George of Mecklenburg, who had either
not heard of the arrangement or were not paying any attention to it,
punched through one of the Alpine passes, the Ehrenburger *Clause,* to
within a few miles of the Tyrolean capital. To avoid possible capture,
Charles fled ignominiously by night to the southeast, finally stopping in
Villach on the border of Carinthia and Italy.[44]

Some have raised the possibility that Ferdinand himself, still embittered
by the succession compact of 1551, engineered this final humiliation of
the Emperor. His concern for his brother nothwithstanding, he had ordered what men there were protecting the Alpine entry points into the
Tyrol to yield to the enemy if they felt themselves hopelessly outnum-
bered and underequipped. Yet, Charles was clearly informed of the military dangers which the ill-guarded passes posed for him and seems to
have regarded the surprise attack as just another unanticipated setback
for which his brother bore no responsibility. Though the Tyrolean defenders actually did allow Duke George's troops to enter the land, they
did so only after negotiations with the invaders that Arras himself permitted them to begin. The administration of Upper Austria had protested
to Charles for some time that they were poorly prepared to protect themselves because of their commitments in Hungary.[45]

Meeting with the princes, their representatives, and Charles's commissioners in Passau at the beginning of June, Ferdinand wanted a quick

agreement which would extricate him and his brother from when he felt had become a very dangerous strategic situation.[46] To get this, he had to appear as trustworthy as possible to the Germans. He was well on the way to winning the confidence of Philip of Hesse, whose release was now the subject of serious negotiation, and of Maurice who, through Zasius, had apologized for the incident at the Ehrenburg pass.[47] But to avoid arousing the suspicions of Charles's emissaries and to reassure the princes, he decided to act in his own name as mediator between the two sides. Charles concurred in this arrangement, thinking that it might serve to confuse his opponents. Its real effect however, was to make him the potential spokesman for the estates as a whole since the basic dispute was between Charles and Maurice.[48] Ferdinand envisioned himself as consulting with the representatives of the estates who would communicate their decisions to Charles and the elector's envoys. He was quick to try to act on the princely complaints that he took seriously. They and their delegates wanted a date set for Philip's release, something not necessarily done at Linz. To avoid having negotiations break down altogether, Ferdinand took the liberty of fixing a time without first consulting Charles.[49]

Ideally, Ferdinand did not want to work out a settlement independent of his brother. Indeed, Charles was on the whole positively inclined toward the king's conduct of the negotiations and complimented him on his handling of the Philip of Hesse question.[50] The princes themselves did not see the brothers as all that far apart, at least in basic policies. In their minds, their present Emperor and their future one were linked inextricably in matters large and small. The impecunious Albrecht Alcibiades resented both Arras who he thought kept Charles from granting him fiefs which he thought were due him and Ferdinand who owed him money since he had assumed Maximilian I and Louis of Hungary's debts to the margrave's father. Just after the Linz meeting, Maurice and Albrecht Alcibiades had presented the king with a document which charged both Habsburgs with destroying the imperial *Kammergericht* through excessive costs and with trying to make the emperorship hereditary.[51]

As he described it, Ferdinand applied himself to the negotiations with the same diligence he would have used to win entry into Paradise.[52] Both Charles's commissioners and the representatives of the other princes agreed that he not only worked extremely hard but was most solicitous of his brother's interests and feelings, even though his own ministers continually reminded him to think in terms of the Turkish threat in Hungary. Upon learning that Henry II had dispatched the bishop of Bayonne to the negotiations even after Maurice had agreed to act as the king's spokesman at Passau, Ferdinand was quick to ask for Charles's advice on how to proceed. When proposals of Albrecht Alcibiades caused difficulties, Charles again was consulted. Maurice was especially stubborn on the timing and conditions of the release of John Frederick, something which Charles now supported. Unwilling to exceed the Emperor's wishes any more than was necessary, Ferdinand again promptly contacted his brother.[53]

Charles had let it be known at the outset of the Passau talks that he would not accept any arrangement before he saw it and that if it caused him difficulties, he would let Ferdinand know. The implication that he might not countenance it at all was clear.[54] Much of what Ferdinand and the princes worked out concerning the treatment of the dissidents did meet with his approval.[55] But though Ferdinand initially tried to put off the discussions of religious matters to a regular diet as his brother had wished, he could not do so. The Passau document called for the lifting of the Augsburg Interim, the recognition of all secularizations which had taken place up to that point, and a full rehearsal by the next diet of how the religious question was to be settled—by a universal or national council, by a theological conference or by the estates themselves. If all this failed, and here was the sticking point with Charles, the agreement sanctioned a permanent religious peace based on the status quo.[56]

Unlike his brother, Ferdinand was willing to go along with this, at least on a temporary basis. He was under no illusion that the Passau agreement was an ideal solution to German difficulties, and he had little faith in the sincerity of the anti-Habsburg signatories. To Charles, at least, he termed the conditions "exhorbitant" and suggested that as soon as they were in a more favorable position, they work toward altering it. However, short-term gains meant everything to him at that point, and he supported the arrangement on those grounds. Though he admitted that Charles's reputation would suffer some by submitting to the treaty, he felt that a pacified Germany would improve the latter's position vis-à-vis France, a consideration which he thought outweighed all others. A hostile Empire would greatly impeded Charles's efforts to rearm. He also hinted at the possible effect of continued German enmity on Philip's future in central Europe.[57]

But Ferdinand's real interests in getting a quick settlement of the princely uprising were his own. The still-rampaging Albrecht Alcibiades was rum-
ored to be moving toward Eger, and the Turks were manoeuvering in
Transylvania. There was no hint in the king's letters to the Emperor that
he intended to help him against the French. That Maurice's deployment in
Hungary would take him out of the French orbit was a happy accident not
a premeditated design.[58]

For all his need for the Emperor to accept the agreement, Ferdinand
deferentially gave him the options of either consenting to it or rejecting
it totally. In the final week of June, however, news from Transylvania
grew worse, and, still anxiously awaiting the Emperor's reaction to the
document, Ferdinand flatly begged him to sanction in without alterations.
He hoped that if Charles accepted the peace, the estates in turn would go
along with a general tax, the oft-discussed "Common Penny," which
he thought would encourage the Hungarians to participate more actively in the defense of Transylvania. Moreover, Charles's rejection of the
treaty would lead to the Empire rejecting him, a situation that would
inevitably, in Ferdinand's eyes, affect his own position.[59]

Observors at Passau were far more pessimistic than Ferdinand himself
about the chances that Charles would accept the agreement.[60] When a
communiqué arrived from the Emperor on July 3, telling of his refusal
to go along with the compact, the king was visibly upset. He postponed
reading the contents of his brother's message to the estates for a day.
When he did so, he promised the Germans that he would use all the persuasive powers at his disposal to change the Emperor's mind. He begged
Maurice to give him eight days of peace to act, and when the elector
refused, threatened to do nothing with Charles at all. This brought the
Saxon around; the two privately agreed that if Charles accepted the treaty
without changes, Maurice and his confederates would do the same. The
elector would not, however, do anything to help Ferdinand until he saw
which way Charles would go.[61]

Charles's refusal had not been hostile—an undercurrent of regret ran
through it and through his messages to his commissioners in Passau on the
subject. He knew well the unhappy consequences which his rejection
of the treaty might have for his brother; he spoke of not wanting to be
the cause either of Ferdinand's ruin or of the German princes and cities
who had to live with troublemakers such as Maurice and Albrecht. But his

conscience and sense of duty were more compelling than even these considerations. He freed Ferdinand to sign the agreement in his own name if he saw it in his interest to do so. Charles's own declaration that he would observe the treaty only if certain conditions were fulfilled would have to be added, however. Furthermore, even if Ferdinand did accept the compact, he would have to declare in writing that neither he nor Maximilian would do anything against the Emperor. In Charles's still suspicious mind, it was the manifest intent of the German princes to separate the family.[62]

Perhaps it was this provision more than any other which led Ferdinand to drop written communications with his brother and, instead, to confront him personally.[63] He left for Villach, arriving there on July 8 to spend the better part of two days and three nights in discussions with the Emperor. The atmosphere of the meeting comes to us almost exclusively from Charles's account. Ferdinand reported tersely two years later that negotiations had been "intense" (*embsig*) and that he had used every ploy conceivable to effect a change of heart in the Emperor. He beseeched him once again to accept the treaty without alteration, claiming that Charles had accepted the very same arrangements in the recesses of earlier diets for apparently selfish reasons. Then military expeditions of the Emperor abroad were at stake; now that it was German interests which were paramount, Charles was nowhere near as flexible. To this the latter correctly objected that his previous concessions had been made only until the next diet and to help Ferdinand in Hungary. This the king admitted. He wept, however, as he described the threat which his lands faced now from the Turks.[64]

But despite this tirade and the genuine feeling of compassion which he had for his brother, Charles stubbornly clung to his position. A religious peace and whatever other grievances the princes had against him could only be discussed at the next diet. Either the electors and the princes could accept his emendations, or Ferdinand could enter into the agreement unchanged in his own name. The Emperor ordered his envoys in Passau to draw up a justification of his position without consulting his brother.[65]

In a pouring rain, the king left Villach on July 11 to return to Passau. Though he believed his efforts to have been in vain, he did his best to put a positive light on his discussions with the Emperor in his report to the estates. Knowing of the Emperor's position, some of them were threatening to leave, a prospect that distressed Ferdinand immeasurably.[66] After deliberating among themselves, the princes came to him and asked if there was any possibility that Charles might be moved from his position on religion. Ferdinand replied that there was none, but that this did not mean that he would cease to work on his brother to accept the treaty. Reports were now coming from Hungary of one Turkish advance after another, and he shipped a map, dirtied when the coach carrying it tipped over in the mud, to illustrate more precisely his plight to his brother. He took the liberty of diverting into Hungary troops whom Charles had recruited in Bohemia for his own purposes. All the while Maurice relentlessly kept up his pressure on Ferdinand, using his promises to go to Hungary to persuade Charles to keep a close eye on John Frederick when the elector was out of his territories. The king did nothing to discourage the wily Saxon from such tactics.[67]

Charles finally met his brother at least half-way. He was not unsympathetic to his Hungarian difficulties; his own agents had reported that Ferdinand's eastern problems were real. He did not object strenuously to Ferdinand's commandeering of the Bohemian troops, and he even echoed a bit of his brother's vocabulary as he spoke of not wishing to see the king's ". . . entire ruin and [that] of his children. . . ."[68] He dallied a bit over the exact date of Philip of Hesse's release, but by August 19, his acceptance of the Passau accord was in German hands. Aside from freeing the landgrave, the agreement called for the free practice of Lutheranism until a national council, presided over by Charles, discussed anew the Augsburg Interim and tried to settle Germany's religious problems. What the Emperor would do if the conclave came to no decision was left open, but he stressed his good intentions. The estates were slowly won to this provision when Charles, by mid-July, had begun to rearm seriously. Their concern also grew about the Hungarian situation.[69] But there was a bitterness in Charles's comment to his brother that he had ratified the Passau agreement strictly out of consideration for the latter's affairs. For himself it held nothing. He sourly expressed the hope that Ferdinand would for once recognize the favor that he was doing him; at least this time, the king could not accuse him of being unresponsive to his needs. He nevertheless warned that if Maurice broke the agreement, Charles would not feel obligated to uphold it. Ferdinand restrainedly thanked him for the gesture, admitting that it had been made for his sake and that of his family alone. He assured him of future devotion.[70]

By September, Maurice and his forces were in Hungary where they managed to fortify Raab and Komorn. Their presence stiffened the successful resistance of Eger to an Ottoman seige and ultimately helped force the Turks to a truce. The mutually profitable cooperation of Ferdinand and the elector did not stop there. Ferdinand assisted the latter against an effort of the newly-freed John Frederick to recapture electoral Saxony in 1553, and both of them worked to check the marauding of Albrecht Alcibiades who had not accepted the Passau treaty.[71]

Thus as in the succession crisis, Ferdinand had once again scored something of a personal triumph at the expense of the Emperor. The German aid he needed came his way as he managed to convince a very dubious brother to yield to his entreaties simply out of dynastic solidarity. The meaning of this episode for Ferdinand's political relationship with Charles and the Empire is a somewhat more complex, and more significant, issue. Had he really, as as been argued, come to differ substantially with his brother on religious matters and to seek a new *modus vivendi* for both Emperor and estates?[72] His behavior puzzled the highly intelligent William of Hesse who at the end of August 1552, with his father not yet released, voiced great suspicion over Habsburg intentions in Germany. Yet, less than two weeks later, having contacted Ferdinand on the matter, he was surprised to find that he could be separated so easily from Charles and was concerned to retain his friendship.[73] Ferdinand was unquestionably most respectful of German feelings both during and after the Passau discussions. And it is also true that he seemed increasingly benign toward Lutherans. In recommending names to Charles for an imperial state council which the latter wished to form, he put forth the name of Ludwig von Stolburg und Kungstein who ". . . although he has something to do with the Lutherans . . . was never seditious."[74] Rumor had it that Ferdinand had argued so strongly for the Protestant position at Villach that, in England in June of 1553, when the duke of Northumberland was looking for a pro-Protestant and pro-French consort for Lady Jane Grey whose succession he was promoting following the death of Edward VI, he sent out a feeler to the king. All such behavior aroused deep suspicion at Charles's court.[75]

Yet, in analyzing Ferdinand's stance on Protestantism in 1552, one must observe a distinction between him as a tactician and a believer. He had always been willing to make temporary concessions to his confessional enemies in order to win their support in Hungary. Given the strong emphasis on the Turkish problem in his correspondence with Charles in 1551-1552 there is no reason to believe that his flexibility at Passau marked any basic change in his normal approach to the Lutherans. Undeniably the agreement called for a religious peace that might very well end with the permanent establishment of the new persuasion and undeniably Ferdinand accepted it. Whether he did so in good faith is an altogether different matter. He did speak of altering the arrangement, although at an indefinite time to come. Ferdinand was a man for whom negotiations were always possible, provided, of course, that he held the trump card of office in his hand.

Nor can it be said that he was moving all that far from the traditional role of the Habsburg Emperors vis-à-vis the imperial estates. It was Charles, now ready to agonize over conscience with his position in Germany a secondary consideration, who had really changed. Ferdinand's arguments with him were cast in a frame of reference in which the German princes, or at least some of them, were indispensible to his well-being, something that Charles once thought as had Maximilian I and Frederick III before him. In his assertion of personal conviction at the expense of his position in the Empire, the older Habsburg had mentally begun his withdrawal to St. Yuste. Ferdinand's concerns on the other hand, had simply inched him much closer to the emperorship.

CHAPTER XIII

A PEACE WON, AN EMPEROR LOST

Though Charles had clearly made his first move to lay down his title and concerns in Germany in 1552, he completed the process irregularly and unpredictably. By so doing, he gave Ferdinand some of the most delicate tactical problems of the latter's career, poised as he now was between his effective responsibility for affairs in the Empire and his formal role as his brother's subordinate. While growing enfeeblement both physical and political became a spiritual burden to the older Habsburg, it became a material trial for the younger, still bound to support his older brother and sovereign even as it became increasingly plain that Charles could do little for him.

Ferdinand's military help for the Emperor grew markedly more erratic, allowing the latter troops from Austria one year, forbidding it the next.[1] The succession agreement lingered as a contentious barrier between them. Ferdinand often reminded his brother that it was the reason for German uncooperativeness, though in the same breath he would protest that he was faithfully observing it. Until Philip's formal declaration of disinterest in the title, however, rumors persisted of secret dealings of the king to break the compact. One of these coupled him with Maurice in an understanding through which no more Spaniards "were to be endured" in Germany. The succession agreement continued to be a drag both on the relations of the two men and their position in Germany. While the princes did not know the precise content of the agreement, they suspected that it limited electoral freedoms in some way.[2] Spanish and Austrian advisors were also made mistrustful of one another because of this issue, as well as other matters.[3] More and more frequently, Ferdinand referred to the "houses" of his family.[4] Yet, so long as Charles remained Emperor, it was he who headed Christendom, and Ferdinand could do nothing but act as

[202]

his subordinate. He was immensely sympathetic to the older man's efforts to recapture Metz, lost to the French in 1552, and generous in his condolences when the undertaking failed.[5] Even in situations where advisors and self-interest alike dictated otherwise, Ferdinand would bow in the end to his brother's wishes.

The still-unresolved question of Württemberg graphically illustrated the last-named situation. As a confederate of John Frederick of Saxony and Philip of Hesse during the Schmalkaldic War, Duke Ulrich, to Ferdinand's way of thinking, had rebelled against his liege lord. The latter figure was Ferdinand himself according to the treaty of Kadan. The Habsburg felt that the duchy should therefore fall back to himself and his heirs. When Ulrich died in 1550, his son and heir, Duke Christoph, vigorously argued that Ferdinand's claims did not apply to him. Charles, on the lookout more than ever for ways to reduce his financial burdens, was anxious to pull his Spanish troops from the fortifications of the duchy they had been occupying since the war. The duke, therefore, tried to work on Ferdinand through the Emperor and his intimate, Arras.[7]

Ministers in both Spain and Austria stood to profit, though in different ways, from the affair. Both sides knew it. One of Ferdinand's confidants, Dr. Jacob Jonas, correctly suspected that Arras was open to bribes from the duke. In 1550, the bishop promised Christoph that he was as ready to serve him as his father, the elder Granvella, had been and enthusiastically accepted some wine, preferable from vineyards around the Neckar, as a gift. He also let it be known through his *major domo* that he would take any game which Christoph could send along to Augsburg where he was then.[8] Ferdinand's advisors, including Jonas, were reputedly just as venal and manipulating the Württemberg affair for the grants of land and money that it might bring them should the duchy fall to Ferdinand. Duke Albrecht of Bavaria, who was serving as a mediator between Christoph and Ferdinand, speculated that the king was actually losing his zest for the territory, but was so under the influence of his subordinates that he could not cooperate with his brother.[9]

By 1551, Charles had an additional reason for treating Christoph gently. A second session of the Council of Trent was ready to open, and he wanted the Protestants to attend. There was no telling what an angered Christoph might do to upset Lutheran sensibilities. In the Netherlands, Mary, who thought once again that Ferdinand was excessively concerned with his own interests, agreed.[10] And Ferdinand ultimately came around to Charles and Arras's way of thinking. At Linz in April 1552, he indicated that he was willing to give a bit on the issue. Talks began at Passau; Albrecht of Bavaria worked out an agreement in which a Habsburg succession in the duchy would take place only if Christoph's male line died out. In lieu of his territorial claims, Ferdinand was to receive 250,000 florins paid over a three-year period which was to begin in 1553.[11] The settlement was along lines which Charles and Arras had envisioned from 1550 on; Ferdinand made it clear that though he deserved every bit of compensation owed him, he had no intention of seriously angering his brother.[12]

Thus, the pressures of courtiers and councilors to the contrary notwithstanding, king ultimately yielded to Emperor. However long-standing the difficulty had been between the two brothers, Ferdinand really had little choice given Charles's unambiguous wishes to divest himself of any responsibility in the duchy. It was not so easy to be submissive, however, to actions that were so tentative, capricious, or narrowly self-focussed that they could hardly serve as the basis for any common policy at all.

The dilemma which this situation posed for Ferdinand became clear when he and Charles tried to create some sort of internal defense organization within the Empire during 1552 and 1553. This idea had been with Charles since the diet in Augsburg in 1547-1548. Ferdinand had not been especially keen on the plan at the time, but his weaknesses and those of his brother after 1552 had made it more appealing to him. Charles dreamed of reviving the Swabian League and actually put out feelers on the matter to the princes without first telling Ferdinand.[13] Despite the slight, Ferdinand wholeheartedly backed him, urging the Emperor to pursue the matter more closely than he actually did. The king himself opened discussions on the question while negotiating in Passau. A year later, when the structure of the organization was under discussion in Memmingen, Ferdinand begged Charles for fuller instructions to aid the work of the imperial representatives. The Emperor sent nothing, however, and this failure, plus other ill-timed gestures on his part hastened the collapse of the talks. Desperate for military assistance, Charles had made an ally out of Margrave Albrecht Alcibiades of Bayreuth, the very man whose depredations the league was supposed to check. The Emperor had also begun to press once again for Philip's election, an act always sure to lower the enthusiasm of the princes for any other idea that their sovereign might propose.[14]

But Ferdinand's interests in any case lay only partially within the western confines that such a league would have had. His membership would have been tied only to his titles in the Tyrol and Ferrette in Alsace, making these the only Habsburg lands which the league would be obligated to defend. Indeed, the prospective members had not wanted Lower Austria to join at all, fearing that they could not avoid defending a territory so exposed to Turkish aggression.[15] But it was the east which weighed most heavily on Ferdinand's mind, not only because of the threat from Constantinople but because of the still-rampaging Albrecht Alcibiades. An awesome figure, once glimpsed riding from a castle in a chain mail coat and rooster-feather headdress on a horse carrying three blunderbusses and two maces, he began to menace Bohemia in the spring of 1553. While in his cups, he had let it be known that he intended to have the Crown of St. Václav for himself. Moving from Franconia through Thuringia and preparing to devastate Braunschweig and Saxony, he raised enough alarm in the kingdom to make Ferdinand fear that his subjects might take their defense into their own hands without bothering to turn to him for leadership.[16]

Even before this situation had arisen, Maurice of Saxony had made the king a very attractive proposition. Faced with his own challenges from the margrave and from his implacably resentful cousin, John Frederick, the ex-elector, Maurice was reading the implications of the contiguity of his territories with Ferdinand's. His conclusion was that he should expand his ties with both the king and Emperor. The arrangement he proposed would have committed him to the defense of all the Habsburg Austrian territories against the Turks, thereby going far beyond the original Saxon-Bohemian *Erbeinigung.* Ferdinand was predictably enthusiastic about the scheme, given exemplary military service in Hungary and the Schmalkaldic War. He also saw it as a way of retaining the slippery elector's loyalty to the house of Habsburg, and begged Charles to support the idea.[17]

But the plan only aroused the Emperor's mistrust, not without some reason. The principle call for the league had come from Maurice, not from Ferdinand, and the Saxon was still courting Henry II of France for his support, an activity open to any number of interpretations as far as Charles was concerned.[18] Ferdinand had come to sound more and more like Maurice's advocate, even though he did his best to present the Wettin's concerns as those of Charles and himself. But most bothersome

of all to the Emperor was the way Ferdinand had jumped into the negotiations with Maurice without first consulting him. So deep were Charles's
misgivings about his brother that he even came to mistrust the latter's
support for the western league.[19] In any case, he felt that the chief military burden in the east would inevitably fall on Ferdinand and himself.
He flatly disagreed with the king who argued that such an organization
would promote the tranquillity of both the Empire and Christendom as
a whole.[20]

Maurice laid a sketch of the league before Ferdinand in the middle of
February 1553; the Habsburg was pleased and asked the Emperor to join.
Charles politely refused. Nevertheless, Ferdinand continued his talks with
Maurice and the representatives of other interested princes throughout
the spring in Eger. Complete agreement among them on all issues that
affected the king's interests was impossible—some present feared that
as members both of the league and of the Empire they would be doubly
obligated to assist Lower Austria against the Turks, so that this and other
problematic questions had to be deferred. However, by June, an active
coalition had developed against Albrecht with Maurice as commander-
in-chief. On the first of July, the so-called League of Eger issued a pro-
clamation against Albrecht which presented Ferdinand and Maurice as
the first defenders of the Empire. Beside them, Charles appeared an almost
inconsequential figure.[21]

Still the unpredictable Emperor could not be ruled out of consideration
altogether. After his initial refusal to enter the league, Charles had changed
his mind, though the conditions which he had set upon his membership
were so restrictive as to render it all but meaningless.[22] Ferdinand was
not completely unsympathetic to the plight which had led Charles to his
flirtation with Albrecht Alcibiades. However, once he and the Saxon elector
had declared themselves against the latter, Ferdinand asked his brother
to place the imperial ban on the margrave. This Charles simply refused to
do. But he continued to tantalize Ferdinand with his continued interest
in the league's affairs, particularly after Maurice was mortally wounded
in a clash with Albrecht at Sievershausen in July 1553. With his chief
antagonist in the princely uprising of 1552 now out of the way, the
Emperor urged his brother to complete the formation of the organization
as quickly as possible and to keep him well-informed of its progress.[23]
Ferdinand, on whose shoulders the chief burden of the war against the

margrave now had fallen, was delighted at his brother's renewed concern for eastern affairs. But Charles still would not outlaw Albrecht.[24]

Nor did the Emperor's relationship with the margrave in any way further another of Ferdinand's efforts to muster princely support in Germany. Even as the king had been negotiating in Eger, yet another league was coming into being in the Empire. Renewed rumors of Philip's imperial candidacy carried by Duke Heinrich of Braunschweig-Wolfen-büttel, back from the siege of Metz, had alarmed many princes. Led by Christoph of Württemberg, William III of Cleves-Jülich, the Count Palatine, and Albrecht of Bavaria, who would serve as Ferdinand's spokesman, this group was purely an affair of the estates. It chief purposes were to mediate between France and Charles as well as to bring about a peace between Albrecht Alcibiades and the Franconian bishops. They also wished to gain a wider acceptance of the Passau accord throughout Germany. The Emperor, therefore, was deliberately excluded, and, not unnaturally, his suspicions were immediately aroused. His membership became even less desirable, at least to Duke Christoph, when in January 1553, Charles told the latter that while he had no desire to make the emperorship hereditary, he knew of no better candidate for the job than Philip.

Ferdinand sent a delegation to these princes meeting in Heilbronn in July 1553, asking them to join him the fight against the margrave. They demurred, given the absence of any indication that Charles would do the same.[25] Maurice's death and with it, the temporary collapse of Ferdinand's Saxon strategy, made it all the more imperative for the king to drive up additional support in Germany. Bavaria, dangerously near to Albrecht's base, supported their Habsburg neighbor's entry, not as King of the Romans, but as another German prince whose western territories warranted his participation.[26]

Yet, though Ferdinand had initiated contacts between himself and the new organization, when the moment came for him to throw his lot in with it, he hesitated. The possible negative reaction of his brother bothered him, and he preferred to postpone discussion of the step until the next diet. Pressure on him to join was heavy, coming from his Bavarian son-in-law and Maximilian, whose pro-German orientation was as lively as ever. Maurice's death had pained the archduke greatly, and his father's reluctance to tie himself to the princes now made him angry.[27]

Ferdinand finally entered the league in August, though precise terms of his membership remained open to clarification. Though he eventually gave Ferdinand's participation his qualified approval, Charles remained leery of the organization since it made no provision for his entry. He reminded his brother that secret negotiations had been the norm for Ferdinand since his dealings with Maurice; it was plain that he did not like it.[28] Ferdinand did his best to be reassuring, claiming that whatever he had done had been due to military pressures on him, not conspiratorial intent. The title of chief of the Empire was still reserved for Charles, he pointed out, and the purpose of the group was to uphold his authority and the laws on which it was based. He also kept Maximilian on a very short leash. When the latter tried to appear personally before a gathering of the new league at Heilbronn in September 1553, his father flatly forbade him to do so.[29] Asking his son if he wanted to destroy all relations with his uncle, he called him a "hothead" who thought neither "...beyond himself nor for himself." Maximilian's fury was boundless. He could not understand Ferdinand's concern for the Emperor, when, in his view, Charles had done so little for him. Yet, Ferdinand remained implacably opposed to his meeting with the princes, and, in the end, he bowed to his father's authority.[30]

But though the need to take into account the Emperor's eccentricities and inconsistencies needlessly complicated Ferdinand's efforts to form German leagues or to participate in them, it did not by itself cause them to fail. Charles was not personally responsible for Maurice's death, and important princes such as Württemberg and the Count Palatine continued to suspect Ferdinand's motives for joining them. They steadfastly refused to mobilize against Albrecht, thus leaving it largely up to the Habsburgs to continue the war against the margrave on his own. Fortunately for Ferdinand, his foe's active support gradually dwindled throughout 1554. In the summer of that year, he fled first to Lorraine and then into France.[31] Rather, it was in the creation of some settlement of German religious differences that the tense balancing act which Ferdinand was performing between his own interests and his brother's feelings and position emerged as truly crucial.

The Passau agreement of 1552 had called for a decisive discussion of the religious question at a future diet. Ferdinand had agreed that this and Turkish aid should be on the agenda for the gathering. The general peace in the Empire that he was trying to stitch together working through leagues was itself predicated on the establishment of confessional harmony—a long-held view of his. He further felt that if anything constructive were to come from the pope and his council, there had to be a renewed effort on the part of the Emperor to reform abuses there. The Lutherans too had to be won to a more flexible posture on the lands they had confiscated from the church, either paying for them or restoring them outright. Charles was not overly-prompt to summon the meeting, however, nor was his brother. Ferdinand's presence was required in his own lands in 1554, and the king also wanted the princes and other members of the estates to have adequate time to prepare for what was obviously to be an important gathering.[32] For their part, the electors and princes also refused to be hurried.

But though both Ferdinand and Charles knew that such a diet was necessary, there were signs that they would not speak with one voice before it. Rumors started making the rounds of German courts at the end of 1553 that Charles would not observe the particulars of the Passau accord, something which distressed Ferdinand considerably since he believed that he would be blamed for such a breach of faith. Unlike Charles, he regarded the compact as a working basis for any future agreement.[33] Whether Charles ever did cancel the treaty unilaterally is not altogether clear. He had made his reservations about it known to Ferdinand from the beginning, and his imperial vice-chancellor, Matthias Seld may have sketched out a revocation as early as 1552. In later years, Arras recalled the existence of such a document, though he said it had not been made public at Ferdinand's request. Philip II, on the other hand, claimed to have heard nothing of it.[34] Whatever its precise status, however, the Passau agreement was certainly to be an issue between them. Shortly before the actual diet opened in Augsburg in 1555, a delegation from the Emperor to Ferdinand urged the latter not to mention the treaty in his proposition to the estates.[35]

But Ferdinand's greatest difficulty with his brother was over the exact relationship which the Emperor would have to the diet and its resolutions. At first Charles apparently expected to attend, since he approved of Augsburg as the meeting place because troops were present for his personal protection. Ferdinand felt that his brother's presence was absolutely necessary if only to dispel the reports of his revocation of the Passau agreement.[36] But by the beginning of 1554, Charles had grown increasingly non-commital about attending, saying that because Ferdinand enjoyed such good will in the Empire and the matters under discussion affected him so directly, it was he who should be present at the gathering from the beginning. By June, he made it clear that he was not coming at all. He was not well, but his chief reasons were his religious reservations, all of which he had laid before Ferdinand two years earlier at Villach. He expressed his confidence that his brother would not consent to anything against his conscience or that would increase religious discord. His commissioners would come with instructions that they should only help Ferdinand. They were to do nothing in Charles's name or through any power which he gave them. Though he was actually in Brussels, he was to be regarded as being in Spain and therefore out of the Empire altogether. Ferdinand, as King of the Romans, was to reach agreement on his own, something which Charles deemed to be perfectly legal. He had, by this time, also given up on Philip's succession in Germany, and he hoped that his absence from the diet would scotch once and for all the idea that he would press for his son's election.[37]

From the outset, Ferdinand was unhappy with such an arrangement. Such an unorthodox method of negotiating, he thought, would only arouse unfriendly suspicions among the princes, especially given Charles's attitude on the religious question. He continued to hope for a change of mind from his brother, however; only at the beginning of January 1555, did he formally accept the powers which Charles wished him to have.[38]

Charles was clearly coming close to a complete abdication of his office and responsibilities. He may have already spoken of it to Ferdinand at their confrontation in Augsburg five years earlier, but war and the negotiation of Philip's English marriage had kept him from pursuing the idea any further.[39] Without an unequivocal statement of resignation, however, it was altogether unrealistic for the Emperor to assume that the estates could even begin to dissassociate him from whatever agreement they reached. Many at the diet had seen Ferdinand and Charles act jointly in the Empire on previous occasions; it strained credibility now to believe that the Emperor would not play the same role in the current agreement as well. One rumor spoke of Ferdinand, Charles, the Pope, Philip, and some German princes as bound together in a plot to suppress Lutheranism.[40] In the area of fact, the Passau agreement had obligated both brothers, and, all in all, they were not so far from one another on the religious question, at least in principle. Charles's general instructions to his commissioners enjoined them to avoid sharpening confessional differences in the Empire without damage to the Catholic position. He continued to argue that the best way to resolve the discord was through a general council, though he was willing to sanction a national colloquy if the estates could not see their way to the larger gathering. There was no sign that he would assent to an unconditional religious peace or hint that he had given up on the eventual reunion of the Catholic and Protestant sides. Ferdinand agreed in substance with all of this.[41] He had thought that a religious colloquy might be held within the framework of the diet, but was quick to abandon the position when Charles opposed it.[42] Throughout the meeting, he would defend orthodox interests tenaciously as befitted a man who, while the gathering was in progress, termed the Spanish Inquisition a "saintly" institution. He asked that a papal legate be with him at all times during the diet to advise him, to fire up lukewarm Catholics among the Germans, and finally, so that if he had to make significant concessions, Rome would know first-hand that they were truly forced from him.[43]

Therefore, it is hardly surprising that the estates continued to believe that Ferdinand held his powers in his brother's name. But from the time of his arrival in Augsburg at the end of December 1555, through the first part of February, the king and the Emperor's commissioners remained at odds over the questions of in whose name the diet was to be conducted and the place of the religious question in it.[44] In truth, Ferdinand was carrying on not one set of negotiations but two—the first with his brother and his emissaries, the second with the estates. It forced him into a night and day pace of work, ". . . contrary to the practices of the other German princes. . ." as one observor noted.[45] He fought stubbornly to have his brother's name incorporated into the meeting's resolutions, pointing out that so long as Charles lived, no negotiations would be valid unless he empowered them and agreed to their conclusions.[46] Since the Emperor in the Netherlands was technically on imperial soil, it defied all logic to deny that Ferdinand was only acting in his stead. True, the recesses of Speier and Nürnberg in 1542 and 1543 had been in Ferdinand's name, but only in the context of the phrase ". . . in place and in the name of his imperial majesty and in our own. . . ."[47] But Charles did not even

want his commissioners to be identified as his own in the imperial proposition to the diet, something which aroused another objection from
Ferdinand.[48]

The form of the proposition, finally laid before the diet in February
1555, represented a compromise on the matter though no one was especially happy with it. Ferdinand had drafted a passage which declared that
Charles had asked his brother to hold the diet in his name. Against the
will of the king's spokesman, Dr. Jonas, Charles's commissioner, Felix
Hornung insisted that it be excised. While the offending formula was not
in the final proposition itself, the prefatory address to the estates, read
by Jonas, described Ferdinand as acting as the Emperor's representative.[49]
As far as he was concerned, and this was true of the estates as well, the
Emperor was still very much a part of the discussions. When they finally
began to deliberate on religious matters in June, members said that it was
their Emperor who had called them together to reestablish peace in the
Empire and had given Ferdinand the power to do this. They spoke of
themselves as being obedient to "both majesties." Ferdinand and his
advisors continued to argue that they were acting only out of a competence given them by Charles.[50]

For all the Emperor's resolve to stay aloof from the diet, he tried to
dictate the order of business. Ferdinand's opening propositions to the diet
in February had called for discussion of religion, Turkish aid, and civil
peace. Charles's representatives, doubtful, in view of Lutheran intransigence shown at Passau and elsewhere, that much in the way of recon-
ciling the faiths could be achieved, asked that the item appear on the
agenda after internal police matters. Ferdinand went along with the request with the support of the electors of Trier and Cologne. The secular
electors and the majority of their princely counterparts were most concerned with religious matters, however, and this was the issue which they
decided to air first. Their sense of urgency did not apply to the pace of
their deliberations. Having been among the first to arrive in Augsburg,
Ferdinand was anxious to hurry discussions along so he could get back
to his own lands where the Turks and Isabella Zapolya were claiming his
attention. However, debate in each of the three chambers of the diet hung
not only on matters of substance but procedural questions as well. The
princes did not give him a formal proposal on the religious question until
June 21, and when they did, it did not indicate that they had found unity

among themselves as he had hoped they would. They had finally resorted to taking separate votes among Protestant and Catholic on issues where they could not agree. The former had called for extending any religious settlement drawn up by the diet to the territorial knights and cities not immediately subject to the Emperor, neither of whom were represented in the body. The adherents of Rome had endorsed a call for church lands whose administrators had changed faiths to remain Catholic property. Some princes were threatening to leave the diet altogether if the king did not give in to their religious wishes; the papal representatives were so alarmed at the tone of the discussions that they began to hope that the king would simply prorogue the meeting. Ferdinand himself was beginning to despair at its outcome. He toyed with the idea of temporizing, but publicly suggested that the diet be prorogued or even disolved. In the latter case, a new one would have to be called.[51]

For all their dilatoriness, however, the princes were anxious to have some confessional accord. Elector August of Saxony, Maurice's successor spoke for many when he said that no one was satisfied with the Augsburg Interim and the mistrust which it had provoked. He argued that understanding between Protestant and Catholic was impossible unless the conditions for suspicion among them were first removed. He also pointed out that effective aid against the Turks could only come when a peace was achieved, something Ferdinand hardly needed to be told. He remained, however, rather cool toward the softened Lutheran attitude, continuing to talk of proroguing the meeting. Whether deliberate or not, it was a clever stratgem. Protestant fears mounted that such a postponement was only another Habsburg trick which would allow Charles to make peace with France and Ferdinand with the Turks. Once this was done, the brothers would be free to turn upon their confessional foes once again as they had done during the Schmalkaldic War. Charles had done something like this at Worms in 1545, postponing the diet to Regensburg in 1546, but invading the Empire instead.[52] But Ferdinand also knew that if he were to enjoy any trust among the estates, some sort of religious peace would have to come from the present gathering. He began to speak of a settlement within the general framework of the Passau agreement. Greater flexibility also emerged among both Protestants and Catholics. The king's willingness to drop any idea of postponing the diet persuaded Elector August and other Protestants to be more compromising. The

Catholic princes had become increasingly worried about trouble with their Lutheran counterparts if a settlement were not worked out.[53] On August 30, Ferdinand took direction of the negotiations firmly in hand. Within three weeks he brought the diet to a conclusion with a skill that even his opponents complimented.[54]

His purpose was to find a religious peace but one which would have a limited impact on the primacy of the Roman church in the Empire. In the latter endeavor, he met with some success though the papacy would be unhappy with the arrangement, especially the provisions for protection of ecclesiastical property.[55] It is true that he accepted as "eternal" the by now familiar *cujus regio, ejus religio* formula which dictated the religious practices of the subjects of the princes. But he also insisted, and won agreement from the estates, that this applied only to the Lutherans and Catholics among them, not to other sects. While he agreed to the toleration of Lutheranism among the knights and the Hanseatic cities who were not official members of the imperial estates, he also won a guarantee that Catholics could practice their faith unmolested in those territories. The *cujus regio* provision was thereby restricted in its use only to those in the estates.

The one thing he could not win the Protestants to was the so-called "ecclesiastical reservation," even with his concession that the religious peace was to be permanent. This provided that if the administration of bishoprics, ecclesiastical foundations, and benefices embraced another faith, the territories associated with these offices would remain possessions of the Catholic church. Under real pressure from Rome and its German supporters, Ferdinand was deeply commited to the principle. The Protestants were equally stubborn in resisting it. He finally got his opponents to allow him to proclaim the reservation in his own name— a favorite device of both himself and the Emperor. This meant that the provision was simply a private expression of the will of the king and therefore not enforceable by the *Reichskammergericht*. It would become one of the more controversial aspects of the settlement. Some Protestants did go along with it, most notably Philip of Hesse, whose five-year captivity had left him a burned-out man, fearful that war with the Catholics would come again. But most did not, so that Ferdinand took yet another step to bring them around. The ecclesiastical principalities contained noblemen and cities who had adopted the Wittenberg reform. Ferdinand

unofficially promised the Protestants at the diet that their cohorts would
not be disturbed in their faith. This, the *Declaratio Ferdinandea,* prompted
heavy criticism from Catholics.[56] The other major issues of the diet—
Turkish aid and the reestablishment of public peace in Germany—were
also covered in the recess. In place of ad hoc leagues, a solid organization
of imperial circles with provision for more efficient leadership was to be
established. It was, however, to be controlled by the estates, not by the
Emperor.[57]

But architect of the Peace of Augsburg though he was, Ferdinand was
not the source of its authority, at least as he and the estates saw it. All
through the most crucial negotiations from June through the middle of
September, Ferdinand had informed the Emperor of their progress and
sought his advice.[58] As late as September 6, the king referred to the
powers which Charles had given him. In discussing a future diet to iron
out issues left unfinished at Augsburg, he spoke of appearing there at
the command of the Emperor in the latter's name. In their last days
together in Augsburg, both Ferdinand and the estates were reminding
one another that he had conducted the negotiations for the Emperor
from whom his powers to do so had come.[59]

Regardless of the legalisms involved, however, Charles had made it
known to Ferdinand in the strongest possible language that he would
tolerate no permanent change in the position of the Catholic faith in the
Empire. Indeed, he was much grieved that he had been able to do so little
to protect it. What he had heard about preliminary negotiations at the
diet on religious matters did not please him. He felt that the participants
had gone far beyond the Passau agreement, at least as he interpreted it,
and beyond the recesses of previous diets as well. He did not blame Ferdinand personally for the shape that the settlement was taking.[60] Nor did
he ever. Even after the recess was promulgated, he said that the king had
done what he could with the type of people he was dealing with; he probably would have done the same had he been involved in the negotiations.
For all the tensions which had been present between them since 1550,
he called Ferdinand a "good brother" and sympathized with his wish to
bring the gathering to an end because of Turkish pressures.[61]

But he made it all but impossible for Ferdinand to do so. Around the
middle of August, Charles had cryptically referred to something he might
have to relay after conferring with Philip. Nothing more was said after

that. However, on September 25, one hour before the Augsburg recess was to be proclaimed, a message arrived from the Emperor to his brother, telling of his intention to abdicate and instructing that the recess not be issued in his name. Once again he pleaded the infirmities of age; he planned to turn the Spanish kingdoms and their possessions over to Philip and the Empire to Ferdinand.[62]

It was nothing more than Ferdinand had wanted, indeed, expected at some future date, but his brother's resolve could not have been more poorly timed. He had never tired of reminding Charles that the diet had been convoked in his name; that the princes knew that he was negotiating on his brother's authority; that anyone in possession of his senses knew that he was only King of the Romans; and that during the Emperor's lifetime, he could do nothing in Germany without the latter's consent. True, he had structured the recess without hearing from Charles, but this had only been because of the pressure of the Turks upon him, a general lack of support from the pope, and Charles's endless military preoccupations with France.[63]

Now that the Emperor was refusing to ratify the Augsburg settlement, its very authoritativeness was open to question. Ferdinand had the choice of disclosing his brother's wishes and thereby seeming to have negotiated for nine months under false pretenses, or wilfully ignoring the Emperor. His response was typically resourceful. Pleading that he could no longer stay owing to the Turks and the need to open a provincial diet of his own, he allowed the text of the recess to be read, then dismissed the Germans without ratifying the document on the grounds that Charles had not answered all the questions he had put to him.[64] The estates did not object unduly, but as such the legality of the settlement remained at issue. Were Charles's plenipotentiary powers to his brother sufficiently comprehensive to draw up an agreement without the former's express ratification? Ferdinand remained evasive. In his own capitulation to the estates made when he officially became Emperor in 1558, he said that the peace was in his name in the place of the Emperor.[65] But for all its problematic features, the outcome at Augsburg pleased him. He thought it was more productive than past gatherings and agreed with Charles that he had done what was possible, the equivalent of success in his psychic economy. Aid against the Turks, more trust between himself and the estates, and peace in the Empire were some of the things that he hoped the settlement would foster.[66]

As far as religious matters went, the heart of the settlement, his wishes would be unfulfilled. Even within Ferdinand's lifetime, complaints about the peace were legion. In 1556, the imperial diet presented him with demands for the abolition of the ecclesiastical reservation, even in the form that had been used to weaken it. He refused, saying he would rather give up military assistance altogether. Despite his desire to create an agreement free of ambiguities, the Protestants were quick to say that the wording of the document had made their situation more difficult. If anything, differing interpretations of the meaning of individual sections of the peace only widened the gap between Protestant and Catholic as the century wore on. His efforts to shore up Catholicism in Austria by using the *cujus regio* principle met with much resistance from the estates.[67]

But looked at in the light of the development of his own political career and the framework in which that took place, the second struggle which he mounted at Augsburg, the one with his brother, shows that he had all but became the leader of his house. From the outset of the diet, it was he, not Charles, who regarded the gathering as not merely desirable but crucial. The abortive efforts of the brothers to establish leagues had disclosed how little was left between them in the way of common policy.[68] It was Ferdinand, not Charles, whose interests were tied to the Empire, something which the older man actually admitted. Charles had really ceased, at least in his own mind, to be a public figure. He could no longer think beyond his own desires. Ferdinand was distressed at this turn of events and so were other members of his family. Mary and Philip fully agreed that the Emperor's precipitate retirement and a new election in Germany might provoke unwelcome moves from the French. It fell to Ferdinand to recall his brother to his sense of duty; Philip was deeply grateful to his uncle for dissuading Charles from leaving Brussels for Spain, a harbinger of his withdrawal in the west.[69] It was Habsburg interests which were at stake, to which the personal whims of an individual member of the dynasty, even if he were the acknowledged head of it, were subordinate. It was Ferdinand who had now come to speak for these concerns, and it was he who had to insure that the power and influence of his family would suffer no loss through the inopportune wishes of a very weary brother.

CHAPTER XIV

TYING THINGS TOGETHER, I: THE DYNASTY

Charles died in September 1558. However, as far as Ferdinand was concerned, the Emperor all but passed from the face of the earth the minute he resolved to rid himself of his official status. Ferdinand did not journey to Brussels in October 1555 for Charles's first ceremonial divestiture of his territories. Indeed, Archduke Ferdinand, representing his father, arrived only after his uncle had completed the ritual.[1] The correspondence between the brothers dropped off dramatically after 1555, and what there was of it was increasingly trivial. To Charles's great distress, Ferdinand continued to press him for 200,000 gulden which, though there was no written agreement to this effect, he insisted his brother owed him according to their 1522 compact. Charles claimed to have met this obligation through the aid he had given Ferdinand against the Turks, in Württemberg, and in securing his election as King of the Romans. He went on to argue that agreements between them had also exempted him from this payment and that he had never asked any satisfaction for Philip's renunciation of the imperial title. Ferdinand kept up his badgering; indeed, his whole attitude toward his brother's finances bordered on the petty. In 1556, when his Spanish daughter-in-law expressed a desire to visit her father, Ferdinand advised Maximilian to depict the trip as the result of Charles's exhaustion. That way, he reasoned, the Emperor would pay for part of it.[2]

Ferdinand did not appear at his brother's funeral, though he commissioned a gargantuan memorial for him held in Augsburg in 1559. When municipal authorities learned that he planned to participate on foot, all the carpenters of the city were commandeered into building a bridge from the imperial residence to the *Frauenkirche* for him to walk upon.

The first procession to the church had 1,500 mourners carrying conventionally sized candles and two hundred poor, especially chosen for the task, bearing as many giant candles. Philip was absent from this ceremony.[3]

The imperial office, however, did not come quite so easily into Ferdinand's hands as Charles passed out of his life. Indeed, the transfer of the dignity was the one serious issue left between them. Ferdinand's objections to having the title come to him so abruptly went beyond the awkwardness that Charles's decision had created for him at Augsburg. 1555 had brought threatening moves from the Turks, and he needed to turn his attention to that corner of Europe once again. According to his decree of election as King of the Romans in 1531, Ferdinand was to become Emperor in the case of an *Erledigung* of the office, meaning Charles's death. This clearly had not happened, and he knew that even in normal circumstances the electors needed much time to deliberate among themselves and to assemble for a formal election, as well as for the delicate negotiations which he would have to carry on with them. Ferdinand also agreed with Philip and Mary that the electors, prompted by the French, might use the opportunity to demand another election altogether, thus putting an end to his plans for both himself and Maximilian. For all his nephew's declared disinterest in the imperial title, Ferdinand also feared that Charles might take the occasion of his renunciation to press his brother, once elected, to work again for Philip's succession.[4]

Though terribly anxious to relieve himself of all his responsibilities, Charles recognized the seriousness of his brother's objections by 1556. He advised Ferdinand to call the electors together at a time the latter felt appropriate and promised to send his representatives to negotiate with the Germans on the transfer of the title to Ferdinand. If the electors could not be won to this arrangement, Charles agreed to retain the title and name of Emperor but to allow Ferdinand to administer the office, a formula the younger Habsburg had suggested a year earlier.[5] A year later, however, stung by insinuations that he had no conscience where his duties were concerned, Charles had second thoughts on the matter. Fearful that his claims both in Burgundy and Italy might be weakened by his father's renunciation, Philip wished more than ever that he not take this step. The final form of the withdrawal was under discussion up to the very last months of the aging emperor's life.[6] Ferdinand, however, had never implied that his service as administrator of the Empire was more than temporary. He extended serious feelers concerning his elevation to the electors in 1556, though he did not meet with them until the following year. In February 1558 he received their recognition; a month later the title was transferred to him in Germany "as if his imperial majesty had already died."[7]

For all their differences, however, Charles and Ferdinand agreed after 1555 that they needed to foster good relations between both sides of their house.[8] Once Ferdinand became Emperor, which made him the head of the dynasty as well, the burden of this responsibility fell to him. He assigned it the highest priority, believing more strongly than ever that dissension with in the family was the one means that enemies of the house of Habsburg had to destroy it.[9] It was a complicated and difficult task since hostilities persisted both in Spain and Austria for many reasons. Intradynastic financial quarrels now visited themselves upon the generations. Philip accused Ferdinand of selling rents that he should not have; Ferdinand would try to make Philip pay debts that Charles had taken over from Maximilian I. As late as 1561, resentment was still present among Philip's advisors, chief among them Arras, that their ruler had lost the emperorship. Both Ferdinand and Maximilian were acutely sensitive to any signs of Spanish ambition in the Empire and were quick to counter them when the appeared. In 1555, members of Charles's entourage in Brussels immediately interpreted Ferdinand's reluctance to take the imperial crown right away as an outright refusal of it, something he swiftly denied. For his part, Philip grew increasingly disturbed at the apparent Protestant sympathies of his cousin and brother-in-law and of Ferdinand's cautious handling of the problem. Finally, the ambitions of the new Emperor and the equally new king of Spain did not always coincide.[10]

But both Ferdinand and Philip brought qualities of character and intelligence to their relationship that augured well for smooth dynastic functioning. Each was exceptionally polite, most certainly by training and probably by nature. The filiopietistic young prince had taken much to heart his father's injunctions in 1548 to maintain close ties to his uncle and cousins, and he began his reign firmly resolved to work well with Ferdinand.[11] Whatever disagreements he had with the latter, he never failed to treat him with utmost deference. Some of this attitude was structurally determined by the subordinate position which Philip occupied in the dynasty, much like the one Ferdinand had held with Charles. It was now Ferdinand who supervised its members, regardless of generational remove or degree of blood relationship. Through Archduke Ferdinand, he, not Maximilian, found a tutor fluent both in Czech and German for the latter's sons. Margaret of Parma, Ferdinand's niece and Philip's half-sister and governor in the Netherlands, deemed it wise to consult her uncle before appointing one of his subjects as her representative in Ghelders. Negotiating a marriage for her son, Alexander, Philip was anxious to have his uncle's approval of the project before going ahead with it.[12] But much of the king of Spain's ability to cooperate with his uncle came from within him.

For his part, Ferdinand's relations with his nephew showed him at his diplomatic best—firm but not inflexible in promoting his own interests, ready to set priorities and to compromise on all but the most central goals, and attuned to the king of Spain's psychological make-up as well as his political concerns. His assertion that Spain's victory in 1557 over France at St. Quentin was no less a triumph than Charles's over the same foe at Pavia was the shrewdest compliment possible to a young man who stood as in awe of his father as Philip did.[13] He claimed that he respected his nephew as much as he did his older brother, and, for all the hierarchical distinctions between them, cooperated with him as a colleague rather than as a subaltern. On occasion Ferdinand's chancellory communicated directly with Spain when it had information thought to be of interest to that kingdom. Even the most casual ambassadorial chit-chat was relayed to Philip if Ferdinand thought it might be useful.[14] In 1556 Philip was allowed to raise troops in the Tyrol and throughout the Empire for Spanish service.[15] Maximilian, too, was reminded by his father of the value of keeping up communications with his cousin.

Wherever possible, Ferdinand used reasoned argument to bring Philip around to his own point of view and scrupulously protected his nephew's independence. Upon hearing in 1562 of plans in Spain to wed the king's son, Don Carlos, to a Portuguese princes rather than to Maximilian's daughter, Archduchess Anna, Ferdinand set about persuading Philip's ambassador in Vienna, the Count de Luna, that his granddaughter was more suitable. Great effort went into convincing de Luna that Philip would find it convenient to engage in negotiations with him. Philip was offered the option of another of Ferdinand's granddaughters for his son should he feel that the older girl would be best married in France. While the Spanish king was weighing this arrangement with a marriage to Mary Stuart for Don Carlos, the Cardinal of Lorraine, the Scottish princess's uncle, urged Ferdinand to get some sort of decision out of his nephew. The Emperor refused, arguing that it was not right to hem Philip in in such a way.[17]

Other things bound uncle and nephew, not the least of which was the trust each had in the religious soundness of the other. Philip was always able to separate Ferdinand's personal faith from his latitudinarian policies and from the confessional adventurism of Maximilian.[18] Indeed, both because of his views and because of the circumstances in which he found himself, Ferdinand was more dependant on his nephew in his defense of orthodoxy than vice-versa. He not only admired the king of Spain for the way he nurtured the Catholic faith in his realms, but he looked to those lands for the well-trained and devout clergy conspicuously absent in the Austrian holdings and eastward. When asking Philip to find a confessor and court preacher for Archduke Charles, he specified that the first should be a Burgundian or Fleming, the second, a Spaniard, since it was these people who provided the best candidates for such offices. Ferdinand turned to Spain and Portugal for funds to support Germans preparing for the Jesuit order in Rome and for the staff of his newly-established Jesuit college in Prague. For a monastery founded in Innsbruck in 1563, he solicited Philip for Jeronimite friars, a group which Ferdinand had always esteemed, and asked the king to incorporate the new foundation into the order in Spain. The scheme did not materialize; it testified eloquently, however, to the Emperor's deep respect for things Spanish.[19] Philip himself was more than glad to accomodate him " . . . in this as in everything."[20]

Ties of a less exalted nature also existed. Ferdinand was very partial to Philip's envoy in Vienna, the Count de Luna, who would represent the affairs of both men at the Council of Trent. The ambassador enjoyed a kind of trust which did much to ease potential tensions between the two rulers. Some of Ferdinand's advisors, particularly his chancellor, George Seld, were in Philip's pay, giving the king of Spain the opportunity to be doubly informed and therefore less vulnerable to surprises from his uncle.[21]

One of the chief causes of trouble between Charles and Ferdinand had been that neither had ever developed much sense of the other's sphere of influence and responsibility. Charles had always expected Ferdinand to support him in the West; Ferdinand had always expected Charles to extricate him from difficulties in Hungary. Bitterness inevitably arose when one brother failed to meet what the other regarded as his obligation to him. This sort of friction was largely absent between Ferdinand and his nephew. As soon as he became Emperor, Ferdinand made it clear that he had no intention of involving himself in Philip's problems with France and the Netherlands where a mutiny against the latter's rule was beginning that would plague him throughout his reign. Philip was quick to return the gesture. He did not ask his uncle to take part in the treaty of Cateau-Cambrésis of 1559 with the French which sanctioned the latter's possession of the once-imperial holdings of Metz, Toul, and Verdun. Ferdinand complained, but did little more.[22] As the titular head of Christendom, he occasionally called upon his nephew for aid in areas which arguably were beyond Spanish concern. He repeatedly tried to extract subsidies against the Turks from the "Burgundian Circle." However, he usually accompanied such requests with promises of compensation and efforts to convince Philip that he was acting in his own interests. He offered to mediate between Henry II and the king of Spain in 1558, hoping to free the latter to move against the Turks. From 1559 through 1561, he couched his pleas to both Philip and Margaret of Parma in the Netherlands for support in meeting a Muscovite attack in Livonia in assurances of reimbursement and reminders that Baltic upheavals would adversely affect trade farther west.[23]

However, more often than not, Ferdinand recognized his nephew's sovereignty in the Netherlands and did not press his claims beyond token levels. In 1562, when some citizens of Cologne protested having some goods confiscated in Brabant, Ferdinand was called upon to work out some solution. While he agreed that the estates of the duchy were part of the Empire, he was also quick to concede that Philip had primary rights there and turned the problem over to him. As far as Ferdinand was concerned, he hoped that an exchange of duty exemptions would solve the difficulty. For his part, Philip had more than financial reasons for welcoming his uncle's hands-off policy in the Netherlands. He had long suspected that his cousins, Maximilian or Ferdinand, had intentions of establishing themselves in the area and always turned a deaf ear to any suggestions that they be made regents there. Maximilian and his son, the future Rudolph II, returned the favor. The fomer steadfastly refused Philip's requests for permission to recruit in Germany, and the latter simply disregarded them.[24]

Short of financially underwriting any part of his nephew's military ventures, Ferdinand was otherwise willing to help him in any way he could. Promises of intelligence from the Empire, especially Lower Saxony which was the most likely source of aid for the Netherlandic dissidents, softened the Emperor's refusal to intervene directly there.[25] He was even more useful to Philip in the Mediterranean, keeping him informed of Venetian and particularly Turkish developments.[26] The Count de Luna used his post in Vienna to relay letters from Constantinople to Spain. Ferdinand urged his ambassador at the Porte to cooperate with Philip's emissaries there.[27] He took over diplomatic functions for him as well. In the process of rebuilding Spanish forces in the Mediterranean after a humiliating defeat at the hands of the Turks in 1560, and heavily burdened with other matters as well, the king decided to seek a truce with Suleiman in 1563. In view of Ferdinand's long-term experience in dealing with the Ottoman court and a peace which Vienna had successfully struck a year earlier there, Philip turned the conduct of his own endeavors over to his uncle. He also promised to ratify anything which Ferdinand concluded. The Emperor gladly accepted the task, and his representative in Constantinople at the time, Albert de Wyss, was able to arrange a peace of eight years. Though he frequently broke the agreement, Philip was delighted to get it. In 1564, Ferdinand's most experienced trouble-shooter among the Turks, Ogiers de Busbecq, won the release of some of Philip's subjects whom the Sultan was holding captive.[28]

In the most long-lived disagreement between the two men, the question of Philip's position in Italy, Ferdinand's ability to defend his interests through reasoned persuasion and willingness to give in on all but central issues warded of what could have been a serious rupture with his nephew. That Charles had intended that his son pay a major role on the peninsula was obvious at least by 1546 when, after extensive consultation with Ferdinand, he invested the prince with Milan. At that time he called the step a means of protecting the Empire, a theme which his son would echo.[29]

Ferdinand had accepted the Italian vicarate for Philip as a way of winning Charles over to the succession agreement of 1551. It was clear even then, however, that he did not intend to let the matter rest. He may have voiced serious objections to the arrangement at the time he was urging the Emperor to keep his title in 1555. In 1556, Giovanni Delfino, papal nuncio to Vienna and very close to Ferdinand, said that Philip's claims in Italy worried his uncle more than did the question of the imperial title itself, an exaggeration to be sure, but a sign of deep concern.[30] Charles may have grown more anxious when, in that same year, he apparently toyed with the idea of creating a hereditary Italian vicarate for Philip and his heirs.[31]

In the spring of 1558, with Ferdinand now Emperor, Arras, Philip's closest adviser on foreign affairs, urged the king to begin pressing his uncle on the imperial vicarate. Their requests were, however, not nearly as incendiary as what Charles had been thinking of two years earlier, referring now only to the Italian provisions in the 1551 succession agreement. Undue emphasis was not to be given even to these, however, and no word of the Spanish overtures was to get to Maximilian. Don Alvaro de Quadra, the bishop of Aquila, was entrusted with the mission to the new Emperor.[32]

Ferdinand's initial reaction was at once evasive, yet clearly negative. Such matters needed much time for thought, he said, especially since he had not completely recovered from a recent illness, a pretext if ever there was one, since he was to prove himself able to hunt from his death bed. He explained that he had accepted the 1551 compact only out of obedience to his brother, even though it would conjure up certain problems, left unspecified, in the Empire. The bishop countered that such dangers were unapparent to Philip who saw the arrangement as a way of conserving imperial authority in Italy. Ferdinand merely repeated his disagreement, and the discussion stopped there.[33]

Ferdinand was very anxious, however, to avoid an open rift with his nephew. He agreed with Philip and Arras that Maximilian should hear nothing of their talks, knowing very well how his son's hostility had complicated relations with the Spanish branch of the house in 1551. He did, however, become more explicit about the problems which he thought the Italian vicarate would bring with it. While not refusing to honor his part of the bargain in "time, place, and season," he reminded Philip of the upheaval against Charles that the 1551 succession agreement had unleashed in Germany and that he had foreseen it at the time. To follow up on the arrangement with Philip now would only confirm the suspicions of the princes that the Habsburgs wished to turn the Empire into a hereditary possession. By this he meant that making Philip an all but independent ruler of the imperial territories in Italy would be akin to treating these holdings in the same proprietary fashion that the Habsburgs did their own patrimony. Legally, he pointed out, the matter would have to go to the diet for decision. He worked on Philip's more narrow Spanish interests as well, pointing out that the vicarate would require the king to live in Italy, pulling him from Iberian, Netherlandic, and English concerns. Not willing to slam the door on his nephew altogether, however, he offered to make him his *locumtenens* on the peninsula and to help him there militarily when he could.[34]

Ferdinand's reaction came as no surprise to Arras—he had had the same experience with him on the matter when he was still King of the Romans.[35] For this reason, he and Philip may have only been on a fishing expedition to begin with. In any case, though not completely persuaded by Ferdinand's reasoning, they did recognize that he would have to go before the diet with their request and that it was no time to do so. They therefore decided not to press their case, waiting until 1562, when the question of Maximilian's election in the Empire arose, to take it up again. Voicing strong support for his cousin, Philip once again contended that the Italian vicarate would only strengthen the former's position in Germany. Ferdinand again demurred, contending that the Empire was not yet ready to have such a question put to it. There the matter stood, as far as he was concerned.[36]

Though the king of Spain refused to communicate directly with his uncle on the subject, claiming that he was not about to beg for what was rightfully his, he seemed to bear Ferdinand no lasting rancour.[37] Not all of this was due to Ferdinand's diplomatic skills. De Luna unfailingly portrayed the Emperor as a man of good will, through the ambassador had some suspicions concerning attitudes in Ferdinand's council. These feelings were confirmed when Ferdinand himself told de Luna that he did not want to confide the substance of their discussions to this body.[38] But short of actually handing him the vicarate, Ferdinand did everything he could to further Philip's position in Italy. In 1560, he invested him with Siena and the right to subinfeudate it if he so wished. Providing a suitable dowry could be arranged, Ferdinand volunteered to marry one of his daughers to the duke of Ferrara, a gesture which he though might force a French candidate to withdraw, thereby helping Philip in the area. In 1564, only a few days before his death, he renewed Philip's title as duke of Milan and extended it to all of the latter's legitimate heirs.[39]

Ferdinand's courtesy to his nephew was amply rewarded in areas which ran the gamut from marital diplomacy to papal relations. In 1559, when Philip heard that the duke of Mantua might marry the daughter of the duke of Ferrara, he felt this might be so prejudicial to Ferdinand's interests that he asked the marquis of Pescara, who was the son-in-law of the Mantuan ruler, to try to divert the duke from such plans. Ferdinand had always been so considerate of him, said the king of Spain, that he wished to see if the Mantuan ruler might be interested in a match with one of the Emperor's daughters. He spoke of himself as delighted to perform these services ". . . knowing that it is all the same thing." A marriage was arranged in Mantua for Archduchess Leonore.[40]

And despite all the German hostility to him, Philip had played a key role in many aspects of his uncle's succession to the imperial office. He had, of course, been as unhappy as Ferdinand, with the precipitate way his father had abandoned his titles, and Ferdinand had consulted with him frequently[41] in the period of delicate negotiation that had followed. At war with the French in the Netherlands in the mid-1550s, Philip hoped to keep the coming transition in Germany as free of interference by Henry II as possible through a victory over him. It was on this advice that Ferdinand did not begin actual meetings with the electors until 1557. Philip's victory over the French at St. Quentin in August of that year created the situation which he and his uncle were longing for. Shortly after, Ferdinand began the negotiations which led to his recognition approximately six months later.[42]

But no sooner had he been accepted as Emperor in Germany than troubles over the dignity came to him from another source—Rome. The deaths of both Julius III and Marcellus II in 1555 had brought to the papacy the irascible Gianpietro Caraffa who took the name of Paul IV. Obsessively resentful of Habsburg political influence in Italy, he believed that Charles V was personally responsible for the rise of Protestantism in Germany. With the latter's withdrawal from office, Paul's hatred was transferred to Ferdinand whose estimate of the pope was at first only mildly negative.[43] Upon hearing of Caraffa's election in

April 1555, Ferdinand regretted the pontiff's pro-French record, but otherwise deemed him to be a learned and worthy man.[44] Paul, of course, had some reason to dislike the younger Habsburg, even though the latter's Italian pretentions were far smaller than his brother's had been. He was central in the creation of the Peace of Augsburg, news of which moved the pope to threaten both Ferdinand and Charles with deposition.[45] But, though he never forgave him for his conciliatory role at Augsburg, Paul's real quarrel with Ferdinand began after the German electors named him Emperor in 1558. Though at the election he resisted the Protestant demand that he no longer promise to defend Christendom *and* the papacy, Ferdinand wanted to avoid as much trouble with his confessional foes as he could. He therefore renewed the Augsburg accord and made no effort to welcome a papal nuncio at his coronation in Aachen in March. Paul objected to the whole procedure vigorously and contended that only he could absolve Charles of his oath of fidelity. He argued that since the pope had transferred the right to elect the Emperor from the Greeks to the Germans, the sovereign could neither resign his new office nor a new one be chosen without at least papal consultation. Charles had compounded the insult by not even notifying the pope officially of his resignation. To the observation that Ferdinand had already been elected, Paul snapped that no Christian would have behaved as the Habsburg had done. Nor, in his view, was any election in which heretics had participated valid. Finally both pope and curia heavily criticized what they saw to be Protestant leanings in Maximilian and Ferdinand's reluctance to counter them forthrightly. Paul compared the Emperor to Eli the priest of Samuel I who did nothing to discipline the sins of his sons.[46] The cardinals around Paul embellished these themes further, implying that while Ferdinand was publicly a blameless Catholic, he shared his son's sympathies. They pointed out that both Maximilian I and Charles V had called themselves mere "elected Emperors" before receiving crowns from the pope.[47]

Ferdinand tried to defend himself in a number of ways. His ambassador to Rome, Martin Guzmán, met the curia halfway by agreeing that the Emperor could not be elected by heretics. He went on to argue, however, that since Charles had not renounced his title but simply abandoned it, the dignity had to fall to Ferdinand. The cardinals received such strained logic coldly. Nor did they accept the more tightly reasoned presentation of Ferdinand's vice-chancellor, George Seld, who contended that the electors were completely independent in secular affairs so long as a clear majority of them voted for the Emperor. Only if he had been chosen by a minority or openly charged with heresy and unbelief could Rome examine his right to be crowned.[48] Two months after Charles died, Ferdinand was still protesting that Paul's quarrel was with his brother rather than himself.[49] Though thoroughly exasperated with the pope, he deeply respected his office and tried his best to mollify the eighty-one year old pontiff. All was to no avail. Paul withdrew his nuncio from Ferdinand's court, thereby breaking formal relations with one of Catholic Christendom's sincerest defenders. Charles's death effected no change in his mood Rather, he redoubled his criticisms of the new Emperor, accusing him of tolerating heretics in his own lands and general carelessness in the stewardship of the church's interests.[50]

Though the German electors assured Ferdinand at a diet in Augsburg in 1559 that Paul's refusal to recognize his election did not trouble them, the Habsburg could not long sustain such a situation, either politically or emotionally. It was now that Philip became very useful to him. Ferdinand's need for an acceptable spokesman in Rome coincided with his nephew's wishes to ingratiate himself with his uncle on the matter of the Italian vicarate.[51] From the papal perspective, the king of Spain, who had openly voiced his reservations about his uncle's accomodating ways in German religious affairs, had truly impeccable confessional credentials. In 1557 both Philip and Paul were equally critical of Ferdinand's decision to allow a theological colloquy among the Germans in Worms. Philip argued that such meetings would weaken the position of Catholicism in the Empire, causing its partisans to vacillate or indeed to follow the lead of Protestantism. He added that such gatherings and the measures they produced would only serve to undermine the work of any future church council. Ferdinand agreed, but since the meeting had grown out of the Passau settlement in 1552, he felt obliged to let it proceed.[52] That the Catholics at the conclave, led by the Jesuit, Peter Canisius, were able to open major disputes among the Protestants themselves was attributed in Rome to Philip's orthodox influence on his uncle. When a bitter attack was launched on the ecclesiastical reservation at the diet in 1559, Philip successfully persuaded the Emperor to defend the arrangement as a way of avoiding papal suspicions about his religious sympathies.[53]

But before the pope in June 1558, Philip stoutly defended his uncle. He depicted him as a man wholeheartedly committed to the Catholic cause and contended, as had Ferdinand, that using force against the heretics in Germany would only unite them against Rome. Like the Emperor, he strongly urged a thorough reform of the papacy itself.[54] Though his presentation made little initial impact, the energetic follow-up work of the Spanish ambassador, Francisco de Vargas, which had Ferdinand's hearty approval, began to take effect. The curia gradually shifted its attitude toward the Emperor, now saying that however it disapproved of his religious policies, it had no complaint about his private religious conduct.[55] Philip advised Ferdinand to keep the affair quiet in Germany. He did feel, however, that his uncle owed the pope some expression of regret for the concessions to Protestantism made at Augsburg, for Maximilian's conduct, and other transgressions such as bestowing church dignities in the Empire before receiving papal confirmation. Philip suggested tha such a gesture be made secretly. Ferdinand, who wanted neither to scandalize Christendom through a permanent break with Rome nor to offend the electors by trivializing their role in his elevation to the imperial office, called the scheme "prudent" and "catholic."[56]

Philip's suggestions had a generally soothing effect on Paul who agreed to open discussions with Ferdinand once again.[57] But before these had gone very far, the volatile pontiff died. Ferdinand saw the way open for improving the quality of whoever held the office and, though he did not say so openly, his own position in Rome as well.[58] The new pope, who took the name Pius IV, quickly accepted the Emperor's offer of a private apology in return for recognition of his election in Germany. The ritual was performed by Ferdinand's new ambassador in Rome, Scipione d'Arco. Nothing was written, as Philip had also advised, since whatever was committed to paper could leak to the Germans and prompt some embarrasing questions from them.[59] Ferdinand did not want a coronation in Italy for fear of the hostility among Protestants it would provoke in the Empire. For all his caution, totally unfounded rumors circulated in 1561 that he had indeed been secretly crowned in Rome.[60] But though he could not receive the sanction of his church in the way he undoubtedly would have preferred, its approval meant a great deal to him. The new papal nuncio, the Polish bishop Stanislaus Hosius, himself in the vanguard of anti-Lutheran activities and shortly to become a cardinal, arrived in Vienna in April

1560. Replying to the envoy's introductory oration, Ferdinand began by asserting his deep faith and his desire to defend papal authority. Suddenly he broke off, overcome by tears. Hosius was so moved that for a few moments, the two wept together. When they finally got control of themselves, Ferdinand confessed that he had only done such a thing once before at the death of his wife. After this scene and private interviews that followed, the bishop was convinced beyond doubt of the Emperor's orthodoxy.[61]

The atmosphere of cordial cooperativeness that Ferdinand fostered with his nephew was perhaps most strikingly evident in the area of religious policy, particularly at the Council of Trent. That Ferdinand could continue this pattern was all the more remarkable since the interests of the two men were by no means the same. Ferdinand's local concessions continued to prompt sharp differences between them, though they were able to agree that in answering the specific challenges which faced the church in each of their lands, they would in some way be supporting the Catholic cause.[62]

Both Charles and Ferdinand had always agreed on the desirability of a general church council, where both secular and spiritual voices would be heard, but neither had been willing to promote it if it was not politically opportune. Philip felt much the same. Of them all, however, it was Ferdinand who had the most at stake in the success of such a gathering, especially after 1555. Faced with genuine confessional heterodoxy in Germany, he saw the conclave as a life and death matter for the lands of himself and his heirs. Philip had an equally strong commitment to the doctrinal unity of Christendom—both he and his uncle were equally hostile to the French national council proposed by the cardinal of Lorraine in 1560. But the crown had a firm grasp on the church in Spain, and Philip could have survived there had the council of 1562-1563 been as abortive as earlier meetings.[63] Even as the gathering was about to get underway, the king of Spain was inquiring in Rome after military support against the French and the German Protestants. Ferdinand, convinced that such moves would fatally undermine the council's chances for success, protested to his nephew strongly. Philip deemed the Emperor's opinion "prudent" and did not pursue his plans.[64]

Where disagreements arose, Ferdinand followed the same strategy as he had in other dealings with his nephew, trying to see as much justice in the opinions and interests of the latter as he could while at the same time moving forward the council in which he had invested so much hope. The notorious dispute between Philip and the French over precedence in the seating order of their delegates is a good case in point. The king of Spain objected strongly to the French contention that their spokesmen had historically occupied more prestigious positions at such councils than their Spanish counterparts. Ferdinand judged Philip's refusal to negotiate this point reasonable; at the same time he proposed a compromise—that the French ambassadors be allowed places nearer the imperial representatives in public meetings and council sessions, but not in processions and other ceremonial occasions where the Spanish would be preferred.[65] The dispute, which dragged on throughout the entirety of the conclave was eventually resolved by Pius IV in favor of the French. Ferdinand continued to act on behalf of his nephew without destroying the chances that the gathering had for coming to some conclusion; Philip was deeply grateful. Privately, however, the Emperor urged him to settle the question with the king of France so that the council might not be dissolved over what he called "human pretension" rather than some more serious issue.[66]

Sometimes circumstances rather than diplomacy settled the differences between them. This was true in their disagreement over the form which the last session of the council was to take. Though the Peace of Augsburg and its predecessor in Passau had brought a tense confessional truce in the Empire, it also brought with it, especially in Austria, the expectation among Protestants there that further toleration was to be won from Ferdinand. Neither Philip nor the Emperor liked this situation, but the latter saw little hope of reestablishing religious unity through force either. When a papal bull announced the recalling of the council to Trent, which had been suspended in 1552, Ferdinand was deeply distressed at its contents. Pius proposed to continue the previous gathering which had taken a particularly strong anti-Protestant stance. The Emperor thought that the only way the Lutherans could be coaxed into participating would be to have the council begin totally anew and not in Trent which they abhorred. By 1561 he feared that Pius's position might provoke the dissidents to war. Philip, however, was at one with the pope on the matter, an attitude which Ferdinand claimed puzzled him. At the beginning of 1561, arguing that Germany was the site of the controversy anyway, he proposed that the council be transferred to Cologne.[67]

The Protestants solved this problem for the Habsburgs by showing little interest in attending any council. The issue of concessions which Ferdinand wanted for his lands was a far more serious issue for him and Philip, however, since it involved a break in ranks between them on a principle which they initially both supported—the right of secular powers to participate in setting the council's agenda.[68]

It was Melanchthon who observed that Protestants could be won back to the church by two doctrinal changes: communion in both kinds and pastoral marriage. After 1556, Ferdinand's territories put a great deal of pressure on him to support the granting of the chalice.[69] As early as 1560, Ferdinand had asked Rome for permission to allow both clerical marriages and communion in both kinds in Germany as a way of eventually having the council celebrated there.[70]

But Ferdinand was not only interested in concessions from Rome and the council; he wanted them to give him more effective instruments for the advancement of the church in his lands. Erasmian as he was, the Emperor believed that only a papacy which had been morally and intellectually reformed could bring those who had wandered back under its sway. If either council or pope chose not to do so, then Ferdinand was prepared to take some initiative. As worried as any of his predecessors about papal prerogative, Pius IV had been reluctant to support such a program. At the end of 1561, Ferdinand resolved to turn to the council. He claimed that he was so concerned to see a reform of monastic life in his own territories that he would go ahead with it regardless of what any authority said.[71]

It had been to avoid just such control of the council's thrust by a secular figure that the papacy had insisted on the right of its legates to set the agenda of the meeting. It had been with just such reforms in mind, among other things, that both Philip and Ferdinand had initially opposed the papal stance. The Emperor's position was summarized in his first "reform libel" of June 1562. He urged that the council order a thorough moral reform of the church and postpone discussion of dogmatic issues until this was done. The document especially stressed the need to improve theological education and to fashion suitable reading material for both clergy and laity. Candidates for clerical benefices were to be more vigorously screened.[72]

These suggestions met with scant oppositon. Indeed, they were incorporated into the final decrees of the council. But Ferdinand had a rather idiosyncratic notion of reform, as far as the council and curia were concerned, for he also included in his "libel" his request for the chalice in Germany, Austria, and the Bohemian lands, and clerical marriage. His interest in the entire program was great enough to convince him that he must compromise with the pope and his legates on the question of who controlled the agenda. In return for getting his requests, especially the chalice, before the body of the council, Ferdinand agreed to let the papal spokesmen present them, in effect signaling that he had given up on the idea that secular powers had as much right to establish the business of the council as did the pope.[73]

Philip was not only suspicious about the concessions his uncle wanted, but, concerned to retain his tight control of the Spanish church, wished to be able to influence the agenda of the council in that direction. The stand-off between uncle and nephew was full of potential trouble not only for their dynasty but for the Catholic world as a whole. To keep Philip and Rome both with him, Ferdinand openly told each side what they wanted to hear. Even as he willingly turned the right of setting the formal agenda of the council over to the papal legates, he voiced continued sympathy for Philip's objections to the procedure, claiming that he himself was worried that Rome's representatives would pour over his propositions so long that they would come to naught.[74]

The first "reform libel" encountered much hostility from both pope and council—the request for the chalice was termed "misguided." Speaking for the papacy, the Jesuit theologian Jaime Lainez argued that the Protestants who had asked for it had done so insincerely, meaning that they had no intention of rejoining the church.[75] Still convinced of the need for their program, Ferdinand and his religious advisors set about amending it. Emerging in June 1563 as the second "reform libel," the reworked document dropped some controversial items such as the request for clerical marriage. It continued to ask for the chalice, however, and for a thoroughgoing reform of papacy and church.[76] Ferdinand bowed to the exclusive right of the papal legates to present his ideas to the council, but not so completely as to give lasting offence to the king of Spain. He urged Philip to continue expressing his ideas on the matter, but reminded him of the general importance of the council, a point of view Philip could not reject out of hand. Indeed, Ferdinand never flatly told Philip to cease his objections to the exclusive right of presentation

of the papal legates to the council, preferring to advise his naturally deliberate nephew to even greater caution. At the same time, he continued
to depict himself as ready to cooperate with the king at the council where-
ever he could. De Luna reported in March 1563 that the Emperor would
even come to Rome if Philip thought it useful.[77]

By November 1563, Philip still wished to continued his objections with
the pope. Having received word from his nephew that he wished his positions to conform with the Emperor's at the council, Ferdinand
felt that they younger man could be talked out of his objections to the
way the agenda had been constructed. Faced with his uncle, Pius, and
the French, all of whom wanted to end the conclave quickly, Philip
decided not to bring the issue to a vote. Certain changes in the final decrees were made to satisfy him; in December 1563, he announced himself content.[78]

The issue of the chalice had been forwarded from the council to Pius,
who granted the concession to Ferdinand in April 1564 for use in Austria and Bohemia.[79] Philip was unhappy with this as well. His own theologians had been telling him that such steps were very serious indeed for
the precedents that they established. Ferdinand repeated the argument
that he had elaborated when they had discussed the question before—
that the religious situation of the respective holdings was so different
that different strategies had to be developed to deal with it. He saw no
other way to save Germany for the church. However, he played upon
Philip's filiopietistic streak to win at least some active sympathy for
his position. Charles V, he claimed, had also requested the chalice at one
point for the troublesome Germans from Paul III. This was an oversimpli-
fied version of what had actually happened since Paul had granted the
chalice on an individual, not general basis, in line with the Augsburg
Interim, but Ferdinand, in any case, was not working on Philip's understanding of history. Philip asked not to be involved in his uncle's religious
policies, and Ferdinand, whose health was failing badly, had little more
to say to him on the matter.[80] Once again, he had been able to realize
the substance of his wishes without alienating his nephew who had good
reason to disagree with him. The consistency of results was in part due
to the pattern of dynastic deference in which Philip had been schooled.
An equal, if not greater part, however, was due to the characteristic blend
of psychological manipulation, reasoned self-interest, and clarity of purpose which Ferdinand applied to the the affairs of his house.

CHAPTER XV

TYING THINGS TOGETHER, II: THE FAMILY

For all the sympathy and similarity of outlook which Ferdinand had with Philip and Charles, a coldly exploitative strain ran through his relationship with them as well. Blood ties were to be used like his loans from the South German merchants—to promote his goals which may or may not have been the same as those of his brother or nephew. With his own children, his self-interest took on a more complex dimension, since it was only through their prosperity that his ambitions for them could be realized. He was therefore much more consistently protective of them than he had ever been of Charles or Philip, unfailingly alert to any possibilities which arose for advancing their welfare.

A time-honored way to accomplish these goals was the dynastic marriage, and Ferdinand was one of the most resourceful matchmakers of his age. All of his daughters who did marry—a few entered the church—did so with reigning sovereigns. Where they were betrothed to fiancés who were not yet of age, their contracts specified that the boy in question would be a legal ruler upon reaching his majority. The one exception in Ferdinand's family to his endless promotion of marital alliances was himself. Widowed just short of his forty-fourth birthday, he did not wed again, unlike most of his contemporaries in similar positions. Part of his disinterest was due to the fact that he never stopped mourning his first wife, but practical considerations also played a part in his thinking. In 1557, he refused to consider marrying a Portugese princess because the size of his present family and the burden of the Turks kep him from taking on any more territorial responsibilities.[1] His children, however, were wed throughout central, eastern, and southern Europe, from Mantua, Ferrara, and Tuscany to Cleves, Bavaria and Poland. These, it should be noted, represented only matches completed, and not the full range of possibilities that Ferdinand's lively imagination generated.

From the standpoint of modern affectional relationship all of these alliances appear rather heartless since their main purposes were political and symbolic. Ferdinand, however, had a good deal of feeling for his daughters especially and sympathy for the situations in which they occasionally found themselves. His oldest child, Elizabeth, and her sister Catherine, had wretched matches with Sigismund Augustus of Poland due to the hostility of their mother-in-law, Queen Bona, and the king's refusal to live with his second Habsburg wife. In Catherine's case, Ferdinand dispatched Maximilian to the Jagellonian court to see if he could do anything to ease the relationship.[2] Nor were his daughters-in-law, at least those who became so through regular marriage negotiations, treated simply as objects in a higher game of diplomatic and property exchanges. He was genuinely fond of his Spanish niece who was Maximilian's wife and concerned himself with her numerous pregnancies and deliveries as much as did her husband. All were part of his family, and both their pleasures and pains were his.[3]

The possibility of gaining additional crowns for his sons through marriage or other means was never far from his mind. At Ferdinand's insistence, Maximilian's wife was designated as a potential heiress to the Spanish crowns in her betrothal agreement with the archduke. Catherine's misery in Poland did not keep her father from thinking of his oldest son as king there once it became likely that Sigismund would have no male offspring.[4] The unusual succession of females in England and Scotland moved Ferdinand to vigorous diplomatic activity on behalf of his two younger sons, Archdukes Ferdinand and Charles. With Mary Stuart, he set the conditions that she remain a Catholic and be accepted as the hereditary ruler of her kingdom. The agreement which he wished to arrange between Charles and Elizabeth would have made the young man administrator of the realm in order, as Ferdinand said, to keep his son near to the seat of power.[5]

Religious considerations were perhaps the most serious strictures on Ferdinand's efforts to advance the fortunes of his children through wedlock. At the diet of Speier in 1544, he and John Frederick of Saxony had agreed upon a union between the elector's son and Archduchess Leonore provided that some confessional accord could be reached throughout the Empire. When John Frederick asked in 1553 if Ferdinand intended to carry through on the arrangement, he refused, claiming that the religious conditions had not been met. Indeed, he had already renounced the agreement in his testament of 1547.[6] Where the marriage was so important that it was positively dangerous not to pursue it, he could adjust his religious reservations to some degree but not indefinitely. This was especially true in his negotiations with Elizabeth of England. The alliance was imperative in his eyes, chiefly because the rulers of both France and Denmark had their eyes on the Tudor queen. The situation raised the possibility that England might come under the control either of a Lutheran or the bitterest enemy of the house of Habsburg. In view of these stakes, he urged his representative to speak cautiously when discussing confessional matters. Ferdinand himself hoped that the religious issue might not loom so large in the negotiations, a not wholly unrealistic attitude since Elizabeth herself had yet to show that she was irrevocably committed to any single persuasion.[7] But in the end, his Catholic loyalties left him unwilling to meet every demand Elizabeth made upon his son. He could also see some advantage in having her marry an Anglican, reasoning that it might harden the Roman opposition in England all the more. Nor was he anxious to have Charles the object of domestic sectarian criticism and discord in his new kingdom.[8]

The other severe limitation on Ferdinand's marital diplomacy was the ever-shaky state of his finances. By the latter half of the 1550s, he was complaining that he could barely meet the daily costs of his own kitchen and cellar and was warning Maximilian not to expect much in the way of subsidies from him.[9] Part of the problem was of course the familiar one—paying for Turkish defence in the face of inflation and ever-dwindling local resources. In 1554, Slavonia had 56,000 households which were assessed 2,324 gulden for military purposes. Only 1,327 of this could be raised. Prices of basic necessities such as bread and cheese had risen dramatically throughout the century and so had borrowing costs.[10] From 1552 to 1555, Ferdinand required 1,270,000 florins in loans, and it was increasingly difficult for him to meet interest payments. From 1556 through 1562, he was loaned another 1,610,083 florins, and finding willing creditors became a problem in itself. In 1563, Maximilian, handling Turkish affairs for his father, found only 10,867 ducats in the war treasury out of which he had to pay a 30,000 ducat tribute to the Porte according to a treaty struck in 1562. After much trouble, he extracted 8,000 from some personal holdings in Carinthia and 120 marks of unminted gold from the archbishop of Salzburg plus some old thalers which had to be converted into ducats in Constantinople.[11]

Though Ferdinand's habits continued to be simple, his lavish court expenditures now had added to them those of his son's establishments and the one of his unmarried daughters at Innsbruck. Maximilian was if anything, more profligate than his father; in 1552, he was counting on a dowry payment from Charles V to meet his obligations against the Turks. When this did not come, to his great annoyance, he was forced to sell "many of his best pieces" as his father put it. In 1551-1552, his household and court expenses amounted to 224,277 florins. For 1564, the last year of Ferdinand's life, outlays in the Tyrol exceeded income from the privinces by 31,000 florins. Over one-half of the total expenses there went for the upkeep of the Innsbruck residence and the territorial administration. The archduchesses, who had gotten along on 30,100 florins in 1553-1555 now required 40,000 for one year alone.[12]

To these sums were added untold hundreds and, in all likelihood, thousands squandered in graft and the dishonest practices of advisors. Foreign observors at Ferdinand's court noted that much irregularity accompanied the disbursing of funds for provisioning his children's households, their servants, and counselors. Monies were not assigned for specific purposes, and many profited from Ferdinand's carelessness in these matters. At least one papal nuncio, Vincenzo Pimpinella, received a monthly allowance of two hundred gulden from Ferdinand when funds from Rome were not forthcoming.[13] In the 1550s, the Habsburg intimates were Johann Trautson, his lord high steward from 1554-1558, his vice-chancellor, Jacob Jonas, and George Gienger, his spokesman at Augsburg in whom he placed much trust. All were of lowly birth, all had been in modest circumstances when they had entered Ferdinand's service, and all subsequently enjoyed a marked improvement in their personal fortunes. Around 1548, Martin Guzmán, one of Ferdinand's most trusted agents, said that of ten men whom his master had recently taken into his employ, eight now had incomes of over 100,000 gulden a year and the other two of over 50,000. Guzmán himself had once received a gift of 30,000 thaler from the then king. After 1559, they began to desert Ferdinand because he had no more to give them; what they took on the side must remain a matter of speculation.[14]

One can only speculate too on why he tolerated this state of affairs. Men such as Gienger and Jonas were openly pro-German, and Ferdinand may have found it politically necessary to keep them up front in his administration. He undoubtedly found them intellectually appealing. Ferdinand was an outgoing man who thoroughly enjoyed the company of those who, like himself, coupled devotion to religion with cosmopolitan sophistication. All of these men at least gave an outward show of these qualities, leading some to think that the Habsburg was blinded by their manners.[15]

It should also be said, however, that Ferdinand's court was no different from any other of his day. Sixteenth-century bureaucrats as a group took their positions in order to profit privately from them, since regular pensions were unknown.[16] And finally, he may have had little choice. His perception of men such as Jonas and Gienger was that they were genuinely competent to perform the tasks he gave them; it was not always easy to find administrators and diplomats with the specific talents the Habsburgs required to carry on their business, much less discipline their fiscal ethics. When in 1547, Charles was searching for men to replace advisors who had recently died, including his imperial vice-chancellor, Jean de Naves, Ferdinand, who thought highly of Naves, was at a loss for suggestions. The only men whom he could think of knew German and Latin but little French and Spanish, or knew Latin better than German, or, for personal reasons did not want to leave their present positions. One of the few competent commanders whom Ferdinand ever had, the Marquis de Marignano, who fought in the ill-fated Buda campaign of 1542, was not beyond profiteering from his service. Ferdinand did not like it, but would not dismiss him permanently either. Charles's high opinion of the marquis, also tempered his severity.[17]

But whatever the reasons for it, Ferdinand's well-known poverty limited the marital prospects of his children at worst and caused them acute embarassment at best. When, in 1548, the duke of Mantua demanded that his Habsburg fiancée be sent to him, both having reached an age where the marriage could be consummated, Ferdinand tried to postpone the journey. He would not have to come up with the final installment of the dowry, which he could not do since he was still paying off nuptial obligations to his sons-in-law Albrecht of Bavaria and Duke William of Cleves. Philip was delegated to detain the Mantuan ruler in Flanders where they were scheduled to meet in order to put off the consummation as long as possible.[18] Mary Stuart's advisors were

reluctant to consider Archduke Charles for that princess on the ground
that the young man was thought to be too impoverished to be consort
to a queen whose own sense of financial reality was hardly well-devel-
oped.[19]

The implications of Ferdinand's straightened circumstances, especially for his sons, were clear. If they were to be worthy prizes for
foreign sovereigns and/or their daughters, it would be due to their territorial titles, not their private fortunes. All of this made Ferdinand's
testamentary disposition of his lands something which he weighed very
heavily. His decision to divide them, with Maximilian receiving Lower
Austria, Bohemia, and Hungary, Ferdinand, the Tyrol and *Vorderösterreich,* and Charles, Styria, Carinthia, Carniola, and Friuli, was one of
the most controversial he ever took, at least as far as scholars are concerned. In some ways he seemed to be contradicting the centralizing
model which he had never rejected in his administration though he had
frequently compromised it. Contemporaries speculated that he saw flaws
in each of the boys—Maximilian's health was poor, Ferdinand was in-
temperate and Charles seemed to be of weak character—and therefore
did not want to entrust only one of them with all his holdings. Yet he
not only divided his lands, but his debts as well, leading some to conclude that the territorial partition was made to enable each son to cover
his share of his father's obligations. Maximilian I had done the same thing
with Charles and Ferdinand, with the latter finally taking the lion's share
of his grandfather's debts in return for more concessions of land from
his brother.[20]

The 1554 testamentary decree which served as the legal basis for
Ferdinand's eventual division also spoke of a divided inheritance as a
way of preventing ill-feeling among the brothers. From his earlier experience with Charles, Ferdinand certainly knew the meaning of this.
However, though Archduke Ferdinand obviously liked the experience
of governing Bohemia and may have asked his father to give him something permanent, there seems to have been no lasting enmity between
the boys.[21] It should furthermore be kept in mind that in resorting to
partible inheritance, Ferdinand was sticking very close to family practice and contemporary princely custom in Germany. Like the testaments
of other sixteenth century territorial princes, the 1554 *Verordnung* as
well as an earlier version of 1543 recommended territorial division only

as a last resort to preserve unity in the family. And like all his German counterparts, Ferdinand enjoined his sons to act in common even if the family lands were divided among them. He himself did his best to minimize possible friction. Incomes from the various Austrian lands were to be equalized even though one brother might receive an intrinsically less productive share than another. For all the burdens which Maximilian, as king of Hungary and Bohemia would have to bear in Turkish defense, Ferdinand bound him to pay the younger archdukes and their legitimate heirs an annual sum from both kingdoms since this was a traditional practice in both realms. Charles and Ferdinand were, however, orderd to aid the king against the Ottomans.[22]

But Ferdinand also had clearly in mind the relationship between his sons' eventual holdings and their capacity to conclude successful marriages. Most problematic of the boys was Archduke Charles, since the marriage contract of Maximilian with his Spanish cousin had specified that he would be king of Bohemia and Archduke Ferdinand removed himself from serious consideration by a morganatic *mésalliance* with Philippine Welser in 1557. Significantly, Ferdinand came to his final decision on the precise division of his inheritance during the negotiations with Mary Stuart in 1563. In listing his son's assets as a husband, he painted a glowing description of his territorial future, pointing out that not even the Emperor Frederick III had held as much land in the southeastern part of the Habsburg patrimony.[23]

Poor or not, the young men were schooled in the ways of command, for only they, besides Ferdinand himself, could provide the personal administration on which the dynastic system, particularly Ferdinand's polyethnic version of it, rested. In 1551, when an army he gathered from all parts of the continent stormed the castle of Lipa in Hungary, the Venetian ambassador, Michele Suriano, mused that the assault would have been far more effective had the king or one of his children led it. Hungarians, Bohemians, and Germans simply did not get along with one another, and Spaniard and Italians were hateful to all. At times, Ferdinand used even his sons-in-law to represent him, especially Albrecht of Bavaria who opened the diet of Regensburg of 1556 in his place. But it was mostly to his own sons he turned or, more precisely, to Maximilian and Ferdinand since Charles was only born in 1540. In 1544, when Maximilian was seventeen and Ferdinand two years younger, they traveled to Speier to be with the Emperor who was to introduce them to the princes formally and assist them in broadening their political horizons.[24]

At times Ferdinand seemed to use the boys simply as informants and diplomatic couriers, but they had more responsible positions as well. In 1546, Maximilian was delegated to open the diet of Upper Lusatia personally and to deal with the Bohemian nobility in Prague since Ferdinand had to hurry to Regensburg for a meeting with Charles. By 1555, all three archdukes were members of the privy council.[25] After 1556, he transferred the military administration of Hungary to Maximilian and began to consult him far more carefully.[26] He kept close watch on the archduke's activities there, especially his negotiations with the Turks, but was in general supportive of the young man's efforts rather than intrusive and critical. He consoled him when he failed and was quick to praise his successes.[27] When he established his new *Hofkriegsrat* in 1556, he made Maximilian his second-in-command, and when he had trouble finding personnel for the new body, it was to his oldest son he turned for further suggestions since Ferdinand himself was not in Vienna.[28]

But though the two boys gladly accepted the political roles that their father cast them in, they lacked some of the intellectual and moral qualities which Ferdinand thought their station demanded. Archduke Ferdinand's aforementioned marriage with Philippine Welser understandably displeased his father, though when the latter chastised the couple, he stressed the secretiveness of their act and the way in which they had transgressed parental will rather than the inequality of their union. Perhaps he could not afford to offend any rich merchant in Augsburg.[29] The 1561 document in which Ferdinand forced the pair to beg his forgiveness specified that no masculine progeny of the match would have any rights in the Habsburg patrimony unless the main male line died out. He did, however, appropriate incomes for any offspring Ferdinand and his wife might produce. Not too long after this, he also granted the archduke and his wife some funds and a residence, Ambras castle in the Tyrol, where the mercurial young Habsburg came to preside over one of the most famous curiosity collections of the late Renaissance.[30]

But it was Maximilian who was his father's main trial, probably because as the first born male of his family, his responsibilities were correspondingly greater. There was much of Ferdinand in his son. Around 1550, Maximilian's face had something of the hyper-excited quality that his father's had once had, and both men had a driving hunger to rule.[31] But where Ferdinand was able to maintain a certain *distance* between the lavish trappings of his court and his most private habits, Maximilian could not. The older man had a hot temper which he had disciplined since youth, but over this lay a personal charm and courtesy which struck all who observed him. Maxmilian was just as volatile, but made little effort to control himself and, to his father's distress, chafed against the deferential postures dictated by the hierarchical organization of his house. He had a bit of his uncle in him too, being far more taciturn than the talkative Ferdinand.[32]

For all his gregariousness, Ferdinand had an air of high seriousness about him. This was reflected in the Erasmian interests of many at his court, the refined musical tastes which he indulged throughout his life, and the generally lofty moral tone which he cultivated in his personal relations. Maximilian as a youth seemed anything but serious and by 1546 and 1547 was already behaving in ways that troubled his father deeply. His favorite pastimes were strumming on a lute and playing with a pet bear.[33] While in camp with his uncle during the Schmalkaldic War, he threw himself into drinking and wenching bouts in Munich and elsewhere in southern Germany and surrounded himself with men whom Ferdinand, in an impassioned plea that he change, called "leves homines." He was openly insubordinate to Charles in 1546, refusing to take the guard duty which his uncle assigned him. Ferdinand angrily accused him of thinking of himself to be more experienced than the Emperor and cited to him an Italian proverb:

> He who thinks he is a stag and really is an ass
> Should take care before jumping over a crevasse.[34]

Maximilian's tastes for the low life left him after his marriage to his Spanish cousin. She bore him fifteen children—the same number his own parents produced—and he appears to have been as faithful to her as his father had been to his wife. But his political and religious attitudes remained very troublesome. His diplomatic indiscretions continued. He was perpetually unsatisfied with financial arrangements made for him, demanding from his father, for example, an income of up to 20,000 thalers a year from Silesia which Ferdinand himself required. Though his marriage was emotionally satisfactory, it brough him few material gains, thus confirming his generally low expectations of the alliance at its outset.[35]

His loathing of everything Spanish except his wife seemed boundless. Even after 1555 and 1556 when Charles made some effort to smooth personal relations between himself and his son-in-law and between the archduke and Philip, Maximilian made little effort to change.[36] His father, as far as he was concerned, had done him little good and his uncle even less. His catalogue of Charles's failings was long. He had hoped to be made regent in the Netherlands, but Philip had been awarded this honor instead. This despite the fact that the archduke's wife, Maria, had once been betrothed to the duke of Orléans who had been promised either Flanders or Milan as part of her dowry. Charles's marriage strategies had been unduly partial to his own children, "unbrotherly,"to use Maximilian's term. Worse yet, he believed that his father's respect for the Emperor had alienated Germany and led to the outright loss of Hungary. Charles's reluctance to place the imperial ban on Albrecht Alcibiades in 1552 and 1553 led his nephew to speculate that he had done so to increase his dependence and that of his brothers on their uncle. All of the archdukes, as well as some of Ferdinand's courtiers, resented the king's original exclusion from the Spanish inheritance. No one, including Maximilian himself, had divined what Ferdinand thought on these matters. All they knew was that he publicly upheld unity with the Emperor in order to secure what he had.[37]

Even after Philip's official renunciation of the imperial succession in 1555, Maxmilian had some idea of combining the German princes and the French in a league against the Spanish. The plan brought forth monumental opposition from Ferdinand whom the archduke then accused of having a too-sensitive conscience. He argued that the king of France and others willingly used underhanded means to preserve what was theirs, and he urged Ferdinand to do the same for what he called the general good. His father flatly refused. He believed Ferdinand's attitude in part to be the product of Spanish advisors whom the latter still had at his court, particularly Martin Guzmán, whom Maximilian detested.[38] The only thing that relieved his hostility toward Spain was his hope that one of his sons might succeed to the crowns there since the heir-apparent, Don Carlos, appeared to be growing steadily more unfit. In 1560, negotiations to send his two oldest sons to be educated at the Spanish court began.[39]

Given the importance which he assigned dynastic cohesion, Ferdinand was deeply concerned about his son's attitude. His answer was to preach steadfastly the need for family solidarity urging Maximilian to treat Philip in a "brotherly" and "trustworthy" way and to understand that intra-Habsburg harmony was "of the greatest necessity." To retain Philip's friendship, Ferdinand even forced a Spanish steward on Maximilian whom both father and son thought incompetent.[40]

But even more serious, at least in terms of Ferdinand's plans for his own offspring, were Maximilian's religious inclinations. Precisely when the archduke began to toy with Protestant ideas is difficult to say. However, by 1555 it was being noised about the Empire that he was about to declare himself a Lutheran and would no longer go to mass. This he never did, indeed, continuing to practice most of the Roman ceremonies and leaving his wife free to observe her strict Catholic devotions. He studied Protestant writings seriously, however, and corresponded with Melanchthon.[41]

His position, however, threatened Ferdinand with what for his was a truly awful choice—between the welfare of his son and that of his religion. As early as his testament of 1543, he had enjoined Maximilian and young Ferdinand to uphold Catholic orthodoxy and to remain within its fold. He did so once again in February 1547 in his critique of Maximilian's personal habits, observing that the sectarianism into which Protestantism was falling was a sign of the error of their beliefs. The devil, he went on to note, was turned out of heaven for *superbia,* and those who rejected good works, contrition, and confession were committing the very same sin.[42] The same thoughts emerged in 1555 in a codicil to his testament of 1554, which now singled Maximilian out as the main concern since it was he who was to inherit and to rule the most territory. Aside from courting the dangers of eternal damnation which the archduke would do if he turned his back on his ancestral faith, his father reminded him of how members of their house had prospered as Catholics. The union of Ferdinand and Isabella had engendered a family which, with the exception of Scotland, had one of their number in every royal house of Europe. He also pointed to the Habsburg possessions in the New World. All this he took to mean that the dynasty owed much to a Catholic divinity.[43]

But just as in the case of his temperament and tastes, Maximilian owed something of his religious leanings to his father as well. Even though

Ferdinand saw nothing positive in Protestantism, as did Maximilian, he did not reject it out of hand. Rather he saw it as symptomatic of certain evils in the church which required correction. No one ever doubted his personal orthodoxy—at least for very long. He had the reputation among contemporary rulers of being the one who spent the most time in the study of religion.[44] This, however, made him not a blind but a critical partisan of Rome, quick to take the papacy and curia to task for their moral and educational failings. The model which he gave to his own family was that of an engaged Catholic but a questioning one, ever watchful lest the earthly custodians of his faith fall short of their high calling. The many Erasmians whom he chose as his theological advisors both reflected and reinforced his views. Few went to the extremes of one of their number, George Cassander, who argued in 1561 that all Christian men who lived as Christians were part of the body of Christ regardless of their rite, but almost all of them could be called moderates in confessional matters. One of the earliest of them was Johann Heigerlin or Johann Faber, who joined Ferdinand in 1523 and who may have received from Erasmus himself the suggestion of the *cuius regio eius religio* formula first adopted at the diet of Speier in 1526. Moreover, the Erasmians were only part of the crazy-quilt mixture of persuasions at Ferdinand's court. One of his treasurers, Hans Hofmann, was believed to be an outright Lutheran, but the Habsburg refused to dismisss him because he was a useful contact with the Protestants. There were strong Catholics, too, as well was Leonhard von Eck a lord high steward, who did not believe much of anything.[45] Ferdinand himself may not have been quite as programmatically latitudinarian as some around him. The Turks did much to force him to compromise his positions, as he himself admitted. At least one source, though Protestant and therefore likely to stress Catholic inclinations to violence, quoted him as saying that if he could defeat the Ottomans, he would reunite Christendom by the sword.[46] Yet, reasoned persuasion was so normal a part of his *modus operandi* in other affairs that one would be thoroughly justified in assuming it characterized his religious attitudes as well. Certainly there is much evidence to support such a conclusion.

To be sure, there were more overtly political reasons for Maximilian to look kindly upon Protestantism. The curia was actively pro-Philip in the imperial succession question, a policy which would have cooled the Habsburg toward the church of Rome even if there had been no alternatives that interested him. But the influence of his father's views in shaping his own should not be underestimated, especially when it was Ferdinand himself who brought to Vienna the man whom he later accused of being more responsible than anyone for his son's heterodoxy—a court preacher named Johannes Pfauser.[47]

On the recommendation of one Kaspar von Nidruck, a Netherlander who, though close to the strict Lutheran Matthias Flacius was a trusted diplomatic agent of Ferdinand's, the king invited the cleric to his capital in 1554. It was said that he was a good preacher. The fact alone that Pfauser had a wife and children should have made him suspect in Ferdinand's eyes, but either the Habsburg was unaware of this or he chose to ignore it. Pfauser's influence on the archduke was powerful and widely known. In 1555, Jan Blahoslav, the most prominent pastor of the Bohemian Brethren whom Ferdinand had all but scourged, came to Vienna in an effort to win the clergyman's sympathy for his coreligionists. Blahoslav believed that Maximilian had accepted Protestantism under Pfauser's tutelage and hoped that through the son, the father could be inclined more sympathetically to the Brethren. The archduke was indeed receptive to his cause, but claimed to have very little influence with his father who had become very bitter about his son's religious tastes.[48]

Pfauser's description of himself as neither Lutheran nor Catholic but treading a middle position was close to the ideas among many of Ferdinand's theological advisors, and his belief in a unified church was at one with the then king's. His sermons, however, stressed scriptural rather than conciliar and patristic authority, and he would have nothing to do with the veneration of saints. By 1555, he had become very popular, regularly drawing crowds to the *Augustinerkirche* who arrived two to three hours in advance of his homilies in order to get a place to hear him.[49] Ferdinand himself seems to have found nothing objectionable in his sermons, but as early as 1554, he was showing a close personal interest in the religious positions of those in Maximilian and Maria's household. Yet, because Maximilian's Protestant sympathies earned him some favor from that quarter in the Empire and Ferdinand did not want to lose it, he moved only slowly to persuade his son of his errors.[50]

A personal interview with Pfauser which he undertook in October 1555, did not go smoothly. The king told the cleric that he stressed faith far more than he did good works and took too strong a christological approach to the question of salvation. Ferdinand indicated that this would have to change. Pfauser refused, and Maximilian came to his defense, driving his father's wrath to a pitch which it rarely reached before others. He refused to continue the discussion when his son claimed that the veneration of saints was useless and idolatrous. However, he did not banish Pfauser from Vienna, allowing him to continue his sermons if he promised to uphold Catholic doctrine. He did have to leave the *Augustinerkirche,* directly adjacent to the *Hofburg,* but Maximilian found another church in the city for him. Ferdinand called upon Bishop Urban of Gurk to serve as his son's court preacher, but nothing had any impact on the archduke.[51]

Pfauser continued on in his customary vein, and Maxmilian's devotion to him continued as well. He regarded the Jesuits as "hypocrites, rascals, and blood-suckers (*Blutmenschen*)," and disputed with them publicly. Through him, Maxmilian got the idea that the order was keeping him from playing any role in Bohemia, where he was the heir-apparent, yet his brother Ferdinand continued on as governor. Ferdinand, of course, was an engaged partisan of the Jesuits, regarding them as the type of clergy needed to rescue the church from the depths into which it had fallen. He would be immensely pleased with the work of the college in Prague which he founded for them in 1556. Consistent with his belief that many of Rome's problems were educational, he was deeply interested in the new German catechism which Peter Canisius was preparing in the early 1550s. Yet, during the diet of Augsburg, while governing in his father's place in Vienna, Maxmilian held up the publication of the catechism, even though it contained an introduction by his father.[52]

Father and son clashed on other religious issues as well. In 1556, it was the question of the education of Maxmilian's children. Ferdinand wanted the Jesuits to supervise it, but Maximilian engaged a certain George Muschler, who taught at the university of Vienna and whose religious orientation was suspicious. Such policies on the part of their father made a Spanish upbringing of the two oldest boys, Rudolph and Ernst, all the more desirable, and they were eventually sent to the court of their second cousin.[53] In June 1557, Maximilian refused to participate publicly in the Ascension Day procession in Vienna. A couple of weeks later, despite his father's plea to the contrary, he did the same thing when asked to appear in the ceremony in Bratislava. He claimed to be ill; Ferdinand did not believe him and asked that he at least take a few steps with him in the march. Maximilian balked, citing conscience, and his father chose not to take part himself under such circumstances.[54] Maximilian's wife became so concerned at her husband's Protestant sympathies that she began to complain to her brother and sister in Spain. They, in turn, called upon Charles to do something from Yuste during the last weeks of his life. The former Emperor sent an envoy to the court of his son-in-law, though, happily for him, he died before he could hear that the mission had been fruitless. Since the archduke actually read theology, Ferdinand imported a Spanish theologian, a Master Gallo, who had made a favorable impression on Maximilian when he had been acting as his uncle's regent in that kingdom. He, too, met with no success.[55]

1558 also brought another interview between Ferdinand and Pfauser, if anything, more furious than the first. We know of this only through the clergyman's somewhat selfdramatizing testimony, but its tone was not wholly inconsistent with Ferdinand's character. Pfauser described him as beginning on a rather low key, urging the preacher not to persist in error and reminding the latter that many outstanding men had made mistakes, then corrected themselves. Pfauser held to his position, only to learn what one Venetian ambassador meant when he described Ferdinand as a man with a fierce desire to be respected. The Emperor grew much sharper, telling the cleric that he was neither learned nor well-born. When the latter still refused to acknowledge his failings, Ferdinand became genuinely abusive. Rattling on in German, Latin, and Italian, he cursed Pfauser, calling him a beast and a monster, and finally ended by spitting in his face with the comment that he would prefer hell with the church to heaven with Luther. Thinking that he had been dismissed, Pfauser moved toward the door but Ferdinand blocked it. Throughout the talk, the Emperor had fingered his dagger and now he clutched it, leading his opponent to think that he might be stabbed. Instead, Ferdinand pulled a sheet of paper from the breast of his tunic. The document contained some articles on religious matters which he asked Pfauser to comment on after reading them. When the latter said that they sounded more like Canisius than Ferdinand, who said he was the author, the Emperor was stung. He angrily accused Pfauser of thinking he did not know how to write, then sent him away. Still, he allowed him to stay on in Vienna.[56]

In Rome, Pius IV began to question the archduke's fitness to be a King of the Romans and future Emperor—with good reason. Meeting with Ferdinand at a diet in Augsburg in 1559, the Protestant estates asked their new Emperor to resign in favor of Maximilian. Ferdinand did his best to keep his disagreements with the archduke confined to religious matters—he was profusely apologetic to the younger man when some of his counselors opened private letters between the two of them— but he did begin to press him on theological issues almost daily. Now the Emperor began threatening his recalcitrant son with total disinheritance in favor of Archduke Ferdinand. Maximilian countered with a request that he be made formal ruler of Bohemia which brought forth a vigorous protest from his younger brother who was still serving as his father's governor in that kingdom. Trying to make remaining in the Catholic faith as attractive as possible, Ferdinand dangled the temptation of a Spanish inheritance before Maximilian's ambitious eyes, pointing out that Philip's only successor at the moment was the feeble Don Carlos. To ease the archduke's financial burdens, he bought the rights to Pardubice in Bohemia for him, which would produce an income of 25,000 gulden a year. To all this Maximilian replied that it did nothing for his conscience.[57]

Mindful of Pius's doubts, Ferdinand described his son as a good Catholic who had been misled by Pfauser. Late in the fall of 1559, he threatened to throw the troublesome clergyman into "the deepest well." Maximilian was so alarmed that he consented to his mentor's removal from his court. However, he thought that his father was persecuting him as well and resented it bitterly. Swearing to Pfauser that he would stay true to his faith, the archduke begged asylum from Elector Frederick of the Palatinate. Neither he nor other Protestant princes with whom the Habsburg communicated offered any help, however, and it was at this point his religious attitudes underwent a change.[58] Maximilian had already shown that he could subordinate religious to dynastic concerns. Representing his father at a meeting of the Austrian estates in 1556 to raise aid against the Turks, he had answered their request that he recognize Protestantism by telling them to worry first about giving him subsidies.[59] By 1561, as Ferdinand was making it clear that he would not work for his election in the Empire unless the archduke's religious beliefs satisfied him, the latter began to give way. In April of that year, he indicated that he would obey his father in worldly matters, but not where his soul was at issue. Even here, his reservations evaporated, with the exception of his desire to enjoy communion in both kinds.[60]

Here Ferdinand saw an area of satisfactory compromise, and, true to form, he began to explore it. He himself, especially after he became Emperor and envisioned himself as following in Charles's footsteps, liked no ritual innovations. However, he seemed to regard communion in both kinds as tolerable so long as it encouraged no further deviance. He was distressed to learn that communion had been celebrated *sub utraque* at the court of his son-in-law William of Cleves during Easter of 1558, but saw no reason to stop it completely so long as no more changes took place.[61]

He began formal negotiations with Pius on the matter in March 1560. By this time, Maximilian had not received communion in three years; he had asked his father's permission to take the chalice, to which Ferdinand had snapped that it was the pope's business, not his, to grant such a dispensation. He pleaded with Pius that Easter was coming and that without papal permission to commune *sub utraque,* the archduke might leave the Roman church altogether. When a papal emissary arrived in Vienna the next month, however, it was without any positive word from Pius on the matter. When the archduke heard of this, he responded in such a way that his father was sure he would formally convert to Protestantism.[62]

Fortunately for the Emperor, Pius's immediate problem was less with the substance of the request than its form. He had been unable to read Ferdinand's handwriting and had been reluctant to turn the letter over to someone who could for fear of breaking secrecy. In October 1561, therefore, Ferdinand sent along another petition, this time with a secretarial copy.[63] The dispensation had become a real matter of state as Ferdinand explained it. An election for a successor to the Hungarian throne was in the offing in which John Sigismund Zapolya, Isabella's son, now prince of Transylvania, was entering the competition. The Hungarian coronation ceremony called for public communion *sub uno* by the new king. Ferdinand had done everything to convince Maximilian to do this, but in vain. With the pope's permission, communion in both kinds would not be heretical. Once again he argued that if Maximilian were forced to disobey Rome in one area, he would do it in others as well. Conversely, if Pius cooperated, the archduke could be kept for his faith. Father and son continued to dispute well through the summer of 1561, forcing the former to defer a diet which he had called in Hungary until Maximilian's religious orientation was settled.[64]

Pius granted the dispensation in December 1561, under very generous terms. Ferdinand had requested it only for the Hungarian coronation; the pope allowed him to use it wherever his conscience saw fit. Hence, he first employed it with the Bohemian coronation in 1562. Not one to drive advantage beyond reason, he promised Pius that he would never use it promiscuously.[65] For his part, Maximilian grew ever closer to his father. In September 1561, he could promise that he would chose educational and clerical supervisors for his sons who were more orthodox in their religious preferences. Finally, in February of the next year, he swore before his father and his privy council and his brothers in Prague that he would not leave the church. This after he and his father had confronted one another for almost twenty straight days and listened to yet another friar.[66] His decision may well have been more a matter of resolution than of conviction as has been observed. But it was all that Ferdinand wanted. He moved swiftly to stage Maximilian's coronation as heir-apparent in Bohemia and Hungary and dropped his objections to his election as King of the Romans in the Empire. It was here that a clear statement of Maximilian's Catholic loyalties was especially important in winning the support of the electors of Mainz and Trier.[67]

For all Ferdinand's worry about Maximilian's religious leanings, he had done much to lay a foundation of good will among the princes on which the archduke's electoral campaign could be built. Indeed, he seemed bent upon a policy of repairing whatever bad feeling among the Germans he or his brother ever created from the moment he became Emperor. By 1559, with the Turks at bay in another truce and Spain and France at peace through the treaty of Cateau-Cambrésis, he felt the Empire was ready for pacification as well. Despite his unhappiness at Elector Frederick's introduction of Calvinism into the Palatinate, he made no effort to force his return to Lutheranism. At Passau in 1552, the Germans had asked that they not be governed by "foreigners," a euphemism for Spaniards. They repeated their request in 1555. Ferdinand finally responded in 1559, promising that the imperial court would be staffed with personnel drawn from Germany and Austria. To ensure internal peace, he encouraged the development of leagues that he and Charles had spoken of for so many years. The League of Landsberg was concerned with safety in the eastern part of the Empire, and a somewhat more limited counterpart came into being in the west through the elector of the Palatinate remained an important opponent of it.[68]

He did his best to harmonize his own need for a strong miitary presence against the Turks with German perceptions of what the could supply. At the diet in Augsburg in 1559, despite an unsuccessful bid for a standing committee of the estates to raise an emergency army in the Empire should he need it, he made no direct requests for aid. Not only did he feel that his truce with the Porte made such support unnecessary for the moment, but he also saw a need for the estates to recover from the burdens that had been placed upon them, particularly if he needed their help again.[69] In all of this, Ferdinand's growing identification with things German was of great help. While he was never the complete German ruler that Maximilian was, he was nevertheless far more sensitive to the princes' values than Charles had ever been and formulated his policies in terms of the impact which they would have have on them. This was true in small matters as well as large. In 1562, after Philip had suggested that one of Ferdinand's youngest daughters, either Johanna or Barbara, be married to the duke of Parma, the Emperor demurred, claiming that such a match would do little to increase his authority in Germany. Having discussed the arrangement with the girls and "other principal persons" in the Empire, he noted that the current duke was the son of a bastard and his mother actually was one. Such persons were looked down upon in Germany—indeed, Ferdinand said they were abhorrent—and the marriage of one of his children to such a mate would only scandalize the princes.[70]

He moved very cautiously into the electoral negotiations for his son, knowing well that he had promised at his own elevation in 1558 that the electors would have a free choice in naming his successor. The wisdom of his efforts to foster good relations with Spain once again became apparent as the elector of Trier stressed this as a condition of his support. Tentative and secret talks with those most sympathetic to the Habsburg cause, such as the elector of Brandenburg, began in 1561. Worried about the increasingly poor state of Ferdinand's health, others began to press him about the sucession, and the Protestants were very anxious to have the religious disposition of their future sovereign settled.[71]

All of this created a favorable climate for the archduke's election. Ferdinand arrived at Frankfurt for a meeting of the *Kurfürsten* where a decision would be taken in October 1562. Other princes and Maximilian drifted in with him.[72] He began his proposition to the electors by recalling for them what they had already said to him—that the Empire should not fall into an interregnum. He asked that they elect a King of the Romans to whom he could agree. Their talks were generally amiable, in part due to the courtesy and tact with which both Habsburgs conducted themselves. Ferdinand's reluctance to deal summarily with Maximilians's religious deviancy now justified itself; both Catholics and Protestants were at least temporarily convinced that their new ruler was a future defender of their persuasion. When news of Maximilian's election was brought to him, Ferdinand appeared before the electors and other members of the estates in the imperial jewels. As he came to the end of his address to the new King of the Romans, he was once more overwhelmed by tears.[73] He recovered quickly enough however, to accept the invitation of the elector Palatine to a local hunt. Two days of sport brought the party sixty-four swine of various sizes, sexes, and ages.[74]

The last hurdle for Maximilian was the attitude of the pope. Pius IV had grown somewhat more favorably disposed toward him since 1561 when rumor reached Rome that the Germans might elect a king without consulting eithter the pope or Emperor. Indeed, he agreed in principle to Maximilian's election when Ferdinand promised to send German bishops to the Council of Trent.[75] But Pius still wanted to examine Maximilian's fitness for the highest secular office in Christendom. The question of the precise need for a papal coronation, something Ferdinand himself had never received, stood open. For all his promises of obedience to Pius, Ferdinand had made no effort to arrange a papal crowning while arranging Maximilian's succession in Germany. A papal nuncio, Delfino, no opponent of the Habsburgs, did appear in Frankfurt, but Maximilian's election took place before his arrival. Thus, when Maximilian asked the pope to recognize his elevation, the latter asked to consider the matter further. When Martin Guzmán travelled to Rome to get the confirmation in December 1562, Pius indicated that he wanted some greater assurance of loyalty from the king. In March 1563, he asked Maximilian for such a declaration both publicly and in writing.[76]

Ferdinand now leaped to the defense of his son. The next month he replied that there was no precedent for such a request and that a simple

written declaration of fidelity would do. He put off his own coronation
to another time, even though Pius invited him to Bologna for it. In general, he now found Maximilian to be thoroughly "reasonable." The latter
volunteered a written guarantee of his loyalty and assured the pope that
he would do for him what his father and uncle had done.[77]

In this situation, Philip once agains did good service for the Austrian
branch of his house. Anxious that his counsin's stature be respected both
within and outside of the Empire, he wanted to see Maximilian firmly
within the bonds of the church of Rome. As he put it, the negotiations
were fraught with implications ". . . for our posterity . . . ;" he set about
trying to win Pius to his uncle and Maximilian's way of thinking. At the
same time, Ferdinand took the opportunity to pressure his son to adopt
even more orthodox religious postures, a development which delighted
the king of Spain. Ferdinand was deeply grateful for his nephew's help,
especially when by September 1563, Philip had succeeded. On 24 December 1563, Maximilian committed his profession of loyalty to paper.[78]

1562 and 1563 were election and coronation years for the Habsburg
heir—Prague in 1562 and Bratislava, where the Hungarian ceremony
took place on September 8, 1563. Neither of these rites went as smoothly as the imperial election. An outbreak of plague somewhat dampened
the Bohemian festivities, and despite efforts to separate the German,
Bohemian, and Hungarian retinues in Bratislava to avoid fighting among
them, some incidents did occur.[79] But Ferdinand had long since accustomed himself to the imperfections of life. And he had much in which
he could rejoice. The most immediate dynastic goal which he had set
for himself—assurance of a Habsburg succession from his line in the two
eastern kingdoms and in the Empire—had been reached. The catastrophe
of an apostasy to Protestantism had been averted. And Maximilian himself seemed more reconciled to him. A few months before his coronation
in Prague, the younger man had thanked Ferdinand for the "fatherly"
way he had treated him and for the burdens which he had shouldered
for his sake.[80] Under the circumstances, as the Emperor would have said,
he could have hardly asked much more.

CHAPTER XVI

AN END AND AN EVALUATION

As late as the middle of the 1550s, there were those who believed that Ferdinand might outlive all his sons.[1] Maximilian had already fallen prey to some of the many illnesses which were to plague him throughout his life; Charles, in general, did not seem robust; and Archduke Ferdinand denied his fleshly appetites only with the greatest difficulty. Their father, on the other hand, had been remarkably free of physical ailments, and gave no sign of abandoning the valetudinarian ways that undoubtedly contributed to his well-being.

But Ferdinand had put uncommon strains upon his body in a lifetime of hectic activity; under such pressures, even the best-endowed of instruments breaks down. With him it began around 1560, when he began to suffer from recurring and long-lasting fevers. Always small, he grew markedly thinner. Repeated bouts of coughing also tormented him. His physicians were baffled and feared for his life. Despite periodic improvements, punctuated with bursts of vigorous activity, especially after the crowning of Maximilian in Bohemia early in 1563, it was clear to others and himself that these remissions were only temporary.[2] In April 1564, he made his oldest son his regent; the following month he confessed that he had been very tired for some time and was not exceedingly weak.[3]

By this time he was bed-ridden and prepared to die. To those who inquired about his health, he replied that he was as well as God allowed. Augustine was read to him regularly, and Maximilian, who cared for him in exemplary fashion, made sure that chamber musicians played for him every day. To the end, his territorial identity stretched the length and breadth of Europe. Apparently mindful of his creative role in the eastern part of the continent, he hoped, vainly, to die on Whitsuntide as had Constantine the Great. But he chose the name of St. James, the apostle to Spain, as the one he wished to have on his lips as he expired. Crisis and death came on the night of July 25. There was no struggle; he had wasted away to the point where he simply seemed to flicker into nothingness, " . . . wie ein Lichtl aus einem Laterndl. . . "[4] in Maximilian's gentle diminutives. As Ferdinand ordered, his coffin went to Prague where he was interred alongside Anna.

The obituary assessments of his family and other conformed nicely to his estimates of himself. Even before Ferdinand died, Elector Frederick of the Palatine, who had had many disagreements with his king and Emperor, had been sincerely saddened at reports of the Habsburg's weakness. While he looked forward to Maximilian as his new ruler, he called Ferdinand the man responsible for the present peace in Germany. Margaret of Parma echoed the sentiments about her uncle's contributions to peace and praised his steadfast Catholicism.[5]

Ferdinand was no pacifist as his calculated promotion of the Schmalkaldic War and his readiness to mount offensives in Hungary against Zapolya, if it seemed advantageous to do so, plainly show. The decorative trappings of war—armour, weaponry and the like—were among his greatest delights. For all that, however, he took little positive pleasure in military campaigning and strategy. That, combined with his talent and taste for reasoned negotiation and his ability to formulate compromises made him a man of peace by sixteenth-century standards as well as his own. During the 1550s, Charles and Philip had criticized Ferdinand's Catholicism on political grounds; Maxmilian seemed near to rejecting it, at least partially for religious reasons; one pope broke off relations with him altogether. Yet, in the end, nephew and papacy came to respect the depth of his confessional commitment, and the son swore practical, if unenthusiastic, allegiance to it. Ferdinand, by contrast, made very few adjustments in his own beliefs. His willingness to permit communion *sub utraque* both in his family and in some of his lands was perhaps the most important exception, but he was very careful to have the permission of Rome before taking such steps. Such an attitude may have been no test of orthodoxy, though there was very little about Ferdinand's religious beliefs that was not orthodox. It was certainly a testimonial to the depth and consistency of his faith, and it was these qualities that impressed contemporaries.

The reactions of his sons and nephew, the king of Spain, would have gladdened him even more. The effort he had spent keeping the Austrian and Spanish branches of his house on good terms gave every sign of bearing long-lasting fruit. Philip spoke of the great love his uncle had shown him and expressed the hope that he would enjoy similar relations with Maximilian. He instructed his representative in Vienna to call upon all three of the dead Emperor's sons. Maximilian was to hear how much his father had done for " . . . our houses, which is all one . . . . " Writing in response to his cousin's condolences, Archduke Ferdinand spoke of " . . . the bond of blood . . . " which united them all.[6]

None of Ferdinand's sons could have rejoiced in the burden of debt he left them. When the three archdukes divided these in May 1565, they totalled 7,604,277 gulden. But he had land and the offices associated with them to bequeath to each of the young men, and none among them would undergo the uncertainties and even humiliation their father had suffered in laying claim to them. Seen as a way of preserving princely rule in one house, the dynastic system had worked handsomely for Ferdinand's sons.

Just how well it worked for their father, its stubborn defender and practicioner, is a more complex question. Clearly it was only through his relationship to Maximilian I and the latter's proprietary right to divide the Habsburg patrimony as he wished that Ferdinand received his foothold in the Austrian lands. But in his expansion of his family's territories to the east, dynastic prerogatives were less useful to him. It was not through the windfalls of marriage contracts, as the old adage has it, that *felix Austria* acquired much of its empire. Rather it was Ferdinand's willingness to pay and, at crucial moments to fight, that legitimized the new dynasty in Bohemia and especially Hungary. If there was any aspect of dynastic connections that made him a respected figure in his new kingdoms, it was his relationship to his Emperor-brother rather than any formal mechanisms of hereditary. In Bohemia, it was only with Charles's help that Ferdinand could tighten his hold on that realm to the point where the succession, while something less than hereditary, was regularized within his family.

Thus, as a way of realizing territorial claims, dynastic prerogatives were of only limited effectiveness in Ferdinand's case—usable where the house of Habsburg had enjoyed a long-term presence, much less so where it was establishing itself in altogether new terrain. As a system of mutual support, Ferdinand was also to find that dynastic connections left much to be desired. For all their professions of family loyalty, and

occasional displays of it, the Habsburg siblings were ruled by the territorial and military imperatives of their own lands far more than by concern for one another. The awesome extent of the sixteenth century
Habsburg land mass should never be read as a sign that local or regional
interests had lost their force. The Mediterranean and Atlantic preoccupations of the king of Spain and duke of Burgundy were not those of
the ruling archduke of Austria and king of Hungary and Bohemia, even
though the two holders of those offices were brothers. For Ferdinand
and Charles to have been the masters of a truly pan-European power,
both would have had to introduce a far greater centralization of political procedures and more careful allotment of resources than either was prepared or willing to do. Even if either man would have accepted limitations on his expenditures defined by something other than his own desires,
each faced diverse military, political, and religious challenges which made
coordinated policies all but impossible. Ferdinand quickly discovered
this at the regional level. He saw very early that geographic contiguity
and individual weakness had linked Austria, Bohemia and Hungary together against the Turks. But his bureaucratic reforms, the practical
expression of that common fate, while long-lasting, were imperfect, due
largely to the pressures which moved him to rationalize his government.
Regardless of his theoretical objections to the process, he was always
willing to go from diet to diet begging aid if the alternative was to be
overrun by the Ottoman armies. Nor did his visions of political reorganization reach beyond the traditional confines of court and estates to
society at large—necessary if he were to make maximum use of the liquid
capital available even in the less than burgeoning economies over which
he presided. For all his complaints about the venality of the Hungarian
nobility, he accomodated their demands within the framework of his
own ambition. The same thing was true in Bohemia. Even as he moved
against the estates there, he did not end their privileges, merely curbed
them.

But for all the weak points in the Habsburg dynastic network as a
system of inter-territorial cooperation, it had served Ferdinand well.
One need only ask what he would have been without it. He would have
been neither a reigning prince in Austria nor a King of the Romans without his brother nor his Habsburg grandfather whose will had mandated
a division of the family's holdings. While Charles's military aid was erratic,

it was potentially the mightiest that Europe could muster. If one lived on the edge of catastrophe as often as Ferdinand did, or thought he did, one fostered such relationships regardless of their inconsistent results. For all the grief that the Spanish branch of his house brought him as he attempted to entrench himself and his sons in central Europe, Ferdinand owed at least part of his success to the general good will of his brother and nephew. One need only look at the career of Maximilian I, who fought wars all over the continent to protect Habsburg interests, to see how advantageous it was to have two fully established branches of the house to tie down potential and actual enemies. While the Turks and the French never gave up their expansionary goals out of fear that Charles and Ferdinand might combine forces, the possibility certainly limited their ambitions. As the weaker of the two brothers by far, Ferdinand certainly profited the most from this situation.

Ferdinand was a master of marshalling all the supportive techniques through which dynastic government renewed and reinforced itself to his own best advantage. The marriages of many of his children gave him access to some of the key houses of central and eastern Europe as well as Italy. When conflict arose among the Habsburgs themselves over the imperial succession, it was Ferdinand who recognized that the ineradicable ties of blood and family religious solidarity would facilitate the work of mending some very nasty wounds. His success depended in part upon the interests and personal qualities that he and Philip II shared, but also on their common ancestry which kept open channnels of communication which might otherwise have been impenetrably blocked. That he had to do this in order to realize his own aims was starkly demonstrated when the German Catholic princes asked for reassurances about Maximilian's relationship with his Spanish cousin before supporting him as King of the Romans.

Ferdinand also understood how to make use of the penalty structure that went along with the rewards of the dynastic system. His true political goal was to keep under control the offices and titles he had won and to insure that his offspring enjoyed them as well. The ties to Spain and good relations with Rome were key instruments in fulfilling this scheme. Thus, when his eldest son differed with him in both policies, his most deeply held ambitions were jeopardized. Like Ferdinand with both his grandfather and his brother, however, Maximilian was made to realize how much of his own purposes depended upon his father's support. It was only after Ferdinand threatened not to work for the archduke's succession in the Empire that the latter rejoined the political and confessional mainstream of his house.

On balance, the house of Austria and its organization had done as much for Ferdinand as he had done for it. His paternal grandfather had delivered him from the limbo of a younger brother of the king of Spain into the role of a territorial ruler. His relationship with Charles had turned him from one among many candidates for the Hungarian and Bohemian crowns into the preferred one. That same connection with the Emperor and then, with Philip had not kept the Turks out of east central Europe, but it had always made the sultan think twice before coming, a significant advantage when one realizes how strained Ferdinand's regular resources were. The system had not worked perfectly for him, but it had functioned effectively in many crucial moments. He had not asked much more of it than that.

NOTES

Notes to Introduction

1. Wolfgang Hilger, *Ikonographie Kaiser Ferdinands I (1503-1564)*, Veröffentlichung der Kommission für Geschichte Österreichs, 3(1969), pp. 124-125 and Tables 25, no. 56; 26, no. 15; 27, no. 85. Pp. 133-140 contains a collection of ambassadorial reports about Ferdinand's person.

2. Ibid., pp. 125-126; Karl Brandi, *Kaiser Karl V. Werden und Schicksal einer Persönlichkeit und eines Weltreiches*, 2 vols. (3rd ed.: Munich: Bruckmann, 1948), 1: 481.

3. August von Kluckhohn, et al., eds., *Deutsche Reichstagsakten, Jüngere Reihe*, 5 vols. (Gotha: Perthes, 1893-1905), 4: 637; Ferdinand to Maximilian, Dec. 27, 1557, Vienna, Haus- Hof-und Staatsarchiv [hereafter called "SA"], *Familienkorrespondenz A*, Karton 2, fo. 136; Ferdinand to Mary, Feb. 22, 1530, *Die Korrespondenz Ferdinands I*, [hereafter called "Korrespondenz"], 3 vols., Veröffentlichungen der Kommission für neuere Geschichte Österreichs, vols. 11, 30-31, 58, eds. Wilhelm Bauer, Robert Lacroix, Christiane Thomas, Herwig Wolfram (Vienna: Holzhausen, 1912-1977, 2^2: 606; Ferdinand to Philip II, July 7, 1563, Archivo General de Simancas [hereafter called "AG"], Secretaria de Estado, *Negociación de Alemania* [hereafter called "Estado, Alemania"], Legajo 652, fo. 30.

4. Wilhelm Bauer, *Die Anfänge Ferdinands I* (Vienna/Leipzig: Braumüller, 1907), pp. 51, 103; James Brodrick, S.J., *Saint Peter Canisius S.J. 1521-1597* (London: Sheed and Ward, 1935), p. 169.

5. Juan Vasquez de Molina to Charles V, Jan. 26, 1557 (copy), Brussels, Archives Générales du Royaume [hereafter called "AGR"], *Manuscrits divers*, 805 A/I, fos. 165-166; Charles to Mary, Jan. 16, 1557, ibid., fo. 149.

6. Ferdinand to Charles, June 13, 1538, SA, *Handschriften, Blau* [hereafter called "Blau"], 597/1, p. 103; Kurt Löcher, *Jakob Seisenegger, Hofmaler Kaiser Ferdinands I* (Munich: Deutscher Kunstverlag, 1962), p.

15; Alfred Stern, "Gabriel Salamanca Graf von Ortenburg," *HZ*, 131 (1925): 33-34; Bauer, *Anfänge*, p. 166.

7. Ferdinand's Instructions to Licenciado Gomez, Oct. 16, 1556 (copy), AGR, *Manuscrits divers,* 805 A/II, fos. 122-123. These folios also carry the alternate numbering, 143-144.

8. Paula Sutter Fichtner, "Of Christian Virtue and a Practicing Prince," *The Catholic Historical Review,* 61 (1975): 413-416; Bernice Hamilton, *Political Thought in Sixteenth Century Spain: A Study of the Political Ideas of Vitoria, Soto, Suárez, and Molina* (Oxford: Clarendon, 1963), p. 67; Ferdinand's Instructions to Chantonnay, July 26, 1549, *Blau,* 597/2, fo. 311.

9. Ferdinand's Instructions to Henri de Hemricourt and Martin de Salinas for Charles, Nov., 1522, *Korrespondenz,* 1: 22-23. On the meaning of the terms "natural" and "rational" especially in sixteenth century Spanish political thought, see Hamilton, *Political Thought,* pp. 11, 13. Also, Ferdinand to Charles, Sept. 7, 1555, *Estado, Alemania,* Legajo 649, fo. 43.

10. " . . . pro dobré /sic/ naše i království tohoto . . . . " Ferdinand to Jan of Pernštejn and Jan Trck, Oct. 25, 1546, *Archiv český, 37 vols.* (Prague: Řiwnáč, 1840-1944), 20: 246; Ferdinand to Jan of Pernštejn, April 17, 1547, ibid., p. 254.

11. Ferdinand's Instructions to Charles de Bredam for Charles V, June 13, 1524, *Korrespondenz,* 1: 170; Ferdinand's Instructions to Joachim de Rye for Charles V, March 11, 1552, Karl Lanz, ed., *Corres- pondenz des Kaisers Karl V [* hereafter called "Lanz, Correspondenz" *],* 3 vols. (Leipzig: Brockhaus, 1844-1846), 3: 124; Ferdinand to Maurice of Saxony, Feb. 12 1552, August von Druffel, ed., *Beiträge zur Reichs- geschichte 1546-1551* [hereafter called "Druffel, Beiträge], Briefe und Akten zur Geschichte des sechzehnten Jahrhunderts, 4 vols. (Munich: Rieger, 1873-1896), 2: 115; Ferdinand's instructions for Martin Guzmán to Charles V, March 3, 1553, Lanz, *Correspondenz,* 3: 550.

12. Gerhard Rill, "Humanismus und Diplomatie: zur Geschichte des Gesandtenwesens unter Ferdinand I.," *MöSA,* 25 (1972): 570-571.

13. Berthold Sutter, introduction to Franz Bernhard von Bucholtz, *Geschichte der Regierung Ferdinands I* [hereafter called "Sutter, intro."], 9 vols. (rpt.;Graz: Akademische Druck-und Verlagsansalt, 1971), 1: 58-59.

14. Ibid., p. 55; Bauer, *Anfänge,* p. 181; Louis II of Hungary to Ferd- inand, Dec. 10, 1522, *Korrespondenz,* 1: 34.

15. Ferdinand to Mary, July 27, 1549, Druffel, *Beiträge*, 1: 268; Ferdinand to Charles, Jan. 27, 1523, *Korrespondenz*, 1: 38; Ferdinand to Charles, Nov. 5, 1524, ibid., p. 106. Also, Lutz Hatzfeld, "Staatsräson und Reputation bie Kaiser Karl V.," *Zeitschrift für Religions-und Geistesgeschichte*, 11 (1959): 35, 46.

16. Ferdinand to Charles, July 7, 1536, *Blau*, 597/1, p. 224; Ferdinand to Charles, Oct. 19, 1544, ibid., 597/2, fos. 125-126.

17. Ferdinand to Charles, June 8, 1552, Lanz, *Correspondenz*, 3: 257; Ferdinand's Instructions to Joachim de Rye for Charles, March 11, 1552, ibid., p. 122.

18. Ferdinand to Charles, Dec. 20, 1537, *Blau*, 597/1: 276; Ferdinand to Charles, Feb. 6, 1538, ibid., p. 283; Ferdinand to Charles, April 6, 1538, ibid., p. 290.

19. Löcher, *Seisenegger*, p. 15.

20. Ferdinand to Maria, Aug. 8, 1527, *Korrespondenz*, 2^1: 105; Ludwig Köchl, *Die kaiserliche Hof-musikkapelle in Wien von 1543 bis 1867* (Vienna: Beck, 1869), pp. 8, 106, 111; Albert Smijers, "Die kaiserliche Hofmusikkapelle von 1543-1619," *Studien zur Musikwissenschaft*, 6 (1919): 139, 143.

R. J. W. Evans, *Rudolf II and His World. A Study in Intellectual History 1576-1612*, (Oxford: Clarendon, 1973), p. 165; Bruno Thomas, "Harnischstudien, III. Stilgeschichte des deutschen Harnisches von 1530 bis 1560," *Jahrbuch des kunsthistorischen Sammlungen in Wien*, N.F., 12 (1938): 175-202.

22. Erich Egg, "Der deutsche König und die neue Kunst. Ferdinand I. der Begrunder der österreichischen Kultur," *Alte und moderne Kunst*, 6, no. 46 (1961): 18-20.

23. Bauer, *Anfänge*, pp. 101-102; Josef Strelka, *Der burgundische Renaissancehof Margarethes von Österreich und seine literarhistorische Bedeutung* (Vienna: Sexl, 1957), pp. 107, 119-120, 123; Joseph von Aschbach, *Geschichte der Wiener Universität*, 3 vols. (repr.: 1 Westmead, Farnborough Hunts., Gregg Press, 1967), 3: 310-311, 335-346; Günther Stökl, "Kaiser Ferdinand I." in *Gestalter der Geschicke Österreichs*, ed., Hugo Hantsch, Studien der wiener katholischen Akademie, 2 (Innsbruck/ Vienna, 1962), pp. 131-132; Fredrich Heer, *Die dritte Kraft. Der europäische Humanismus zwischen den Fronten der konfessionellen Zeitalter* (Frankfurt a. M.: Fischer, 1959), pp. 130, 314, 428; Paula Sutter Fichtner, "The Disobedience of the Obedient. Ferdinand I and the Papacy, 1555-

1564," *The Sixteenth Century Journal*, 11 (1980): 26-27.

24. Hilger, *Ikonographie*, p. 139; Ferdinand to Charles, April 2, 1539, *Blau*, 597/1, pp. 348-349; Ferdinand to Charles, May 16, 1543, ibid., 597/ 2, fo. 88.

25. William Bousma, *Concordia Mundi: the Career and Thought of Guillaume Postel 1510-1581* (Cambridge, Mass.: Harvard, 1957), pp. 6-7, 13-15, 20-21; Jan Kvačala, "Wilhelm Postell, seine Geistesart und seine Reformgedanken," *ARG*, 9 (1911-1912): 224, 226, and 15 (1918); 157-158, Peter Canisius to Ioanni de Polanco, S.J., Jan. 5, 1554, *Beati Petri Canisii Societatis Jesu, Epistolae et Acta*, ed. Otto Braunsberger, 8 vols. (Freiburg i.B.: Herder, 1896-1923), 1: 449-450.

26. Ferdinand to Charles, Nov. 4, 1531, *Korrespondenz*, 3^2: 361-362.

27. J. H. Elliot, *The Old World and the New 1492-1650* (Cambridge: Cambridge University Press, 1970), p. 17; John M. Headley, "The Habsburg World Empire and the Revival of Ghibellinism," *Medieval and Renaissance Studies*, 7 (1978): 114.

28. Hilger, *Ikonographie*, pp. 125, 138; Bauer, *Anfänge*, pp. 102-103; Ferdinand's Instructions to Martin de Salinas for Charles V, April 2, 1525, *Korrespondenz*, 1: 289; Ferdinand to Charles, May 26, 1540, *Blau*, 597/1, pp. 393-394.

29. Alphons Lhotsky, *Die Geschichte der Sammlungen*, Festschrift des kunsthistorischen Museums zur Feier des fünfzigjährigen Bestandes, 2 vols. (Vienna: Berger, 1941-1945), 2^1: 142, 154.

30. Helmut Goetz, "Die geheimen Ratgeber Ferdinands I. (1503-1564). Ihre Persönlichkeit im Urteil der Nuntien und Gesandten," *QuF*, 42/43 (1963): 462, 476, 483-485, 488.

31. Ferdinand to Charles, Feb. 26, 1545, *Blau*, 597/2, fo. 136.

32. Karl Oberleitner, ed., "König Ferdinand's Instruction an Marx Treitssauerwein wegen Fortsetzung der Herausgabe des Weisskunigs, Theuerdank's, der Ehrenporte, der Genealogie des österreichischen Kaiserhauses und der Schriften Stabius," *Beilage zum Archiv für Kunde österreichischer Geschichte. Notizenblatt*, 8(1858): 286-288.

33. Sutter, intro., p. 131; Karl Brandi, "Berichte und Studien zur Geschichte Karls V.," pt. 2, *Nachrichten von der Gesellschaft der Wissenschaften zu Göttingen*, Phil.-hist. Klasse, nos. 3-4 (1930): 272.

34. Ferdinand to Mary, July 4, 1534, Bucholtz, *Regierung*, 5: 113.

35. For a representative sample of family correspondence on this matter see *Estado, Alemania*, Legajo 649.

36. David Hunt, *Parents and Children in History: the Psychology of Family Life in Early Modern France* (New York: Harper Torchbook, 1972), pp. 149, 154-155.

37. E.g., Charles to Ferdinand, Feb. 15, 1516, *Korrespondenz,* 1: 4; Ferdinand to Charles, Aug. 10, 1552, Lanz, *Correspondenz,* 3: 447; Ferdinand to Charles, Aug. 20, 1555, ibid., p. 676; Hilger, *Ikonographie,* p. 137.

38. Ferdinand to Charles, Oct. 22, 1538, *Blau,* 597/1: 327; Ferdinand to Charles, Aug. 10, 1552, Lanz, *Correspondenz,* 3: 447; Ferdinand to Charles, Sept. 26, 1555, ibid., p. 687.

39. Charles's Instructions to Joachim de Rye for Ferdinand, Mar. 3, 1552, Lanz, *Correspondenz,* 3: 98-99; Ferdinand's Instructions to Joachim de Rye for Charles, Mar. 11, 1552, ibid., p. 118.

40. Bucholtz, *Regierung,* 7: 198; Ferdinand to Charles, April 27, 1536, *Blau,* 597/1: 202-203.

41. Ferdinand to Charles, Nov. 9, 1546, *Blau,* 597/2, fo. 192; Ferdinand to Charles, Nov. 29, 1546, ibid., fo. 194.

42. Ferdinand to Charles, May 22, 1556, Lanz, *Correspondenz,* 3: 702; Ferdinand to Mary, July 4, 1534, Bucholtz, *Regierung,* 5: 113.

43. Ferdinand to Charles, June 27, 1552, Lanz, *Correspondenz,* 3: 303; Ferdinand to Maximilian, June 15, 1559 (?), SA, *Familienkorrespondenz,* A, Karton 2, fo. 170.

44. Druffel, *Beiträge,* 1: 669-670.

45. Ferdinand to Charles, Sept. 1, 1525, *Korrespondenz,* 1: 326.

46. Ferdinand to Maurice of Saxony, Apr. 1, 1552, Lanz, *Correspondenz,* 3: 152; Bucholtz, *Regierung,* 7: 198.

47. Paula Sutter Fichtner, "Dynastic Marriage in Sixteenth-Century Habsburg Diplomacy and Statecraft: an Interdisciplinary Approach," *American Historical Review,* 81 (1976): 243-265.

48. Alfons Huber, "Die Erwerbung Siebenbürgens durch Ferdinand I. im Jahre 1551 u. Bruder Georgs Ende," AöG, 75 (1889): 508-509; Count de Luna to Philip II, Nov. 15, 1560, *Colección de documentos inéditos para la historia de espava,* 112 vols. (rpt.: Vaduz: Kraus, 1966), 98: 257-258: Instructions of Gonsalez Perez to Mos de Yerge, Jan. 19, 1564, *AG, Estado, Alemania,* Legajo 652, fo. 191.

49. Ferdinand to Philip II, Nov. 19, 1562, *Documentos inéditos,* 98: 337.

50. Ferdinand to Charles, March 24, 1552, *Blau,* 597/3, fo. 209; Ferdinand to Charles, Apr. 27, 1552, ibid., fo. 216.

51. Ferdinand to Charles, July 2, 1552, Lanz, *Correspondenz,* 3: 341.

Notes to Chapter I

1. Maximilian to Margaret, Jan. 1, 1516, *Correspondance de l' empreur Maximilien Ièr et de Marguerite d'Autriche,* ed. M. le Glay, 2 vols. (Paris: Renouard, 1839), 2: 335-338.

2. Brandi, *Karl V,* 1: 43-50, *passim.*

3. Bauer, *Anfänge,* p. 11; Sutter, intro., p. 21.

4. Bauer, *Anfänge,* pp. 17, 50-51; Hilger, *Ikonographie,* p. 198.

5. Bauer, *Anfänge,* p. 45; Theodor B. Kassowitz, *Die Reformvorschläge Kaiser Ferdinands I auf dem Konzil von Trient* (Vienna/Leipzig: Braumüller, 1906), pp. 7-8.

6. Ferdinand of Aragon to his ambassador to Maximilian, Sept. 22, 1513, AG, *Patronato Real,* Legajo 16, fo. 22; Ferdinand of Aragon to Maximilian, 1513?, ibid., Legajo 53, fo. 82; Ferdinand of Aragon's Instructions to Don Pedro Urrea, n.d., *Estado, Alemania,* Legajo 635, fo. 19; Ferdinand of Aragon's Instructions to Juan de Luca for Maximilian, AG, *Estado, Flandes,* Legajo 496, fos. 39, 41, 44-45. Cf. Sutter, intro., p. 22. See also Erich König, "Zur Hauspolitik Maximilians I. in den Jahren 1516 und 1517," in *Festgabe Hermann Grauert zur Vollendung des 60. Lebensjahres* (Freiburg i. B.: Herder, 1910), p. 201.

7. König, "Hauspolitik," p. 202; Oswald Redlich, "Die Pläne einer Erhebung Österreichs zum Königreich," *Zeitschrift des historischen Vereins für Steiermark,* 26 (1931): 94-99; Bauer, *Anfänge,* p. 24.

8. Bauer, *Anfänge,* pp. 40, 69-70.

9. Gustav Turba, *Geschichte des Thronfolgerechts in allen habsburgischen Ländern bis zur pragmatischen Sanktion Karls VI* (Vienna/Leipzig: Fromme, 1903), p. 157, note 4; Bucholtz, *Regierung,* 1: 63-64, 67.

10. Charles to Ferdinand, Feb. 15, 1516, *Korrespondenz,* 1:4; Charles to Ferdinand, Sept. 17, 1517, ibid., p. 7; Memorandum of the Bishop of Badajoz to the Cardinal [Cisneros] of Spain, March 8, 1516 (copy), AGR, *Manuscrits divers,* 175 Abis, fo. 12.

11. Brandi, *Karl V,* 1: 70; Sutter, intro., p. 28.

12. Sutter, intro., pp. 25, 28; Hermann Baumgarten, *Geschichte Kaiser Karls V,* 3 vols. (Stuttgart: Cotta, 1885), 1: 77-78; Bauer, *Anfänge,* pp. 57-59; Brandi, *Karl V,* 1: 116.

13. Laurent Vital, "Premier voyage de Charles-Quint en Espagne de 1517 à 1518," *Collection des voyages des souverains des Pays Bas,* 4 vols. (Brussels: Hayez, 1874-1882), 3: 272, 282.

14. Baumgarten, *Karl V,* 1: 135, note; Alfons Huber, *Geschichte Österreichs,* 7 vols. (Gotha: Perthes, 1885-1938), 3: 482; Georg Kirchmair, *Georg Kirchmairs Denkwürdigkeiten 1519-1553,* ed., Theodor von Karajan, Fontes Rerum Austriacarum, Scriptores, 1^1 (1885): 451.

15. Baumgarten, *Karl V,* 1: 135-139; Bauer, *Anfänge,* pp. 75-76; Headley, "Ghibbelinism," pp. 97-98.

16. Alphons Lhotsky, *Das Zeitalter des Hauses Österreich. Die ersten Jahre der Regierung Ferdinands I (1520-1527)* (Vienna/Cologne/Graz: Böhlaus, 1917), p. 72.

17. SA, *Haus-Archiv, Familien-Akten,* Karton 97, fo. 4.

18. Charles to Ferdinand, March 5, 1519, *Korrespondenz,* 1:11; Bauer, *Anfänge,* pp. 76-77.

19. Bauer, *Anfänge,* pp. 46, 87-89, 113; Antonín Rezek, "Zur Kaiserwahl 1519," *Forschungen zur deutschen Geschichte,* 23 (1883): 342; X. Liske, "Der Congress zu Wien im Jahre 1515," ibid., 7 (1867): 503.

20. Turba, *Thronfolgerecht,* p. 159. I am using the modern terminology for these areas. What is today called Lower Austria (*Niederösterreich*) was in the sixteenth century known as "Österreich unter der Enns." At that time "Niederösterreich" included not only the present province of that name but also modern Upper Austria ("Österreich ob der Enns" in the sixteenth century), Styria, Carinthia, and Carniola. Each of these territories had their own estates. "Oberösterreich" or Upper Austria in the sixteenth century referred to the Tyrol along with "Vorderösterreich" which encompassed Habsburg holdings and protectorates in Switzerland and southwest Germany. See Eduard Rosenthal, "Die Behördeorganisation Kaiser Ferdinands I. Das Vorbild der Verwaltungsorganisation in den deutschen Territorien," *AöG,* 69 (1887): 65, note 1.

21. Hans Pirchegger, *Geschichte und Kulturleben Deutschösterreichs von 1526 bis 1792* (Vienna/Leipzig: Braumüller, 1931), p. 2; Huber, *Geschichte Österreichs,* 3: 490-491; Bauer, *Anfänge,* pp. 44, 151; Bucholtz, *Regierung,* 1: 159.

22.   Lhotsky, *Haus Österreich*, p. 117.

23.   Baumgarten, *Karl V*, 2: 112; Turba, *Thronfolgerecht*, p. 161.

24.   Ferdinand to Charles, Jan. 28, 1530, *Korrespondenz*, 2^2: 584-585.

25.   Gerda Koller, "Die Hochzeit Ferdinands I in Linz," *Linz aktiv*, 24 (1967): 23, 25; Ferdinand to Margaret, July 12, 1526, *Korrespondenz*, 1: 399-400; Ferdinand to Maria, Oct. 15, 1529, ibid., 2^2: 521-522; Ferdinand to Maria, 21 Jan. 1530, ibid., p. 574.

26.   Sutter, intro., p. 52.

27.   Koller, "Hochzeit," pp. 23-24.

28.   Aschbach, *Wiener Universität*, 3:5.

29.   Karl Oberleitner, "Österreichische Finanzen und Kriegswesen unter Ferdinand I 1522-1564," *AöG*, 22 (1860): 13-14. The following coinages and equivalencies were current in sixteenth century central Europe:

5 rhenish florins = 5 1/3 imperial gulden

4 Hungarian gulden = 5 1/3 imperial gulden

1 Bohemian groschen = 2 1/2 imperial gulden

1 ducat = 1 2/3 imperial gulden

The *Pfund* or pound was considered to have the same value as the imperial gulden in Vienna. Bohemian groschen were sometimes measured in units of sixty called *kop* (Germ. *Schock*). See Alphons Huber, "Studien über die finanziellen Verhältnisse Österreichs unter Ferdinand I.," *MIöG*, Ergänzungsband 4 (1893): 188, note 1, 199, 201, 212, 218. See also Huber, *Geschichte Österreichs*, 3: 493; Bauer, *Anfänge*, pp. 220-221; Karl Eder, *Das Land ob der Enns vor der Glaubensspaltung*, Studien zur Reformationsgeschichte Oberösterreichs, 2 vols. (Linz: Im Buchlanden, 1932-1936), 1: 45.

30.   Michael Mayr, "Der Generallandtag der österreichischen Erbländer zu Augsburg (December 1525 bis März 1526)," *Zeitschrift des Ferdinandeums*, 38 (1893/1894): 24; Kirchmair, *Denkwürdigkeiten*, p. 433. It was estimated at the diet of Nürnber 2 in 1522 that it would cost one gulden a day to keep a driver and four wagon horses. An average wage for an artisan in central Europe was considered to be six gulden for thirty days. See *Reichstagsakten*, Jüngere Reihe, 3: 111, 115.

31.   Paul W. Roth, "Münzwesen und Türkennot," *Die wirtschaftlichen Auswirkungen der Türkenkriege*, ed. Othmar Pickl, Grazer Forschungen zur Wirtschafts-und Sozialgeschichte, 1 (1971): 333, 337.

32. Friedrich Engel-Janosi, "Zur Geschichte der wiener Kaufmannschaft von der Mitte des 15. bis zur Mitte des 16. Jahrhunderts," *Mitteilungen des Vereines für Geschichte der Stadt Wien*, 6 (1926): 42-43; Otto Brunner, "Eine handelspolitische Denkschrift der Stadt Wien an König Ferdinand I," *MIöG*, Ergänzungsband 11 (1929): 483-484.

33. Engel-Janosi, "Kaufmannschaft," pp. 46-48; Othmar Pickl, "Der Handel Wiens und Wiener Neustadts mit Böhmen, Mähren, Schlesien, und Ungarns in der ersten Hälfte des 16. Jahrhunderts," *Der Außenhandel Ostmitteleuropas 1450-1650,* ed. Ingomar Bog (Cologne/Vienna: Böhlau, 1971), pp. 320, 322-323.

34. Hugo Hantsch, *Die Geschichte Österreichs,* 2 vols. (Graz/Vienna: Styria, 1947-1953), 1: 254; Huber, *Geschichte Österreichs,* 3: 501.

35. Baumgarten, *Karl V,* 2: 392; Theodor Wiedemann, *Geschichte der Reformation und Gegenreformation im Lande under der Enns,* 5 vols. (Prague, Tempsky, 1879-1886), 1: 41-42; Ernst Tomek, *Kirchengeschichte Österreichs,* 2 vols. (Innsbruck/Vienna: Tyrolia, 1935-1949), 2: 238; Johann Loserth, *Die Reformation and Gegenreformation in den innerösterreichischen Ländern im 16. Jahrhundert* (Stuttgart: Cotta, 1898), p. 22; Georg Loesche, *Geschichte des Protestantismus in Österreich* (Leipzig: Manz, 1930), p. 56; Grete Mecenseffy, *Geschichte des Protestantismus in Österreich* (Graz/Cologne: Böhlaus, 1946), p. 20.

36. Tomek, *Kirchengeschichte,* 2: 238-239; Ferdinand Hirn, *Geschichte der tiroler Landtage von 1518 bis 1525,* Erläuterungen und Ergänzungen zu Janssens's Geschichte des deutschen Volkes, ed. Ludwig Pastor, 4, no. 5 (1905): 80; Loserth, *Reformation in Innerösterreich,* pp. 25-26.

37. Ferdinand to Charles, April 2, 1525, *Korrespondenz,* 1: 286; Loesche, *Protestantismus,* p. 56.

38. Ferdinand to Andreas da Burgo, July 7, 1529 (excerpts), AG, *Estado, Alemania,* Legajo 635, fo. 53.

39. Baumgarten, *Karl V,* 2: 388-389; Ferdinand to Charles, March 14, 1525, ibid., p. 272; Ferdinand to Charles, April 2, 1525, ibid., p. 286. On Johann Faber see, Adalbert Horawitz, "Johann Heigerlin (genannt Faber), Bischof von Wien, bis zum Regensburger Convent," *Sitzungsberichte der phil.- hist. Klasse der kaiserlichen Akademie der Wissenschaften zu Wien,* 107 (1884): 113, 119.

40. Ferdinand's Instructions for Alonso Goncalez de Meneses to Charles, May 4, 1525, *Korrespondenz,* 1: 299-300; Ferdinand to Charles,

June 17, 1525, ibid., pp. 303-305; Bernhard von Cles to Ferdinand, Aug. 28, 1525, SA, *Große Korrespondenz*, Fasc. 25/a, fo. 52.

41.   Ferdinand's Instructions for Alonso Goncalez de Meneses to Charles, May 4, 1525, *Korrespondenz*, 1: 299-300; Ferdinand to Margaret, Sept. 14, 1525, ibid., p. 331; Ferdinand to Charles, Aug. 24, 1525, ibid., p. 319.

42.   Huber, *Geschichte Österreichs*, 3: 509-510; Ferdinand to Margaret, Sept. 14, 1525, *Korrespondenz*, 1: 331; Hantsch, *Geschichte Österreichs*, 1: 252.

43.   Rosenthal, "Behördeorganisation," p. 60, note 1; Kurt Kaser, *Deutsche Geschichte im Ausgange des Mittelalters, 1438-1519*, 2 vols. (Stuttgart/Berlin: Cotta, 1912), 2: 311-313, 418-419; Huber, *Geschichte Österreichs*, 3: 463.

44.   Alexander Novotny, "Ein Ringen um ständische Autonomie zur Zeit der erstarkenden Absolutismus (1519-1522)," *MIöG*, 7 (1963): 355; Kirchmair, *Denkwürdigkeiten*, pp. 441-444; Bauer, *Anfänge*, p. 83.

45.   Huber, *Geschichte Österreichs*, 3: 486-487; Otto Stolz, *Grundriß der österreichischen Verfassungs- und Verwaltungsgeschichte* (Innsbruck/Vienna: Tyrolia, 1951), p. 130.

46.   Loserth, *Reformation in Innerösterreich*, pp. 28-29.

47.   Hans Ankwicz-Kleehoven, *Der wiener Humanist Johannes Cuspinian* (Graz/Cologne: Böhlaus, 1959), p. 204; Bucholtz, *Regierung*, 1: 182, 495-496.

48.   Siegmund von Herberstein, *Selbstbiographie 1486-1553*, ed. Theodor von Karajan, *FRA*, 1(1855):257.

49.   Victor von Kraus, "Zur Geschichte Oesterreichs unter Ferdinand I, 1519-1522," *Neunter Jahresbericht des leopoldstädter Communal-Real- und Obergymnasiums in Wien*, no. 11 (1873): 78 and note 1; Tomek, *Kirchengeschichte*, 2: 223.

50.   Ferdinand to Charles, Nov. 5, 1522, *Korrespondenz*, 1: 31.

51.   Baumgarten, *Karl V*, 1:135-139.

Notes to Chapter II

1.   Ferdinand to Charles, April 24, 1524, *Korrespondenz*, 1: 129.

2.   Huber, *Geschichte Österreichs*, 4: 201-202.

3.   Stern, "Salamanca," pp. 19-21; Bauer, *Anfänge*, p. 168; Turba, *Thronfolgerecht*, p. 157, note 1.

4. Oscar Mitis, "Vom burgundischen Hof Ferdinands I. in Österreich," *Jahrbuch für Landeskunde von Niederösterreich*, New Series 21 (1928): 157-159; *Reichstagsakten*, Jüngere Reihe, 3: 111, 115.

5. Stern, "Salamanca," p. 23.

6. von Kraus, "Ferdinand I," xxvi, doc. 11; Bauer, *Anfänge*, pp. 84, 131, 173, Stern, "Salamanca," p. 28; Kirchmair, *Denkwürdigkeiten*, pp. 461-462.

7. Charles to Ferdinand, Mar. 25, 1523, *Korrespondenz*, 1: 46; Charles to Ferdinand, June 20, 1523, ibid., pp. 68-69; Ferdinand to Margaret, Dec. 1523, ibid., p. 77; Ferdinand to Charles, Dec. 18, 1523, ibid., p. 92; Bauer, *Anfänge*, p. 204.

8. Stern, "Salamanca," p. 28; Arwed Richter, *Der Reichstag zu Nürnberg 1524* (Leipzig: Fock, 1888), p. 17.

9. Quoted in Baumgarten, *Karl V*, 2: 320.

10. A copy of the imperial instructions without date is in Vienna, SA, *Belgien, PA* 4, Konv. 1, fos. 23-26.

11. Ferdinand to Charles, June 12, 1524, *Korrespondenz*, 1: 147; Ferdinand to Charles, July 11, 1524, ibid., pp. 206-207.

12. Charles to Ferdinand, Oct. 4, 1524, ibid., pp. 223-224; Charles to Ferdinand, Dec. 16, 1524, pp. 246-247.

13. Hermann Baumgarten, "Differenzen zwischen Karl V. und seinem Bruder Ferdinand im Jahre 1524," *DZG*, 2 (1889): 15.

14. Ferdinand to Charles, Oct. 16, 1525, *Korrespondenz*, 1: 334; Mayr, "Generallandtag," pp. 7-9.

15. Karl Baumgarten, *Karl V und die deutsche Reformation*, Schriften des Vereins für Reformationsgeschichte, 27 (1889): 46.

16. Mecenseffy, *Protestantismus in Österreich*, pp. 22-23; Charles to Ferdinand, Mar. 30, 1526, *Korrespondenz*, 1: 376-377.

17. Ferdinand to Charles, April 30, 1526, *Korrespondenz*, 1: 383.

18. Stern, "Salamanca," pp. 34-35; Engel-Janosi, "Wiener Kaufmannschaft," *Alemania*, pp. 38-39; Ferdinand to Charles, April 2, 1539, *Blau*, 597/1, p. 352; AG, *Estado*, Legajo 637, fos. 27-83.

19. Hajo Holborn, *A History of Modern Germany*, 3 vols. (New York: Knopf, 1959-1969), 1: 38-39.

20. Hermann Wiesflecker, *Kaiser Maximilian I. Das Reich, Österreich und Europa an der Wende zur Neuzeit*, 3 vols. to date (Vienna: Verlag für Geschichte und Politik, 1971- -), 2: 136-137, 175-201; Karl Nehring,

Matthias Corvinus, Kaiser Friedrich III und das Reich. Zum hunyadisch-habsburgischen Gegensatz im Donauraum (Munich: Oldenburg, 1975), p. 59.

21. *Reichstagsakten,* Jüngere Reihe, 3: 124-125; Bauer, *Anfänge,* p. 3; Leopold von Ranke, *Über die Zeiten Ferdinands I und Maximilians II,* Sämtliche Werke, 54 vols. (Leipzig: Duncker, 1868-1890), 7: 21.

22. Baumgarten, *Karl V,* 2: 312-314; Richter, *Reichstag zu Nürnberg,* pp. 65-66.

23. Baumgarten, *Karl V,* 1: 135-139; Baumgarten, ibid., 2: 181-182; Brandi, *Karl V,* 1: 162.

24. Leopold von Ranke, *Deutsche Geschichte im Zeitalter der Reformation* (repr.: Cologne, Phaidon, n.d.), p. 263.

25. Richter, *Reichstag zu Nürnberg,* pp. 11-12.

26. Ferdinand to Charles, ?, 1524, Bucholtz, *Regierung,* 2: 52; Richter, *Reichstag zu Nürnberg,* ch. 8; Karl Brandi, *Deutsche Geschichte im Zeitalter der Reformation und Gegenreformation* (Munich: Bruckmann, 1960), p. 121.

27. Richter, *Reichstag zu Nürnberg,* pp. 68-69, 71, 79.

28. Ibid., pp. 121-122; Brandi, *Karl V,* 1: 164.

29. Bucholtz, *Regierung,* 2: 50-51.

30. Richter, *Reichstag zu Nürnberg,* p. 68.

31. Bucholtz, *Regierung,* 2: 45-47, 50-51; Brandi, *Karl V,* 1: 163; Ferdinand to Charles, April 24, 1524, *Korrespondenz,* 1: 126-127; Ferdinand to Charles, April 27, 1524, ibid., p. 128.

32. Ernst Laubach, "Karl V., Ferdinand I. und die Nachfolge im Reich," *MIöG,* 29 (1976): 4-5.

33. Ferdinand's Instructions for Henri de Hemricourt and Martin de Salinas for Charles, Nov. 1522, *Korrespondenz,* 1: 25-29; Ferdinand's Instructions for Charles de Bredam for Charles, June 13, 1524, ibid., 152-153, 158, 162, 169.

34. Johann von der Leiter to Duke William of Bavaria, Dec. 20, 1523, *Reichstagsakten,* Jüngere Reihe, 4: 629; Burchain of Isenhagen to Dukes Otto and Ernst of Lüneburg, Dec. 25, 1523, ibid., p. 630; Richter, *Reichstag zu Nürnberg,* pp. 48-49.

35. Ferdinand to Charles, Jan. 27, 1523, *Korrespondenz,* 1: 37; Ferdinand to Charles, May 12, 1523, ibid., p. 59; Loserth, *Reformation in Innerösterreich,* p. 24; Karl Hofmann, "Die Konzilsfrage auf den deutschen

Reichstagen von 1521-1524," (diss: Mannheim, 1932), pp. 33, 72.

36. Richter, *Reichstag zu Nürnberg,* pp. 35-36, 46, 49-50, 93-94, 101, note 3, 130; Hannart to Charles, March 13, 1524, Lanz, *Correspondenz,* 1: 98.

37. Hannart to Charles, March 13, 1524, Lanz, *Correspondenz,* 1: 98; Hannart to Margaret, Feb. 18-26, 1524, *Reichstagsakten,* Jüngere Reihe, 4: 693-694; Ferdinand to Charles, April 27, 1524, *Korrespondenz,* 1: 126-127.

38. Baumgarten, *Karl V,* 2: 343.

39. Ibid., p. 341.

40. Stephen Fischer-Galati, *Ottoman Imperialism and German Protestantism 1521-1555* (Cambridge: Harvard, 1959), p. 23; Richter, *Reichstag zu Nürnberg,* p. 110; Ferdinand to Charles, April 27, 1524, *Korrespondenz,* 1: 116; Ferdinand to Charles, June 13, 1524, ibid., p. 186; Charles to Ferdinand, July 8, 1524, ibid., pp. 199-201.

41. Ferdinand to Charles, Oct. 14, 1524, *Korrespondenz,* 1: 226; Ferdinand to Charles, Sept. 1, 1525, ibid., p. 323; Charles to Ferdinand, June 25, 1525, ibid., p. 306; Charles to Ferdinand, Oct. 31, 1525, ibid., p. 340.

42. Ferdinand to Charles, Nov. 1, 1524, ibid., p. 231; Ferdinand's Instructions for Charles de Bredam to Charles, June 13, 1524, ibid., pp. 164-165; Brandi, *Karl V,* 1: 164.

43. Charles to Ferdinand, April 15, 1524, ibid., pp. 104-105, 107.

44. Ferdinand's Instructions for Charles de Bredam to Charles, June 13, 1524, ibid., pp. 164-165. Cf. Ferdinand's Instructions for Anton de Croy and Charles de Bredam to Margaret, June 4, 1529, *Korrespondenz,* 2^2: 424-425.

45. Bernhard of Cles to Ferdinand, Sept. 19, 1523, *Große Korrespondenz,* Fasc. 25/a, fo. 7; Bernhard of Cles to Ferdinand, Sept. 23, 1523, ibid., fo. 13; Gabriel Sanchez to Ferdinand, Aug. 24, 1523, ibid., fos. 183-184.

46. Ferdinand's Instructions for Charles de Bredam to Charles, June 13, 1524, *Korrespondenz,* 1: 171-172.

47. Ferdinand to Charles, Nov. 1, 1524, ibid., p. 382; Ferdinand to Charles, Nov. 5, 1524, ibid., p. 106; Ferdinand to Margaret, Nov. 18, 1524, ibid., p. 241.

48. Ferdinand to Charles, Mar. 14, 1525, ibid., p. 274; Sutter, intro., 125-126; Ranke, *Deutsche Geschichte,* p. 409; Johannes Dantiscus to King

Sigismund of Poland, March 16, 1525, *Acta Tomiciana*, 16 vols. (Poznań: Mersbach, 1852-1960), 7: 195.

49. Ferdinand to Charles, March. 14, 1525, *Korrespondenz*, 1: 275; Ferdinand to Charles, Sept. 1, 1525, ibid., p. 324; Ferdinand to Charles, April 2, 1525, ibid., p. 289.

50. Ferdinand to Charles, May 20, ibid., p. 287; Ferdinand's Instructions for Gabriel Salamanca to Charles, ibid., pp. 360, 362.

51. Charles to Ferdinand, March 26-31, 1525, ibid., pp. 278, 280; Charles to Ferdinand, June 25, 1525, ibid., p. 308; Ferdinand to Charles, Sept. 1, 1525, ibid., pp. 324, 326; Ferdinand to Margaret, Dec. 12, 1525, ibid., p. 353; Bucholtz, *Regierung,* 2: 296.

52. Ferdinand's Instructions for Henri de Hemricourt and Martin de Salinas to Charles, Nov. 1522, ibid., pp. 22-25; Ferdinand to Charles, May 12, 1523, ibid., p. 52; Ferdinand's Instructions for Charles de Bredam for Charles, June 13, 1524, ibid., p. 180; Ferdinand to Charles, June 13, 1524, ibid., p. 181; Bauer, *Anfänge,* pp. 230-231.

53. Charles to Ferdinand, Feb. 6, 1525, *Korrespondenz*, 1: 254-255; Bauer, *Anfänge,* pp. 230-231; Sutter, intro., p. 126.

54. Bauer, *Anfänge,* pp. 234-235.

55. Charles to Ferdinand, June 25, 1525, *Korrespondenz,* pp. 307-308; Baumgarten, *Karl V,* 2: 551.

56. Ferdinand to Charles, Sept. 1, 1525, *Korrespondenz,* 1: 325.

Notes to Chapter III

1. Ferdo Hauptmann, "Ungarn, Habsburg und die kroatische Staatsidee im 16. und 17. Jahrhundert," *Südostdeutsches Archiv,* 12 (1969): 63.

2. Stanko Guldescu, *A History of Medieval Croatia* (The Hague: Mouton, 1964), pp. 152, 273, note 3, 306; Christopher Frangipani (Frankopan) to Ferdinand, March 1, 1523, SA, *Große Korrespondenz* 25/a, fo. 176; Bishop of Trieste to Ferdinand, March 16, 1523, ibid., fos. 236-237.

3. Bálint Hóman and Gyula Szekfű, *Magyar Történet,* 8 vols. (Budapest: Király magyar egyetemi nyomda, n.d.), 2: 576, 595; Huber, *Geschichte Österreichs,* 3: 519-520; Ludwik Kolankowski, "Polityka ostatnich Jagiellonów," *Kwartalnik historyczny,* 25 (1911); 57.

4. Ankwicz-Kleehoven, *Cuspinian,* pp. 216-217.

5. Gernot Heiß, "Politik und Ratgeber der Königin Maria von Ungarn in den Jahren 1521-1531," *MIöG,* 82 (1974): 128-129.

6. Ibid., pp. 127, 135-138; Wilhelm Fraknói, *Ungarn vor der Schlacht Mohacs, 1524-1526,* trans. J. H. Schwicker (Budapest: Lauffer, 1886), pp. 15, 49, 122-123, 211, note 2, 212, note 1; Hóman/Szekfű, *Magyar Történet,* 2: 606; Huber, *Geschichte Österreichs,* 3: 525; Ferdinand's Instructions for Charles de Bredam to Charles, June 13, 1524, *Korrespondenz,* 1: 165.

7. Josef Janáček, *České dějiny: doba předbělohorské 1526-1527* (Prague: Academia, 1968), p. 262, tables 10 and 11; Jan Heřman, "Zemské berni rejstříky z 1. 1523 a 1529," *Československý časopis historický,* 10 (1962): 248, 253.

8. R. R. Betts, "Social and Constitional Development in Bohemia," in R. R. Betts, *Essays in Czech History* (London: Athlone, 1969), pp. 45-46.

9. *Československá vlastivěda,* ed. Václav Novotný, 12 vols. (Prague: Sfinx, 1929-1936) 4: 294-329; Ernest Denis, *Fin de l'indépendence bohême* (2nd ed.: Paris: Leroux, 1930), 1: 212-224; Huber, *Geschichte Österreichs,* 3: 413-416; W. W. Tomek, *Geschichte Böhmens* (Prague: Řivnáč, 1865), pp. 335, 337, 341; Kenneth J. Dillon, *King and Estates in the Bohemian Lands 1526-1564,* Studies Presented to the International Commission for the History of Representatives and Parliamentary Institutions, 57 (Brussels: Editions de la librairie encyclopédique, 1976): 8.

10. *Vlastivěda,* 4: 316; Huber, *Geschichte Österreichs,* 3: 522, 532.

11. *Reichstagsakten,* Jüngere Reihe, 3: 341-342, note 1; Hans Übersberger, *Österreich und Russland seit dem Ende des 15. Jahrhunderts* (Vienna/Leipzig: Braumüller, 1906), pp. 181-182.

12. Ferdinand to Charles, Sept. 2, 1522, *Korrespondenz,* 1:17.

13. Antonín Rezek, "Úmluvy sjezdu vídenského z 1. 1515 a jich význam pro volbu českou 1. 1526," *Časopis českého musea,* 55 (1881); Petr of Rožmberk to Zdeněk Lev Rožmital, 1523, *Archiv český,* 12: 69; Jindřich, Jost, and Petr of Rožmberk to Ferdinand, May, 1525, ibid., pp. 92-96.

14. Andrea da Burgo to Ferdinand, March 22, 1523, SA, *Große Korrespondenz,* Fasc. 25/a, fo. 245; Johannes Schneidpöck to Ferdinand, 23-24 January 1524, ibid., fo. 35; Antonín Rezek, *Zvolení a korunování Ferdinanda I. za krále českého* (Prague: J. Otto, 1878), p. 505, note 2. The author's German translation of this, *Geschichte der Regierung Ferdinands I. in Böhmen,* was published in the same year by Otto in Prague.

15.   Bauer, *Anfänge*, p. 177.

16.   *Reichstagsakten*, Jüngere Reihe, 3:29. '

17.   Ibid., p. 97; Bauer, *Anfänge*, p. 132.

18.   Anon. report to Ferdinand, 1523, SA, *Große Korrespondenz*, Fasc. 25/a, fo. 205; Bishop of Trieste to Ferdinand, March 16, 1523, ibid., fos. 236-237; Christopher Frangipani (Frankopan) to Ferdinand, March, 1523, ibid., fo. 176; Hauptmann, "Kroatische Staatsidee," p. 65.

19.   Ferdinand's Instructions to Antonio de Padua, Nov. 6, 1523, AG, *Patronato Real*, Legajo 57, fo. 171/1.

20.   Andrea da Burgo to Ferdinand, Mar. 7, 1523, *Große Korrespondenz*, Fasc. 25/a, fo. 212; Andrea da Burgo to Ferdinand, March 22, 1523, ibid., fo. 245; Andrea da Burgo to Ferdinand, ibid., April 12, 1523, fo. 296.

21.   Andrea da Burgo to Ferdinand, Mar. 22, 1523, ibid., fo. 245; Andrea da Burgo to Ferdinand, April 16, 1523, ibid., fo. 301; Andrea da Burgo to Ferdinand, May 30, 1523, ibid., fo. 137. Cf. Karl Stoegemann, "Über die Briefe des Andrea da Burgo, Gesandten König Ferdinands an den Cardinal und Bischof von Trient," *Sitzungsberichte der Wiener Akademie der Wissenschaften*, phil.-hist. Klasse, 14 (1857): 163-164, 166.

22.   Huber, *Geschichte Österreichs*, 3: 522; Richter, *Reichstag zu Nürnberg*, pp. 112-113; Ferdinand to Charles, Dec. 18, 1523, *Korrespondenz*, 1: 89; Ferdinand to Margaret, May 25, 1523, ibid., p. 64ff; Ankwicz-Kleehoven, *Cuspinian*, p. 218; Kolankowski, "Polityka," p. 58; Janusz Pajewski, *Stosunki polsko-wągierskie i niebezpieczeństwo tureckie w latach 1516-1526*, Rozprawy historyczne towarzystwa naukowego Warszawskiego, 9 (1930): 40.

23.   See the reports of Schneidpöck to Ferdinand, *Große Korrespondenz*, fasc. 25/a, May 1, 1524, fos. 331-332 and June 5, 1524, fos. 340-343. Cf. the report of the papal nuncio, Campeggi to Jacobo Sadoleto, Aug. 22, 1524, *Monumenta Vaticana Hungariae. Relationes Oratorum Pontificiorum 1524-1526* (Budapest: n. publ., 1884), p. 28; Louis of Hungary to Sigismund of Poland, 1525, *Acta Tomiciana*, 7: 161.

24.   *Monumenta Vaticana Hungariae*, p. 190.

25.   *Reichstagsakten*, Jüngere Reihe, 3: 212; Chieregati to Isabella d'Este, Nov. 28, 1522, ibid., p. 861.

26.   Wolfgang Steglich, "Die Reichstürkenhilfe in der Zeit Karls V," *Militärgeschichtliche Mitteilungen*, 11 (1972): 8, 19-21; Bauer, *Anfänge*, pp. 185-187. Cf. Fischer-Galati, *Ottoman Imperialism*, p. 20.

27. Fischer-Galati, *Ottoman Imperialism,* pp. 22-23; Baumgarten, *Karl V,* 2: 387.

28. *Reichstagsakten,* Jüngere Reihe, 3: 60-61.

29. Ferdinand to Charles, Nov. 5, 1522, *Korrespondenz,* 1: 32; Ferdinand's Instructions for Henri de Hemricourt and Martin de Salinas to Charles, Nov. 22, ibid., p. 26; Ferdinand to Charles, Jan. 27, 1523, ibid., p. 36; Andrea da Burgo to Ferdinand, July 3, 1523, SA, *Große Korrespondenz,* 25/a, fo. 20; Andrea da Burgo to Ferdinand, May 5, 1523, ibid., fo. 5; Andrea da Burgo to Ferdinand, May 12, 1523, ibid., fo. 46; Ferdinand to Margaret, May 12, 1524, *Korrespondenz,* 1: 130-131: Ferdinand to Charles, June 10, 1524, ibid., pp. 144-145; Ferdinand to Charles, Dec. 4, 1525, ibid., p. 351.

30. Ferdinand to Charles, April 2, 1525, *Korrespondenz,* 1: 287; Charles to Ferdinand, Oct. 31, 1525, ibid., pp. 339, 341.

31. Frankói, *Ungarn vor Mohács,* pp. 55-56, 269, note, 2, 270; Antonio Burgio to Jacobo Sadoleto, Feb. 18, 1526, *Monumenta Vaticana Hungariae,* p. 324; Antonio Burgio to Jacobo Sadoleto, March 27, 1526, ibid., p. 349.

32. Marino Sanuto, *I Diarii,* 58 vols. (Venice: Visentini, 1894), 41; 298, 374; Ferdinand to Bernard Trumpić, Aug. 4, 1526, *Monumenta Spectantia Historiam Slavorum Meridionalium,* 45 vols. (Zagreb: Dionička tiskare, 1868-1950), 35: 11, Ferdinand to Nicholas Jurisić, Aug. 4, 1526, ibid., p. 13; Louis to Ferdinand, June 6, 1526, *Korrespondenz,* 1: 391.

33. Ferdinand to Charles, May 25, 1526, *Korrespondenz,* 1: 388; Ferdinand to Margaret, July 16, 1526, ibid., pp. 402-403; Charles to Ferdinand, July 27, 1526, ibid., pp. 411, 414-415; Antonio Burgio to Jacobo Sadoleto, July 26, 1526, *Monumenta Vaticana Hungariae,* p. 427; Antonio Burgio to Jacobo Sadoleto, July 10, 1526, ibid., p. 417. For a detailed discussion of Ferdinand's behavior prior to Mohács see my "An Absence Explained: Archduke Ferdinand of Austria and the Battle of Mohács," *Austrian History Yearbook,* 2 (1966): 11-17.

34. Fichtner, "Absence," pp. 13-14.

35. Walter Friedensburg, *Der Reichstag zur Speier 1526,* Historische Untersuchungen, No. 5 (Berlin: Gaertner, 1887), 426-427, 429-431; Fischer-Galati, *Ottoman Imperialism,* pp. 24-26.

36. Charles to Ferdinand, July 27, 1526, *Korrespondenz,* 1: 419-20.

37.   Fichtner, "Absence," p. 16.

38.   Ferdinand to Louis, Sept. 7, 1526, *Urkunden und Actenstücke zur Geschichte der Verhältnisse zwischen Österreich, Ungern* /sic/ *und der Pforte im XVI und XVII. Jahrhunderts,* ed. Anton von Gévay, 3 vols. (Vienna: Schaumberg, 1840), 11: 2.

39.   Ferdinand to Maria, Sept. 9, 1526, *Korrespondenz,* 1: 446.

40.   Ferdinand to Charles, Sept. 22, 1526, ibid., pp. 460-461; Rezek, "Úmluvy," pp. 390-391.

41.   W. F. A. Bernhauer, ed. and trans., *Sulaiman des Gesetzgebers Tagebuch auf seinem Feldzuge nach Wien im Jahre 93 5/6 d.h. J. 1529 n. Chr.* (Vienna: Gerold, 1858), p. 1; Ferdinand to Charles, Sept. 22, 1526, *Korrespondenz,* 1: 464-465, 467.

42.   Ferdinand to Mary, Sept. 9, 1526, *Korrespondenz,* 1: 446; Ferdinand to Mary, Sept. 11, 1526, ibid., pp. 447-448; Ferdinand's Instructions for Johann von Lamberg, Sept. 17, 1526, ibid.: 450; Ferdinand to Margaret, Sept. 22, 1526, ibid., p. 468.

43.   Margaret to Ferdinand, Oct. 2, 1526, ibid., pp. 471-472; Charles to Ferdinand, 23/30 Nov. 1526, ibid., p. 488; Charles's Instructions to Don Antonio Mendoza, Dec., 1526, AG, *Patronato Real,* Legajo 57, fo. 168.

Notes to Chapter IV

1.   Alfons Huber and Alfons Dopsch, *Österreichische Reichsgeschichte* (2nd ed.: Prague/Vienna: Tempsky, 1901), p. 147; Ernst Hellbling, *Österreichische Verfassungs-und Verwaltungsgeschichte* (Vienna: Springer, 1956), pp. 211-212.

2.   Rezek, *Regierung,* pp. 53-54; Rezek, "Úmluvy," p. 400; Huber, *Geschichte Österreichs,* 3: 543.

3.   Baumgarten, *Karl V,* 2: 576; Bucholtz, *Regierung,* 2: 411-413.

4.   Ferdinand to Adam of Hradec, Sept. 10, 1526, in Rezek, *Regierung,* p. 152; L. Kupelwieser, *Die Kämpfe Österreichs mit den Osmanen vom Jahre 1526 bis 1537* (Vienna/Liepzig: Braumüller, 1899), p. 3; Ferdinand and Anna's Instructions to their ambassadors, Sept. 24, 1526, *Die böhmische Landtagsverhandlungen und Landtagsbeschlüsse vom Jahre 1526 bis auf de Neuzeit,* 11 vols. (Prague: königlicher böhmische Landesausschuß, 1877-1941), 1: 67-68, 87.

5. Charles to Ferdinand, Nov. 23-30, 1526, *Korrespondenz*, 1: 489.

6. Rezek, *Regierung*, pp. 21-22, 65-66, 122.

7. Stanislaus Smolka, "Ferdinand des Ersten Bemühungen um die Krone von Hungarn," *AöG*, 57 (1878): 110.

8. Bertold Bretholz, *Neuere Geschichte Böhmens* (Gotha: Perthes, 1920), pp. 7, 79-80; Ranke, *Deutsche Geschichte*, p. 430; Denis, *Premiers Habsbourgs*, p. 20.

9. Hellbling, *Verfassungsgeschichte*, pp. 213-214; Huber, *Geschichte Österreichs*, 3: 546-547; Rezek, *Regierung*, pp. 89-94.

10. Tomek, *Geschichte Böhmens*, p. 338; Turba, *Thronfolgerechts*, p. 154.

11. Rezek, *Regierung*, pp. 135-136.

12. Bucholtz, *Regierung*, 2: 446-447; Ferdinand to Mary, March 6, 1527, *Korrespondenz*, 2^1: 26.

13. Bretholz, *Geschichte Böhmens*, 11-12; Rezek, *Regierung*, p. 140.

14. Huber-Dopsch, *Reichsgeschichte*, p. 149; Rezek, *Regierung*, pp. 72-73, 112-115; Bucholtz, *Regierung*, 2: 526-527; Tomek, *Geschichte Böhmens*, p. 329.

15. Ferdinand to the Moravian Diet, *Archiv český*, 11: 403.

16. Rudolf Dvořák, *Dějiny Moravy*, 5 vols. in 1 (Brno: Musejní spolek, 1899-1905), pp. 385-400; František Kameníček, "Účastenství moravanů pří valkách tureckých r. 1526 d. r. 1568," *Sborník historický*, 4 (1886): 16-17.

17. Ferdo Šišić, *Die Wahl Ferdinands I. von Österreich zum König von Kroatian* (Zagreb: Suppan, 1917), p. 11; Smolka, "Bemühungen," pp. 26-27; Ignaz Fessler and Ernst Klein, *Geschichte von Ungarns*, 10 vols. (2nd. ed.: Leipzig, Brockhaus, 1866-1883), 3: 401.

18. Šišić, *Wahl*, pp. 16, 20.

19. Huber, *Geschichte Österreichs*, 3: 443; Liske, "Congress zu Wien," p. 526; Uebersberger, *Österreich und Russland*, pp. 75, 218-219; Heiß, "Ratgeber," p. 144.

20. Smolka, "Bemühungen," pp. 24-25, 33-34; Huber, *Geschichte Österreichs*, 3: 551, 553; Franz Krones, *Handbuch der Geschichte Österreichs*, 5 vols. (Berlin: Hofmann, 1879), 3: 184-185; Eduard Richter, "Die Haltung der ungarischen Bergstädte nach der Doppelwahl von 1526," *MIöG*, 32 (1911): 501; Baumgarten, *Karl V*, 2: 576: Liske, "Congress zu Wien," p. 525.

21.   Liske, "Congress zu Wien," pp. 508, 511, 513, 521, 524; Turba, *Thronfolgerechts*, p. 345.

22.   Smolka, "Bemühungen," p. 40.

23.   Otto Friedrich Winter, "Das Register Ferdinands I. als Quelle zu seiner ungarischen Politik," *MöSA*, 7 (1954): 559.

24.   Fessler-Klein, *Geschichte von Ungarn*, 3: 408-409; Šišić, *Wahl*, p. 21, Smolka, "Bemühungen," p. 48.

25.   Šišić, *Wahl*, pp. 23-24; Ferdinand to Margaret, Nov. 24, 1526, *Korrespondenz*, 1: 493-494; Josef Rohrmoser, *Diplomatische Verhandlungen zwischen Ferdinand I und Johann Zapolya* (Czernowitz: Eckhardt, 1862), pp. 8-10.

26.   Winter, "Register," pp. 526-566 and 567, notes 54-60; Smolka, "Bemühungen," pp. 48, 63-64; Heiß, "Ratgeber," p. 150, note 53; Huber-Dopsch, *Reichsgeschichte*, p. 151; Hóman-Szekfű, *Magyar történet*, 3: 17, 68-69; *Monumenta Hungariae Historica: Monumenta Comitialia Regni Hungariae*, 12 vols. (Budapest: királyi tudományegytem kőnyvnyomd, 1874-1917), 1: 61-62.

27.   Huber, *Geschichte Österreichs*, 3: 554; Šišić, *Wahl*, pp. 34-36.

28.   Kiszling, *Die Kroaten: der Schicksalsweg eines Südslawenvolkes* (Graz/Cologne: Böhlaus, 1956), p. 24; Hauptmann, "Croatische Staatsidee," p. 67.

29.   ". . . nosque in maximo esse apparatus, quo non modo Hungariam defendere, sed hostes (deo favente) longe a suis limitibus profligare, ipsosque serenissimos fratrem et sororem nostros, in possessione suorum . . . regnorum imponere valeamus." SA, *Belgica, D.B.*, Fasc. 233, fo. 161. See also Ferdinand to the Croatian estates, Jan. 19, 1527 in *Acta Comitialia Regni Croatiae, Dalmatiae, et Slavoniae*, Monumenta Spectantia Slavorum Meridionalium, 33 (1912): 83.

30.   Smolka, "Bemühungen," pp. 124-131; Ferdinand's Instructions for Jörg Truchseß *et al.*, Nov. 20, 1526, Bucholtz, *Regierung*, 9: 2, 7; Ferdinand to Charles, Dec. 31, 1526, *Korrespondenz*, 1: 507.

31.   Bucholtz, *Regierung*, 3: 197, 201.

32.   Ferdinand to Mary, Jan. 21, 1527, *Korrespondenz*, 2^1: 7-8; Mary to Ferdinand, Feb. 9, 1527, ibid., p. 17.

33.   Mary to Ferdinand, Feb. 9, 1527, ibid., p. 17; Ferdinand to Mary, Feb. 9, 1527, ibid., pp. 15-16; Mary to Ferdinand, Feb. 14, 1527, ibid., p. 20; Ferdinand to Mary, March 5, 1527, ibid., pp. 24-25; Ferdinand to Mary, April 7, 1527, ibid., p. 49; Heiß, "Ratgeber," p. 153.

34. Ferdinand to Mary, March 5, 1527, *Korrespondenz,* 2¹: 24-25; Ferdinand to Mary, March 6, 1527, ibid., p. 26.

35. Smolka, "Bemühungen," pp. 139, 149; Uebersberger, *Österreich und Russland,* p. 221.

36. Steglich, "Reichstürkenhilfe," pp. 27, 33; Charles to Ferdinand, March 6, 1527, *Korrespondenz,* 2¹: pp. 27-28; Charles to Ferdinand, April 26, 1527, ibid., p. 62.

37. Ferdinand to Mary, April 7, 1527, ibid., p. 50; Ferdinand to Mary, May 14, 1527, pp. 70-73; Mary to Ferdinand, May 20, 1527, ibid., p. 75.

38. Ferdinand to Margaret, May 27, 1527, ibid., p. 80; Ferdinand to Charles, May 30, 1527, ibid., p. 82; Ferdinand to Charles, May 31, 1527, ibid., pp. 87-88; Charles to Ferdinand, July 31, 1527, ibid., p. 99.

39. "... bons maris ne perdent volontiers temps, quant la oportunité la done...." Ferdinand to Mary, Sept. 21, 1527, ibid., p. 128.

40. Rohrmoser, *Diplomatische Verhandlungen,* p. 12.

41. Ferdinand to Charles, May 31, 1527, *Korrespondenz,* 2¹: 86; *Böhmische Landtagsverhandlungen,* 1: 67-68.

42. Charles to Ferdinand, Sept. 8, 1527, *Korrespondenz,* 2¹: 120-121; Ferdinand to Margaret, Oct. 4, 1527, ibid., p. 138.

43. Charles to Ferdinand, Sept. 8, 1527, ibid., p. 122; Ferdinand to Charles, Nov. 23, 1527, ibid., pp. 155-156; Baumgarten, "Differenzen," pp. 1-2.

44. Mary to Ferdinand, May 20, 1527, *Korrespondenz,* 2¹: 86.

Notes to Chapter V

1. Rosenthal, "Behördeorganisation," p. 179.

2. Ibid., pp. 65, 161, note 2, 260-261, 176.

3. Hans Voltelini, "Die Wiener Stadt- u. Stadtgerichtsordnung Ferdinands I. von 1526," *Mitteilungen des Vereines für Geschichte der Stadt Wien,* 9/10 (1929-1930): 107-108.

4. Huber, *Reichsgeschichte,* p. 226.

5. Thomas Fellner and Heinrich Kretschmayr, *Die österreichische Zentralverwaltung,* 2 vols. (Vienna: Holzhausen, 1907), 1: 38-39, 141; Mayr, "Generallandtag," pp. 49-50; Rosenthal, "Behördeorganisation," pp. 82-83, 85, note 1, 99; Oskar Regele, "Der österreichische Hofkriegsrat 1556-1848," *MöSA,* Ergänzungsband 1 (1949): 14-16; Firnhaber, "Militärwesen," p. 130.

6.   Rosenthal, "Behördeorganisation," pp. 68, 84, 155, 163-164, 172; Sutter, intro., p. 66.

7.   Fellner, *Zentralverwaltung*, 1: 69, 141; Rosenthal, "Behördeorganisation," pp. 116-117, 120-121, 127, 132, 186, note 1, 189; Theodor Mayer, "Das Verhältnis der Hofkammer zur ungarischen Kammer bis zur Regierung Maria Theresias," *MIöG*, Ergänzungsband 9 (1915): 197, 199-200, 203.

8.   Rosenthal, "Behördeorganisation," p. 127; Huber, *Reichsgeschichte*, pp. 185, 191-192, 199-200; Hermann Bidermann, *Geschichte der österreichischen Gesamt-Staatsidee 1526-1804* (Innsbruck: Wagner, 1867), pp. 17, 20; Bretholz, *Neuere Geschichte Böhmens*, 1: 45-46; Alfred Fischel, "Kaiser Ferdinands I. Versuch zur Einführung einer rein landesfürstlichen Verwaltung in Mähren, (1528)," *Zeitschrift des deutschen Vereines für die Geschichte Mährens und Schlesiens*, 17 (1913): 259-273.

9.   Bidermann, *Gesamt-Staatsidee*, pp. 3-5, 8-10; R. R. Betts, "Constitutional Development and Political Thought in Eastern Europe," *The New Cambridge Modern History*, 12 vols. (Cambridge: University Press, 1957-1968), 2: 467.

10.   Bidermann, *Gesamt-Staatsidee*, p. 10.

11.   Ibid., p. 6.

12.   Ferdinand to Charles, Sept. 13, 1540, *Blau*, 597/1: 438.

13.   Ferdinand to Charles, Oct. 5, 1548, ibid., 597/2, fo. 272; Ferdinand to Charles, Feb. 12, 1554, Drüffel, *Beiträge*, 4: 373; Charles to Ferdinand, April 8, 1554, ibid., p. 449.

14.   Ferdinand to Suleiman, July 15, 1529, Gévay, *Urkunden*, 1^3: 23; Ferdinand to Suleiman, July 23, 1529, ibid., p. 26; Ferdinand's Instructions for Joseph von Lamberger and Nikolaus Jurischitsch, May 27, 1530, ibid., 1^4: 4.

15.   Oberleitner, "Finanzlage," p. 13.

16.   Wilhelm Bauer, "Ein handelspolitischer Projekt Ferdinand I. aus dem Jahre 1527," *Beiträge zur neueren Geschichte Österreichs*, 1 (1906): 14-17; Pickl, "Auswirkungen," pp. 87-88, 91-92.

17.   *Böhmische Landtagsverhandlungen*, 1: 255; Rosenthal, "Behördeorganisation," pp. 282-283; Oberleitner, "Finanzlage," p. 13.

18.   Ferdinand to Mary, July 15, 1528, *Korrespondenz*, 2^1: 267-268; Bucholtz, *Regierung*, 9: 149.

19.   Bucholtz, *Regierung*, 4: 497-508; Miloslav Volf, "Královský

důchod a uvĕ̆r v XVI století," *Ččh*, 48/49 (1947-1948): 146-148; Dillon, *Kings and Estates*, pp. 43, 52.

20. Rezek, *Regierung*, p. 5; Volf, "Královsky důchod," pp. 129, 140.

21. Denis, *Premiers Habsbourgs*, p. 42.

22. Mayer, "Ungarische Kammer," pp. 194-195.

23. Heiß, "Ratgeber," p. 152. Bornemisza died in 1527.

24. Franz Salamon, *Ungarn im Zeitalter der Türkenherrschaft*, trans. Gustav Jurány (Leipzig: Haessel, 1887), pp. 78, 80.

25. *Korrespondenz*, 2^1: 187, editors' note; Ferdinand to Mary, May 31, 1528, ibid., pp. 228-229.

26. Salamon, *Türkenherrschaft*, pp. 53-56; Hóman-Szekfű, *Magyar Történet*, 3: 159, 201.

27. Margaret's Instructions for Claude Vaytel to Ferdinand, June 6, 1528, *Korrespondenz*, 2^1: 233, 238.

28. Heiß, "Ratgeber," pp. 146-147.

29. Tomek, *Kirchengeschichte*, 2: 250-251; Eder, *Land o.d. Enns*, 2: 19-20. Once Ferdinand came to an agreement with the estates in 1527, he returned the church silver.

30. Mecenseffy, *Protestantismus in Österreich*, pp. 23-25.

31. Bucholtz, *Regierung*, 4: 475; Tomek, *Kirchengeschichte*, 2: 244, 246; Wiedemann, *Reformation unter der Enns*, 1: 66 and note 1; *Reichstagsakten*, Jüng. Reihe, 4^1: 870-871, note 1.

32. Ferdinand Hrejsa, *Dějiny křest'anství v Československů*, 6 vols. (Prague: evangelická faculta boholslovecká, 1947-1948), 5: 23.

33. Adalbert Hudak, "Der Hofprediger Johannes Henckel und seine Beziehungen zu Erasmus von Rotterdam," *Kirche im Osten*, 2 (1959): 107, 109-110.

34. Huber, *Geschichte Österreichs*, 4: 103; Loesche, *Geschichte des Protestantismus*, p. 384.

35. Mary to Ferdinand, April 15, 1527, *Korrespondenz*, 21: 58.

36. Mary to Ferdinand, ibid.: 214-216.

37. Loesche, *Geschichte des Protestantismus*, p. 448.

38. Ferdinand to Mary, July 15, 1528, *Korrespondenz* 2^1: 268-270.

39. Mary to Ferdinand, Aug. 4, 1528, ibid., p. 276; Heiß, "Ratgeber," p. 173. Heiß incorrectly dates the diet as occurring in 1529.

40. Heiß, "Ratgeber," pp. 153, 169; Smolka, "Bemühungen," pp. 96, 98; Mary to Ferdinand, July 11, 1528, *Korrespondenz*, 2^1: 266; Ferdinand to Mary, July 27, 1528, ibid., p. 274.

41.   Ferdinand to Charles, Jan. 10, 1538, *Blau,* 597/1, p. 344.

42.   Günther Probszt-Obstorff, "Königin Maria und die niederungarischen Bergstädte," *Zeitschrift für Ostforschung,* 15 (1966): 626, 632-633;
Ferdinand to Charles, April 2, 1539, *Blau,* 597/1, p. 352.

43.   Gernot Heiß, "Die ungarische, böhmischen, und österreichischen
Besitzungen der Königin Maria (1505-1558) and ihre Verwaltung," pt. 1,
MöSA, 27 (1974): 71: Heiß, "Ratgeber," pp. 168, 172.

44.   Ferdinand to Mary, Feb. 3, 1528, *Korrespondenz,* 2^1: 186-188;
Ferdinand's Instructions for Joseph Lamberger, May 31, 1528, ibid., pp.
229-230; Mary to Ferdinand, July 5, 1528, ibid., pp. 257-258; Mary to
Ferdinand, June 12, 1528, ibid., p. 247.

45.   Ferdinand to Mary, June 28, 1528, ibid., pp. 250-251; Ferdinand
to Mary, June 29, ibid., pp. 252-253; Mary to Ferdinand, July 9/10, 1528,
ibid., pp. 261-262. Heiß, "Besitzungen," p. 70. The author speculates
that Mary may have believed herself to be barren.

46.   Ferdinand to Mary, July 27, 1528, *Korrespondenz,* 2^1: 275.

47.   Heiß, "Ratgeber," pp. 175-176 and "Besitzungen," p. 71.

48.   Heiß, "Besitzungen," p. 93; Rezek, *Regierung,* p. 144.

49.   Probszt-Obstorff, "Königin Maria," pp. 660-662, 678-679, 681.

Notes to Chapter VI

1.   Laubach, "Nachfolge," pp. 16-19.

2.   Huber, *Geschichte Österreichs,* 3: 13.

3.   Fessler-Klein, *Geschichte Ungarns,* 3: 430, 433; Uebersberger,
Österreich und Russland, p. 239.

4.   Roger B. Merriman, *Suleiman the Magnificent 1520-1566* (rpt.;
New York: Cooper Square, 1966), p. 103; Ferdinand to Mary, Feb. 5,
1529, *Korrespondenz,* 2^2: 368.

5.   Bucholtz, *Regierung,* 3: 257; Günther Stökl, "Siegmund Freiherr
von Herberstein. Diplomat und Humanist," *Ostdeutsche Wissenschaft.
Jahrbuch des ostdeutschen Kulturrates,* 2^2: 7(1960): 77; Margaret to Ferdinand, May 1529, *Korrespondenz,* 2^2: 406; Ferdinand to Charles, July 28,
1529, ibid., p. 458; V.-L Bourilly, "Antonio Rincon et la politique orientale
de Francois Ier, (1522-1541)," *Revue historique,* 113 (1913): 77-78.

6.   *Böhmische Landtagsverhandlungen,* 1: 299; Huber, *Geschichte
Österreichs,* 4: 18.

7. Margaret to Ferdinand, 13/14 June, 1529, *Korrespondenz,* 2² : 432-433; *Monumenta Hungarica Historica, Diplomataria,* 41 vols. (Budapest: Eggenberger, 1857-1919), 1: 71-72.

8. Charles's Instructions to William de Montfort for Ferdinand, April 3, 1529, *Korrespondenz,* 2² : 387-388, 391; Ferdinand to Gattinara, Feb. 9, 1529, *Reichstagsakten,* Jüngere Reihe, 4¹ : 504, note 2.

9. Charles to Ferdinand, April 3/4, 1529, *Korrespondenz,* 2² : 391-393; Charles to Ferdinand, Feb. 16, 1529, ibid., pp. 371-372; Ferdinand to Margaret, May 30, 1529, ibid., pp. 417-418; Ferdinand to Charles, Aug. 28, 1529, ibid., p. 478; Ferdinand to Charles, July 1, 1529, ibid., p. 445; Steglich, "Reichstürkenhilfe," p. 47; Bourilly, "Rincon," pp. 65-67.

10. Ferdinand to Mary, Feb. 19, 1529, *Korrespondenz,* 2² : 374-375; Ferdinand to Mary, March 5, 1529, ibid., p. 379.

11. Bucholtz, *Regierung,* 3: 258-259; *Reichstagsakten,* Jüngere Reihe, 4¹ : 551; Johannes Kühn, *Die Geschichte des Speyerer Reichstags 1529,* Schriften des Vereins für Reformationsgeschichte, no. 146 (1929): 169-170.

12. Fischer-Galati, *Ottoman Imperialism,* p. 34; *Reichstagsakten,* Jüngere Reihe, 4¹ : 614; Kühn, *Speyerer Reichstag,* p. 153.

13. Kühn, *Speyerer Reichstag,* pp. 89-91, 255; Holborn, *Modern Germany,* 1: 208.

14. Kühun, *Speyerer Reichstag,* pp. 25, 27, 132, 244-245.

15. Ibid., pp. 148, 204-205, 215; Fischer-Galati, *Ottoman Imperialism,* pp. 34-35.

16. Bucholtz, *Regierung,* 4: 565; Huber, *Geschichte Österreichs,* 4: 28-29; Ferdinand to Mary, April 24, 1529, *Korrespondenz,* 2² : 399; Kühn, *Speyerer Reichstags,* pp. 14, 239.

17. Ferdinand to Charles, July 28, 1529, *Korrespondenz,* 2² : 456-457; Ferdinand to Charles, Aug. 28, 1529, ibid., p. 478; Ferdinand to Charles, Sept. 18, 1529, ibid., pp. 497-498.

18. Mary to Ferdinand, June 17, 1529, ibid., pp. 448-449.

19. Kuppelwieser, *Kampf,* p. 16; Huber, *Geschichte Österreichs,* 4: 20; Bucholtz, *Regierung,* 3: 263-266; Ferdinand to Clement VII, SA, *Belgien, PA* 7, Fasc. 2, fo. 52.

20. Ferdinand to Mary, Aug. 18, 1529, *Korrespondenz,* 2² : 473; Ferdinand to Mary, Aug. 2, 1529, ibid., p. 462; Charles to Ferdinand, Sept. 23, 1529, ibid., pp. 500-508; Charles to Ferdinand, Oct. 9, 1529, ibid., pp. 518-519; Charles to Margaret, July 24, 1529, ibid., p. 453.

21. Fischer-Galati, *Ottoman Imperialism,* p. 35; Charles to Ferdinand, Sept. 5, 1529, *Korrespondenz,* 2^2 : 485; Steglich, "Reichstürkenhilfe," pp. 37, 39.

22. Ferdinand to Mary, Oct. 15, 1529, *Korrespondenz,* 2^2 : 522; Ferdinand to Charles, Oct. 19, 1529, ibid., pp. 523-524.

23. Ferdinand to Charles, Oct. 24, 1529, ibid., p. 527; Ferdinand to Charles, Nov. 12, 1529, ibid., pp. 536-537.

24. Ferdinand to Charles, Dec. 9, 1529, ibid., p. 543; Charles to Ferdinand, Jan. 11, 1530, ibid., pp. 551-552.

25. Ferdinand to Mary, Jan. 17, 1530, ibid., p. 568; Ferdinand to Charles, Jan. 28, 1530, ibid., p. 590; Ferdinand to Mary, March 25, 1530, ibid., pp. 618-619.

26. Ferdinand to Charles, Jan. 28, 1530, ibid., pp. 579-582.

27. Mary to Ferdinand, ibid., pp. 599-600; Brandi, *Deutsche Reformation,* pp. 190-191.

28. Charles to Ferdinand, Jan. 11, 1530, ibid., pp. 555, 563.

29. Ferdinand to Charles, Jan. 28, 1530, ibid., pp. 588-589.

30. AGR, *Allemande,* fasc. 766, fo. 435; cf. Laubach, "Nachfolge," pp. 28-9. Baumgarten, *Karl V und die deutsche Reformation,* pp. 80-81; Ascan Westermann, *Die Türkenhilfe und die politisch-kirchlichen Parteien auf dem Reichstag zu Regensburg 1532,* Heidelberger Abhandlungen zur mittleren and neueren Geschichte, no. 25 (1910): 11.

31. Christiane Thomas, " 'Moderación de Poder': zur Entstehung der geheimen Vollmacht für Ferdinand I. 1531," *MöSA,* 27 (1974): 132.

32. Lanz, *Correspondenz,* 1: 412-414.

33. Otto Winckelmann, *Der Schmalkaldische Bund 1530-1532 und der Nürnberger Religionsfriede* (Straßburg: Heitz, 1892), p. 12; Heinrich Lutz, "Karl V und Bayern. Umrisse einer Entscheidung," *Zeitschrift für bayerische Landesgeschichte,* 32 (1959): 21-23; Westermann, *Türkenhilfe,* p. 24; Kühn, *Speyerer Reichstag,* p. 122.

34. Bucholtz, *Regierung,* 3: 538; Ranke, *Deutsche Geschichte,* pp. 607, 612.

35. Götz Freiherr von Pölnitz, *Anton Fugger,* 2 vols. (Tübingen: Mohr, 1958-1963), 1: 209-210.

36. Thomas, " 'Moderación'," pp. 125-130.

37. Charles to Ferdinand, Feb. 12, 1531, *Blau,* 595, fo. 62.

38. Thomas, " 'Moderación'," p. 116.

39. Winckelmann, *Schmalkaldischer Bund,* pp. 82, 114; Bucholtz, *Regierung,* 4: 157-158.

40. Winckelmann, *Schmalkaldischer Bund,* pp. 135-136.

41. Ferdinand to Charles, April 27, 1531, *Korrespondenz,* 3^1: 114; Charles to Ferdinand, June 13, 1531, Lanz, *Correspondenz,* 1: 479.

42. Charles to the Counts of Nassau and Neunar, July 1531, Lanz, *Correspondenz,* 1: 515.

43. Fischer-Galati, *Ottoman Imperialism,* p. 54.

Notes to Chapter VII

1. Kupelwieser, *Kampf,* pp. 78-79; Fessler-Klein, *Geschichte Ungarns,* 3: 444.

2. Copy of an ambassadorial report to Ferdinand, Feb. 26, 1531, AG, *Estado, Alemania,* Legajo 635, fo. 126.

3. Rohrmoser, *Diplomatische Verhandlungen,* pp. 19, 25; Uebersberger, *Österreich und Russland,* pp. 245-247.

4. Rohrmoser, ibid., p. 28; Kupelwieser, *Kampf,* pp. 74-75; Bucholtz, *Regierung,* 4: 97; Huber, *Geschichte Österreichs,* 4: 31, 38-39.

5. Ferdinand to Charles, March 27, 1531, *Korrespondenz,* 3^1: 83; Ferdinand to Charles, Dec. 10, 1531, ibid., 3^2: 436; Charles to Ferdinand, Jan. 2, 1532, Lanz, *Correspondenz,* 1: 642.

6. Ferdinand to Charles, Jan. 28, 1530, *Korrespondenz,* 2^2: 585; Ferdinand to Charles, March 17, 1531, ibid., 3^1: 75-76; Charles to Ferdinand, July 29, 1531, ibid., 3^2: 227; Charles to Ferdinand, Nov. 25, 1531, ibid., pp. 410-411; *Böhmische Landtagsverhandlungen,* 1: 344-345.

7. Pickl, "Handel Wiens," pp. 334-335.

8. Ferdinand to Charles, April 27, 1531, *Korrespondenz,* 31: 482; Bucholtz, *Regierung,* 9: 157.

9. Pickl, "Handel Wiens," p. 328; Ferdinand to Mary, Jan. 4, 1531, *Korrespondenz,* 3^1: 2.

10. Ferdinand to Mary, June 22, 1531, *Korrespondenz,* 3^1: 162.

11. Fessler-Klein, *Geschichte Ungarns,* 3: 447-448.

12. Bucholtz, *Regierung,* 4: 552.

13. Bucholtz, ibid., pp. 559-560; Fessler-Klein, *Geschichte Ungarns,* 3: 450-451; SA, *Hungarica,* Fasc. 20, fos. 12, 25.

14. SA, *Hungarica,* fasc. 20, fo. 48; Bucholtz, *Regierung,* 4: 558-559.

15. *Monumenta Hungarica Historica: Comitialia,* 1: 236-237, 284, 399-400; *Acta Regni Croatia,* 1: 288; Gévay, *Urkunden,* 1^4: 7; Mary to Ferdinand, May 5, 1531, *Korrespondenz,* 3^1: 121.

16. *Monumenta Hungarica Historica: Comitialia,* 1: 432, 434, 451; Christine Turetschek, *Die Türkenpolitik Ferdinands I von 1529-1532,* Dissertationen der Universität Wien, No. 10 (Vienna: Notring, 1978), pp. 221-222.

17. Ferdinand to Charles, Jan. 28, 1530, *Korrespondenz,* 2^2: 583-589.

18. Bucholtz, *Regierung,* 4: 565; Fischer-Galati, *Ottoman Imperialism,* pp. 44-45.

19. Charles to Ferdinand, April 3, 1531, *Korrespondenz,* 3^1: 93-96; Ferdinand to Charles, April 27, 1531, ibid., pp. 110-113; Winckelmann, *Schmalkaldische Bund,* p. 115.

20. Ferdinand to Mary, Aug. 17, 1531, *Korrespondenz,* 3^2: 243; Mary to Ferdinand, Sept. 2, 1531, ibid., p. 249; Charles to Ferdinand, Sept. 19, 1531, ibid., pp. 256-257.

21. Ferdinand to Mary, Sept. 25, 1531, ibid., pp. 261-263.

22. Charles to Ferdinand, 26/28 Sept. 1531, ibid., p. 271; Anna to Bishop Bernhard of Cles, Sept. 28, 1531, SA, *Belgica, PA* 13, fo. 38; Anna to Bernhard of Cles, Sept. 29,1531, ibid., fo. 40.

23. Sanuto, *Diarii,* 55: 52; Charles to Ferdinand, Oct. 1, 1531, *Korrespondenz,* 3^2: 549.

24. Ferdinand to Mary, Oct. 5, 1531, *Korrespondenz,* 3^2: 310.

25. Ferdinand to Mary, Nov. 24, 1531, ibid., p. 407; Sanuto, *Diarii,* 55: 257.

26. Kühn, *Speyerer Reichstag,* pp. 129-130, 224-225.

27. Peter Rassow, *Die Kaiser-Idee Karls V. dargestellt an der Politik der Jahre 1528-1540,* Historische Studien, no. 217 (Berlin: Ebering, 1932), pp. 85, 90-91; Winckelmann, *Schmalkaldische Bund,* pp. 221, 286 (note 445), 254, 223; Ranke, *Deutsche Geschichte,* p. 666.

28. Ferdinand to Mary, April 22, 1532, Gévay, *Urkunden,* 1^5: 76-77; Fischer-Galati, *Ottoman Imperialism,* pp. 53-54.

29. Winckelmann, *Schmalkaldische Bund,* p. 22. Privately, however, Charles did not place much value on a treaty with Zapolya. At the end of July 1531, he admitted to Ferdinand that any agreement with the voivode would be of little use since the principal foe in the east was the sultan. Charles to Ferdinand, July 29, 1531, *Korrespondenz,* 3^2: 227.

30. Ferdinand to Mary, June 8, 1532, Gévay, *Urkunden*, 1^5: 78-79; Ferdinand to Mary, June 22, 1532, ibid., pp. 81-84; Ferdinand to Mary, June 25, 1532, ibid., p. 85; Anna to Bernhard of Cles, Aug. 26, 1532, SA, *Belgien, PA* 13, Konv. 5, fo. 68.

31. Westermann, *Türkenhilfe*, pp. 110-111.

32. Kupelwieser, *Kampf*, pp. 91-92; Bucholtz, *Regierung*, 4: 103-104; Kameniček, "Učastenství," p. 28; Charles to Empress Isabella, Aug. 26, 1532, AG, *Estado, Alemania*, Legajo, 636, fo. 67.

33. Kőszeg is about sixty miles north-east of Graz. Kupelwieser, *Kampf*, p. 108; Winckelmann, *Schmalkaldische Bund*, p. 256; Huber, *Geschichte Österreichs*, 4: 40-41, 45-46; Ferdinand to Mary, Oct. 2, 1532, Gévay, *Urkunden*, 2^1: 51-52; Charles's Instructions for Pedro de la Cuerra to the Pope, Oct. 4, 1532, AG, *Estado, Alemania*, Legajo 636, fo. 231.

34. Alexis Thurzó to Ferdinand, Oct. 13, 1532, SA, *Hungarica*, fasc. 21, fo. 42; Alexis Thurzó to Ferdinand, Oct. 17, 1532, ibid., fo. 48.

35. Ferdinand to Mary, Oct. 21, 1532, Gévay, *Urkunden*, 2^1: 53; Ferdinand to Mary, Oct. 31, 1532, ibid., p. 54; Ferdinand to Charles, Oct. 30, 1532, Lanz, *Correspondenz*, 2: 19.

36. Alexis Thurzó to Ferdinand, Nov. 20, 1532, SA, *Hungarica*, fasc. 21, fo. 138; Alexis Thurzó to Ferdinand, Dec. 12, 1532, ibid., fasc. 21, fo. 13; Ferdinand to Mary, Nov. 25, 1532, Gévay, *Urkunden*, 2^1: 57, 59-60; Huber, *Geschichte Österreichs*, 4: 46-47.

37. Merriman, *Suleiman*, pp. 118-125.

38. Bourilly, "Rincon," p. 277.

Notes to Chapter VIII

1. Viktor Bibl, *Maximilian II. Der rätselhafte Kaiser* (Hellerau bei Dresden: Avalun, 1929), p. 29.

2. Ibid., p. 29; Joseph Hirn, *Erzherzog Ferdinand II. von Tirol*, 2 vols. (Innsbruck: Wagner, 1885-1888), 1: 4.

3. Report of the marriage between Queen Elizabeth and the king of Poland, July 14-19, 1538, AGR, *Allemande*, fasc. 538, fos. 76-78.

4. Report of Count Veit von Thurn, SA, *Haus-Archiv, Familien-Akten*, Karton 60, Konv. 2, fo. 8.

5. Bibl, *Rätselhafter Kaiser*, p. 29.

6. Robert Holtzmann, *Kaiser Maximilian II bis zu seiner Thronbesteigung 1527-1564* (Berlin: Schwetschke, 1903), p. 28.

7. Ferdinand to Charles, July 13, 1538, *Blau,* 597/1, pp. 313, 315-316; Ferdinand to Charles, June 23, 1540, ibid., p. 408.

8. Hanns von Lamberg to Ferdinand, April 4, 1532, SA, *Haus-Archiv, Familien-Akten,* Karton 53, Konv.1, fo. 1; Veit von Thurn to Ferdinand, May 4, 1546, ibid., fo. 8.

9. Hirn, *Ferdinand von Tirol,* 1: 5, 7-8.

10. Turba, *Thronfolgerechts,* pp. 288, 345, 167; Anton Gindely, "Über die Erbrechte des Hauses Habsburg auf die Krone von Ungarun in der Zeit von dem Jahre 1526-1687," *AöG,* 51 (1873): 205-206.

11. Ferdinand to Charles, Dec. 20, 1537, *Blau,* 597/1, p. 275.

12. Rosenthal, "Behördeorganisation," pp. 232-235, 136-137, 139-140; Oberleitner, "Finanzlage," pp. 23, 27, 31.

13. Rosenthal, "Behördeorganisation," p. 70; Ferdinand to Charles, Nov. 15, 1539, *Blau,* 597/1, p. 382.

14. Rosenthal, "Behördeorganisation," pp. 232-233; Bucholtz, *Regierung,* 5: 113. Cf. Harry A. Miskimin, *The Economy of Later Renaissance Europe* (London: Cambridge, 1977), pp. 1-19.

15. Ferdinand to Charles, Dec. 20, 1537, *Blau,* 597/1, p. 274; Ferdinand to Charles, May 15, 1538, ibid., p. 301.

16. Ferdinand to Charles, June 26, 1536, ibid., p. 220.

17. Ferdinand to Charles, April 9, 1535, ibid., p. 162; Ferdinand to Charles, April 12, 1537, ibid., p. 252; Ferdinand to Charles, July 3, 1536, ibid., p. 223; Ferdinand to Charles, July 24, 1536, ibid., p. 229; Ferdinand to Charles, March 6, 1536, ibid., pp. 194-196; Ferdinand to Charles, July 17, 1536, ibid., p. 227.

18. Ferdinand to Charles, June 7, 1535, ibid., p. 166; Ferdinand to Charles, July 8, 1537, ibid., p. 259; Ferdinand to Charles, April 12, 1537, ibid., p. 252; Ferdinand to Charles, July 24, 1536, ibid., p. 229.

19. Winckelmann, *Schmalkaldische Bund,* pp. 130-131; Fischer-Galati, *Ottoman Imperialism,* p. 58.

20. Ferdinand to Antonio de Leyva, April 16, 1534, AG, *Estado, Alemania,* Legajo 637, fo. 6.

21. Bucholtz, *Regierung,* 4: 232-233; Ranke, *Deutsche Geschichte,* p. 678; Ferdinand to Charles, Aug. 3, 1534, *Blau,* 597/1, p. 138.

22. Brandi, *Reformation und Gegenreformation,* pp. 209-210; Otto Winckelmann, "Über die Bedeutung der Verträge von Kadan und Wien (1534-1535) für die deutschen Protestanten," *Zeitschrift für Kirchengeschichte,* 11 (1890): 217, 220.

23.   Ferdinand to Charles, July 10, 1534, *Blau,* 597/1, pp. 133-134; Ferdinand to Charles, Aug. 3, 1534, ibid., p. 137; Ferdinand to Charles, Aug. 8, 1534, ibid., p. 141; Ferdinand to Charles, Oct. 2, 1534, ibid., p. 142; Ferdinand to Charles, Nov. 3, 1534, ibid., p. 148; Bucholtz, *Regierung,* 4: 305-306.

24.   Ferdinand to Charles, Oct. 8, 1534, *Blau,* 597/1, p. 143; Ferdinand to Charles, April 9, 1535, ibid., pp. 163-164.

25.   Ferdinand to Charles, Feb. 9, 1536, ibid., p. 192; Ferdinand to Charles, May 1, 1536, ibid., p. 207; Ferdinand to Charles, July 7, 1536, ibid., pp. 225-226; Winckelmann, "Verträge," pp. 234-236; O. Waltz, "Der Wiener Vertrag vom 22. November, 1535," *Forschungen zur deutschen Geschichte,* 13 (1873): 376-378; (N.N.) Wille, "Zum Religionsartikel des Friedens von Kadan 1534," *Zeitschrift für Kirchengeschichte,* 8 (1885): 56-57; Ranke, *Deutsche Geschichte,* p. 779.

26.   Charles to Ferdinand, Dec. 9, 1531, *Korrespondenz,* 3[2]: 430-431; Walter Fuchs, "Baiern und Habsburg, 1534-1536," *ARG,* 41 (1948): 6-7; Bucholtz, *Regierung,* 4: 268-269.

27.   Ferdinand to Charles, Jan. 20, 1535, *Blau,* 597/1, pp. 154-155; Ferdinand to Charles, June 7, 1535, ibid., p. 168.

28.   Rohrmoser, *Diplomatische Verhandlungen,* pp. 16, 23-24, 26.

29.   Fuchs, "Baiern und Habsburg," pp. 10-11.

30.   Ferdinand to Charles, April 9, 1535, *Blau,* 597/1, p. 161a; Ferdinand to Charles, Oct. 22, 1535, ibid., pp. 181-182; Ferdinand to Charles, June 13, 1536, ibid., p. 215.

31.   Ferdinand to Charles, Mar. 7, 1536, ibid., pp. 197-198; Ferdinand to Charles, April 9, 1535, ibid., p. 165; Fuchs, "Baiern und Habsburg," pp. 3-4, 24, 27-30.

32.   Ferdinand to Charles, Mar. 6, 1541, *Blau,* 597/1, p. 462; Ferdinand to Charles, Nov. 22, 1545, ibid., 597/2, fo. 150; Ferdinand to Charles, Mar. 5, 1537, ibid., 597/1, pp. 241, 257; Ferdinand to Charles, June 4, 1542, ibid., 597/2, fo. 42.

33.   Bibl, *Rätselhafter Kaiser,* pp. 30-31; Holtzmann, *Maximilian II,* pp. 18-19, 23, 26.

34.   Walter Rosenberg, *Der Kaiser und die Protestanten in den Jahren 1537-1539,* Schriften des Vereins für Reformationsgeschichte, 20, no. 77 (1903-1904), p. 59.

35.   Hirn, *Ferdinand von Tirol,* 1: 7; D. Eduard Böhl, *Beiträge zur Geschichte der Reformation in Österreich* (Jena: Fischer, 1902), p. 109.

36.   Ranke, *Deutsche Geschichte*, p. 778; Rosenberg, *Kaiser und Protestanten*, p. 59.

37.   Ferdinand to Andrea Burgo, July 8, 1529 (excerpt), AG, *Estado, Alemania*, Legajo 635, fo. 53.

38.   Eder, *Land ob der Enns*, 2: 50.

39.   Rosenberg, *Kaiser und Protestanten*, pp. 29-32; Loesche, *Protestantismus in Österreich*, p. 359; Tomek, *Kirchengeschichte Österreichs*, 2: 299.

40.   Rudolf Till, "Glaubensspaltung in Wien," *Wiener Geschichtesblätter*, 21 (1966): 4.

41.   Winckelmann, "Verträge," pp. 221, 236-237.

42.   Ferdinand to Charles, Aug. 18, 1537, *Blau*, 597/1, pp. 263-264; Ferdinand to Charles, Feb. 8, 1538; ibid., p. 284; Ferdinand to Charles, April 29, 1538, ibid., p. 299; Ferdinand to Charles, July 29, 1540, ibid., pp. 423-424; Ferdinand to Charles, Aug. 24, 1540, ibid., p. 432.

43.   Karl Ausserer, "Kardinal Bernhard von Cles und die Papstwahl des Jahres 1534," *MIöG*, 35 (1914): 116, 121.

44.   Ibid., pp. 129-130; Ferdinand to Charles, Oct. 22, 1535; *Blau*, 597/1, p. 181; Ferdinand to Charles, July 13, 1535, ibid., p. 170; Ferdinand to Charles, Oct. 7, 1535, ibid., p. 177; Ferdinand to Charles, June 21, 1536, ibid., p. 218; August Korte, *Die Konzilspolitik Karls V in den Jahren 1538-1543*, Schriften des Vereins für Reformationsgeschichte, 22, no. 85 (1905), pp. 13, 23, 29.

45.   Ferdinand to Charles, Nov. 3, 1537, *Blau*, 597/1, p. 271; Ferdinand to Charles, June 3, 1538, ibid., pp. 306-307; Ferdinand to Charles, June 28, 1538, ibid., p. 310.

46.   Rosenberg, *Kaiser und Protestanten*, p. 29. Paul returned the insult. In 1537, he refused Ferdinand aid against the Turks, and, in 1539, confirmed Zapolya's appointees to bishoprics in Hungary and even sent them financial assistance. Ferdinand to Charles, April 12, 1537, *Blau*, 597/1, p. 249; Ferdinand to Charles, April 17, 1538, ibid., p. 294; Ferdinand to Charles, April 29, 1538, ibid., p. 300; Bucholtz, *Regierung*, 4: 336.

47.   Ferdinand to Charles, Aug. 25, 1538, *Blau*, 597/1, p. 322; Ferdinand to Charles, Oct. 22, 1538, ibid., pp. 331-332.

48.   Ferdinand to Charles, Mar. 2, 1538, ibid., p. 286; Ferdinand to Charles, June 3, 1538, ibid., p. 305; Ferdinand to Charles, Aug. 1, 1538, ibid., p. 318.

49. Ferdinand to Charles, Jan. 6, 1538, ibid., p. 278; Rosenberg, *Kaiser und Protestanten,* pp. 7-8.

50. Rosenberg, *Kaiser und Protestanten,* pp. 46, 49, 61.

51. Ibid., p. 65; Fischer-Galati, *Ottoman Imperialism,* pp. 67-69.

52. Fischer-Galati, *Ottoman Imperialism,* pp. 71, 73; Ferdinand to Charles, "last day of Feb." 1539, *Blau,* 597/1, p. 348; Ferdinand to Charles, May 3, 1539, ibid., p. 357; Ferdinand to Charles, Apr. 9, 1535, ibid., p. 165; Ferdinand to Charles, Aug. 27, 1535, ibid., p. 174.

53. Rosenberg, *Kaiser und Protestanten,* pp. 9-10, 13.

54. Ibid., pp. 17-18; Ferdinand to Charles, s.d. May, 1536, *Blau,* 597/ 1, p. 210; Ferdinand to Charles, April 12, 1537, ibid., pp. 246-247.

55. Rosenberg, *Kaiser und Protestanten,* p. 16; Ranke, *Deutsche Geschichte,* p. 797; Ferdinand to Charles, May 15, 1538, *Blau,* 597/1, p. 302; Ferdinand to Charles, July 8, 1537, ibid., pp. 257-259; Ferdinand to Charles, Aug. 18, 1537, ibid., p. 264.

56. Ferdinand to Charles, Nov. 3, 1537, ibid., p. 266; Ferdinand to Charles, Oct. 22, 1538, ibid., p. 331; Ferdinand to Charles, April 6, 1538, ibid., p. 289; Ferdinand to Charles, July 29, 1540, ibid., p. 424.

57. Ferdinand to Charles, Nov. 17, 1539, ibid., pp. 384-385; Ferdinand to Charles, Jan. 26, 1540, ibid., p. 392; Ferdinand to Charles, Sept. 6, 1540, ibid., p. 434.

58. Ferdinand to Charles, Jan. 10, 1539, ibid., p. 342; Ferdinand to Charles, Aug. 4, 1539, ibid., p. 370; Ferdinand to Charles, Sept. 5, 1539, ibid., p. 380; Ferdinand to Charles, Nov. 5, 1539, ibid., p. 381.

59. Ferdinand to Charles, June 21, 1539, ibid., pp. 363-364; Ferdinand to Charles, June 2, 1540, ibid., pp. 396-397.

60. Ferdinand to Charles, June 16, 1540, ibid., p. 403; Ferdinand to Charles, June 23, 1540, ibid., pp. 407-409; Ferdinand to Charles, July 10, 1540, ibid., p. 415; Ferdinand to Charles, Sept. 13, 1540, ibid., p. 436.

61. Ferdinand to Charles, July 10, 1540, ibid., p. 416; Ferdinand to Charles, July 29, 1540, ibid., p. 423; Ferdinand to Charles, Sept. 6, 1540, ibid., p. 433.

62. Brandi, *Karl V,* 1: 376.

Notes to Chapter IX

1. Heinrich Kretschmayer, "Ludovico Gritti," *AöG,* 83 (1897); 25-26, 34-36, 42, 57, 66, 70-72, 81-83; Bucholtz, *Regierung,* 4: 141; Holtzmann,

Maximilian II, p. 30; Ferdinand to Charles, Oct. 8, 1534, *Blau,* 597/1, p. 147.

2. Holtzmann, *Maximilian II,* pp. 30-31; Ferdinand to Charles, Aug. 27, 1535, *Blau,* 597/1, p. 172; Andreas Cornaro, "Eine Reise des Kardinals Bernhard von Cles zu Kaiser Karl V. nach Neapel im Jahre 1536 nach seinen Briefen an Ferdinand I," *Römische historische Mitteilungen,* 2 (1957/1958): 56-58.

3. Ferdinand to Charles, Oct. 2, 1534, *Blau,* 597/1, p. 145; Ferdinand to Charles, Nov. 3, 1534, ibid., p. 147; Ferdinand to Charles, Aug. 27, 1535, ibid., p. 173.

4. Ferdinand to Charles, April 27, 1536, ibid., p. 202; Ferdinand to Charles, June ?, 1536, ibid., p. 221; Ferdinand to Charles, June 7, 1536, ibid., pp. 166-167; Ferdinand to Charles, April 30, 1536, ibid., p. 204.

5. Gunther Rothenberg, *The Austrian Military Border in Croatia 1522-1747,* Illinois Studies in the Social Sciences, 48 (1960): 23; Ferdinand to Bernhard von Cles, Sept. 7, 1535, Bucholtz, *Regierung,* 9: 64; Ferdinand to Charles, Oct. 7, 1535, *Blau,* 597/1, p. 178.

6. Ferdinand to Charles, Dec. 15/16, AG, *Estado, Alemania,* Legajo 637, fo. 23; Huber, *Geschichte Österreichs,* 4: 58-59.

7. Thomas Nádasdy, Alexis Thurzó *et al.* to Charles, AGR, *Allemande,* fasc. 766, fo. 493; Ferdinand to Charles, July 12, 1534, *Blau,* 597/1, pp. 135-136.

8. Memorandum from Charles's chancellory on the report of Cornelius Scepperus from Constantinople, 1533, AGR, *Allemande,* fasc. 766, fos. 228-232; Ferdinand to Charles, Jan. 20, 1535, *Blau,* 597/1, pp. 153-154; Ferdinand to Charles, April 9, 1535, ibid., p. 161; Ferdinand to Charles, July 8, 1537, ibid., p. 255; Kretschmayer, "Gritti," pp. 54-55.

9. Ferdinand to Charles, July 8, 1537, *Blau,* 597/1, p. 256.

10. Huber, *Geschichte Österreichs,* 4: 60-62; Rosenberg, *Kaiser und Protestanten,* p. 23; Ferdinand to Charles, Nov. 3, 1537, *Blau,* 597/1, p. 270.

11. Rosenberg, *Kaiser und Protestanten,* p. 23; Ferdinand to Charles, Nov. 3, 1537, *Blau,* 597/1, p. 268; Ferdinand to Charles, Dec. 20, 1537, ibid., pp. 273-274; Ferdinand to Charles, Feb. 6, 1538, ibid., pp. 282-283; Ferdinand to Charles, Feb. 8, 1538, ibid., p. 283; Huber, *Geschichte Österreichs,* 4: 60-62.

12. Ferdinand to Charles, Mar. 2, 1538, *Blau,* 597/1, p. 285; Ognjeslav Utjesenović, *Lebensgeschichte des Cardinals Georg Utiesenović [sic]*

genannt Martinuzzi (Vienna: Braumüller, 1881), p. 45; Szekfű, *Magyar történet,* 4: 37.

13. Gindely, "Erbrechte," pp. 206-207; Huber, *Reichsgeschichte,* p. 170.

14. Ferdinand to Charles, June 3, 1538, *Blau,* 597/1, p. 307; Ferdinand to Charles, Jan. 10, 1539, ibid., p. 343; Ferdinand to Charles, Aug. 1, 1538, ibid., pp. 317-318; Utjesenović, *Utiesenović,* pp. 47-48; Ferdinand to Charles, Nov. 15, 1538, *Blau,* 597/1, pp. 334-336.

15. Ferdinand to Charles, Feb. 15, 1539, *Blau,* 597/1, p. 345.

16. Ferdinand to Charles, April 2, 1539, ibid., pp. 349-351; Ferdinand to Charles, Aug. 8, 1539, ibid., pp. 374-375; Ferdinand to Charles, Aug. 4, 1539, ibid., p. 370; Ferdinand to Charles, July 10, 1540, ibid., p. 412.

17. Ferdinand to Charles, July 8, 1539, ibid., pp. 365-366; Ferdinand to Charles, ibid., Aug. ?, 1539, ibid., pp. 375-376; Ferdinand to Charles, Nov. 15, 1539, ibid., p. 382.

18. Ferdinand to Charles, Aug. 18, 1540, ibid., pp. 429-431; Utjesenović, *Utiesenović,* pp. 33, 52; Bucholtz, *Regierung,* 5: 146; Huber, "Erwerbung," p. 486.

19. Bucholtz, *Regierung,* 5: 131, 136-137; bishop of Modena to Cardinaal Farnese, Sept. 3, 1540, *Monumenta Hungarica: Diplomataria,* 16: 112; Ranke, *Deutsche Geschichte,* pp. 858-859.

20. Utjesenović, *Utiesenović,* pp. 49-50; Huber, *Geschichte Österreichs,* 4: 71; Übersberger, *Österreich und Russland,* pp. 254-255; bishop of Modena to Cardinal Farnese, Sept. 3, 1540, *Monumenta Hungarica: Diplomataria,* 16: 112.

21. Ferdinand to Charles, Aug. 24, 1540, *Blau,* 597/1: 432; Ferdinand to Charles, Sept. 13, 1540, ibid., p. 436.

22. Bucholtz, *Regierung,* 5: 143; Ferdinand to Charles, Sept. 6, 1540, *Blau,* 597/1, p. 434; Ferdinand to Charles, Sept. 13, 1540, ibid., p. 435.

23. Utjesenović, *Utiesenović,* p. 52; Alexander Gonfallenero to Cardinal Farnese, Jan. 4, 1541, *Monumenta Hungarica: Diplomataria,* 16, p. 25; Oberleitner, "Finanzwesen," p. 76.

24. Ferdinand to Charles, Nov. 8, 1540, *Blau,* 597/1: 442-443; 446; Huber, *Geschichte Österreichs,* 4: 69.

25. Ferdinand to Charles, Feb. 7, 1541, *Blau,* 597/1, pp. 456-457; Ferdinand to Charles, Feb. 25, 1541, ibid., p. 460; Otto Zinkeisen, *Geschichte*

des osmanischen Reiches in Europa, 7 vols. (Hamburg: Perthes, 1840-1863), 2: 841; Ferdinand to Mary, March 15, 1541, SA, *Belgica, PA* 12, fos. 5-6; Árpád Károlyi, "A német birodalom nagy hadi vállalata Magyarországon 1542," *Századok,* 16: 289-290, note 1; Fischer-Galati, *Ottoman Imperialism,* p. 77.

26. Bishop of Modena to Cardinal Farnese, April 19, 1541, *Monumenta Hungarica: Diplomataria,* 16: 127; Alexis Thurzó to Archbishop Francis Frankopan, June 4, 1541, ibid., p. 130; Sanzioto Cardinal Farnese, April 17, 1541, *Nuntiaturberichte aus Deutschland,* ed. Preussisches historische Institut in Rom, Part 1, 1534-1559, 12 vols. (Gotha: Perthes, 1892-1970), 7: 41; Morone to Cardinal Farnese, May 15, 1541, ibid., p. 55; Ferdinand to Mary, May 17, 1541, SA, *Belgica, PA* 12, fo. 25.

27. Paul Heidrich, *Karl V und die deutschen Protestanten am Vorabend des Schmalkaldischen Krieges,* 2 parts. Frankfurter historische Forschungen, nos. 5 and 6 (1911-1912), 1: 16-17.

28. Sanzio to Cardinal Farnese, June 24, 1541, *Nuntiaturberichte,* 7: 69-70; Morone to Cardinal Farnese, June 25, 1541, ibid., p. 71.

29. Fischer-Galati, *Ottoman Imperialism,* pp. 79, 83; Huber, *Geschichte Österreichs,* 4: 76.

30. Fischer-Galati, *Ottoman Imperialism,* pp. 83-84; Sir Charles Oman, *The Art of War in the Sixteenth Century* (New York: Dutton, 1927), p. 695; Ferdinand to Mary, SA, *Belgica, PA* 12, fos. 32-33; Ferdinand to Mary, Sept 24, 1541, ibid., fo. 40; Ferdinand to Charles, Aug. 26, 1541, *Blau,* 597/1, p. 469.

31. Verallo to Cardinal Farnese, Sept. 5, 1541, *Nuntiaturberichte,* 7: 162; Ferdinand to Charles, Sept. 1541, *Blau,* 597/1, pp. 471-472; Ferdinand to Mary, Oct. 31, 1541, SA, *Belgica, PA* 12, fo. 45; Ferdinand to Mary, Oct. 26, 1541, SA, *Belgica, PA* 7, fo. 10; Károlyi, "A német birodalom," pp. 357, 362, 366.

32. Walter Björkman, *Ofen zur Türkenzeit,* Abhandlungen aus dem Gebiet der Auslandskunde, Series B, 2 (Hamburg, 1920): 16 and note 10; Ferdinand to Charles, Dec. 28, 1541, ibid., p. 476; Ferdinand to Mary, Nov. 26, 1541, SA, *Belgica, PA* 12, fo. 47; Utjesenović, *Utiesenović,* p. 59; Huber, *Geschichte Österreichs,* 4: 82-84.

33. Heidrich, *Karl V und die deutschen Protestanten,* 1: 55. John Ferderick of Saxony and Philip of Hesse to Maurice of Saxony, Oct. 24, 1541, *Politische Korrespondenz des Herzogs und Kurfürsten Moritz von*

Sachsen, ed. Erich Brandenburg, 2 vols. (Leipzig: Teubner, 1900), 1: 224; Bucholtz, *Regierung,* 5: 163-165.

34. Marnolz to Mary, Sept. 26, 1541, SA, *Belgica, PA* 41, fo. 12.

35. Ferdinand to Mary, Dec. 28, 1541, ibid., *PA* 12, fo. 51; Ferdinand to Charles, Dec. 28, 1541, ibid., *PA* 7, fo. 7; Bucholtz, *Regierung,* 5: 167; Oman, *Sixteenth Century,* pp. 78-79, 87; d'Alençon to Francis I, Mar. 3, 1542 in Károlyi, "A német birodalom," p. 585, note 1; Bishop of Modena to Cardinal Farnese, June 4, 1542, *Monumenta Hungarica: Diplomataria,* 16: 135.

36. Bishop of Modena to Cardinal Farnese, Nov. 11, 1540, *Monumenta Hungarica: Diplomataria,* 16; 121; Verallo to Cardinal Farnese, Oct. 1, 1541, *Nuntiaturberichte,* 7: 170; Oman, *Sixteenth Century,* pp. 115-129, 130-149, 196, 688, 693; J. R. Hale, "Armies, Navies, and the Art of War," *New Cambridge Modern History,* 2: 482; Károlyi, "A német birodalom," pp. 567-568.

37. Károlyi, "A német birodalom," pp. 374-375.

38. Ferdinand to Charles, Mar. 2, 1538, *Blau,* 597/1, p. 287; Nicolo Tiepolo *et al.* to the Doge, May 24, 1538, *Venetianische Depeschen vom Kaiserhofe,* ed. Historische Commission der kaiserlichen Akademie der Wissenschaften, 4 vols. (Vienna: Tempsky, 1889-1901), 1: 71-72; Ferdinand to Charles, April 29, 1538, *Blau,* 597/1: 296; Ferdinand to Charles, April 17, 1538, ibid., p. 295; Ferdinand to Charles, Aug. 1, 1538, ibid., p. 319.

39. Ferdinand to Charles, Aug. 24, 1540, ibid., p. 431, Ferdinand to Charles, Sept. 6, 1540, ibid., p. 433.

40. Adolf Hasenclever, "Johann von Naves aus Luxemburg, Reichsvizekanzler unter Kaiser Karl V," *MIöG,* 26 (1905): 305-306; Jean de Naves to Charles, Nov. 12, 1541, Lanz, *Correspondenz,* 2: 328-329; Ferdinand to Charles, Nov. 9, 1541, in Árpád Károlyi, "Kiadatlan levelek a német birodalom magyarországi nagy hadi vállalatának történetéhez, 1542," *Történelmi Tár* (1880): 496. For a detailed account of the 1542 campaign see my "Dynasticism and Its Limitations: the Habsburgs and Hungary, 1542," *East European Quarterly,* 4 (1971): 389-407.

41. Mary to Charles, March 23, 1542, SA, *Belgica, PA* 41, fo. 118; Zinkeisen, *Osmanisches Reich,* 2: 849; Bucholtz, *Regierung,* 5: 165.

42. Charles to Naves, Jan. 11, 1542, Lanz, *Correspondenz,* 2: 335; Ferdinand to Charles, Mar. 4, 1542, Károlyi, "Kiadatlan levelek," p. 505.

43.   Charles to Ferdinand, Dec. 29, 1541 in Károlyi, "Kiadatlan levelek," p. 498-499. Charles to Ferdinand, Mar. 14, 1542, ibid., pp. 508-
509; Charles to Granvella, Dec. 28, 1541, SA, *Belgica, PA* 46, fo. 233;
Károlyi, "A német birodalom," pp. 378-384.

44.   Ferdinand to Charles, June 4, 1542, Károlyi, "Kiadatlan levelek,"
pp. 520-521; Charles to Ferdinand, May 10, 1542, ibid., pp. 515-516;
Károlyi, "A német birodalom," pp. 628-630.

45.   Christian Meyer, "Die Feldhauptmannschaft Joachim II im Türkenkriege von 1542," *Zeitschrift für preussische Geschichte und Landeskunde,* 16 (1879): 481; Hermann Traut, *Kurfürst Joachim II. von Brandenburg und der Türkenfeldzüge vom Jahre 1542* (Gummersbach: Luyken,
1892), p. 26.

46.   Ferdinand to Charles, April 13, 1542, Károlyi, "Kiadatlan levelek," pp. 510-512; Ferdinand to Charles, June 4, 1542, ibid., p. 521; Ferdinand to Charles, May 24, 1542, SA, *Belgica, PA* 7, fos. 67-68; Henri
Pirenne, *Historie de Belgique,* 7 vols. (Brussels: Lamertin, 1908-1932),
3: 90-93, 95, 134, 136; Felix Rachfall, "Die Trennung der Niederlande
vom deutschen Reiche," *Westdeutsche Zeitschrift für Geschichte und
Kunst,* 19 (1900): 88, claims that there is no evidence that any imperial
jurisdiction was exercised in the so-called Burgundian circle after its formation in 1512.

47.   Jakob May, *Der Kurfürst, Cardinal und Erzbischof Albrecht II
von Mainz und Magdeburg,* 2 vols. (Munich: Franz, 1865-1875), 2: 394;
Conrad Varrentrapp, *Hermann von Wied und sein Reformationsversuch in
Köln* (Leipzig: Duncker and Humblot, 1878), p. 221; Julius Traugott
Jacob von Könneritz (posthumous papers), "Erasmus von Könneritz in
dem Kriegszuge gegen die Türken 1542," *Archiv für die sächsische Geschichte,* 8 (1870): 80-88.

48.   Traut, *Joachim,* pp. 68-69; Heidrich, *Karl V und die deutschen
Protestanten,* 1: 88-100, *passim.*

49.   Traut, *Joachim,* p. 63; Ferdinand to Mary, July 27, 1542, SA,
Belgica, PA 12, fo. 114; Ferdinand to Mary, Aug. 12, 1542, ibid., fos.
120-121, 124-125; Ferdinand to Mary, Aug. 25, 1542, ibid., fo. 126;
Pirenne, *Histoire,* 3: 103.

50.   Heidrich, *Karl V und die deutschen Protestanten,* 1: 101; Ferdinand to Charles, Sept. 27, 1542, Károlyi, "Kiadatlan levelek," pp. 533-
534.

51. Károlyi, "A német birodalom," p. 639; Meyer, "Feldhauptmannschaft," pp. 481-482; Traut, *Joachim,* p. 33; Fischer-Galati, *Ottoman Imperialism,* p. 67.

52. Georg Voigt, *Moritz von Sachsen, 1541-1547* (Leipzig: Tauschnitz, 1876), p. 43; Bucholtz, *Regierung,* 5: 167; Károlyi, "A német birodalom," p. 626; Könneritz, "Könneritz," p. 87.

53. Könneritz, "Könneritz," p. 92; Moritz Nubes to Stephen Roth, July 21, 1542 in Otto Clemen, " Zum Türkenfeldzug des Kurfürsten Joachim II von Brandenburg," *Jahrbuch für brandenburgische Kirchengeschichte,* 34 (1939): 94; Traut, *Joachim II,* pp. 77, 79.

54. Traut, *Joachim II,* pp. 95-96; Alexis Thurzó to Joachim, July 26, 1542, Károlyi, "Kiadatlan levelek," pp. 527-529; Károlyi, "A német birodalom," p. 625.

55. Károlyi, "A német birodalom," pp. 633, 640; Traut, *Joachim II,* pp. 38, 96-98; Könneritz, "Könneritz," p. 93; Meyer, "Feldhauptmannschaft," p. 506.

56. Meyer, "Feldhauptmannschaft," p. 522; Traut, *Joachim II, p.* 112; report of Hans Ungnad in Lanz, *Correspondenz,* 2: 376. Cf. Voigt, *Moritz von Sachsen,* p. 49.

57. Verallo to Cardinal Farnese, Oct. 26, 1542, *Nuntiaturberichte,* 7: 269.

58. Ferdinand to Mary, Oct. 21, 1542, SA, *Belgica, PA* 12, fo. 132, Meyer, "Feldhauptmannschaft," pp. 507-508; Bucholtz, *Regierung,* 5: 170-171.

59. Verallo to Cardinal Farnese, June 8, 1542, *Nuntiaturberichte,* 7: 212; Verallo to Cardinal Farnese, Sept. 22, 1542, ibid., pp. 218-219; Verallo to Farnese, Sept. 22, 1542, ibid., p. 256.

60. Bucholtz, *Regierung,* 5: 171; report of Verallo of letters of Francis Frankopan, Oct. 13, 1542, *Monumenta Hungarica: Diplomataria,* 16: 158-159.

61. Charles to Ferdinand, Nov. 3, 1542, Károlyi, "Kiadatlan levelek," p. 537; Ferdinand to Charles, May 31, 1543, *Blau,* 597/2, fo. 90; Ferdinand to Charles, July 29, 1543, ibid., fo. 76.

62. Merriman, *Suleiman,* p. 268; Ferdinand to Charles, July 23, 1543, *Blau,* 597/2, fo. 94.

63. Ferdinand to Charles, Oct. 3, 1543, *Blau,* 597/2, fo. 101; Ferdinand to Charles, Oct. 18, 1543, ibid., fo. 102.

64. Ferdinand to Charles, Oct. 19, 1544, ibid., fo. 125; Ferdinand to Charles, Dec. 11, 1544, ibid., fo. 128; Ferdinand to Charles, Feb. 11, 1545, ibid., fo. 132.

65. Ferdinand to Charles, Oct. 18, 1543, ibid., fo. 102; Ferdinand to Charles, Feb. 11, 1545, ibid., fo. 132; Huber, *Geschichte Österreichs*, 4: 89; Huber, "Finanzielle Verhältnisse," p. 214.

66. Ferdinand to Charles, Oct. 14, 1544, *Blau*, 597/2, fo. 124; Ferdinand to Charles, Nov. 21, 1545, ibid., fo. 149; Ferdinand to Charles, Nov. 22, 1545, ibid., fo. 150; Ferdinand to Charles, April 14, 1546, fo. 166, 168; Charles to Ferdinand, Sept. 1545, AG, *Estado, Flandes*, Legajo 501, fo. 149.

67. Ferdinand to Charles, Feb. 14, 1545, *Blau*, 597/2, fo. 135; Ferdinand to Chares, Dec. 21, 1545, ibid., fo. 159; Merriman, *Suleiman*, pp. 269-270.

69. Bucholtz, *Regierung*, 5: 180-181, 183; *Geschichte Österreichs*, 4: 88; Karlowitz to Ferdinand, Nov. 1542, Károlyi, "Kiadatlan levelek," pp. 539-540; Maurice of Saxony agreed. Maurice to Ferdinand, Nov. 1542, ibid., pp. 538-539.

69. Heiß, "Besitzungen," pp. 92-93; Ferdinand to Charles, Dec. 2, 1548, *Blau*, 597/2, fo. 290; Helmut Goetz, "Die Finalrelation des venezianischen Gesandten Michele Suriano, 1555," *QuF*, 41 (1961): 274-275, 287-289.

70. Ferdinand to Charles, Jan. 19, 1541, *Blau*, 597/1, p. 542.

71. Ferdinand to Charles, Dec. 29, 1542, ibid., fo. 84; Huber, "Erwerbung," p. 488.

72. Huber, "Erwerbung," p. 490.

73. Ibid., pp. 502-505, 513-545, *passim;* Ferdinand to Charles, Jan. 2, 1552, *Blau*, 597/3, fo. 64.

74. Alfons Huber, "Die Verhandlungen Ferdinand I mit Isabella von Siebenbürgen 1551-1555," *AöG*, 78 (1892): 5-6, 14, 34.

75. Ibid., pp. 5, 9-10, 37, note 2.

76. Ibid., p. 19; Henry II to Sigismund Augustus, Dec. 29, 1552 (copy), AGR, *Allemande*, fasc. 801, fo. 352; Prothonotary of Poitiers to Mary, 1553, ibid., fasc. 802, fos. 480-481; Ferdinand to Charles, Dec. 10, 1552, Lanz, *Correspondenz*, 3: 523-525; Ferdinand to Charles, Jan. 26, 1553, ibid., p. 537; Ferdinand to Charles, Dec. 29, 1553, ibid., pp. 603-604.

77. Huber, "Verhandlungen," pp. 37-38.

78. Goetz, "Finalrelation," p. 315.

79. Huber, "Verhandlungen," pp. 38-39; Ferdinand to Charles, Oct. 29, 1553, *Blau,* 597/3, fo. 238.

80. Ferdinand to Maximilian, Jan. 20, 1557, SA, *Familienkorrespondenz A,* Karton 2, fos. 128-129; Ferdinand to Maximilian, Jan. 17, 1559?, ibid., fo. 156; Ferdinand to Maximilian, Dec. 7, 1559?, ibid., fo. 171; Josef Žontar, "Michael Cernović, Geheimagent Ferdinands I. und Maximilians II., und seine Berichtenstattung," *MöSA,* 24 (1971): 183-184, 195-197; report to Granvella, AG, *Estado, Flandes,* Legajo 522, fo. 79.

81. Goetz, "Finalrelation," p. 270.

82. Győző Ember, "Ungarns Außenhankel mit dem Westen um die Mitte des XVI Jahrhunderts," in *Außenhandel Ostmitteleuropas,* pp. 93, 95, 101-103; László Makkai, "Der ungarische Viehhandel 1550-1650," ibid., pp. 490-491; 499, 501; Pickl, "Auswirkungen," pp. 93, 126.

83. Goetz, "Finalrelation," pp. 274-275, 287-289, 314, and note 290.

84. Berthold Picard, *Das Gesandtschaftswesen Ostmitteleuropas in der frühen Neuzeit,* Wiener: Archiv für Geschichte des Slawentums und Osteuropas, 6 (Vienna, 1967): 118.

Notes to Chapter X

1. Bucholtz, *Regierung,* 4: 423.

2. Ferdinand to Vojtěch of Pernštejn, May 25, 1530, *Archiv česky* 20: 351; Ferdinand to Jan of Pernštejn, Sept. 5, 1538, ibid., pp. 418-419; Ferdinand to Jan of Pernštejn, Dec. 6, 1542, ibid., pp. 464-465, 468-469.

3. Ferdinand to Jan of Lippého, Jan of Pernštejn, *et al.,* Dec. 20, 1533, ibid., p. 31; Ferdinand to Jan of Pernštejn, May 2, 1534, ibid., p. 34; Ferdinand to Jan of Pernštejn, June 27, 1529, ibid., p. 539; Ferdinand to Jan of Pernštejn, May 15, 1534, ibid., 20: 34-35.

4. Dillon, *King and Estates,* pp. 46-47; Bretholz, *Neuere Geschichte Böhmens,* 1: 80-82; Bucholtz, *Regierung,* 4: 451-454; Wácslav. W. Tomek, *Dějěpis města Prahy,* 12 vols. (Prague: Řiwanč, 1855-1901), 11: 63, 65-66, 69, 81, 101; Ludwig Schlesinger, *Geschichte Böhmens* (Prague/Leipzig: Calve'sche Buchandlung/Brockhaus, 1869), pp. 439-440.

5. J. K. Zeman, "The Rise of Religious Liberty in the Czech Reformation," *Central European History,* 6 (1973): 141-142; Denis, *Premiers*

Habsbourgs, pp. 20, 70. On sects in Moravia in the first part of the sixteenth century see Otakar Odložilík, "Jednota bratří Habrovanských," *Ččh,* 29 (1923): 15-16.

6. Ferdinand to Jan of Pernštejn, Feb. 24, 1545; *Archiv český,* 20: 223; Hrejsa, *Dějiny krest'anstvi,* 5:8, Otakar Odložilík, "A Church in a Hostile State: the Unity of Czech Brethren," *Central European History,* 6 (1973): 116.

7. Hrejsa, *Dějiny křest'anstvi,* 5: 13, 27, Odložilík, "Jednota bratří," p. 16; Betts, *Cambridge Modern History,* 2: 200; Dillon, *Kings and Estates,* pp. 76-77.

8. Goetz, "Finalrelation," p. 280; Eduard Šimek, "Die Zusammenhänge zwischen Währung und Handel in Böhmen des 16. Jahrhunderts," in Bog, *Außenhandel,* p. 242; Ferdinand to Mary, Jan. 21, 1530, *Korrespondenz,* 2² : 572; Ferdinand to Mary, March 25, 1530, ibid., pp. 618-619.

9. Quoted in Hans Sturmberger, "Türkengefahr und österreichische Staatlichkeit," *Südostdeutsche Archiv,* 10 (1967): 136.

10. Ferdinand to Mary, Jan. 28, 1530, *Korrespondenz,* 2² : 590; Krones, *Handbuch,* 3: 206.

11. For the period 1539-1550, archducal possessions in Lower Austria showed a net profit of 10,557 pounds whereas the Styrian domains ran a deficit of 497 pounds from 1531-1539. For the years 1537 to 1541, the Hungarian treasury showed a profit of 51,103 florins. Oberleitner, "Finanzen," pp. 81, 199-201.

12. Hirn, *Ferdinand von Tirol,* 1: 10; Hanns Leo Mikoletzky, "Der Haushalt des kaiserlichen Hofes zu Wien (vornehmlich im 18. Jahrhundert)," *Carinthia I,* 146 (1956): 668-670; Oberleitner, "Finanzen," pp. 224-228. Cf. Huber, "Finanziellen Verhältnisse," p. 20); Friedrich Firnhaber, "Der Hofstaat König Ferdinands im Jahre 1554," *Archiv für Kunde österreichischer Geschichtsquellen,* 26 (1861): 3.

13. Firnhaber, "Hofstaat," pp. 13-28; Oberleitner, "Finanzen," 90, 224-228; SA, *Haus-Archiv, Familien Akten,* Karton 97, fo. 50.

14. SA, *Haus-Archiv, Familien Akten,* Karton 97, fos. 6, 56-7, 63-5.

15. Janáček, *Doba předbělohorská,* pp. 259-261, tables 3a, 3b.

16. Oberleitner, "Finanzen," pp. 65-66, 74-75, 77, 89, note 75.

17. Huber, *Reichsgeschichte,* pp. 210-211; Bucholtz, *Regierung,* 4: 522-523; Dillon, *Kings and Estates,* p. 41; *Landtagsverhandlungen,* 2: 14.

18. Johann Loserth and Franz Freiherr von Mensi, "Die Prager Ländertagung von 1541/1542," *AöG,* 103 (1913): 438-40, 552; Josef Polišensky,

"Bohemia, the Turk, and the Christian Commonwealth (1462-1620)," *Byzantinoslavica,* 14 (1953): 93.

19. Polišenský, "Christian Commonwealth," 94.

20. Leonhard von Muralt, ed., *Quellen zur Geschichte der Täufer in der Schweiz. Zürich,* vol. 1 (Zürich: Hirzel, 1952): 255; Manfred Krebs, ed., *Quellen zur Geschichte der Täufer, IV: Baden und Pfalz,* Quellen und Forschungen zur Reformationsgeschichte, 23 (Gütersloh, 1951): 395; Karl Schornbaum, ed., *Quellen zur Geschichte der Täufer, II: Bayern,* Ibid., p. 547; Grete Mecenseffy, "Herkunft oberösterreichischen Täufer," *ARG,* 57 (1956): 252-258; Hrejsa, *Dějiny křest'anství,* 5: 123.

21. Hrejsa, *Dějiny křest'anství,* p. 103; Denis, *Premiers Habsbourgs,* pp. 91-94, 157; Dillon, *Kings and Estates,* pp. 71, 100-101.

22. Betts, *Cambridge Modern History,* 2: 471-472.

23. Ferdinand to Charles, Sept. 23, 1544, *Blau,* 597/2, fo. 123; Bucholtz, *Regierung,* 6: 347.

24. Bucholtz, *Regierung,* 4: 456-460; Dillon, *Kings and Estates,* p. 85.

25. Ferdinand to Charles, Nov. 9, 1541, *Blau,* 597/1: 479-481.

26. Fischer-Galati, *Ottoman Imperialism,* p. 85.

27. Ibid., pp. 86-87; Heidrich, *Karl V und die Protestanten,* 1: 120, 122, 144; Bucholtz, *Regierung,* 5: 41; Jaroslav Springer, *Beiträge zur Geschichte des Wormser Reichstags 1544 und 1545* (diss.: Leipzig, 1882), pp. 20, 24.

28. Ferdinand to Charles, Aug. 13, 1544, *Blau,* 597/2, fo. 120; Ferdinand to Charles, Dec. 6, 1543, ibid., fo. 110; Ferdinand to Charles, June 26, 1543, ibid., fo. 92; Ferdinand to Charles, July 6, 1543, ibid., fo. 93; Ferdinand to Charles, Feb. 11, 1545, ibid., fo. 133.

29. Heidrich, *Karl V und die Protestanten,* 1: 107; Brandi, *Karl V,* 1: 429.

30. Ferdinand to Charles, Nov. 9, 1541, *Blau,* 597/1: 479-481; Ferdinand to Charles, Aug. 26, 1542, ibid., 597/2, fo. 56; Ferdinand to Charles, Nov. 8, 1545, ibid., fo. 147.

31. Ferdinand to Charles, Nov. 8, 1545, ibid., fo. 148; Ferdinand to Charles, April 16, 1546, ibid., fo. 167; Ferdinand to Charles, Feb. 18, 1546, ibid., fos. 165-166; Ferdinand to Charles, April 14, 1546, ibid., fo. 146; Ferdinand to Charles, April 14, 1546, ibid., fo. 167; Heidrich, *Karl V und die Protestanten,* 2: 96-97.

32.   Bucholtz, *Regierung,* 5: 546-547; Ferdinand to Charles, April 14, 1546, *Blau,* 597/2, fo. 148; Heidrich, *Karl V und die Protestanten,* 2: 149.

33.   On the potential hazards of the campaign see the remarks of Alvise Mocenigo and Bernardo Navager in *Venetianische Depeschen,* 1: 498.

34.   Charles to Ferdinand, May 1, 1546, Druffel, *Beiträge,* 1: 10; Ferdinand to Charles, Oct. 24, 1546, SA, *Belgien, PA* 8, fo. 283; Ferdinand to Charles, Nov. 16, 1546, ibid., fo. 303.

35.   Bucholtz, *Regierung,* 6: 357; Voigt, *Moritz von Sachsen,* p. 211; Verallo to Farnese, July 19, 1546, *Nuntiaturberichte,* 1^9: 125; Charles to Ferdinand, Aug. 17, 1546; SA, *Belgien, PA* 6, Konv. 1, fo. 38.

36.   Paula Sutter Fichtner, "When Brothers Agree: Bohemia, the Habsburgs, and the Schmalkaldic Wars, 1546-1547," *Austrian History Yearbook,* 11 (1975): 69-70; Bretholz, *Neuere Geschichte,* p. 152; Ferdinand to Charles, Aug. 28, 1546, *Blau,* 597/2: fo. 175.

37.   Bretholz, *Neuere Geschichte,* p. 165; Ferdinand to Charles, Nov. 18, 1542, *Blau,* 597/2, fo. 75; Ferdinand to Charles, Aug. 24, 1543, ibid., fo. 100; Ferdinand to Charles, Nov. 16, 1543, ibid., fo. 108.

38.   Ferdinand to Charles, Oct. 24, 1546, *Blau,* 597/2, fo. 188; Ferdinand to Charles, Aug. 28, 1546, ibid., fos. 174-175; Ferdinand to Charles, Oct. 24, 1546, ibid., fo. 188.

39.   Ferdinand to Charles, Oct. 24, 1546, ibid., fo. 187; Ferdinand to Charles, Oct. 31, 1546, ibid., fo. 189; Ferdinand to Charles, Nov. 4, 1546, ibid., fos. 190-191; Ferdinand to Charles, Nov. 11, 1546, Nov. 11, fo. 193; Ferdinand to Charles, Nov. 16, 1546, fos. 193-194.

40.   Voigt, *Moritz,* pp. 181, 184-185; Bretholz, *Neuere Geschichte,* pp. 164-165.

41.   Bretholz, *Neuere Geschichte,* p. 165; Karel Tieftrunk, *Odpor českých stavů proti Ferdinandovi I. 1. 1547* (Prague: Řiwnać, 1872), pp. 64-65.

42.   Adolf Bachmann, *Geschichte Böhmens,* 2 vols. (Gotha: Perthes, 1905), 2: 498-499; Tieftrunk, *Odpor,* pp. 27, 29.

43.   Bretholz, *Neuere Geschichte,* pp. 149-150.

44.   Fichtner, "Brothers," pp. 70-71.

45.   Ferdinand to Charles, Jan. 8, 1547, *Blau,* 597/2, fo. 206; Ferdinand to Charles, Dec. 18, 1546, ibid., fo. 197.

46.   Ferdinand to Charles, Oct. 31, 1546, ibid., fo. 189; Ferdinand to Charles, Oct. 29, 1546, ibid., fo. 187; Ferdinand to Charles, Nov. 8, 1546,

ibid., fo. 192; Ferdinand to Charles, Dec. 26, 1546, ibid., fo. 198.

47. Ferdinand to Charles, Dec. 30, 1546, ibid., fo. 199; Ferdinand to Charles, Sept. 4, 1546, ibid., fo. 176.

48. Charles to Ferdinand, Oct. 9, 1546, Druffel, *Beiträge*, 1: 23.

49. Huber, *Geschichte Österreichs*, 4: 121-122; Tieftrunk, *Odpor*, pp. 64-65; Tomek, *Město Prahy*, 11: 306; Krones, *Handbuch*, 3: 207.

50. "...une perpetuelle obeissance, sehurte pour moy et mes hoirs et successeurs en ce royaulme et autres mes pays...." Ferdinand to Charles, Dec. 30, 1546, *Blau*, 597/2, fo. 200.

51. Ferdinand to Charles, Jan. 2, 1547, SA, *Belgien, PA* 9, fo. 1; Ferdinand to Charles, Jan. 10, 1547, ibid., fo. 18.

52. Ferdinand's announcement of Anna's death (sketch) SA, *Haus-Archiv, Familien-Akten*, Karton 60, Konv. 3, fo. 1; *Landtagsverhandlungen*, 2: 53, 57; Voigt, *Moritz von Sachsen*, p. 282.

53. Voigt, *Moritz von Sachsen*, p. 282; Bretholz, *Neuere Geschichte*, p. 172.

54. Voigt, *Moritz von Sachsen*, p. 284; Ferdinand to Charles, Jan. 8, 1547, *Blau*, 597/2, fo. 207; Ferdinand to Charles, Jan. 24, 1547, ibid., fos. 211-212.

55. Bretholz, *Neuere Geschichte*, pp. 172-173; *Landtagsverhandlungen*, 2: 59-60; Ferdinand to Charles, Feb. 8, 1547, *Blau*, 597/2, fo. 218.

56. Franz Martin Pelzel (Pelcl), *Geschichte der Böhmen*, 2 vols. (Prague/Vienna: Schönfeld, 1782), 2: 592; Bucholtz, *Regierung*, 6: 377; Huber, *Geschichte Österreichs*, 4: 125; Ferdinand to Charles, Feb. 20/21, 1547, SA, *Belgien, PA* 9, fo. 52.

57. Bretholz, *Neuere Geschichte*, pp. 184-187, 196; Huber, *Geschichte Österreichs*, 4: 125-126; Tieftrunk, *Odpor*, p. 126.

58. Ferdinand to Charles, Mar. 4, 1547, SA, *Belgien, PA* 9, fo. 86; *Landtagsverhandlungen*, 2: 132.

59. Charles to Ferdinand, Feb. 19, 1547, Lanz, *Correspondenz*, 2: 541; Charles to Ferdinand, Mar. 10, 1547, ibid., p. 545; Ferdinand to Charles, March 20, 1547, SA, *Belgien, PA* 9, fos. 102-103; Luis Avila y Zuñiga, *Comentaria de la guerra de Alemania*, Bibliotheca de autores españoles, 285 vols. (Madrid: Rivadeneyra, 1848-1980), 1: 435-436; Alois Mocenigo in Joseph Fiedler, ed., *Relationen venetianischer Botschafter über Deutschland und Österreich im sechzehnten Jahrhundert*, *FRA*, 30 (Vienna, 1870): 105-106.

60. Bretholz, *Neuere Geschichte,* pp. 184-185; Tieftrunk, *Odpor,* 100-101; Charles to the Bohemian Estates, March 22, 1547 in Friedrich Hortleder, *Von Anfang und Fortgang . . . deß teutschen Kriegs Keyser Carls deß Fünfften wider die Schmalkaldische Bundoberste,* 3 vols. (Frankfurt a.M.: Hoffmann, 1618), 2: 572-573); Tomek, *Město Prahy,* 11: 340.

61. Ferdinand to Charles, April 1, 1547, SA, *Belgien, PA* 9, fo. 118; Charles to Ferdinand, April 2, 1547, Druffel, *Beiträge,* 1: 55-56.

62. Bucholtz, *Regierung,* 6: 368-387; Bretholz, *Neuere Geschichte,* pp. 201-202.

63. Tieftrunk, *Odpor,* pp. 197-198.

64. Verallo to Farnese, May 3, 1547, in *Nuntiaturberichte,* 1[9]: 551; Bavé to Mary, May 7, 1547, SA, *Belgien, PA* 74, fo. 126; Tomek, *Město Prahy,* 11: 360-361.

65. Pelzel, *Geschichte Böhmens,* 2: 574-575.

66. Alvise Mocenigo and Lorenzo Contarini to the Doges, May 13, 1547, *Venetianische Depeschen,* 2: 257-258; Alvise Mocenigo to the Doges, May 26, 1547, ibid., p. 270; Bretholz, *Neuere Geschichte,* p. 205-206; Avila, *Comentario,* p. 446; Charles to Ferdinand, June 17, 1547, SA, *Belgien, PA* 6, Konv. 2, fo. 69.

66. Sixtus of Ottersdorf, *O pokřeni stavů městského léta 1547,* ed. Josef Janáček (Prague: Melantrich, 1950), p. 38.

67. Ranke, *Deutsche Geschichte,* pp. 1006-1007; Huber, *Geschichte Österreichs,* 4: 129; Ferdinand to Jan of Pernštejn, June 9, 1547, *Archiv český,* 20: 258.

69. Ferdinand to Charles, June 5, 1547 in Bucholtz, *Regierung,* 9: 425-426; Ferdinand to Charles, June 17, 1547, ibid., p. 429.

70. Charles to Ferdinand, June 12, 1547, Lanz, *Correspondenz,* 2: 583; Charles to the Bohemian delegation, June 17-30, 1547, Druffel, *Beiträge,* 1: 60-61.

71. Ferdinand to Charles, June 19, 1547, SA, *Belgien, PA* 9, fos. 142-144; Ferdinand to Maurice of Saxony, June 17, 1547, *Landtagsverhandlungen,* 2: 305; Charles to Ferdinand, June 28, 1547, Druffel, *Beiträge,* 1: 63, Bretholz, *Neuere Geschichte,* p. 213.

72. Ferdinand to Mary, July 10, 1547, SA, *Belgien, PA* 12, fos. 280-281; report of Lorenzo Contarini of 1548 in E. Albéri, ed., *Relazione degli ambasciatori veneti al Senato,* 15 vols. (Florence: Società editrice fiorentina, 1839-1863), 1[1]: 428-429; Ferdinand to Charles, July 14, 1547, SA, *Belgien, PA* 9, fo. 148.

73.   Bucholtz, *Regierung,* 6: 418-420; Huber, *Geschichte Österreichs,* 4: 133.

74.   Tieftrunk, *Odpor,* p. 14; Bretholz, *Neuere Geschichte,* p. 176.

75.   Ferdinand to William of Bavaria, June 15, 1547, *Landtagsverhandlungen,* 2: 302; *Vlastiveda,* 4: 362; Bretholz, *Neuere Geschichte,* pp. 217-218; Bucholtz, *Regierung,* 6: 427 and 9: 445; Dillon, *King and Estates,* p. 147.

76.   The figure on the cost of the war is from an anonymous document beginning "Le roy avoit fait son compte. . . ." *Blau,* 597/2, fo. 221. Also Tieftrunk, *Odpor,* p. 127; Dillon, *King and Estates,* p. 136; Huber, *Geschichte Österreichs,* 4: 131-132; Bretholz, *Neuere Geschichte,* p. 218.

77.   Tomek, *Město Prahy,* 11: 393 and note 25; Anton Gindely, "Geschichte der böhmischen Finanzen von 1526 bis 1618," *Denkschriften der kaiserlichen Akademie der Wissenschaften: phil.- hist. Klasse,* 7 (1868): 91, 94, table 2; Toman, *Böhmisches Staatsrecht,* pp. 21-22; Antonín Rezek, "Beiträge zur Geschichte der Confiscation vom Jahre 1547," *Zprávy o zasedání královské české společnosti nauk* (1876): 140, 142.

78.   Erasmus von Windischgrätz to the representatives of Styria, May 26, 1556, in Johann Loserth "Ständische Beziehungen zwischen Böhmen und Innerösterreich im Zeitalter Ferdinands I," *Mitteilungen des Vereins für Geschichte der Deutschen in Böhmen,* 50 (1912): 36-40; Dillon, *King and Estates,* p. 164; Toman, *Böhmisches Staatsrecht,* p. 23.

79.   František Kavka, "Die Habsburger und der böhmische Staat bis zum Mitte des 18. Jahrhunderts," *Historica,* 8 (1964): 48-49.

80.   Volf, "Královský důchod," pp. 129-131.

81.   Michele Suriano in Goetz, "Finalrelation," p. 278; Hirn, *Ferdinand von Tirol,* 1: 23, 35-40.

82.   Goetz, "Finalrelation," pp. 276-277; Dillon, *King and Estates,* pp. 144-145.

83.   Verallo to Farnese, July 15, 1547, *Nuntiaturberichte,* 1[10]: 46-47.

84.   Josef Janáček, "Zrušení cechů roku 1547," *Ččh,* 7 (1959): 231-242, *passim* and the same author's *Remeslná výroba v českých městech v 16. století* (Prague: Československé akademie věd, 1961), pp. 226-228; Polišenský, "Bohemia and the Turk," p. 94.

85.   "VInCItVr eLeCtor PrInCeps a Caesare SaXVs obrVItVr saeVIs RegIa Praga MaLIs," in Sixtus of Ottersdorf, *O pokoření,* p. 160.

Notes to Chapter XI

1. Report of Tiepolo, Corner, *et al.*, June 13, 1538, *Venetianische Depeschen*, 1: 126; Ferdinand to Charles, Oct. 21, 1545, *Blau*, 597/2, fo. 145.

2. Ferdinand to Charles, Dec. 6, 1543, *Blau*, 597/2, fo. 109; Ferdinand to Charles, Feb. 18, 1543, ibid., fo. 86.

3. E.g., Ferdinand to Charles, Nov. 18, 1542, ibid., fos. 77, 82; Ferdinand to Charles, Aug. 26, 1542, ibid., fo. 55; Ferdinand to Charles, Aug. 24, 1543, ibid., fos. 99-100; Ferdinand to Charles, Feb. 18, 1542, ibid., fos. 1-2.

4. Ferdinand to Charles, Feb. 1, 1546, ibid., fo. 163; Ferdinand to Charles, Feb. 18, 1543, ibid., fos. 85, 88; Ferdinand to Charles, Aug. 9, 1548, ibid., fo. 277.

5. Fischer-Galati, *Ottoman Imperialism,* pp. 81-83; Ferdinand to Charles, Dec. 6, 1543, *Blau*, 597/2, fo. 110.

6. Heidrich, *Karl V und die Protestanten,* 2: 8, 55-57; Ferdinand to Charles, Feb. 11, 1545, *Blau*, 597/2, fos. 130-131, 133. Ferdinand had little choice in the matter after he rejected his brother's suggestion that their sister Mary temporarily represent them with the argument that it was unheard of for a woman to represent the Emperor! Springer, *Wormser Reichstag,* p. 18.

7. Adolf Hasenclever, "Die Politik der Schmalkaldener vor den Ausbruch des schmalkaldischen Krieges," (diss.: Berlin, 1901), p. 39.

8. Ferdinand to Charles, Jan. 6, 1549, Druffel, *Beiträge,* 4: 189-190; Ferdinand to Charles, Sept.6, 1547, *Blau*, 597/2: fo. 267.

9. The Queen of Poland, Bona Sforza had had a long-standing quarrel over Neapolitan claims with the Habsburgs and chose to vent her ire on her daughter-in-law. Part of her revenge, at least according to the Polish ambassador, had been to try to block consummation of the marriage. Ferdinand to Charles, Feb. 18, 1543, *Blau*, 597/2, fo. 85; Ferdinand to Charles, Mar. 22, 1543, ibid., fo. 87; Ferdinand to Charles, June 26, 1543, ibid., fo. 91; Ferdinand to Charles, Jan. 12, 1544, ibid., fo. 115; Ferdinand to Charles, Feb. 4, 1544, ibid., fo. 117; Ferdinand to Charles, Sept. 23, 1544, ibid., fo. 123.

10. Ferdinand to Charles, Sept. 27, 1548, ibid., fos. 279-280; Ferdinand to Charles, Oct. 5, 1548, ibid., fo. 282; Ferdinand to Charles, Nov. 24, 1548, ibid., fos. 288-289; Ferdinand to Charles, July 18, 1547, ibid., fo.

260; Ferdinand to Charles, Aug. 18, 1547, ibid., fo. 261; Ferdinand to Charles, Dec. 2, 1548, ibid., fo. 290.

11. Ferdinand to Charles, Dec. 18, 1546, ibid., fo. 197; Ferdinand to Charles, Dec. 30, 1546, ibid., fo. 199; Ferdinand to Charles, Dec. 18, 1546, ibid., fo. 197; Ferdinand to Charles, Jan. 18, 1547, ibid., fo. 209; Cf. Ferdinand to Charles, April 29, 1551, ibid., 597/3, fo. 38. See also Gustav Turba, "Beiträge zur Geschichte der Habsburger. II. Zur Reichs-und-Hauspolitik der Jahre 1548 bis 1558," *AöG*, 90 (1901): 5.

12. Mary to Ferdinand, May 5, 1551, Druffel, *Beiträge*, 1: 638; Arras to Mary, May 26, 1552, ibid., p. 647; Charles to Ferdinand, Aug. 15, 1551, Lanz, *Correspondenz*, 3: 69-70.

13. Ferdinand to Charles, Oct. 21, 1545, *Blau*, 597/2, fo. 145.

14. Holtzmann, *Maximilian II*, pp. 45-46; Ferdinand to Charles, Oct. 21, 1545, *Blau*, 597/2, fos. 145-146.

15. Ferdinand to Charles, Jan. 18, 1547, *Blau*, 597/2, fos. 210-211; *Papiers d'état du cardinal de Granvelle*, ed. Charles Weiss, 9 vols. (Paris: Imprimerie royale, 1841-1852), 3: 313.

16. Ranke, *Deutsche Geschichte*, p. 830. Cf. Laubach, "Nachfolge," p. 37 and Brandi, *Karl V*, I: 353.

17. *Papiers d'état de Granvelle*, 3: 313-314.

18. Ferdinand to Charles, Aug. 9, 1548, *Blau*, 597/2, fos. 275-277; Ferdinand to Charles, Feb. 15, 1549, ibid., fo. 300; Ferdinand to Charles, Feb. 21, 1549, ibid., fos. 300-301.

19. Laubach, "Nachfolge," p. 35.

20. Ibid., pp. 34-35; Bucholtz, *Regierung*, 5: 548-550.

21. Ferdinand to Philip, Aug. 2, 1545, ibid., fo. 165.

22. Laubach, "Nachfolge," p. 36.

23. Charles's Instructions for Chantonnay, July 12, 1549, Druffel, *Beiträge*, I: 245-246; Charles's Instructions for Philip, Jan. 18, 1548, *Papiers d'état de Granvelle*, 3: 273-274.

24. Bartholomäus Sastrow, *Lauf meines Lebens*, ed. Christfried Coler (Berlin: Rütten and Loening, 1956), pp. 214-216.

25. Ferdinand to Charles, *Blau*, 597/2, fo. 325 summarized in Druffel, *Beiträge*, 1: 305. The Druffel summary is deceptive inasmuch as it does not mention this agreement between Ferdinand and Charles.

26. ". . . la schosse que plus tasche l'homme en ce monde . . ." Ferdinand to Mary, July 27, 1549, Druffel, *Beiträge*, 1: 268.

27. Charles's Instructions for Chantonnay, July 12, 1549, ibid., p. 245; Peter Rassow, *Forschungen zur Reichsidee im 16. und 17. Jahrhundert,* Arbeitsgemeinschaft für Forschung des Landes Nordrhein-Westfalen, Geistewissenschaft, 10 (1955), pp. 11-12.

28. Bibl, *Maximilian II,* p. 50; Walter Goetz, *Maximilians II. Wahl zum römischen Könige 1562.* (Würzburg: Becker, 1891), p. 16.

29. Bibl, *Maximilian II,* p. 51; Arras to Mary, July 22, 1550, Druffel, *Beiträge,* 1: 449.

30. Arras to Mary, July 29, 1550, Druffel, *Beiträge,* 1:458; Bruno Thomas, "Kaiser Ferdinands I. Harnisch von Kunz Lochner," *Jahrbuch der kunsthistorischen Sammlungen in Wien,* 50 (1953): 136.

31. Arras to Mary, July 29, 1550, Druffel, *Beiträge,* 1: 458; Bibl, *Maximilian II,* p. 52; Mary to Charles, Aug. 10, 1550, SA, *Belgien, PA* 75, fo. 66 (copy).

32. Charles to Mary, Dec. 16, 1550, Lanz, *Correspondenz,* 3: 20.

33. Charles and Ferdinand's accounts of the negotiations down to the middle of December, on which the following narrative is based, largely concur. See Ferdinand to Charles, Dec. 14, 1550, ibid., pp. 11-15; Charles to Mary, Dec. 16, 1550, ibid., pp. 15-20.

34. Bibl, *Maximilian II,* p. 52, Marillac to Henry II of France, Feb. 16, 1551, Druffel, *Beiträge,* 1: 574; Henry II to Marillac (?), Feb. 11, 1551, ibid., p. 574.

35. Laubach, "Nachfolge," pp. 42-45. Arras's sketch of this proposal is in SA, *Belgien, PA* 54, Konv. 5, fos. 210, 215.

36. Ferdinand to Mary, c. 14 Feb.?, 1551, Druffel, *Beiträge,* 3¹: 162-165. Cf. SA, *Belgien, PA* 85, Konv. 2 B, fo. 25 and Laubach, "Nachfolge," pp. 45-46.

37. Mary to Ferdinand, n.d. Feb.-Mar. 1551, Druffel, *Beiträge,* 3¹: 176; Ferdinand to Mary, Feb.-Mar. 1551, ibid., pp. 176-178.

38. Charles to Ferdinand, Feb.-Mar. 1551, ibid., pp. 180-183. Cf. Rassow, *Forschungen,* pp. 12-13.

39. Charles to Ferdinand, Feb.-Mar. 1551, Druffel, *Beiträge,* 3¹: 180. Mary's sketch of the latter proposal, ibid., p. 191.

40. Ferdinand's proposals on Philip's position in Italy, ibid., pp. 197-200; Turba, "Beiträge, II," pp. 9-10; Heinrich Lutz, *Christianita Afflicta. Europa, das Reich und die päpstliche Politik im Niedergang der hegemonie Kaiser Karls V.* (Göttingen: Vandenhoeck and Ruprecht, 1964), p. 204. For text of the agreement see Druffel, *Beiträge,* 3¹: 161-165, 176-207.

41. Laubach, "Nachfolge," pp. 47-48.

42. Bibl, *Maximilian II*, pp. 54-55.

43. Mary to Ferdinand, Mar. 1551, Druffel, *Beiträge*, 3¹: 203-204; Marillac to Henry II, Mar. 3, 1551, ibid., 1: 586; Marillac to Henry II, Mar. 10, 1551, ibid., p. 591; Karl Brandi, "Passauer Vertrag und Augsburger Religionsfriede," *HZ*, 95 (1905): 237-238.

44. Walter Friedensburg, "Karl V. und Maximilian II. (1551). Ein venetianischer Bericht über vertrauliche Äußerungen des Letzteren," *QuF*, 4: 72-73, 77.

45. Rassow, *Forschungen*, p. 12; Ferdinand to Mary, SA, *Belgien, PA* 85, Konv. 2 B, fo. 30. Summary in Druffel, *Beiträge*, 3¹: 204.

46. "Relacion de los documentos sobre el vicaratio del imperio," AG, *Estado, Alemania*, Legajo 646, fo. 252.

47. Lutz, *Christianitas*, p. 85.

48. Ibid., and Stökl, "Ferdinand I.," p. 128. See also Ferdinand to Mary, n.d. 1551, Druffel, *Beiträge*, 3¹: 161.

49. Laubach, "Nachfolge," p. 33; Lutz, *Christianitas*, pp. 85-86; Memoire of Arras in Druffel, *Beiträge*, 3¹: 189; Ferdinand to Charles, Nov. 25, 1549, *Blau*, 597/2, fo. 325; Bucholtz, *Regierung*, 5: 850.

50. Ferdinand to Charles, June 3, 1551, *Blau*, 597/3, fos. 44-45, 47-48; Ferdinand to Charles, Aug. 12, 1551, ibid., fo. 49.

51. Ferdinand to Charles, July 28, 1551, ibid., fo. 48; Ferdinand to Charles, Aug. 12, 1551, ibid., fo. 49.

52. Ferdinand to Charles, Aug. 10, 1552, Lanz, *Correspondenz*, 3: 447; Charles's Instructions for Joachim de Rye for Ferdinand, Mar. 3, 1552, ibid., pp. 98-99; Ferdinand to Charles, Sept. 26, 1555, ibid., p. 687.

53. Heinrich of Meissen to Charles, Aug. 1552, AGR, *Allemande*, fasc. 800, fo. 171.

54. Brandi, "Passauer Vertrag," p. 235.

55. Ibid., p. 226; Lutz, *Christianitas*, p. 134.

56. Lutz, *Christianitas*, pp. 134-135.

57. For a selection of Zasius's letters, see Druffel, *Beiträge*, 4. He was especially active during 1553-1554. On Philip's feelings see Arras to Mary, Oct. 8, 1552, ibid., 2: 776-777.

58. Zasius to Ferdinand, Aug. 24, 1553, Druffel, *Beiträge*, 4: 248; S. Ißleib, Von Passau bis Sievershausen, 1552-1553," *Neues Archiv für sächsische Geschichte*, 8 (1887): 69: Zasius to Ilsunger, Crat, and other Austrian privy councillors, Oct., 1552, Druffel, *Beiträge*, 2: 802.

59. Goetz, *Maximilian II*, p. 27.

60. Zasius to Maximilian II, Nov. 4, 1553, Druffel, *Beiträge*, 4: 316-317; Zasius to Maximilian, Oct. 26, 1553, ibid., pp. 311-312.

61. Bucholtz, *Regierung*, 7: 533.

62. Zasius to Maximilian, Nov. 4, 1553, Druffel, *Beiträge*, 4: 316-317.

63. Bucholtz, *Regierung*, 7: 533; Ferdinand to Gamez (his ambassador in Spain), Dec. 10, 1552, Druffel, *Beiträge*, 2: 830-831; Ferdinand to Pedro Lasso, June 24, 1554, ibid., 4: 492; Ferdinand to Charles, April 26, 1554, SA, *Belgien, PA* 10, fos. 41-42. Cf. Lutz, *Christianitas*, p. 231.

64. Goetz, *Maximilian II*, p. 27; Lutz, *Christianitas*, pp. 408-409.

65. Ferdinand to Charles, Oct. 21, 1545, *Blau*, 597/2, fos. 145-146.

66. Charles to Ferdinand, Dec. 9, 1553, Druffel, *Beiträge*, 4: 333; Charles to Ferdinand, Feb. 3, 1554, Lanz, *Correspondenz*, 3: 606.

67. E. Harris Harbison, *Rival Ambassadors at the Court of Queen Mary* (Princeton: Princeton University Press, 1940), pp. 70-71.

68. Turba, "Beiträge, II," pp. 5-8; Lutz, *Christianitas*, pp. 207-208; Harbison, *Rival Ambassadors*, pp. 58-59, note 4.

69. Lutz, *Christianitas*, pp. 206-207; Harbison, *Rival Ambassadors*, p. 71, note 29; Arras's Instructions to Simon Renard, Aug. 14, 1553, Druffel, *Beiträge*, 4: 238-239, note 3.

70. Ferdinand's Instructions for Guzmán, July 27, 1553, Druffel, *Beiträge*, 4: 221.

71. Gamez to Ferdinand, Oct. 22, 1553, ibid., pp. 307-308; Ferdinand to Charles, Oct. 29, 1553, AGR, *État et audience*, fasc. 46, fo. 95.

72. Maximilian to Albrecht of Bavaria, Dec. 11, 1553, ibid., 4: 338; Maximilian to Albrecht of Bavaria, Feb. 15, 1554, ibid., p. 374; Zasius to Ferdinand, Feb. 17, 1554, ibid., p. 375.

73. Maximilian to Albrecht of Bavaria, Feb. 22, 1554, ibid., p. 377.

74. Charles to Ferdinand, Dec. 9, 1553, ibid., pp. 333-334.

75. Ferdinand to Charles, Dec. 29, 1553, Lanz, *Correspondenz*, 3: 596-597; Charles to Ferdinand, Feb. 3, 1554, ibid., pp. 606-607.

76. Ferdinand to Charles, Feb. 26, 1554, Druffel, *Beiträge*, 4: 379; Lutz, *Christianitas*, p. 211.

77. Lutz, *Christianitas*, pp. 182, 216-217.

78. Wiesflecker, *Kaiser Maximilian*, 2: 400.

79. E.g. Sutter, intro., pp. 142-143; Lutz, *Christianitas*, pp. 137-138.

80. Ferdinand to Charles, April 19, 1551, *Blau*, 597/3, fo. 42. Cf. Ferdinand to Charles, Oct. 24, 1531, *Korrespondenz*, 3^2: 336.

Notes to Chapter XII

1. Ferdinand to Charles, March 17, 1547, *Blau,* 597/2, fo. 241; Ferdinand to Charles, Sept. 27, 1542, ibid., fo. 65; Ferdinand to Charles, Dec. 18, 1546, ibid., fo. 196; Ferdinand to Charles, Jan. 18, 1547, ibid., fos. 209-210; Ferdinand to Charles, Feb. 8, 1547, ibid., fo. 218; Ferdinand's Instructions to Charles, Aug. 18, 1547, ibid., fos. 263-264.

2. Ferdinand to Charles, Feb. 19, 1547, ibid., fos. 222-223.

3. Ranke, *Deutsche Geschichte,* p. 867; Fichtner, "Disobedience," pp. 24-25.

4. E.g. Ferdinand to Charles, Oct. 4, 1545, *Blau,* 597/2, fo. 143.

5. Ferdinand to Charles, Aug. 24, 1543, ibid., fo. 99; Ferdinand to Charles, Nov. 16, 1543, ibid., fo. 107; Ferdinand to Charles, June 15, 1547, ibid., fo. 250; Heidrich, *Karl V und die Protestanten,* 2: 63.

6. Ferdinand to Charles, Mar. 11, 1542, *Blau,* 597/2, fos. 21-22; Ferdinand to Charles, July 8, 1542, ibid., fo. 46.

7. Ferdinand to Charles, Nov. 9, 1541, ibid., 597/1: 478-479; Heidrich, *Karl V und die Protestanten,* 1: 49, 67, 71, 76, 83.

8. Ferdinand to Charles, April 13, 1542, *Blau,* 597/2, fos. 28-29; Ferdinand to Charles, April 24, 1542, ibid., fo. 33; Ferdinand to Charles, June 4, 1542, ibid., fo. 44; Ferdinand to Charles, Oct. 24, 1543, ibid., fos. 104-105.

9. Ferdinand to Charles, Mar. 6, 1541, ibid., 597/1: 462.

10. Ferdinand to Charles, Oct. 21, 1545, ibid., 597/2, fos. 143-144; Ferdinand to Charles, Nov. 16, 1543, ibid., fo. 107.

11. Ferdinand to Charles, Mar. 1, 1545, ibid., fos. 137-138.

12. Ferdinand to Charles, Oct. 24, 1543, ibid., fo. 104; Ferdinand to Charles, Feb. 18, 1543, ibid., fo. 95.

13. Ferdinand to Charles, Aug. 26, 1542, ibid., fos. 55-56.

14. Ferdinand to Charles, June 17, 1547, ibid., fo. 251-252; Ferdinand to Charles, June 5, 1547, ibid., fo. 248; Holborn, *Germany,* 1: 230; Ranke, *Deutsche Geschichte,* p. 1000.

15. Ferdinand to Charles, Mar. 1, 1545, *Blau,* 597/2, fo. 138; Ferdinand to Charles, Dec. 9, 1546, ibid., fo. 195; Gustav Turba, "Verhaftung und Gefangenschaft des Landgrafen Philipp von Hesse," *AöG,* 83 (1897): 111.

16. Charles to Ferdinand, Feb. 2, 1547, Lanz, *Correspondenz,* 2: 529; Turba, "Verhaftung," pp. 110-111; S. Ißleib, "Die Gefangennahme

des Landgrafen Philipp von Hessen 1547," *Neues Archiv für sächsische Geschichte und Altertumskunde*, 11 (1889): 180-186.

17.   Ferdinand to Charles, Dec. 9, 1546, *Blau*, 597/2, fo. 195.

18.   Ferdinand to Charles, Dec. 30, 1546, ibid., fo. 199; Ferdinand to Charles, Feb. 20, 1547, ibid., fo. 225. Maurice even begged the future Philip II to intercede on behalf of his father-in-law with the Emperor. Maurice to Philip, n.d., AG, *Estado, Alemania*, Legajo 646, fo. 110 (copy).

19.   Ferdinand to Charles, June 5, 1547, *Blau*, 597/2, fo. 247.

20.   Ferdinand to Charles, June 17, 1547, ibid., fo. 251. Cf. Bucholtz, *Regierung*, 6: 63-65. See also Gerhard Bonwetsch, *Geschichte des passauischen Vertrages von 1552*, (Göttingen: Dietrich, 1907), p. 23 and note 4.

21.   Holborn, *Germany*, 1: 230; Karl Erich Born, "Moritz von Sachsen und die Fürstenverschwörung gegen Karl V," *HZ*, 191 (1960): 22-23; Ferdinand to Charles, July 14, 1547, *Blau*, 597/2, fos. 254-255.

22.   Peter Rassow, "Die Reichstage zu Augsburg in der Reformationszeit," in Hermann Rinn, ed., *Augusta 955-1955. Forschungen und Studien zur Kultur-und Wirtschaftsgeschichte Augsburgs* (Augsburg: Rinn, 1955), p. 278.

23.   Ferdinand's Instructions for Charles, Aug. 18, 1547, *Blau*, 597/2, fo. 275; Ferdinand to Charles, Feb. 19, 1547, ibid., fo. 223; Horst Rabe, *Reichsbund und Interim. Die Verfassungs-und Religionspolitik Karls V. und der Reichstag von Augsburg* (Cologne/Vienna: Böhlau, 1971), pp. 128-129, 131, 135, 273-294, 432-433.

24.   Ferdinand's Instructions to Chantonnay, July 26, 1549, *Blau*, 597/2, fo. 309; Ferdinand to Charles, Jan. 2, 1549, Druffel, *Beiträge*, 1: 186-187; Fischer-Galati, *Ottoman Imperialism*, p. 99; Ranke, *Deutsche Geschichte*, pp. 1030-1032; Holborn, *Germany*, 1: 231.

25.   Ferdinand to Charles, June 21, 1549, Druffel, *Beiträge*, 1: 236; Ferdinand to Charles, Sept. 27, 1547, *Blau*, 597/2, fo. 281; Ferdinand to Charles, Oct. 15, 1548, ibid., fos. 273-274; Ferdinand to Charles, June 21, 1548, Druffel, *Beiträge*, 4: 234-235; Rabe, *Reichsbund*, pp. 432-434.

26.   Ferdinand to Charles, Nov. 5, 1551, Druffel, *Beiträge*, 1: 791-792; Ferdinand to Charles, Dec. 12, 1551, ibid., pp. 852-854; Ferdinand to Charles, Dec. 2, 1551, Lanz, *Correspondenz*, 3: 185-186.

27.   Goetz, *Maximilian II*, p. 18; Born, "Moritz von Sachsen," p. 43; Heinrich von Meissen to Ferdinand, Mar. 22, 1552, Druffel, *Beiträge*, 2: 278-279.

28. For an excellent discussion of relations between Maurice and the Habsburgs during this period see Born, "Moritz von Sachsen," pp. 25-26, 47, 56, 62-63.

29. Arras to Mary, Nov. 17, 1551, Druffel, *Beiträge,* 1: 802; Charles to Ferdinand, Nov. 23, 1551, ibid., pp. 828-829.

30. Druffel, *Beiträge,* 3^2: 340-342; Born, "Moritz von Sachsen," pp. 52-53; Rabe, *Reichsbund,* 443, 445.

31. Charles's Secret Instructions for Joachim de Rye, Mar. 13, 1552, Lanz, *Correspondenz,* 3: 107; Arras to Mary, Druffel, *Beiträge,* 2: 164; Charles to Mary, Feb. 24, 1552, ibid., pp. 151-152. In his *Geschichte des passauischen Vertrages,* pp. 27-28, Bonwetsch argued that Ferdinand's warnings about Maurice were so unclear that they had a "calming" effect on the Emperor. While it is true that the king did not categorically implicate the Saxon, his news that various anti-Habsburg coalitions were in the making should have been enough to alert Charles that trouble was afoot. Cf. Bucholtz, *Regierung,* 7: 23-25.

32. Maximilian to Gamez, Mar. 1, 1552, Lanz, *Correspondenz,* 3: 97 (excerpt). The selection in Lanz does not identify Maximilian's correspondee. This is in Druffel, *Beiträge,* 2: 181, note 1. See also Arras to Joachim de Rye, March 4, 1552, ibid., p. 193. See also Charles to Mary, March 21, 1552, Lanz, *Correspondenz,* 3: 131.

33. Born, "Moritz von Sachsen," p. 54; Ferdinand's Instructions for Joachim de Rye to Charles, Mar. 11, 1552, Lanz, *Correspondenz,* 3: 119-121.

34. Ferdinand's Instructions for Joachim de Rye to Charles, Mar. 11, 1552, Lanz, *Correspondenz,* 3: 124; Bucholtz, *Regierung,* 7: 53; Charles to Ferdinand, March 3, 1552, Lanz, *Correspondenz,* 3: 100; Mary to Ferdinand, April 9, 1552, Druffel, *Beiträge,* 2: 345-346; Ferdinand to Mary, May 2, 1552, ibid., 448-450.

35. Mary to Arras, Feb. 8, 1552, Druffel, *Beiträge,* 2: 106.

36. Ferdinand to Charles, Dec. 12, 1551, Bucholtz, *Regierung,* 7: 28-29.

37. G. Fischer, "Ferdinand I. und Karl V. im Jahre 1552," *Jahrbücher der kgl. Akademie gemeinnütziger Wissenschaften zu Erfurt,* NF 32 (1906): 190-193; Ferdinand to Maurice, Feb. 12, 1552, Druffel, *Beiträge,* 2: 115-118.

38. Bonwetsch, *Passauer Vertrag,* pp. 20-21; Fischer, "Ferdinand und Karl," p. 190.

39.   Ferdinand's Instructions for Joachim de Rye to Charles, Mar. 11, 1552, Lanz, *Correspondenz*, 3: 122-123; Charles's Instructions for Joachim de Rye to Ferdinand, Mar. 3, 1552, ibid., pp. 100, 104; Charles to Ferdinand, Mar. 11, 1552, Druffel, *Beiträge*, 2: 226-227.

40.   Charles to Ferdinand, Mar. 11, 1552, Druffel, *Beiträge*, 2: 230-231; Ferdinand to Charles, Mar. 14, 1552, ibid., p. 244; Ferdinand's Memorandum for Lazarus Schwendi to Charles, April 23, 1552, ibid., p. 421; Ferdinand's Instructions for Joachim de Rye for Charles, Mar. 11, 1552, Lanz, *Correspondenz*, 3: 123; Charles's Instructions to Joachim de Rye for Ferdinand, Mar. 22, 1552, ibid., p. 140; Charles to Ferdinand, April 25, 1552, ibid., p. 185.

41.   Ferdinand's Instructions for Martin Guzmán to Charles, April 13, 1552, Lanz, *Correspondenz*, 3: 165-167; Heinrich of Meissen to Ferdinand, April 10/11, 1552, Druffel, *Beiträge*, 2: 364; Bonwetsch, *Passauer Vertrag*, p. 45.

42.   Bonwetsch, *Passauer Vertrag*, pp. 52-53, 58-59; Ferdinand to Maurice, April 1, 1552, Lanz, *Correspondenz*, 3: 152; Ferdinand's Instructions to Joachim de Rye, Mar. 11, 1552, ibid., p. 123; Ferdinand's Resolutions to the Princes and their Representatives at Linz, April 28, 1552, Druffel, *Beiträge*, 3²: 402-406.

43.   Charles to Ferdinand, April 4, 1552, Bucholtz, *Regierung*, 7: 61-65; Ferdinand to Charles, April 5, 1552, Druffel, *Beiträge*, 2: 330-331; Ferdinand to Charles, April 9, 1552, ibid., pp. 344-345; Ferdinand's Instructions to Martin Guzmán, ibid., p. 273.

44.   Bonwetsch, *Passauer Vertrag*, pp. 62-63.

45.   Fischer, "Ferdinand und Karl," pp. 183-184, 197, 199, 201-202; Bonwetsch, *Passauer Vertrag*, pp. 65-66; Charles's Instructions for Joachim de Rye to Ferdinand, Mar. 22, 1552, Druffel, *Beiträge*, 2: 283; The Governor, Government and Councillors of Upper Austria to Ferdinand, April 9/10, 1552, ibid., pp. 311-312; Charles to Albrecht of Bavaria, May 25, 1552, ibid., p. 507.

46.   Ferdinand to Charles, June 6, 1552, Lanz, *Correspondenz*, 3: 234-235.

47.   S. Ißleib, "Die Gefangenschaft Philipps von Hessen 1547 bis 1552," *Neues Archiv für sächsische Geschichte und Altertumskunde*, 14 (1893): 266; Philip to William of Hesse and his advisors, April 16, 1552, Lanz, *Correspondenz*, 3: 173; Zasius to Ferdinand, Druffel, *Beiträge*, 2: 504.

48. Lutz, *Christianitas,* p. 89; Bonwetsch, *Passauer Vertrag,* p. 111.

49. Ferdinand to Charles, June 3, 1552, Lanz, *Correspondenz,* 3: 218; Ferdinand to Charles, June 6, 1552, ibid., pp. 232-233.

50. Charles to Joachim de Rye, June 7, 1552, ibid., p. 247; Charles to Ferdinand, June 8, 1552, ibid., p. 252.

51. Margrave Albrecht of Bayreuth to Albrecht of Bavaria, June 6, 1552, Druffel, *Beiträge,* 2: 566-567; Druffel, *Beiträge,* 3^2: 395 and 396, note 2.

52. Ferdinand to Charles, June 22, 1552, Lanz, *Correspondenz,* 3: 282.

53. Joachim de Rye to Charles, June 15, 1552, ibid., p. 269; Ferdinand to Charles, May 30, 1552, ibid., p. 210; Ferdinand to Charles, June 3, 1552, ibid., p. 219; Ferdinand to Charles, June 8, 1552, ibid., p. 257; Ferdinand to Charles, June 17, 1552, ibid., p. 272; Ferdinand to Charles, June 22, 1552, ibid., pp. 284-285; Joachim of Brandenburg's Counsellors to the Elector, June 18, 1552, Druffel, *Beiträge,* 2: 609.

54. Charles to Ferdinand, June 7, 1552, ibid., p. 245.

55. Bonwetsch, *Passauer Vertrag,* pp. 129-130, 132.

56. Charles to Ferdinand, June 2, 1552, Lanz, *Correspondenz,* 3: 240-241; Protocol of Württemberg at Passau, June 6, 1552, Druffel, *Beiträge,* 3: 480; Holborn, *Germany,* 1: 239-240.

57. Ferdinand to Charles, June 22, 1552, Lanz, *Correspondenz,* 3: 282-283, 288-289; Ferdinand to Charles, Aug. 10, 1552, ibid., p. 441.

58. Mordeisen and Carlowitz to Maurice, June 24, 1552, Druffel, *Beiträge,* 2: 628; Ferdinand to Charles, June 22, 1552, Lanz, *Correspondenz,* 3: 283, 289-292.

59. Ferdinand to Charles, June 22, 1552, Lanz, *Correspondenz,* 3: 288; Ferdinand to Charles, June 28, 1552, ibid., pp. 305-306; Ferdinand to Mary, June 26, 1552, *Blau,* 597/3, fos. 158-159.

60. Christof von d. Strassen to Elector Joachim of Brandenburg, June 18, 1552, Druffel, *Beiträge,* 2: 608.

61. Bonwetsch, *Passauer Vertrag,* pp. 149-151; Protocol of William Hund (Bavarian councillor at Passau), Druffel, *Beiträge,* 3: 468; Maurice of Saxony to Mordeisen and Carlowitz, July 12, 1552, ibid., 2: 665.

62. Charles to Ferdinand, June 30, 1552, Lanz, *Correspondenz,* 3: 325-326.

63. Bucholtz, *Regierung,* 7: 96-97.

64. Ferdinand's Instructions to Heinrich of Meissen, July 15, 1554, AGR, *Allemande*, fasc. 801, fo. 7; Charles to Mary, July 16, 1552, Druffel, *Beiträge*, 2: 682-684; Charles to Joachim de Rye and Matthew Seld, July 11, 1552, Lanz, *Correspondenz*, 3: 361.

65. Ferdinand's Instructions for [Henry of] Plauen to Maurice, July 15, 1552, Druffel, *Beiträge*, 3: 538-539, note 1; Charles's Declaration to the Estates, July 14, 1552, ibid., pp. 535-536; Bonwetsch, *Passauer Vertrag*, p. 155; Gustav Wolf, "Der Passauer Vertrag und seine Bedeutung für die nächstfolgende Zeit," *Neues Archiv für sächsische Geschichte und Altertumskunde*, 15 (1894): 253.

66. Lutz, *Christianitas*, p. 91; Ferdinand to Mary, July 17, 1552, *Blau*, 597/3, fo. 164; Bonwetsch, *Passauer Vertrag*, p. 157.

67. Ferdinand to Charles, July 15, 1552, Lanz, *Correspondenz*, 3: 370-371; Ferdinand to Charles, July 28, 1552, ibid., pp. 396-397; Ferdinand to Charles, Aug. 8, 1552, ibid., p. 433; Maurice to Ferdinand, Aug. 1, 1552, Druffel, *Beiträge*, 2: 714.

68. Charles to Ferdinand, July 31, 1552, Lanz, *Correspondenz*, 3: 456; Lazarus Schwendi to Charles, Aug. 22, 1552, ibid., p. 470; Wolf, "Passauer Vertrag," pp. 258-259.

69. Fischer-Galati, *Ottoman Imperialism*, pp. 105-106; Bonwetsch, *Passauer Vertrag*, pp. 188, 190.

70. Charles to Ferdinand, Sept. 1, 1552, Lanz, *Correspondenz*, 3: 483-484; Ferdinand to Charles, Sept. 12, 1552, ibid., p. 489.

71. Born, "Moritz von Sachsen," p. 63; Ißleib, "Passau bis Sievershausen," pp. 42-43.

72. Lutz, *Christianitas*, pp. 81-82.

73. Landgrave William of Hesse to Maurice, Aug. 23, 1552, Druffel, *Beiträge*, 2: 743-744; William of Hesse to Maurice, Sept. 5, 1552, ibid., pp. 753-754.

74. Ferdinand to Charles, Aug. 5, 1552, Lanz, *Correspondenz*, 3: 415-416.

75. Lutz, *Christianitas*, p. 705.

Notes to Chapter XIII

1. Ferdinand to Charles, April 26, 1554, Druffel, *Beiträge*, 4: 457; Ferdinand to Charles, Feb. 5, 1555, *Blau*, 597/3, fos. 274-275.

2. Ferdinand to Charles, April 26, 1553, Druffel, *Beiträge*, 4: 130-

131; Margrave Albrecht to Maurice of Saxony, June 10, 1553, ibid., pp. 171-172; Ferdinand to Charles, Aug. 17, 1553, Lanz, *Correspondenz*, 3: 582-583; Bernhard Sicken, "Der Heidelberger Verein (1553-1556), *Zeitschrift für württembergische Landesgeschichte,* 32 (1973): 324.

3. Nicolaus von Pollweiler to Ferdinand, Sept. 26, 1553, Druffel, *Beiträge,* 4: 267-268.

4. Ferdinand to Charles, Oct. 27, 1552, Lanz, *Correspondenz,* 3: 509; Ferdinand to Charles, Aug. 17, 1553, ibid., p. 583.

5. Ferdinand's Instructions for Martin Guzmán to Charles, Mar. 3, 1553, ibid., p. 550; Ferdinand to Charles, Oct. 27, 1552, ibid., p. 509; Ferdinand to Charles, Jan. 26, 1553, ibid., pp. 535-536.

6. Ferdinand to Charles, Aug. 28, 1546, *Blau,* 597/2, fos. 175-176; Viktor Ernst, ed. *Briefwechsel des Herzogs Christoph von Wirtemberg* [sic], 4 vols. (Stuttgart: Kohlhammer, 1899-1907), 1: x-xii; Charles to Ferdinand, Aug. 15, 1551, Lanz, *Correspondenz,* 3: 69-70.

7. Protocol of Christoph of Württemberg's agent Eisslinger's interview with Arras, May 2, 1551, Ernst, *Briefwechsel,* 1: 173.

8. Duke Christoph of Württemberg to Albrecht of Bavaria, Aug. 30, 1551, ibid., p. 269; Bishop of Arras to Christoph of Württemberg, Nov. 19, 1550, ibid., p. 42; Eisslinger to Duke Christoph, Dec. 29, 1550, ibid., p. 103; Eisslinger to Duke Christoph, Dec. 17, 1550, ibid., p. 89.

9. Johannes Fessler to Duke Christoph, Dec. 2, 1550, ibid., p. 70; Duke Christoph's Instructions for Kaspar Berg, July 6, 1551, ibid., p. 222; Ludwig of Frauenberg's Report to Duke Christoph, Mar. 20, 1551, ibid., p. 149; Eisslinger to Duke Christoph, Dec. 17, 1550, ibid., p. 88; Kaspar Berg to Duke Christoph, July 15, 1551, ibid., pp. 234-235; Bishop of Arras to Duke Christoph, July 18, 1551, ibid., p. 237.

10. Ernst, ibid., xiv-xv; Mary to Ferdinand, May 5, 1551, Druffel, *Beiträge,* 1: 638.

11. Christoph Friedrich von Stälin, *Wirtembergische* /sic/ *Geschichte,* 4 vols. (Stuttgart: Cotta, 1873), 4: 529-530; 532-533, 538; Ferdinand to Charles, Oct. 17, 1552, Lanz, *Correspondenz,* 3: 503-504; Charles to Ferdinand, Nov. 15, 1552, ibid., pp. 514-515, 517.

12. Ferdinand to Charles, Dec. 9, 1552, ibid., pp. 518-519; Ferdinand to Charles, Dec. 10, 1552, ibid., pp. 520-521.

13. Viktor Ernst, "Eine kaiserliche Werbung, die Erneuerung des schwäbischen Bundes betreffend 1552," *Württembergische Vierteljahreshefte für Landesgeschichte,* N'F. 8 (1899): 214-215; Wolf, "Passauer Vertrag," pp. 257-258.

14. Lutz, *Christianitas,* pp. 186, 198; Wolf, "Passauer Vertrag," p. 269.

15. Ferdinand to Charles, Dec. 16, 1552, Lanz, *Correspondenz,* 3: 527; Lutz, *Christianitas,* p. 119.

16. Ißleib, "Von Passau," pp. 81, note 129, 83; Lutz, *Christianitas,* p. 201; Ferdinand to Charles, June 12, 1553, Druffel, *Beiträge,* 4: 176; Ferdinand to Charles, June 14, 1553, *Blau,* 597/3, fo. 220.

17. Ferdinand to Charles, Dec. 16, 1552, Lanz, *Correspondenz,* 3: 525-526; Ferdinand to Charles, Feb. 14, 1553, ibid., p. 539.

18. Lutz, *Christianitas,* p. 189.

19. Ferdinand to Charles, Aug. 7, 1552, Lanz, *Correspondenz,* 3: 431; Ferdinand to Charles, Oct. 17, 1552, ibid., p. 505; Ferdinand to Charles, Dec. 9, 1552, ibid., p. 519; Ferdinand to Gamez, Dec. 16, 1552, Druffel, *Beiträge,* 2: 838-839; Wolf, "Passauer Vertrag," p. 261.

20. Charles to Ferdinand, Nov. 15, 1552, Lanz, *Correspondenz,* 3: 517.

21. Wolf, "Passauer Vertrag," pp. 267, 279-280; Lutz, *Christianitas,* pp. 201-203.

22. Lutz, *Christianitas,* pp. 193, 201-203.

23. Lutz, *Christianitas,* p. 212; Charles to Ferdinand, July 23, 1553, Druffel, *Beiträge,* 4: 216-217.

24. Ferdinand to Charles, July 26, 1553, Druffel, *Beiträge,* 4: 221; Ferdinand to Albrecht of Bavaria, Aug. 2, 1553, ibid., p. 233; Lutz, *Christianitas,* p. 212.

25. Lutz, *Christianitas,* p. 187; Bucholtz, *Regierung,* 7: 135-136; Sicken, "Heidelberger Verein," pp. 328-330, 333-334, 340-341.

26. Brandi, "Passauer Vertrag," p. 241.

27. Brandi, "Passauer Vertrag," pp. 240-241; Druffel, *Beiträge,* 4: 213-214, note 1; Maximilian to Albrecht of Bavaria, Sept. 4, 1553, ibid., pp. 253-254.

28. Charles to Ferdinand, Dec. 9, 1553, Druffel, *Beiträge,* 4: 334; Charles to Ferdinand, Feb. 3, 1554, Lanz, *Correspondenz,* 3: 606-607.

29. Ferdinand to Charles, Sept. 10, 1553, Druffel, *Beiträge,* 4: 257; Ferdinand to Charles, Aug. 27, 1553, *Blau,* 597/3, fo. 231; Ferdinand to Charles, Dec. 29, 1553, Lanz, *Correspondenz,* 3: 598-599.

30. Maximilian to Albrecht of Bavaria, Sept. 4, 1553, Druffel, *Beiträge,* 4: 253-254.

31. Lutz, *Christianitas,* pp. 188, 215; Bucholtz, *Regierung,* 7: 148-149, 154.

32. Ferdinand's Instructions for Martin Guzmán to Charles, Mar. 3, 1553, Lanz, *Correspondenz,* 3: 554; Ferdinand to Charles, Dec. 29, 1553, ibid., pp. 600-601; Ferdinand to Charles, Sept. 15, 1554, ibid., pp. 644-645; Charles to Ferdinand, July 23, 1553, Druffel, *Beiträge,* 4: 217-218.

33. Ferdinand to Charles, Dec. 29, 1553, Lanz, *Correspondenz,* 3: 602-603.

34. Lutz, *Christianitas,* p. 220; Ferdinand to Charles, Oct. 27, 1552 in Gustav Turba, "Beiträge zur Geschichte der Habsburger. III. Zur deutschen Reichs-und Hauspolitik der Jahre 1553 bis 1558," *AöG,* 90 (1901): 236, 241-242; Granvelle (Arras) to Pfintzing, Nov. 23, 1568, AGR, *Manuscrits divers,* 187 A, fo. 221 (copy); Philip II to Granvelle, Mar. 12, 1569, ibid., fo. 222 (copy); Granvelle to Philip, 1569 ?, ibid., fo. 223 (copy).

35. Lutz, *Christianitas,* p. 221.

36. Charles to Ferdinand, July 23, 1553, Druffel, *Beiträge,* 4: 217-218; Ferdinand to Charles, Dec. 29, 1553, Lanz, *Correspondenz,* 3: 602.

37. Charles to Ferdinand, Feb. 3, 1554, Lanz, *Correspondenz,* 3: 608; Charles to Ferdinand, June 8, 1554, ibid., pp. 622-624; Turba, "Beiträge. III.," pp. 244, 247.

38. Druffel, *Beiträge,* 4: 546, note 4; Ferdinand to Charles, Jan. 4, 1555, ibid., p. 557.

39. Martin Guzmán to Ferdinand, Oct. 12, 1555, Druffel, *Beiträge,* 4: 750.

40. Prior Brenz of Stuttgart to Christoph of Württemberg, Feb. 26, 1555, Ernst, *Briefwechsel,* 3: 91; Christoph of Württemberg to Wilhelm von Grumbach, June 25, 1555, ibid., p. 246; Eisslinger to Christoph of Württemberg, Aug. 28, 1555, ibid., p. 304.

41. Gustav Wolf, *Der Augsburger Religionsfriede* (Stuttgart: Göschen, 1890), pp. 9, 15-16.

42. Lutz, *Christianitas,* pp. 225-226, 330-331.

43. Ibid., p. 360; Wilhelm Maurenbrecher, "Beiträge zur deutschen Geschichte 1555-1559," *HZ,* 50 (1883): 9; Granvelle, *Papiers d'état,* 4: 429.

44. Lutz, *Christianitas,* p. 325.

45. Turba, "Beiträge. III.," p. 253.

46. Ibid., p. 248.

47. Quoted in Lutz, *Christianitas,* p. 233.

48. Heinrich Lutz and Alfred Kohler, eds., *Das Reichstagsprotokoll des kaiserlichen Kommissars Felix Hornung vom Augsburger Reichstag*

1555, Österreichische Akademie der Wissenschaften, Phil.-hist. Klasse. Denkschriften, 103 (Vienna, 1971), pp. 35-36.

49. Ibid., pp. 46-47.

50. Ibid., pp. 68, 77; Lutz, *Christianitas,* pp. 363-365.

51. Ferdinand to Charles, July 9, 1555, Lanz, *Correspondenz,* 3: 663-664; Bucholtz, *Regierung,* 7: 173, 194; Lutz, *Christianitas,* pp. 330-331; Wolf, *Augsburger Religionsfriede,* pp. 38-39, 94, 111.

52. Bucholtz, *Regierung,* 7: 194; Wolf, *Augsburger Religionsfriede,* p. 145; Ferdinand to Charles, Aug. 20, 1555, Lanz, *Correspondenz,* 3: 667.

53. Ferdinand to Charles, July 30, 1555, Lanz, *Correspondenz,* 3: 672; Ferdinand to Charles, Aug. 27, 1555, ibid., p. 678; Christoph of Württemberg to Wilhelm von Münchingen and Hieronymous Gerard, Aug. 24, 1555, Ernst, *Briefwechsel,* 3: 296.

54. Lutz, *Christianitas,* pp. 425-426.

55. Ibid., p. 371; Wolf, *Augsburger Religionsfriede,* p. 141.

56. Wolf, *Augsburger Religionsfriede,* pp. 153-154, 158-160, 167; Bucholtz, *Regierung,* 7: 197, 203-204; Lutz, *Christianitas,* p. 429; Maurenbrecher, "Beiträge zur deutschen Geschichte," pp. 4-6; Martin Heckel, "Autonomia und Pacis Compositio: der Augsburger Religionsfriede in der Deutung der Gegenreformation," *Zeitschrift der Savigny-Stiftung für Rechtsgeschichte,* kanonistische Abteilung, 45 (1959): 158; Lewis Spitz, "Particularlism and Peace. Augsburg, 1555," *Church History,* 25 (1956): 113, 120.

57. Lutz, *Christianitas,* p. 432; Fischer-Galati, *Ottoman Imperialism,* p. 109.

58. Ferdinand to Charles, July 9, 1555, Lanz, *Correspondenz,* 3: 663-665; Ferdinand to Charles, July 30, 1555, ibid., pp. 669-673; Ferdinand to Charles, Aug. 20, 1555, ibid., p. 677; Ferdinand to Charles, Aug. 27, 1555, ibid., p. 678.

59. Lutz, *Hornung,* pp. 125, 152, note 436, 162; Wilhelm von Münchingen and Hieronymous Gerard to Christoph of Württemberg, Sept. 24, 1555, Ernst, *Briefwechsel,* 3: 337.

60. Charles to Ferdinand, April 8, 1555, Druffel, *Beiträge,* 4: 647; Charles to Ferdinand, April 10, 1555, Lanz, *Correspondenz,* 3: 649-650 (Druffel, 4, dates this April 11.) Also Charles to Ferdinand, July 7, 1555, ibid., pp. 695-696.

61. Charles to Ferdinand, Sept. 19, 1555, Lanz, *Correspondenz, 3*: 681; Gamez to Ferdinand, Oct. 6, 1555, Druffel, *Beiträge,* 4: 746; Turba, "Beiträge. III.," p. 254.

62. Charles to Ferdinand, Aug. 15, 1555, Lanz, *Correspondenz, 3*: 674-675; Turba, "Beiträge. III.," p. 250; Ferdinand to Maximilian, Sept. 24, 1555, SA, *Familienkorrespondenz A,* Karton 2, fo. 118.

63. Ferdinand to Charles, April 17, 1555, Lanz, *Correspondenz, 3*: 650-651; Ferdinand to Charles, Sept. 24, 1555, ibid., pp. 638-684.

64. Turba, "Beiträge. III.," p. 251.

65. Ibid., pp. 250, 252; Brandi, "Passauer Vertrag," p. 263, note 3.

66. Ferdinand to Maximilian, Sept. 15, 1555, SA, *Familienkorrespondenz* A, Karton 2, fos. 114-115; Ferdinand to Maximilian, Sept. 27, 1555 ?, ibid., fo. 117; Lutz, *Christianitas,* p. 436.

67. Bucholtz, *Regierung,* 7: 221-222; Lutz, *Christianitas,* p. 225; Heckel, "Autonomia," pp. 159, 191, 210-211.

68. Daniel, "Augsburg Confession," p. 103; Maurenbrecher, "Beiträge zur deutschen Geschichte," pp. 10-12.

69. Lutz, *Christianitas,* p. 191.

70. Martin Guzmán to Ferdinand, Sept. 20, 1555, Druffel, *Beiträge,* 4: 751; Lutz, *Christianitas,* pp. 416-417.

Notes to Chapter XIV

1. Turba, "Beiträge, III.," p. 257; Maurenbrecher, "Beiträge zur deutschen Geschichte," p. 24.

2. Turba, "Beiträge, III.," p. 256; Charles to Ferdinand, Jan. 18, 1557, AGR, *Manuscrits divers,* 805 A/II, fos. 120-121 (141-142); Ferdinand to Maximilian, April 12, 1556, SA, *Familienkorrespondenz A,* Karton, 2, fo. 122.

3. "Aigentliche/und Warhaffte Beschreibung/weß herzlichen Besingknuß/so die Roem. kay. May. Kaiser u. jrer May. lieben Brüder unnd Herrn Kayser Carlen dem fünfften... ordenlich und zierlich gehalten ...," SA, *Familien-Akten,* Karton 60, Konv. 6, fo. 62; Bruno Thomas, "Die Augsburger Funeralwaffen Kaiser Karls V," *Zeitschrift für historische Waffenkunde,* 18 (1959): 29-31, 33.

4. Ferdinand to Charles, Aug. 21, 1555, *Blau,* 597/3, fo. 316; Turba, "Beiträge, III.," pp. 264-267.

5. Ferdinand to Charles, Aug. 21, 1555, *Blau,* 597/3, fo. 317; Charles to Ferdinand, Aug. 8, 1556, Lanz, *Correspondenz,* 3: 708-709.

6. Philip II to Ruy Gomez de Silva, Mar. 11, 1557 (copy), AGR, *Manuscrits divers,* 805 A/II, fo. 147 (172); Charles to Juan Vazquez de Molina, May 3, 1558, ibid., fo. 375 (434).

7. Turba, "Beiträge, III.," p. 257.

8. Charles to Ferdinand, Oct. 19, 1555, Lanz, *Correspondenz,* 3: 689; Ferdinand to Charles, Oct. 31, 1555, ibid., p. 691.

9. Ferdinand to Maximilian, June 4, 1557, SA, *Familienkorrespondenz A,* Karton 2, fo. 131.

10. Ferdinand's Instructions for Licenciado Gamez, Oct. 16, 1556 (copy), AGR, *Manuscrits divers,* 805 A/II, fos. 122-123 (143-144); Arras to Gonzalo Perez, Nov. 23, 1561, AG, *Estado, Flandes,* Leg. 521, fo. 45; Maurenbrecher, "Beiträge zur deutschen Geschichte," p. 23.

11. Wilhelm Maurenbrecher, "Beiträge zur Geschichte Maximilians II, 1548-1562," *HZ,* 32 (1874): 271; Granvelle, *Papiers d'état,* 3: 273-274; Philip to Ferdinand, Nov. 21, 1557, *Documentos inéditos,* 2: 506-507.

12. On Philip's obedience to his father see Charles Petrie, *Philipp II von Spanien,* trans. Ursula Gmelin, (Stuttgart: Kohlhammer, 1965), pp. 62-63; Ferdinand to Maximilian, June 15, 1557, Margaret of Parma to Philip II, Oct. 4, 1559, *Correspondance de Marguerite d'Autriche, duchesse de Parme, avec Philippe II,* ed. L. -P. Gachard, 3 vols. (Brussels: Muquardt, 1867-1881), 1: 44-46; Granvelle to Philip II, Dec. 12, 1562, AG, *Estado, Flandes,* Legajo, 524, fo. 32/1.

13. Ferdinand to Philip, Aug. 25, 1557, *Documentos inéditos,* 2: 491.

14. Ferdinand to Philip, Nov. 30, 1556, ibid., p. 450; Ferdinand to Philip, Aug. 25, 1557, ibid., p. 491; Ferdinand to Philip, Jan. 12, 1558, ibid., p. 511; Count de Luna to Philip, Oct. 20, 1562, ibid., 98: 371.

15. Ferdinand's Repy to Philip, Dec. 10, 1556, ibid., 2: 458.

16. Ferdinand to Maximilian, June 4, 1557, SA, *Familienkorrespondenz A,* Karton 2, fo. 131.

17. Ferdinand to Philip, Jan. 14, 1562, AG, *Estado, Alemania,* Legajo 651, fo. 1; Count de Luna to Philip, Jan. 4, 1562, ibid., fo. 34; Ferdinand's Instructions to Martin Guzmán for Philip, n.d. (1562?), ibid., fo. 104/1; Ferdinand to Martin Guzmán, Aug. 19, 1563, ibid., Legajo, 652, fo. 35; Count de Luna to Philip, Jan. 19, 1562, *Documentos inéditos,* 98: 272.

18. Count de Luna to Philip, Aug. 29, 1562, *Documentos inéditos,* 98: 360-361; Philip to Count de Luna, Sept. 1562, ibid., p. 361.

19. Ferdinand to Count de Luna, s.d., 1563, ibid., p. 452; Ferdinand to Philip, Nov. 23, 1559, ibid., 2: 553; Ferdinand to Philip, May 17, 1563, ibid., 98: 439.

20. Philip to Ferdinand, July 21, 1563, ibid., 98: 466.

21. Count de Luna to Philip, Oct. 8, 1560, ibid., p. 174; Philip to Ferdinand, March (April?) 2, 1563, ibid., p. 423; Count de Luna to Philip, Aug. 16, 1562, ibid., pp. 354, 357; Philip to Count de Luna, July 4, 1562, ibid., p. 345; Count de Luna to Philip, Mar. 29, 1562, ibid., p. 310. Philip maintained a network of agents throughout the Empire.

22. Marvin R. O'Connell, *The Counter Reformation,* (New York: Harper Torchbooks, 1974), p. 35; Ferdinand to Philip, Mar. 13, 1558, SA, *Belgien, PA* 102a, fo. 12.

23. Maurenbrecher, "Beiträge zur deutschen Geschichte," p. 56; Ferdinand to Margaret of Parma, June 17, 1561, AGR, *Allemande,* fasc. 102, fo. 73; Ferdinand to Margaret of Parma, Jan. 23, 1561, ibid., fo. 96; Ferdinand to Margaret of Parma, May 24, 1561, ibid., fo. 65; Ferdinand to Philip, Aug. 17, 1559, *Documentos inéditos,* 98: 95-98; Ferdinand to Philip, July 28, 1560, ibid., pp. 160-161.

24. Ferdinand to Margaret of Parma, Dec. 4, 1562, AGR, *Allemande,* fasc. 102, fo. 31; Ferdinand to Margaret of Parma, Feb. 27, 1562, ibid., fasc. 92, fos. 59, 61-62; Petrie, *Philipp II,* p. 109; Evans, *Rudolph II,* p. 96.

25. Ferdinand to Philip, Mar. 13, 1558, SA, *Belgien, PA* 102a, fo. 12; Count de Luna to Philip, Jan. 12, 1560, *Documentos inéditos,* 98: 109-110. Margaret of Parma performed the same services for Ferdinand from the Netherlands. See Margaret of Parma to Wolfgang Bryning, Jan. 29, 1560, AGR, *Allemande,* fasc. 92, fo. 70.

26. Ferdinand to Philip, Nov. 20, 1563, *Documentos inéditos,* 101: 34; sketch of a report to Philip, Oct. 22, 1552, AG, *Estado, Flandes,* Legajo 504, fo. 201.

27. Count de Luna to Philip, Jan. 19, 1562, *Documentos inéditos,* 98: 277; Count de Luna to Philip, n.d., ibid., pp. 298-299; Ferdinand to his ambassador, s.d., 1563, AG, *Estado, Alemania,* Legajo 652, fo. 64; extract of Ferdinand's orders to his ambassador in Constantinople, April 11, 1564, ibid., fo. 196.

28. John Lynch, *Spain under the Habsburgs,* 2 vols. (Oxford: Blackwell, 1965-1969), 1: 222; Philip to Ferdinand, May 4, 1563, *Documentos*

inéditos, 98: 431-432; Ferdinand to Philip, May 27, 1563, ibid., p. 441; Philip to George Seld (Ferdinand's vice-chancellor), July 21, 1563, ibid., pp. 465-466; Joseph von Hammer-Purgstall, *Histoire de l'empire ottoman,* 12 vols. trans. J. -J. Hellert (Paris: Bellizard, 1835-1838), 6: 165. Ferdinand to Philip II, Jan. 19, 1564, ibid., 101: 63.

29.   AG, *Patronato Real,* Legajo 44, fo. 1/LV. According to the agreement, however, Ferdinand was to retain control over feudatory rights to Mantua, Monferrat, Florence, Piedmont and the holdings of the dukes of Ferrara. See Druffel, *Beiträge,* 3^1: 197 and Maurenbrecher, "Beiträge zur deutschen Geschichte," p. 21.

30.   Maurenbrecher, "Beiträge zur deutschen Geschichte," pp. 23, 28.

31.   Lutz, *Christianitas,* p. 419.

32.   Maurenbrecher, "Beiträge zur deutschen Geschichte," pp. 57-58.

33.   The bishop of Aquila to Philip, June 13, 1558, *Documentos inéditos,* 98: 14-15.

34.   Maurenbrecher, "Beiträge zur deutschen Geschichte," pp. 59-60; Ferdinand to Philip, July 22, 1558, *Documentos inéditos,* 98: 24-26.

35.   Arras to the bishop of Aquila, n.d., AG, *Estado, Alemania,* Legajo 649, fo. 193.

36.   Philip to the Count de Luna, Jan. 28, 1562, *Documentos inéditos,* 98: 284; Count de Luna to Philip, Feb. 25, 1562, ibid., pp. 293-295; Count de Luna, to Philip, Aug. 29, 1562, ibid., p. 362.

37.   Philip to the Count de Luna, Sept. 1562, ibid., p. 365; Philip to the Count de Luna, July 4, 1562, ibid., pp. 344-345.

38.   Count de Luna to Philip, Mar. 29, 1562, ibid., p. 309; Count de Luna to Philip, Aug. 29, 1562, ibid., p. 362.

39.   AG, *Patronato Real,* Legajo 46, fos. 46-49/IV and Legajo 44, fo. 15/II; Ferdinand to Philip, Nov. 19, 1562, *Documentos inéditos,* 98: 377-378.

40.   Philip to the Count de Luna, 17, Feb., 1559, AG, *Estado, Alemania,* Legajo 650, fo. 128; Philip to Ferdinand, Sept. 4, 1560, ibid., fo. 158; Don Jorge Manriquez to Philip, Jan. 1560, ibid., fo. 73.

41.   Maurenbrecher, "Beiträge zur deutschen Geschichte," pp. 25, 50.

42.   Turba, "Beiträge, III.," p. 274.

43.   Eduard Reimann, "Der Streit zwischen Papstthum und Kaiserthum im Jahre 1558," *Forschungen zur deutschen Geschichte,* 5 (1865): 299.

44.   Ferdinand to Maximilian, April 21, 1555 ?, SA, *Familienkorrespondenz, A,* Karton 2, fos. 83-84.

45. Heinrich Lutz, "Bayern und der Laienkelch, 1548-1556," *QuF*, 34 (1954): 214.

46. Josef Grisar, "Die Stellung der Päpste zum Reichstag und Religionsfrieden von Augsburg 1555," *Stimmen der Zeit*, 156 (1954/1955): 454; Hans Erich Feine, "Papst, erste Bitte, und Regierungsantritt des Kaisers seit dem Ausgang des Mittelalters," *Zeitschrift der Savigny-Stiftung für Rechtsgeschichte*, 51, kanonistische Abt. 20 (1931): 46-47; Joseph Schmid, "Die deutsche Kaiser-und Königswahl und die römische Curie in den Jahren 1558-1620," *Historisches Jahrbuch der Görres-Gesellschaft*, 6 (1885): 14-55 ff.; Reimann, "Streit," p. 302.

47. Reimann, "Streit," p. 304; Schmid, "Kaiserwahl," pp. 11, 16; Eduard Reimann, "Papst Paul IV und das Kaiserthum," *Abhandlungen der schlesischen Gesellschaft für väterlandischen Kultur*, phil.-hist. Abt. (1871): 30.

48. Bishop of Aquila to ?, June 13, 1558, *Documentos inéditos*, 98: 16; Eduard Reimann, "Die römische Königswahl von 1562 und der Papst," *Forschungen zur deutschen Geschichte*, 8 (1868): 4.

49. Schmid, "Kaiserwahl," pp. 29-30.

50. Ibid., pp. 30, 33; Reimann, "Streit," p. 307; Bishop of Aquila to Philip II, June 13, 1558, *Documentos inéditos*, 98: 14.

51. Reimann, "Paul IV," p. 34; Maurenbrecher, "Beiträge zur Geschichte Maximilians," pp. 266-267.

52. Philip II to Ferdinand, May 18, 1557, *Documentos inéditos*, 98: 476-477; Ferdinand to Philip, June 8, 1557, ibid., pp. 478-481.

53. Maurenbrecher, "Beiträge zur deutschen Geschichte," pp. 38, 72-73.

54. Schmid, "Kaiserwahl," pp. 22-23.

55. Ibid., pp. 24, 27-28; Ferdinand to Philip, Jan. 3, 1559, *Documentos inéditos*, 2: 521-522.

56. Reimann, "Paul IV," p. 32; Philip to Ferdinand, May 12, 1559, *Documentos inéditos*, 2: 524-525; Ferdinand to Philip, May 17, 1559, ibid., p. 530.

57. Maurenbrecher, "Beiträge zur Geschichte Maximilians," p. 269.

58. Ferdinand to Maximilian, Mar. 20, 1559 ?, SA, *Familienkorrespondenz, A*, Karton 2, fo. 165; Reimann, "Paul IV," pp. 35-36.

59. Reimann, "Paul IV," p. 39.

60. Count de Luna to Philip, Mar. 13, 1560, *Documentos inéditos*, 98: 136; Frederick III of the Palatinate to Christoph of Württemberg,

Mar. 20, 1561, *Briefe Friedrich des Frommen Kurfürsten von der Pfalz*, ed. August Kluchhohn, 2 vols. in 3 (Braunschweig: Schwetschke, 1868-1872), 1: 169.

61. Kassowitz, *Reformvorschläge*, pp. 7-8.

62. Ferdinand to Philip, Dec. 30, 1562, *Documentos inéditos*, 98: 580.

63. Delfino to Charles Borromeo, Oct. 18, 1560, AG, *Estado, Alemania*, Legajo 650, fo. 217.

64. Count de Luna to Philip, Jan. 19, 1562, *Documentos inéditos*, 98: 275; Philip to the Count de Luna, Mar. 11, 1562, ibid., p. 301.

65. Ferdinand to Philip, Dec. 30, 1562, ibid., pp. 580-581.

66. Philip to Ferdinand, May 12, 1563, ibid., pp. 435-436; Ferdinand to Philip, July 17, 1563, AG, *Estado, Alemania*, Legajo 652, fo. 31; James W. Thompson, *The Wars of Religion in France* (repr: New York, Ungar, n.d.), pp. 261-262.

67. Hartmann Grisar, "Jakob Lainez und die Frage des Laienkelches auf dem Concil von Trient," pt. 2, *Zeitschrift für katholische Theologie*, 6 (1882); 80; David P. Daniel, "The Influence of the Augsburg Confession in South-East Central Europe," *Sixteenth Century Journal*, 11 (1980): 102; Count de Luna to Philip, Dec. 28, 1560, *Documentos inéditos*, 98: 190; Ferdinand to Martin Guzmán, AG, *Estado, Alemania*, Legajo 650, fo. 40; Pedro de Labitra to Philip, Feb. 3, 1561, ibid., *Flandes*, Legajo 521, fo. 88.

68. Ferdinand to Philip, Dec. 30, 1562, *Documentos inéditos*, 98: 576.

69. Till, "Glaubensspaltung," pp. 5-6; Grisar, "Lainez," pt. 2, p. 80.

70. Ferdinand to Philip, June 27, 1560, *Documentos inéditos*, 98: 561.

71. Ferdinand to Philip, June 27, 1560, ibid., p. 561; Kassowitz, *Reformvorschläge*, p. 50; Ferdinand to George Gienger, Feb. 24, 1562 in Theodor von Sickel, "Das Reformations-libell des Kaisers Ferdinand I. vom Jahre 1562 bis zur Absendung nach Trient," *AöG*, 45 (1871): 15.

72. Hubert Jedin, *Geschichte des Konzils von Trient*, 4 vols. in 5 (Freiburg: Herder, 1949-1970), 4[1]: 157-158; Philipp Helle, *Die Konferenzen Morones mit Kaiser Ferdinand I (Mai 1563) und ihre Einwirkung auf den Gang des Trienter Konzils* (Bonn: Carl Georgi, 1911), pp. 8-9.

73. Helle, *Morone*, pp. 16, 30-31, 33; Jedin, *Trient*, 4[1]: 158; Grisar, "Lainez," pt. 2, p. 86.

74. Ferdinand to Philip, Dec. 30, 1562, *Documentos inéditos,* 98: 576, 578-579.

75. Grisar, "Lainez," pt. 2, p. 42.

76. Helle, *Morone,* pp. 17, 19-21, 25.

77. Count de Luna to Philip, Mar. 9, 1563, *Documentos inéditos,* 98: 408; Ferdinand to Count de Luna, s.d., 1563, ibid., pp. 448-452; Count de Luna to Philip, Mar. 31, 1563, ibid., p. 422.

78. Philip to Ferdinand, Mar. (April ?) 2, 1563, ibid., p. 423; Ferdinand to Philip, Nov. 9, 1563, ibid., 101: 5; Philip to Count de Luna, Nov. 15, 1563, ibid., pp. 11-12; Philip to Count de Luna, Dec. 6, 1563, ibid., p. 42.

79. Till, "Glaubensspaltung," p. 6.

80. Jedin, *Trient,* 4[1]: 164; Philip to Ferdinand, April 23, 1564, *Documentos inéditos,* 101: 71.

Notes to Chapter XV

1. Fichtner, "Dynastic Marriage," p. 261; Juan Vasquez de Molina to Charles, Jan. 26, 1557, AGR, *Manuscits divers,* 805 A/I (copy), fos. 165-166.

2. Walter Pillich, "Königin Katharina von Polen in Linz," *Historisches Jahrbuch der Stadt Linz* (1966): 169-198. Sigismund claimed that Catherine was epileptic. She left Poland in 1567, never to return and died in Linz in 1570. See also Ferdinand to Maximilian, Mar. 20, 1559 ?, SA, *Familienkorrespondenz, A,* Karton 2, fo. 164.

3. Ferdinand to Charles, April 24, 1552, Druffel, *Beiträge,* 2: 425; Ferdinand to Maximilian, Jan. 17, 1559 ?, SA, *Familienkorrespondenz, A,* Karton 2, fo. 156; Ferdinand to Maximilian, Oct. 14, 1559, ibid., fo. 150.

4. Ferdinand to Maximilian, Mar. 20, 1559 ?, SA, *Familienkorrespondenz, A,* Karton 2, fo. 164; Maximilian to Albrecht of Bavaria, Oct. 29, 1554, Druffel, *Beiträge,* 4: 536-537.

5. Count de Luna to Philip II, May 24, 1561, *Documentos inéditos,* 98: 220-221; Ferdinand's Instructions to George von Hellfenstein, SA, *Familien-Akten,* Karton 21, fasc. 3, fos. 72-73.

6. John Frederick the Elder to Ferdinand, July 31, 1553, Druffel, *Beiträge,* 4: 230. See also Ferdinand to Charles, Dec. 1, 1554, ibid., pp. 544-545.

7.   Fichtner, "Dynastic Marriage," p. 245; Ferdinand's Instructions to Caspar Breuner, Aug. 1, 1559, SA, *Familien-Akten,* Karton 21, fasc. 3, fos. 1, 4; Ferdinand to Maximilian, June 24, 1559, ibid., fasc. 2, fo. 162; Joel Hurstfield, "The Search for Compromise in England and France," in Joel Hurstfield, ed., *The Reformation Crisis* (New York: Harper Torchbooks, 1966), p. 97.

8.   Ferdinand to Philip, June 23, 1559, *Documentos inéditos,* 2: 544-545; Ferdinand to Caspar Breuner, June 22, 1559, SA, *Familien-Akten,* Karton 21, fasc. 2, fo. 153.

9.   Ferdinand to Maximilian, April 21, 1555 ?, SA, *Familienkorrespondenz, A,* Karton 2, fo. 83; Ferdinand to Maximilian, June 15, 1559 ?, ibid., fo. 169.

10.   Hauptmann, "Kroatische Staatsidee," pp. 67-68; Karl Oberleitner, "Die Finanzlage Niederösterreichs im 16. Jahrhundert," *Archiv für Kunde österreichescher Geschichtsquellen,* 30 (1864), p. 42.

11.   Oberleitner, "Finanzen," pp. 97, 106.

12.   Ibid., pp. 218-219, note 1, p. 229; Ferdinand's Memorandum to Charles on Maximilian, *Blau,* 597/3, fo. 85.

13.   Goetz, "Finalrelation," p. 282, Gerhard Müller, "Vincenzo Pimpinella am Hofe Ferdinands I 1529, 1532," *QuF,* 40 (1960): 71-72.

14.   Goetz, "Ratgeber," p. 489; Goetz, "Finalrelation," pp. 299-300; Ferdinand to Charles, Jan. 12, 1544, *Blau,* 597/2, fo. 114; Hilger, *Ikonographie,* p. 138.

15.   Goetz, "Finalrelation," pp. 299-300; Hilger, *Ikonographie,* p. 138; Goetz, "Finalrelation," p. 293.

16.   Hellbling, *Verfassungsgeschichte,* p. 229.

17.   Ferdinand to Charles, April 13, 1542, *Blau,* 597/2, fo. 32; Ferdinand to Charles, Nov. 18, 1542, ibid., fo. 77.

18.   Ferdinand to Charles, Dec. 9, 1548, ibid., fo. 292.

19.   Antonia Fraser, *Mary Queen of Scots* (London: Panther, 1970), pp. 257-258.

20.   Goetz, "Finalrelation," pp. 297-298; Huber, "Finanziellen," pp. 186-187.

21.   Sutter, intro., p. 175; Hirn, *Ferdinand von Tirol,* 1: 43, 46, Ferdinand to Maximilian, Ferdinand, and Charles, Feb., 1547, Bucholtz, *Regierung,* 9: 466-467; Ferdinand to Maximilian, July 9, 1552 ?, SA, *Familienkorrespondenz, A,* Karton 2, fo. 72.

22.   Hirn, *Ferdinand von Tirol,* 1: 42-43; Franz Ferdinand Schrötter,

Abhandlungen aus dem österreichischen Staatsrecht und Freiheitsbriefen, 5 vols. (Vienna: Kraus, 1762-1766), 5: 452-457, 468-469, 483-485. For a representative sample of the testaments of German ruling houses see Hermann Schulze, ed., *Die Hausgesetze der regierenden deutschen Fürstenhäuser,* 3 vols. (Jena: Fischer, 1862-1883). On the growth of partitive inheritance in Germany see the same author's *Das Recht der Erstgeburt in den deutschen Fürstenhäusern und seine Bedeutung für die deutsche Staatsentwicklung* (Leipzig: Avenarius und Mendelsohn, 1851). See also Lhotsky, *Sammlungen,* 2¹: 154.

23. "... que ha algos dias que ha tomado determinacion en el dicho repartimiento, dando al dicho Archiduque /Charles/ los ducados de stiria, carinthia, y carniola y assimismo el condado de goricia, que el Emperador Frederico de buena memoria al principio de su imperio no tuvo otros ni mejores, y aun no tenia entonces el... condado de goricia en su poder ..." Ferdinand's Reply to the Bishop of Rennes, Aug. 2, 1563, AG, *Estado, Alemania,* Legajo 652, fo. 18.

24. Goetz, "Finalrelation," pp. 290, 292-293; Bucholtz, *Regierung,* 7:221; Holtzmann, *Maximilian,* p. 36.

25. Holtzmann, *Maximilian,* pp. 46-47; Goetz, "Finalrelation," p. 299; Ferdinand to Maximilian, Sept. 1, 1556 ?, SA, *Familienkorrespondenz,* A, Karton 2, fo. 127; Ferdinand to Maximilian, Jan. 20, 1557, ibid., fo. 128; Ferdinand to Charles, Mar. 15, 1554, *Blau,* 597/3, fo. 250.

26. Ferdinand to Charles, May 22, 1556, Lanz, *Correspondenz,* 3: 700-701; Ferdinand to Maximilian, Feb. 20, 1558 ?, SA, *Familienkorrespondenz, A,* Karton, 2, fo. 142; Ferdinand to Maximilian, Dec. 11, 1559, ibid., fo. 152; Rosenthal, "Behördeorganisation," p. 149, note. 4.

27. Ferdinand to Maximilian, Jan. 12, 1557, SA, *Familienkorrespondenz, A,* Karton 2, fo. 126; Ferdinand to Maximilian, Oct. 2, 1555, ibid., fo. 120; Ferdinand to Maximilian, Feb. 1, 1559, ibid., fo. 160.

28. Friedrich Firnhaber, "Zur Geschichte des österreichischen Militärwesens," *Archiv für Kunde österreichischer Geschichtsquellen,* 30 (1864): 97, 130.

29. Gisela Üllenberg, "Augsburger Frauen. Agnes Bernauer und Philippine Welser," in *Augusta 955-1955. Foschungen und Studien zur Kultur-und Wirtschaftsgeschichte Augsburgs,* (Augsburg: Rinn, 1955), pp. 141-142.

30. Fichtner, "Dynastic Marriage," p. 256.

31. *Renaissance in Österreich. Schloß Schallaburg.* Katalog desieder-
ö

niederösterreichischen Landesmuseums, New Series, No. 57 (Vienna, 1974), item. no. 281.

32. Bibl, *Maximilian II*, p. 43; Goetz, "Finalrelation," p. 295.

33. Brodrick, *Peter Canisius*, pp. 169-170.

34. ". . . qui asino e et cervo se crede/ al saltar del fosco se vede . . . ." Ferdinand to Maximilian, Ferdinand, and Charles, Feb., 1547, Bucholtz, *Regierung*, 9: 468-469; Holtzmann, *Maximilian*, pp. 51-54.

35. Bibl, *Maximilian II*, p. 49; Goetz, *Maximilian II*, p. 36; Ferdinand to Maximilian, Jan. 20, 1557, SA, *Familienkorrespondenz, A*, Karton 2, fo. 129; Maximilian to Albrecht of Bavaria, Jan. 13, 1554, Druffel, *Beiträge*, 4: 360-361.

36. Maurenbrecher, "Beiträge zur deutschen Geschichte," pp. 18-19; Charles to Ferdinand, Mar. 18, 1556, Lanz, *Correspondenz*, 3: 697.

37. Bibl, *Maximilian II*, pp. 44-45; Turba, "Beiträge, 2," pp. 69-70; Goetz, "Finalrelation," pp. 297, 304-306.

38. Goetz, "Finalrelation," p. 304; Lutz, *Christianitas*, pp. 480, 499.

39. Goetz, *Maximilian II*, p. 116; Erwin Mayer-Löwenschwerdt, "Der Aufenthalt der Erzherzöge Rudolf und Ernst in Spanien 1564-1571," *Sitzungsberichte der Akademie der Wissenschaften in Wien*, phil. -hist. Klasse, 206 (1927): 8; Peter Rassow, "Karls V Tochter Maria als Eventual-Erbin des spanischen Reiches," *ARG*, 49 (1958): 167-168.

40. Ferdinand to Maximilian, June 10, 1552, SA, *Familienkorrespondenz, A*, Karton 2, fo. 74.

41. Councillors of Christoph of Württemberg to Christoph, June 20, 1555, Ernst, *Briefwechsel*, 3: 238; Maurenbrecher, "Geschichte Maxilians," p. 257.

42. Holtzmann, *Maximilian*, p. 56; Bucholtz, *Regierung*, 9: 466-467.

43. There are three copies of this codicil in SA, *Familienkorrespondenz, A*, Karton 2. The one used for this passage, fos. 92-97, has Ferdinand's signature.

44. Goetz, "Finalrelation," pp. 302-303.

45. Heer, *Dritte Kraft*, pp. 417, 428-429; Goetz, "Ratgeber," pp. 468-469, 472; Rafael de Hornedo, "Carlos V y Erasmo," *Miscelánea Comillas*, 30 (1958): 239, note 138, and 240.

46. Ferdinand to Philip, 1 Sept. 1558 (copy), AGR, *Allemande*, fasc. 102, fo. 5; Anton Gindely, ed., *Quellen zur Geschichte der böhmischen Brüder, FRA: Diplomataria et Acta*, 19 (1859): 144.

47. Maurenbrecher, "Geschichte Maximilians," pp. 252-253; Bibl, *Maximilian II*, p. 71; Mayer-Löwenschwerdt, "Aufenthalt," p. 12.

48.   Gindely, *Quellen*, pp. 147, 167.

49.   Bibl, *Maximilian II*, pp. 72-73.

50.   Charles V to Philip, Feb. 16, 1554, AG, *Estado, Flandes*, Legajo 508, fo. 37; Maurenbrecher, "Geschichte Maximilians," p. 263. Cf. Joseph Schlecht, "Das geheime Dispensbreve Pius IV für die römische Königskrönung Maximilians II," *Historisches Jahrbuch*, 14 (1893): 5. Philip of Hesse recommended Maximilian's election as King of the Romans in 1562 believing that the latter would soft-pedal the religious issue in Germany. Philip of Hesse to Elector Frederick III of the Palatinate, March/April, 1562 (excerpt) in Walter Heinemeyer, ed. *Politisches Archiv des Landgrafen Philip des Großmütigen von Hessen*, Veröffentlichungen der historisches Kommission für Hessen und Waldeck, 24^2 (Marburg, 1959): 168.

51.   Bibl, *Maximilian II, pp. 75-76; Gindely, Quellen*, pp. 141-142, 145.

52.   Ferdinand to Philip, Sept. 1, 1557, *Documentos inéditos*, 2: 497-498; Bibl, *Maximilian II*, pp. 72-73; Maurenbrecher, "Geschichte Maximilians," p. 257; Gindely, *Quellen*, pp. 131, 134.

53.   Bibl, *Maximilian II*, p. 77; Goetz, *Maximilian II*, p. 117.

54.   Bibl, *Maximilian II*, p. 83; Gindely, *Quellen*, pp. 183-184.

55.   Maurenbrecher, "Geschichte Maximilians," p. 264.

56.   Goetz, "Finalrelation," p. 295; Gindely, *Quellen*, pp. 172-173.

57.   Ferdinand to Maximilian, Aug. 29, 1559, SA, *Familienakten, A*, Karton 2, fo. 144; Bibl, *Maximilian II*, pp. 90-93; Maurenbrecher, "Geschichte Maximilians," p. 278.

58.   Bucholtz, *Regierung*, 7: 502-503. Pfauser finally left Vienna in 1560.

59.   Bibl, *Maximilian II*, p. 77.

60.   Goetz, *Maximilian II*, pp. 110-111; Maurenbrecher, "Geschichte Maximilians," pp. 278-279, 281.

61.   Ferdinand to Philip, Aug. 29, 1558, SA, *Belgica, PA* 102a, fo. 16.

62.   Schlecht, "Dispensbreve," pp. 6-7, Bibl, *Maximilian II*, p. 95.

63.   Schlecht, "Dispensbreve," p. 13.

64.   Count de Luna to Philip, Aug. 20, 1561, *Documentos inéditos*, 98: 236-237.

65.   Schlecht, "Dispensbreve," pp. 16-17, 19, 34.

66.   Count de Luna to Philip, Sept. 15, 1561, *Documentos inéditos*, 98: 245; Count de Luna to Philip II, Feb. 19, 1562, ibid., p. 290; Jedin, *Trient*, 4^1: 145; Bibl, *Maximilian II*, p. 101.

67. Eduard Reimann as cited in Maurenbrecher, "Geschichte Maximilians," p. 222; Goetz, *Maximilian II*, pp. 101-102, 104, 110, 117.

68. Ferdinand to Maximilian, Mar. 20, 1559, SA, *Familienkorrespondenz, A*, Karton 2, fo. 165; Kluckhohn in *Briefe Friedrich des Frommen*, 1: lxiii; Ferdinand to Elector Frederick III, July 13, 1563, ibid., pp. 417-419; Lutz, *Christianitas*, p. 468; Bucholtz, *Regierung*, 7: 227-228; Margaret of Parma to Philip, Oct. 4, 1559, *Correspondence*, 1: 38.

69. Ferdinand's statement to the diet, April ?, 1559 (copy), AGR, *Allemande*, fasc. 806, fos. 22-25.

70. Ferdinand to Philip, Nov. 19, 1562, *Documentos inéditos*, 98: 378.

71. Count de Luna to Philip, Mar. 2, 1561, ibid., p. 197; Goetz, *Maximilian II*, pp. 55, 64, 73, 81, 124, 134-135.

72. Excerpts from Arras's letters of Oct. 30, 1562, AG, *Estado, Flandes*, Legajo 521, fo. 132.

73. Duke of Arechot to ?, Nov. 3, 1562, ibid., *Alemania*, Legajo 651, fo. 217; Arras to Gonsalvo Perez, Nov. 3, 1562, ibid., *Flandes*, Legajo 522, fo. 33; Duke of Arechot to Margaret of Parma, Dec. 3, 1562, ibid., fo. 104; Goetz, *Maximilian II*, pp. 183, 198.

74. Elector Frederick III to Duke Johann Wilhelm of Saxony, Dec. 14, 1562, *Briefe Friedrich des Frommen*, 1: 363.

75. Goetz, *Maximilian II*, p. 167; Peter Pierson, *Philip II of Spain* (London: Thames and Hudson, 1973), pp. 115-116.

76. Reimann, "Römische Königswahl," pp. 4, 6, 8, 17; Feine, "Erste Bitte," p. 49.

77. Reimann, "Römische Königswahl," pp. 8-9, 13; Ferdinand to Philip, July 2, 1563, AG, *Estado, Alemania*, Legajo 652, fo. 30.

78. Reimann, "Römische Königswahl," p. 15; Philip's Instructions for Martin Guzmán, Dec. 9, 1562, AG, *Estado, Alemania*, Legajo 651, fos. 96, 102. Philip to Martin Guzmán, Dec. 11, 1562, Documentos inéditos, 98: 383; Philip to Maximilian, April 6, 1563, ibid., p. 425; Ferdinand to Philip, Oct. 10, 1563, ibid., p. 514.

79. "Nuevas de augusta y praga, Sept. 13 ?, 1562, AG, *Estado, Alemania*, Legajo 651, fo. 161; Friedrich Firnhaber, "Die Krönung Kaiser Maximilians II. zum König von Ungarn 1563," *AöG*, 22 (1860): 313, 317, 326-327.

80. Maximilian to Ferdinand, May 11, 1562, in Heinrich Kretschmayer, "Maximilian II. an Ferdinand I. Linz 11 May (1562)," *MIöG*, 18 (1897): 622-623.

Notes to Chapter XVI

1. Goetz, "Finalrelation," p. 297.

2. Queen Catherine of Poland to Ferdinand, Dec. 12, 1563?, SA, *Familienkorrespondenz, A,* Karton 1, fo. 153; Hilger, *Ikonographie,* p. 139; Sutter, intro., p. 157; Ferdinand to the Queen of Portugal, Jan. 16, 1563, *Documentos inéditos,* 2: 585-586; Count de Luna to Philip II, Aug. 20, 1561, ibid., 98: 237; Vice-chancellor Seld to Granvella (Arras), May 26, 1563, AG, *Estado, Flandes,* Legajo 524, fo. 61.

3. Ferdinand to Philip II, May 23, 1564, *Documentos inéditos,* 101: 75; Bibl, *Maximilian II,* p. 115.

4. Bibl, *Maximilian II,* pp. 116-117; M . . . y, Freiherr von, "Die letzten Lebenstage Kaiser Ferdinands I," *Archiv für Geographie, Historie, Stasts-und Kriegskunst,* 8 (1817): 61-62.

5. Elector Frederick III to Duke John William of Saxony, Feb. 9, 1564, *Briefe,* 1: 485-486; Margaret of Parma to Philip II, Aug. 13, 1564, AG, *Estado, Flandes,* Legajo 525, fo. 169.

6. Philip's Instructions to Count de Fuensalida, Sept. 4, 1564, *Documentos inéditos,* 101: 85; Archduke Ferdinand to Philip, Dec. 3, 1564, ibid., p. 90; Philip to the Duke of Parma, AG, *Estado, Flandes,* Legajo 525, fo. 54.

WORKS CITED

I. Archival sources

Brussels. Archives générales du royaume. *Archives d'état. Allemande.*
Fascicles 38, 92, 102, 766, 800, 801, 802, 806, 839.
Manuscrits divers. Fascicles 175/Abis, 187A, 187A, 805A/I, 805A/II.
Papiers d'état et l'audience. Fascicle 46.

Simancas. Archivo general de Simancas. *Secretaria de estado. Negociación
de Alemania.* Legajos 635, 636, 637, 646, 649, 650, 651, 652.
Secretaria de estado. Negociación de Flandes. Legajos 496, 501, 504, 508,
521, 522, 524, 525.
Patronato real. Legajos 16, 44, 46, 53, 57.

Vienna. Haus, Hof, -und Staatsarchiv. *Belgien, D D. B.* Fascicle 223.
Belgien, Politisches Archiv. Fascicles 4, 6, 7, 8, 9, 10, 12, 13, 41, 46,
54, 74, 75, 85, 102a.
Grosse Korrespondenz. Fascicle 25a.
Handschriften. Blau. 595, 597/1, 597/2, 597/3.
Haus-Archiv. Familien-Akten. Cartons 21, 53, 60, 97.
Haus-Archiv. Familienkorrespondenz. A. Cartons 1, 2.
Hungarica. Fascicles. 20, 21.

II. Published sources

Acta Tomiciana. 16 vols. Poznań: Merzbach, 1852-1960.
E. Albèri, ed. *Relazioni degli ambasciatori veneti al Senato.* 15 vols. Flor-
ence: società editrice fiorentina, 1839-1863.
Archiv český. 37 vols. Prague: Řivnáč, 1840-1944.
Avila y Zuñiga, Luis. *Comentaria de la guerra de Alemania.* Bibliotheca de
autores españoles, 1. Madrid: Rivadeneyra, 1852.

Bauer, Wilhelm, Robert Lacroix, Christiane Thomas, Herwig Wolfram, eds. *Die Korrespondenz Ferdinands I.* Veröffentlichungen der Kommission für neuere Geschichte Österreichs. 11, 30-31, 58. Vienna: Holzhausen, 1912-1977.

Bernhauer, W. F. A., ed. and trans. *Sulaiman des Gesetzgebers Tagebuch auf seinem Feldzuge nach Wien im Jahre 93 5/6 D.H. = j. 1529 n. Chr.* Vienna: Gerold, 1858.

Die böhmische Landtagsverhandlungen und Landtagsbeschlüße vom Jahre 1526 bis auf die Neuzeit. 11 vols. Prague: königlicher böhmische Landesausschuß, 1877-1941.

Brandenburg, Erich, ed. *Politische Korrespondenz des Herzogs und Kurfürsten Moritz von Sachsen.* 2 vols. Leipzig: Teubner, 1900.

Canisius, Peter. *Beati Petri Canisii Societatis Jesu, Epistolae et Act.* Ed. Otto Braunsberger. 8 vols. Freiburg i. Breisgau: Herder, 1896-1923.

Colección de documentos inéditos para la historia de España. 112 vols. 1842-1895; rpt. Vaduz: Krauss, 1966.

Collection des voyages des souverains des Pays Bas. 4 vols. Brussels: Hayez, 1874-1882.

Druffel, August von, ed. *Beiträge zur Reichsgeschichte 1546-1555.* 4 vols. Munich: Rieper, 1873-1896.

Ernst, Viktor, ed. *Briefwechsel des Herzogs Christoph von Wirtemberg.* 4 vols. Stuttgart: Kohlhammer, 1899-1907.

Fiedler, Joseph, ed. *Relationen venetianischer Botschafter über Deutschland und Österreich im sechzehnten Jahrhundert.* Fontes Rerum Austriacarum. 30. Vienna: Gerold, 1870.

Gachard, L. P., ed. *Correspondance de Marguerite d'Autriche, duchesse de Parme avec Philippe II.* 3 vols. Brussels: Muquardt, 1867-1881.

Gévay, Anton von, ed. *Urkunden und Actenstücke zur Geschichte der Verhältnisse zwischen Österreich, Ungern [sic] und der Pforte in XVI und XVII. Jahrhunderts.* 3 vols. Vienna: Schaumberg, 1840.

le Glay, M., ed. *Correspondance de l'empreuer Maximilien Ièr. et de Marguerite d'Autriche.* 2 vols. Paris: Renouard, 1839.

Gindely, Anton, ed. *Quellen zur Geschichte der böhmischen Brüder.* Fontes Rerum Austriacarum. 19. Vienna: Gerold, 1859.

Goetz, Helmut, ed. "Die Finalrelation des venezianischen Gesandten Michele Suriano 1555," *Quellen und Forschungen aus italienischen Archiven und Bibliotheken.* 41 (1961): 235-322.

Heinemeyer, Walter, ed. *Politisches Archiv des Landgrafen Philip des Großmütigen von Hessen.* Veröffentlichungen der historischen Kommission für Hessen und Waldeck. 24¹, 24². Marburg: Elwert Kommissionsverlag, 1954, 1959.

Herberstein, Siegmund von. *Selbstbiographie.* Ed. Theodor von Karajan. Fontes Rerum Austriacarum. 1. Vienna: Gerold, 1855.

Hortleder, Friedrich. *Vom Anfang und Fortgang deß teutschen Krieges Keyser Carls deß Fünfften wider die Schmalkaldische Bundsoberste* . . . . 3 vols. Frankfurt a. M.: Hoffmann, 1618.

Károlyi, Árpád, ed. "Kiadatlan levelek a német birodalom magyarországi nagy hadi vállalatának történetéhez, 1542." *Történelmi tár.* (1880): 490-540.

Kirchmair, Georg. *Georg Kirchmairs Denkwürdigkeiten 1519-1553.* Ed. Theodor von Karajan. Fontes Rerum Austriacarum. 1. Vienna: Gerold, 1855.

Kluckhohn, August, ed. *Briefe Friedrich des Frommen Kurfürsten von der Pfalz.* 2 vols. in 3. Braunschweig: Schwetschke, 1868-1872.

_____ and A. Wrede, eds. *Deutsche Reichstagsakten.* Jüngere Reihe. 5 vols. Gotha: Perthes, 1893-1905.

Könneritz, Julius T. J., ed. "Erasmus von Könneritz in dem Kriegszuge gegen die Türken 1542." *Archiv für die sächsischen Geschichte,* 8 (1870): 82-101.

Krebs, Manfred, ed. *Quellen zur Geschichte der Täufer, IV: Baden und Pfalz.* Quellen und Forschungen zur Reformationsgeschichte. 23. Gütersloh: Bertelsmann, 1951.

Kretschmayr, Heinrich, ed. "Maximilian II. an Ferdinand I. Linz 11. May (1562)." *Mitteilungen des Institus für österreichische Geschichtsforschung,* 18 (1897): 620-623.

Lanz, Karl, ed. *Correspondenz des Kaisers Karl V.* 3 vols. Leipzig: Brockhaus, 1844-1846.

Lutz, Heinrich and Alfred Kohler, eds. *Das Reichstagsprotokoll des kaiserlichen Kommissars Felix Hornung vom Augsburger Reichstag 1555.* Österreichische Akademie der Wissenschaften. Philosophische-historische Klasse. Denkschriften. 103. Vienna: Böhlaus, 1971.

Monumenta Hungariae Historica: Monumenta Comitialia Regni Hungariae. 12 vols. Budapest: király tudományegytem könyvnyomd, 1874-1917.

Monumenta Hungariae Historica: Diplomataria. 41 vols. Budapest: Eggenberg, 1857-1919.

Monumenta Spectantia Historiam Slavorum Meridionalium. 45 vols. Zagreb: jugoslavenská akademia znajosti, 1868-1950.

Monumenta Vaticana Hungariae. Relationes Oratorum Pontificiorum 1524-1526. Budapest: n.p., 1884.

Muralt, Leonhard von. ed. *Quellen zur Geschichte der Täufer in der Schweiz. Zürich.* Zürich: Hirzel, 1952.

Nuntiaturberichte aus Deutschland. Ed., Prussian Historical Academy in Rome. pt. 1. 12 vols. Gotha: Perthes, 1892-1970.

Oberleitner, Karl, ed. "König Ferdinand's Instructions an Marx Treitssauerwein wegen Fortsetzung der Herausgabe des Weiss Kunigs, Theuerdank's, der Ehrenporten, der Genealogie des österreichischen Kaiserhauses und der Schriften des Stabius." *Beilage zum Archiv für Kunde österreichischer Geschichte.* Notizenblatt, 8 (1858): 286-288.

Sanuto, Marino. *I. Diarii.* 58 vols. Venice: Visentini, 1879-1902.

Sastrow, Bartholomäus, *Lauf meines Lebens.* Ed. Christfried Coler. Berlin: Rütten and Loening, 1956.

Schornbaum, Karl, ed. *Quellen zur Geschichte der Täufer, II: Bayern.* Quellen und Forschungen zur Reformationsgeschichte. 23 Gütersloh: Bertelsmann, 1951.

Schulze, Hermann, ed. *Die Hausgesteze der regierenden deutschen Fürstenhäuser.* 3 vols. Jena: Fischer, 1862-1883.

Sixt z Ottersdorfu. *O pokření stavů městského léta 1547.* Ed. Josef Janáček. Prague: Melantrich, 1950.

Venetianische Depeschen vom Kaiserhofe. 4 vols. Vienna: Tempsky, 1889.

Weiss, Charles, ed. *Papiers d'état du cardinal de Granvelle.* 9 vols. Paris: imprimerie royale, 1841-1852.

III. Books

Ankwicz-Kleehoven, Hans. *Der Wiener Humanist Johannes Cuspinian.* Graz/Cologne: Böhlaus, 1959.

Aschbach, Joseph von. *Geschichte der Wiener Universität.* 3 vols. 1865-1888. rpt.; 1 Westmead, Farnborough Hunts: Gregg, 1967.

Augusta 955-1955. Forschungen und Studien zur Kultur-und Wirtschaftsgeschichte Augsburgs. Augsburg: Rinn, 1955.

Bauer, Wilhelm. *Die Anfänge Ferdinands I.* Vienna/Leipzig: Braumüller, 1907.

Baumgarten, Hermann. *Geschichte Kaiser Karls V.* 3 vols. Stuttgart: Cotta, 1885.

——————. *Karl V und die deutsche Reformation.* Halle: Verein für Reformationsgeschichte, 1889.

Betts, R. R. *Essays in Czech History.* London: Athlone, 1969.

Bibl, Viktor. *Maximilian II. Der rätselhafte Kaiser.* Hellerau bei Dresden: Avalun, 1929.

Bidermann, Hermann. *Geschichte der österreichischen Gesammt-Staatsidee 1526-1804.* Innsbruck: Wagner, 1867.

Björkmann, Walther. *Ofen zur Türkenzeit.* Abhandlungen aus dem Gebiet der Auslandskunde. 2nd ser. 2. Hamburg: Friederichsen, 1920.

Böhl, D. Eduard. *Beiträge zur Geschichte der Reformation in Österreich.* Jena: Fischer, 1902.

Bog, Ingomar, ed. *Der Außenhandel Ostmitteleuropas 1450-1650.* Vienna/Cologne: Böhlau, 1971.

Bonwetsch, Gerhard. *Geschichte des Passauischen Vertrages von 1552.* Göttingen: Dietrich, 1907.

Bousma, William. *Concordia Mundi: the Career and Thought of Guillaume Postel (1510-1581).* Cambridge, Mass.: Harvard, 1957.

Brandi, Karl. *Deutsche Geschichte im Zeitalter der Reformation und Gegenreformation.* 1927. rpt.; Munich: Bruckmann, 1960.

——————. *Kaiser Karl V. Werden und Schicksal einer Persönlichkeit und eines Weltreiches.* 2 vols. 3rd ed. Munich: Bruckmann, 1937.

Bretholz, Berthold. *Neuere Geschichte Böhmens.* Gotha: Perthes, 1920.

Brodrick, James. *Saint Peter Canisius S.J. 1521-1597.* London: Sheed and Ward, 1935.

Bucholtz, Franz Berhard von. *Geschichte der Regierung Ferdinands I.* 9 vols. 1831-1838. rpt. with intro. by Berthold Sutter; Graz: Akademische Druck-und Verlagsanstalt, 1971.

Československá vlastivěda. 12 vols. Prague: Sfinx, 1929-1936.

Denis, Ernst. *La Fin de l'indépendance bohême.* 2 vols. 2nd. ed. Paris: Leroux, 1930.

Dillon, Kenneth. *Kings and Estates in the Bohemian Lands 1526-1564.* Studies Presented to the International Commission for the History of Representative and Parliamentary Institutions. 57. Brussels: editions de la librairie encyclopédique, 1976.

Dvořák, Rudolf. *Dějiny Moravy.* 5 vols. in 1. Brno: musejní spolek, 1899-1905.

Eder, Karl. *Das Land ob der Enns vor der Glaubensspaltung.* 2 vols. Linz: im Buchlanden, 1932-1936.

Elliot, John H. *The Old World and the New 1492-1650.* Cambridge: Cambridge University, 1970.

Evans, R. J. W. *Rudolf II. and His World. A Study in Intellectual History 1576-1612.* Oxford: Oxford University, 1973.

Fellner, Thomas and Heinrich Kretschmayr. *Die österreichische Zentralverwaltung.* Vienna: Holzhausen, 1907.

Fessler, Ignaz and Ernst Klein. *Geschichte von Ungarn.* 10 vols. 2nd ed. Leipzig: Brockhaus, 1866-1883.

Fischer-Galati, Stephen. *Ottoman Imperialism and German Protestantism, 1521-1555.* Cambridge, Mass.: Harvard, 1959.

Fraknói, Wilhelm. *Ungarn vor der Schlacht Mohács, 1524-1526.* trans. J. H. Schwicker. Budapest: Lauffer, 1886.

Fraser, Antonia. *Mary Queen of Scots.* London: Panther, 1970.

Friedensberg, Walter. *Der Reichstag zur Speier 1526.* Historische Untersuchungen. 5. Berlin: Gaertner, 1887.

Goetz, Walter. *Maximilians II. Wahl zum römischen Könige 1562. Mit besonderer Berücksichtigung der Politik Kursachsens.* Würzburg: Becker, 1891.

Guldescu, Stanko. *History of Medieval Croatia.* The Hague: Mouton, 1964.

Hamilton, Bernice. *Political Thought in Sixteenth-Century Spain: A Study of the Political Ideas of Vitoria, Soto, Suárez, and Molina.* Oxford: Clarendon, 1963.

Hammer-Purgstall, Joseph von. *Histoire de l'empire ottoman.* trans. J. -J. Hellert. 12 vols. Paris: Bellizard, 1835-1838.

Hantsch, Hugo. *Die Geschichte Österreichs.* 2 vols. Graz/Vienna: Styria, 1947-1953.

Harbison, E. Harris. *Rival Ambassadors at the Court of Queen Mary.* Princeton: Princeton University, 1940.

Hasenclever, Adolf. *Die Politik der Schmalkaldaner vor dem Ausbruch des Schmalkaldischen Krieges.* Diss.: Berlin, 1901.

Heer, Friedrich. *Die dritte Kraft. Der europäische Humanismus zwischen den Fronten des konfessionellen Zeitalters.* Frankfurt a.M.: Fischer, 1959.

Heidrich, Paul. *Karl V und die deutschen Protestanten am Vorabend des Schmalkaldischen Krieges.* 2 parts. Frankfurter historische Forschungen. Nos. 5 and 6 (1911-1912).

Hellbling, Ernst C. *Österreichische Verfassungs-und Verwaltungsgeschichte.* Vienna: Springer, 1956.

Helle, Philipp. *Die Konferenzen Morones mit Kaiser Ferdinand I (Mai 1563) und ihre Einwirkung auf den Gang des Trienter Konzils.* Bonn: Georgi, 1911.

Hilger, Wolfgang. *Ikonographie Kaiser Ferdinands I. (1503-1564).* Veröffentlichung der Kommission für Geschichte Österreichs. 3. Vienna: Böhlaus, 1969.

Hirn, Ferdinand. *Geschichte der tiroler Landtage von 1518 bis 1525. In Erläuterungen und Ergänzungen zu Janssen's Geschichte des deutschen Volkes.* 4 (1905).

Hirn, Joseph. *Erzherzog Ferdinand II. von Tirol.* 2 vols. Innsbruck: Wagner, 1885-1888.

Hofmann, Karl. *Die Konzilsfrage auf den deutschen Reichstagen von 1521-1524.* Diss.: Mannheim, 1932.

Holborn, Hajo. *A History of Modern Germany.* 3 vols. New York: Knopf, 1959-1969.

Holtzmann, Robert. *Kaiser Maximilian II. bis zur seiner Thronbesteigung (1527-1564).* Berlin: Schwetschke, 1903.

Hóman, Bálint and Gyula Szekfű. *Magyar történet.* 8 vols. Budapest: király magyar egytemi nyomda, n. d.

Hrejsa, Ferdinand. *Dějiny křešt'anství v Československu.* 6 vols. Prague: evangelická fakulta bohoslovecká, 1947-1948.

Huber, Alfons. *Geschichte Österreichs.* 7 vols. Gotha: Perthes, 1885-1938.

_____ and Alfons Dopsch. *Österreiche Reichsgeschichte.* 2nd ed. Prague/Vienna: Tempsky, 1901.

Hunt, David. *Parents and Children in History: The Psychology of Family Life in Early Modern France.* New York: Harper Torch, 1972.

Janáček, Josef. *České dějiny: doba předbělohorská 1526-1547.* Prague: academia, 1968.

_____. *Řemeslná výroba v českých městech v 16. století.* Prague: československé akademie ved, 1961.

Jedin, Hubert. *Geschichte des Konzils von Trient.* 4 vols. in 5. Freiburg i. B.: Herder, 1949-1975.

Kaser, Kurt. *Deutsche Geschichte im Ausgange des Mittelalters (1438-1519).* 2 vols. Stuttgart/Berlin: Cotta, 1912.

Kassowitz, Theodor. *Die Reformvorschläge Kaiser Ferdinands I. auf dem Konzil von Trient.* Vienna/Leipzig: Braumüller, 1906.

Kiszling, Rudolf. *Die Kroaten: der Schichsalsweg eines Südslawenvolkes.* Graz/Cologne: Böhlaus, 1956.

Köchel, Ludwig von. *Die kaiserliche Hof-musikkapelle in Wien von 1543 bis 1867.* Vienna: Beck, 1869.

Korte, August. *Die Konzilspolitik Karls V in den Jahren 1538-1543.* Halle: Verein für Reformationsgeschichte, 1905.

Krones, Franz von. *Handbuch der Geschichte Österreichs.* 5 vols. Berlin: Hofmann, 1879.

Kühn, Johannes. *Die Geschichte des Speyerer Reichstags 1529.* Leipzig: Verein für Reformationsgeschichte, 1929.

Kupelwieser, L. *Die Kämpfe Österreichs mit den Osmanen vom Jahre 1526 bis 1537.* Vienna/Leipzig: Braumüller, 1899.

Lhotsky, Alphons. *Die Geschichte der Sammlungen. 1 Hälfte: von den Anfängen bis zum Tode Kaiser Karls VI. 1740.* Festschrift des kunsthistorischen Museums zur Feier des fünfzigjährigen Bestands. 2. Vienna: Berger, 1941-1945.

_____. *Das Zeitalter des Hauses Österreich. Die ersten Jahre der Regierung Ferdinands I. 1520-1527.* Veröffentlichung der Kommission für Geschichte Österreichs. 4. Vienna/Cologne/Graz: Böhlaus, 1971.

Löcher, Kurt. *Jakob Seisenegger, Hofmaler Kaiser Ferdinands I.* Munich: deutscher Kunstverlag, 1962.

Loesche, Georg. *Geschichte des Protestantismus in Österreich.* Leipzig: Manz, 1930.

Loserth, Johann. *Die Reformation und Gegenreformation in den innerösterreichischen Ländern im 16. Jahrhundert.* Stuttgart: Cotta, 1898.

Lutz, Heinrich. *Christianitas Afflicta. Europa, das Reich, und die päpstliche Politik im Niedergang der Hegemonie Kaiser Karls V. (1552-1556).* Göttingen: Vandenhoek and Ruprecht, 1964.

Lynch, John. *Spain under the Habsburgs.* 2 vols. Oxford: Blackwell, 1965-1969.

May, Jakob. *Der Kurfürst, Cardinal und Erzbischof Albrecht II von Mainz und Magdeburg.* Munich: Franz, 1865.

Mayer-Löwenschwerdt, Erwin. *Der Aufenthalt der Erzherzöge Rudolf und Ernst in Spanien.* Akademie der Wissenschaften in Wien, philosophisch-historische Klasse, Sitzungsberichte. 206, No. 5 (1927).

Mecenseffy, Grete. *Geschichte des Protestantismus in Österreich.* Graz/Cologne: Böhlaus, 1956.

Merriman, Roger B. *Suleiman the Magnificent 1520-1566.* 1944. rpt.; New York: Cooper Square, 1966.

Miskimin, Harry A. *The Economy of Later Renaissance Europe.* Cambridge: Cambridge University, 1977.

Nehring, Karl. *Matthias Corvinus, Kaiser Friedrich III. und das Reich. Zum hunyadisch-habsburgischen Gegensatz im Donauraum.* Munich: Oldenbourg, 1975.

The New Cambridge Modern History. 12 vols. Cambridge: Cambridge University, 1957-1968.

O'Connell, Marvin R. *The Counter-Reformation 1560-1610.* New York: Harper Torch, 1974.

Oman, Sir Charles W. C. *A History of the Art of War in the Sixteenth Century.* New York: Dutton, 1927.

Pajewski, Janusz. *Stosunki polsko-węgierskie i niebezpieczństwo tureckie w latach 1516-1526.* Rozprawy historyczne towarzystwa naukowego Warszawskiego. 9. Warsaw: towarzystwo naukowego Warszawskiego, 1930.

Pelzel, Franz Martin. *Geschichte der Böhmen.* 3rd ed. 2 vols. Prague/ Vienna: Schönfeld, 1782.

Petrie, Charles. *Philipp II. von Spanien.* trans. Ursula Gmelin. Stuttgart: Kohlhammer, 1965.

Picard, Bertold. *Das Gesandtschaftswesen Ostmitteleuropas in der frühen Neuzeit.* Wiener Archiv für Geschichte des Slawentums und Osteuropas. 6. Graz/Vienna/Cologne: Böhlaus, 1967.

Pickl, Othmar, ed. *Die wirtschaftlichen Auswirkungen der Türkenkriege.* Grazer Forschungen zur Wirtschafts-und Sozialgeschichte. 1. Graz: Lehrkanzel für Wirtschafts-und Sozialgeschichte der Universität Graz, 1971.

Pierson, Peter. *Philip II of Spain.* London: Thames and Hudson, 1975.

Pirchegger, Hans. *Geschichte und Kulturleben Deutsch-österreichs von 1526 bis 1792.* Vienna/Leipzig: Braumüller, 1931.

Pirenne, Henri. *Histoire de Belgique.* 7 vols. Brussels: Lamertin, 1908-1932.

Pölnitz, Götz von. *Anton Fugger.* 2 vols. Tübingen: Mohr, 1958-1963.

Rabe, Horst. *Reichsbund und Interim. Die Verfassungs-und Religionspolitik Karls V. und der Reichstag von Augsburg 1547/1548.* Cologne/ Vienna: Böhlaus, 1971.

Ranke, Leopold von. *Deutsche Geschichte im Zeitalter der Reformation.* Cologne: Phaidon, n.d.

Ranke, Leopold von. *Über die Zeiten Ferdinands I und Maximilians II.* in Sämmtliche Werke. 8. Leipzig: Duncker, 1868-1890.

Rassow, Peter. *Forschungen zur Reichsidee im 16. und 17. Jahrhundert.* Arbeitsgemeinscchaft für Forschung des Landes Nordrhein-Westfalen, Geisteswissenschaften. 10. Cologne: Westdeutscher Verlag, 1955.

_____. *Die Kaiser-Idee Karls V dargestellt an der Politik der Jahre 1528-1540.* Historische Studien. 217. Berlin: Ebering, 1932.

Regele, Oskar. *Der österreichische Hofkriegsrat 1556-1848.* MIöG. Ergänzungsband, 1 (1949).

Renaissance in Österreich. Schloß Schallaburg. Katalog des niederösterreichischen Landesmuseums. New Series. 57. Vienna: niederösterreichische Landesregierung, 1974.

Rezek, Antonín. *Zvolení a korunování Ferdinanda I. za krále českého.* Prague: Otto, 1878.

Richter, Arwed. *Der Reichstag zu Nürnberg 1524.* Leipzig: Fock, 1888.

Rohrmoser, Josef. *Diplomatische Verhandlungen zwischen Ferdinand I und Johann Zapolya.* Czernowitz: Eckhardt, 1862.

Rosenberg, Walter. *Der Kaiser und die Protestanten in den Jahren 1537-1539.* Halle: Verein für Reformationsgeschichte, 1903-1904.

Rothenberg, Gunther. *The Austrian Military Border in Croatia 1552-1747.* Urbana, Ill.: University of Illinois, 1960.

Salamon, Franz. *Ungarn im Zeitalter der Türkenherrschaft.* trans. Gustav Jurány. Leipzig: Haessel, 1887.

Schlesinger, Ludwig. *Geschichte Böhmens.* Prague/Leipzig: Calve'sche Buchhandlung/Brockhaus, 1869.

Schrötter, Ferdinand. *Abhandlungen aus dem österreichischen Staatsrecht und Freiheitsbriefen.* 5 vols. Vienna: Krauß, 1762-1766.

Schulze, Hermann. *Das Recht der Erstgeburt in den deutschen Fürstenhäusern und seine Bedeutung für die deutsche Staatsentwicklung.* Leipzig: Avenarius and Mendelsohn, 1851.

Šišić, Ferdinand von. *Die Wahl Ferdinands I. von Österreich zum König von Kroatien.* Zagreb: Suppan, 1917.

Springer, Jaroslav. *Beiträge zur Geschichte des Wormser Reichstags 1544 und 1545.* Diss.: Leipzig, 1882.

Stälin, Christoph Friedrich von. *Wirtembergische Geschichte.* 4 vols. Stuttgart: Cotta, 1873.

Stolz, Otto. *Grundriß der österreichischen Verfassungs-und Verwaltungsgeschichte.* Innsbruck/Vienna: Tyrolia, 1951.

Strelka, Josef. *Der burgundische Renaissancehof Margarethes von Österreich und seine literarhistorische Bedeutung.* Vienna: Sexl, 1957.

Thompson, James Westfall. *The Wars of Religion in France 1559-1576.* 1909. rpt.; New York, Ungar, n.d.

Tieftrunk, Karel. *Odpor českých stavů proti Ferdinandovi I. 1. 1547.* Novočeská bibliotheka. 19. Prague: Řiwáč, 1872.

Tomek, Ernst. *Kirchengeschichte Österreichs.* 2 vols. Innsbruck/Vienna: Tyrolia, 1935-1949.

Tomek, Wácslaw Wladiwoj. *Dějepis města Prahy.* 12 vols. Prague: Řiwnáč, 1855-1901.

Traut, Hermann. *Kurfürst Joachim II. von Brandenburg und der Türkenfeldzug vom Jahre 1542.* Gummersbach: Luyken, 1892.

Turba, Gustav. *Geschichte des Thronfolgerechts in allen habsburgischen Ländern bis zur pragmatischen Sanktion Kaiser Karls VI.* Vienna/Leipzig: Fromme, 1903.

Turetschek, Christine. *Die Türkenpolitik Ferdinands I von 1529-1532.* Vienna: Notring, 1968.

Uebersberger, Hans. *Österreich und Russland seit dem Ende des 15. Jahrhunderts.* Vienna/Leipzig: Braumüller, 1906.

Utjesenović, Ognjeslav. *Lebensgeschichte des Cardinals Georg Utiesenović genannt Martinuzzi.* Vienna: Braumüller, 1881.

Varrentrapp, Conrad. *Hermann von Wied und sein Reformations-Versuch in Köln.* Leipzig: Duncker und Humblot, 1878.

Voigt, Georg. *Moritz von Sachsen 1541-1547.* Leipzig: Tauschnitz, 1876.

Westermann, Ascan. *Die Türkenhilfe und die politisch-kirchlichen Parteien auf dem Reichstag zu Regensburg 1532.* Heidelberger Abhandlungen zur mittleren und neueren Geschichte. 25. Heidelberg: Winter, 1910.

Wiedemann, Theodor. *Geschichte der Reformation und Gegenreformation im Lande unter der Enns.* 5 vols. Prague: Tempsky, 1879-1886.

Wiesflecker, Hermann. *Kaiser Maximilian I. Das Reich, Österreich und Europa an der Wende zur Neuzeit.* 3 vols. to date. Vienna: Verlag für Geschichte und Politik, 1971 -.

Winckelmann, Otto. *Der Schmalkaldische Bund 1530-1532 und der Nürnberger Religionsfriede.* Straßburg: Heitz, 1892.

Wolf, Gustav. *Der Augsburger Religionsfriede.* Stuttgart: Göschen, 1890.

Zinkeisen, Johann W. *Geschichte des osmanischen Reiches in Europa.* Hamburg: Perthes, 1840-1863.

IV. Articles

Ausserer, Karl. "Kardinal Berhard von Cles und die Papstwahl des Jahres 1534." *MIöG,* 35 (1914): 114-139.

Bauer, Wilhelm. "Ein handelspolitisches Projekt Ferdinands I. aus dem Jahre 1527." *Beiträge zur neueren Geschichte Österreichs,* 1 (1906): 14-17.

Baumgarten, Hermann. "Differenzen zwischen Karl V. und seinem Bruder Ferdinand im Jahre 1524." *DZG,* 2 (1889): 1-16.

Born, Karl Erich. "Moritz von Sachsen und die Fürstenverschwörung gegen Karl V." *HZ,* 191 (1960): 18-66.

Bourilly, V. -L. "Antonio Rincon et la politique orientale de Francois Ier, (1522-1541)." *Revue historique,* 113 (1913): 64-83, 268-308.

Brandi, Karl. "Berichte und Studien zur Geschichte Karls V." parts 1 and 2. Gesellschaft der Wissenschaft zu Göttingen. Philologisch-historische Klasse. *Nachrichten.* (1930-1933).

_____. "Passauer Vertrag und Augsburger Religionsfriede." *HZ,* 95 (1905): 206-264.

Brunner, Otto. "Eine handelspolitische Denkschrit der Stadt Wien an König Ferdinand I." *MIöG,* Ergänzungsband. 11 (1929): 474-496.

Clemen, Otto. "Zum Türkenfeldzug des Kurfürsten Joachim II von Brandenburg." *Jahrbuch für brandesburgische Kirchengeschichte,* 34 (1939): 88-96.

Cornaro, Andreas. "Eine Reise des Kardinals Berhard von Cles zu Kaiser Karl V. nach Neapel im Jahre 1536 nach seinen Briefen an Ferdinand I." *Römische historische Mitteilungen,* 2 (1957-1958): 51-71.

Daniel, David P. "The Influence of the Augsburg Confession in South-East Central Europe." *The Sixteenth Century Journal,* 11 (1980): 99-114.

Egg, Erich. "Der deutsche König und die neue Kunst. Ferdinand I. der Begrunder der österreichischen Kultur." *Alte und moderne Kunst,* 6, no. 46 (1961): 16-20.

Ember, Győző. "Ungarns Außenhandel mit dem Westen um die Mitte des XVI. Jahrhunderts." in Bog, *Außenhandel:* 86-104.

Engel-Janosi, Friedrich. "Zur Geschichte der Wiener Kaufmannschaft von der Mitte des 15. bis zur Mitte des 16. Jahrhunderts." *Mitteilungen des Vereines für Geschichte der Stadt Wien,* 6 (1926): 36-71.

Ernst, Viktor. "Ein kaiserliche Werbung, die Erneuerung des schwäbischen Bundes betreffend." *Württembergische Vierteljahreshefte für Landsgeschichte, NS 8 (1899): 214-223.*

Feine, Hans Erich. "Papst, Erste Bitte u. Regierungsantritt des Kaiser seit dem Ausgang des Mittelalters." *Zeitschrift der Savigny-Stiftung für Rechtsgeschichte* 51, kanonistische Abteilung, no. 20 (1931): 1-101.

Fichtner, Paula Sutter. "An Absence Explained: Archduke Ferdinand of Austria and the Battle of Mohács." *Austrian History Yearbook,* 2 (1966): 11-17.

——————. "Of Christian Virtue and a Practicing Prince: Emperor Ferdinand I and His Son Maximilian." *The Catholic Historical Review,* 61 (1975): 409-416.

——————. "The Disobedience of the Obedient: Ferdinand I and the Papacy, 1555-1564." *The Sixteenth Century Journal,* 11 (1980): 25-34.

——————. "Dynastic Marriage in Sixteenth-Century Habsburg Diplomacy and Statecraft: an Interdisciplinary Approach." *American Historical Review,* 81 (1976): 243-265.

——————. "Dynasticism and its Limitations: the Habsburgs and Hungary, 1542." *East European Quarterly,* 4 (1971): 389-407.

——————. "When Brothers Agree: Bohemia, the Habsburgs, and the Schmalkaldic Wars, 1546-1547." *Austrian History Yearbook,* 11 (1975): 67-78.

Firnhaber, ‌‌‌rich. "Zur Geschichte des österreichischen Militärwesens." *Archiv für Kunde österreichischer Geschichtsquellen,* 30 (1864): 91-178.

——————. "Der Hofstaat König Ferdinands im Jahre 1554." *Archiv für Kunde österreichischer Geschichtsquellen,* 26 (1861): 3-28.

——————. "Die Krönung Kaiser Maximilians II. zum Könige von Ungarn, 1563." *AöG,* 22 (1860): 305-338.

Fischel, Alfred. "Kaiser Ferdinands I. Versuch zur Einführung einer rein landesfürstlichen Verwaltung in Mähren (1528)." *Zeitschrift des deutschen Vereines für die Geschichte Mährens und Schlesiens,* 17 (1913): 259-273.

Fischer, G. "Ferdinand I. und Karl V. im Jahre 1552." *Jahrbücher der kg. Akademie gemeinnütziger Wissenschaften zu Erfurt,* NS 32 (1906): 179-203.

Friedensburg, Walter. "Karl V und Maximilian II (1551). Ein venetianischer Bericht über vertrauliche Äußerungen der Letzteren." *QuF*, 4 (1902): 72-81.

Fuchs, Walther Peter. "Baiern und Habsburg 1534-1536." *ARG*, 41 (1948): 1-32.

Gindely, Anton. "Geschichte der böhmischen Finanzen von 1526 bis 1618." *Denkschriften der kaiserlichen Akademie der Wissenschaften.* Phil. -hist. Klasse, 7 (1868): 89-167.

————— . "Über die Erbrechte des Hauses Habsburg auf die Krone von Ungarn in der Zeit von dem Jahre 1526-1687." *AöG*, 51 (1873): 195-240.

Goetz, Helmut. "Die geheimen Ratgeber Ferdinands I. (1503-1564). Ihre Persönlichkeit im Urteil der Nuntien und Gesandten." *QuF*, 42-43 (1963): 453-494.

Grisar, Hartmann, "Jakob Lainez und die Frage des Laienkelches auf dem Concil von Trient." part 1. *Zeitschrift für katholische Theologie*, 5 (1881): 672-720; part 2. Ibid., 6 (1882): 39-112.

Grisar, Josef. "Die Stellung der Päpste zum Reichstag und Religionsfrieden von Augsburg 1555." *Stimmen der Zeit*, 80 (1954/1955): 440-462.

Hasenclever, Adolf. "Johann von Naves aus Luxemburg, Reichsvizekanzler unter Kaiser Karl V." *MIöG*, 26 (1905): 280-328.

Hatzfeld, Lutz. "Staatsräson und Reputation bie Kaiser Karl V." *Zeitschrift für Religions-und Geistesgeschichte*, 11 (1959): 32-58.

Hauptmann, Ferdo. "Ungarn, Habsburg und die kroatische Staatsidee im 16. und 17. Jahrhundert." *Südostdeutsches Archiv*, 12 (1969): 62-72.

Headley, John M. "The Habsburg World Empire and the Revival of Ghibellinism." *Medieval and Renaissance Studies*, 7 (1978): 93-127.

Heckel, Martin. "Autonomia und Pacis Compositio. Der Augsburger Religionsfriede in der Deutung der Gegenreformation." *Zeitschrift der Savigny-Stiftung für Rechtsgeschichte*. Kanonistische Abteilung, 45 (1959): 141-248.

Heiß, Gernot. "Politik und Ratgeber der Königin Maria von Ungarn in den Jahren 1521-1531." *MIöG*, 82 (1974): 119-180.

————— . "Die ungarischen, böhmischen und österreichischen Besitzungen der Königin Maria (1505-1558) und ihre Verwaltung." *MöSA*, 27 (1974): 61-100.

Heřman, Jan. "Zemské berni rejstříky z 1. 1523 a 1529." *Československý časopis historický,* 10 (1962): 248-257.

Horawitz, Adalbert. "Johann Heigerlin (genannt Faber), Bischof von Wien bis zum Regensburger Convent." *Sitzungsberichte der phil. -hist. Klasse der kaiserlichen Akademie der Wissenschaften zu Wien,* 107 (1884): 83-220.

Hornedo, Rafael de. "Carlos V y Erasmo." *Miscelánea comillas,* 30 (1958): 201-247.

Huber, Alfons. "Die Erwerbung Siebenbürgens durch Ferdinand I. im Jahre 1551 u. Bruder Georgs Ende." *AöG,* 75 (1889): 483-545.

——————. "Studien über die finanziellen Verhältnisse Österreichs unter Ferdinand I." *MIöG.* Ergänzungsband, 4 (1893): 181-247.

——————. "Die Verhandlungen Ferdinands I. mit Isabella v. Siebenbürgen 1551-1555." *AöG,* 78 (1892): 1-39.

Hudak, Adalbert. "Der Hofprediger Johannes Henck und seine Beziehungen zu Erasmus von Rotterdam." *Kirche im Osten,* 2 (1959): 106-113.

Hurstfield, Joel. "The Search for Compromise in England and France." In *The Reformation Crisis.* Ed. Joel Hurstfield. (New York: Harper Torch, 1966), pp. 95-106.

Ißleib, S. "Die Gefangennahme des Landgrafen Philip von Hessen 1547." *Neues Archiv für sächsische Geschichte,* 11 (1890): 177-244.

——————. "Die Gefangenschaft Philipps von Hessen 1547 bis 1552." *Neues Archiv für sächsische Geschichte,* 14 (1893): 211-266.

——————. "Von Passau bis Sievershausen, 1552-1553." *Neues Archiv für sächsische Geschichte,* 8 (1887): 41-103.

Janáček, Josef. "Zrušeni cechů roku 1547." *Ččh,* 7 (1959): 231-242.

Kameníček, František. "Učastenství Moravanů při valkach tureckých r. 1526 d. r. 1568." *Sborník historický,* 4 (1886): 15-19, 65-77, 157-175, 193-206, 271-284.

Károlyi, Árpád. "A német birodalom nagy hadi vállalata Magyarországon 1542." *Századok,* 14 (1880): 265-299, 357-387, 445-465, 558-589, 621-655.

Kavka, František. "Die Habsburger und der böhmische Staat bis zur Mitte des 18. Jahrhunderts." *Historica,* 8 (1964): 35-64.

König, Erich. "Zur Hauspolitik Maximilians I. in den Jahren 1516 und 1517." in *Festgabe Hermann Grauert zur Vollendung des 60. Lebensjahres.* (Freiburg i. Br.: Herder, 1910): 191-204.

Kolankowski, Ludwik. "Polityka ostatnich Jagiellonów." *Kwartalnik historyczny*, 25 (1911): 55-63.

Koller, Gerda. "Die Hochzeit Ferdinands I. in Linz." *Linz aktiv* 24 (1967): 19-26.

Kraus, Victor von. "Zur Geschichte Oesterreichs unter Ferdinand I. 1519-1522." *Neuenter Jahresbericht des Leopoldstädter Communal-Real-und Obergymnasiums in Wien*, No. 11 (1873): 1-114.

Kretschmayr, Heinrich. "Ludovico Gritti." *AöG*, 83 (1897): 1-106.

Kvačala, J. "Wilhelm Postell, seine Geistesart und seine Reformgedanken." part 1. *ARG*, 9 (1911/1912): 285-330; part 2. ibid., 11 (1914): 200-227; part 3. ibid., 15 (1918): 157-203.

Laubach, Ernst. "Karl V., Ferdinand I. und die Nachfolge im Reich." *MöSA*, 29 (1976): 1-51.

Liske, X. "Der Congress zu Wien im Jahre 1515." *Forschungen zur deutschen Geschichte*, 7 (1867): 463-558.

Loserth, Johann. "Ständische Beziehungen zwischen Böhmen und Innerösterreich im Zeitalter Ferdinands I." *Mitteilungen des Vereines für Geschichte der Deutschen in Böhmen*, 50 (1911/1912): 1-41.

—————. and Franz von Mensi. "Die Prager Ländertagung von 1541/1542." *AöG*, 103 (1913): 433-546.

Lutz, Heinrich. "Bayern und der Laienkelch 1548-1556." *QuF*, 34 (1954): 203-235.

—————. "Karl V und Bayern. Umrisse einer Entscheidung." *Zeitschrift für bayerische Landesgeschichte*, 22 (1959): 13-41.

Makkai, László. "Die ungarische Viehhandel 1550-1650." In Bog, *Außenhandel*: 483-506.

Maurenbrecher, Wilhelm. "Beiträge zur deutschen Geschichte 1555-1559." *HZ*, 50 (1883): 1-83.

—————. "Beiträge zur Geschichte Maximilians II. 1548-1562." *HZ*, 32 (1874): 221-297.

Mayer, Theodor. "Das Verhältnis der Hofkammer zur ungarischen Kammer bis zur Regierung Maria Theresias." *MIöG*. Ergänzungsband, 9 (1915): 178-263.

Mayr, Michael. "Der Generallandtag der österreichischen Erbländer zu Augsburg (December 1525 bis März 1526)." *Zeitschrift des Ferdinandeums*. 3rd Series, 38 (1893/1894): 1-154.

Mecenseffy, Grete. "Herkunft oberösterreichischer Täufer." *ARG*, 47 (1956): 252-258.

Meyer, Christian. "Die Feldhauptmannschaft Joachim II im Türkenkriege von 1542." *Zeitschrift für preussische Geschichte und Landeskunde,* 16 (1879): 480-538.

Mikoletzky, Hanns Leo. "Der Haushalt des kaiserlichen Hofes zu Wien (vornehmlich im 18. Jahrhundert)." *Carinthia I,* No. 146 (1956): 658-683.

Mitis, Oscar. "Vom burgundischen Hof Ferdinands I. in Österreich." *Jahrbuch für Landeskunde von Niederösterreich,* NS 21 (1928): 153-163.

Müller, Gerhard. "Vincenzo Pimpinella am Hofe Ferdinands I. 1529-1532." *QuF,* 40 (1960): 65-88.

M...y, Freiherr von. "Die letzten Lebenstage Kaiser Ferdinands I." *Archiv für Geographie, Historie, Staats-und Kriegskunst,* 8 (1817): 60-62.

Novotny, Alexander. "Ein Ringen um ständische Autonomie zur Zeit des erstarkenden Absolutismus (1519-1522)." *MIöG,* 71 (1963): 354-369.

Oberleitner, Karl. "Die Finanzlage Niederösterreichs im 16. Jahrhundert." *Archiv für Kunde österreichischer Geschichtsquellen,* 30 (1864): 3-90.

—————— . "Österreichisches Finanzen und Kriegswesen unter Ferdinand I: 1522-1564." *AöG,* 22 (1860): 1-233.

Odložilík, Otakar. "A Church in a Hostile State: the Unity of Czech Brethren." *Central European History,* 6 (1973): 111-127.

—————— . "Jednota bratří habrovanských." *Ččh,* 29 (1923): 1-70, 301-357.

Pickl, Othmar. "Die auswirkungen der Türkenkriege auf den Handel zwischen Ungarn und Italien im 16. Jahrhundert." In Pickl, *Wirtschaftliche Auswirkungen:* 71-130.

—————— . "Der Handel Wiens and Wiener Neustadts mit Böhmen, Mähren, Schlesien und Ungarns in der ersten Hälfte des 16. Jahrhunderts." In Bog, *Außenhandel:* 320-341.

Pillich, Walter. "König Katharina von Polen in Linz." *Historisches Jahrbuch der Stadt Linz,* (1966): 169-198.

Polišensky, Josef. "Bohemia, the Turk and the Christian Commonwealth (1462-1620)." *Byzantinoslavica,* 14 (1953): 82-108.

Probszt-Obstorff, Günther. "Königin Maria und die niederungarischen

Bergstädte." *Zeitschrift für Ostforschung,* 15 (1966): 621-703.

Rachfall, Felix. "Die Trennung der Niederlande vom deutschen Reiche." *Westdeutsche Zeitschrift für Geschichte und Kunst,* 19 (1900): 79-119.

Rassow, Peter. "Karls V. Tochter Maria als Eventual-Erbin des spanischen Reiche." *ARG,* 49 (1958): 161-168.

—————. "Die Reichstage zu Augsburg in der Reformationszeit." In *Augusta 955-1955:* 273-282.

Redlich, Oswald. "Die Pläne einer Erhebung Österreichs zum Königreich." *Zeitschrift des historischen Vereins für Steiermark,* 26 (1931): 87-99.

Reimann, Eduard. "Papst Paul IV und das Kaiserthum." *Abhandlungen der schlesischen Gesellschaft für väterlandischen Kultur.* Phil. -hist. Abteilung (1871): 25-40.

—————. "Die römische Königswahl von 1562 und der Papst." *Forschungen zur deutschen Geschichte,* 8 (1868): 1-19.

—————. "Der Streit zwischen Pappstthum und Kaiserthum im Jahre 1558." *Forschungen zur deutschen Geschichte,* 5 (1865): 291-335.

Rezek, Antonín. "Beiträge zur Geschichte der Confiscation vom Jahre 1547." *Zprávy o zasedání královské české společnosti nauk* (1876): 138-143.

—————. "Úmluvy sjezdu vídeňského z 1. 1515 a jich význam pro volbu čskou 1. 1526." *Časopis českého musea,* 55 (1881): 385-403.

—————. "Zur Kaiserwahl 1519." *Forschungen zur deutschen Geschichte,* 23 (1883): 336-348.

Richter, Eduard. "Die Haltung der ungarischen Bergstädte nach der Doppelwahl von 1526." *MIöG,* 32 (1911): 501-505.

Rill, Gerhard. "Humanismus und Diplomatie. Zur Geschichte des Gesandtenwesens unter Ferdinand I." *MöSA,* 25 (1972): 565-580.

Rosenthal, Eduard. "Die Behördeorganisation Kaiser Ferdinands I. Das Vorbild der Verwaltungsorganisation in den deutschen Territorien." *AöG,* 69 (1887).

Roth, Paul. "Münzwesen und Türkennot." In Pickl, *Wirtschaftliche Auswirkungen:* 333-337.

Schlecht, Joseph. "Der geheime Dispensbreve Pius IV für die römische Königskrönung Maximilians II." *Historisches Jahrbuch der Görres-Gesellschaft,* 14 (1893): 1-38.

Schmid, Joseph. "Die deutsche Kaiser-und Königswahl und die römische

Curie in den Jahren 1558-1620." *Historisches Jahrbuch der Görres-Gesellschaft,* 6 (1885): 3-41, 161-207.

Sicken, Bernhard. "Der Heidelberger Verein (1553-1556)." *Zeitschrift für württembergische Landesgeschichte,* 32 (1973): 320-435.

Sickel, Theodor von. "Das Reformations-libell des Kaisers Ferdinand I. vom Jahre 1562 bis zur Absendung nach Trient." *AöG,* 45 (1871): 1-96.

Šimek, Eduard. "Die Zusammenhänge zwischen Währung und Handel im Böhmen des 16. Jahrhunderts." In Bog, *Außenhandel:* 229-245.

Smijers, Albert. "Die kaiserliche Hofmusikkapelle von 1543-1619." *Studien zur Musikwissenschaft,* part 1. 6 (1919): 139-186.

Smolka, Stanislaus. "Ferdinand des Ersten Bemühungen um die Krone von Hungarn." *AöG,* 57 (1878): 1-172.

Spitz, Lewis. "Particularism and Peace. Augsburg 1555." *Church History,* 25 (1956): 110-126.

Steglich, Wolfgang. "Die Reichstürkenhilfe in der Zeit Karls V." *Militärgeschichtliche Mitteilungen,* 11 (1972): 7-55.

Stern, Alfred. "Gabriel Salamanca Graf von Ortenburg." *HZ,* 131 (1925): 19-40.

Stoegmann, Karl. "Über die Briefe des Andrea da Burgo, Gesandten König Ferdinands an den Cardinal und Bischof von Trient." *Sitzungsberichte der Wiener Akademie der Wissenschaften,* 24 (1857): 159-252.

Stökl, Günther. "Kaiser Ferdinand I." In *Gestalter der Geschicke Österreichs,* ed. Hugo Hantsch. Studien der Wiener katholischen Akademie, 2 (1962): 127-141.

—————. "Siegmund von Herberstein. Diplomat und Humanist." *Ostdeutsche Wissenschaft. Jahrbuch des ostdeutschen Kulturrates,* 7 (1910): 69-80.

Sturmberger, Hans. "Türkengefahr und österreichische Staatlichkeit." *Südostdeutsches Archiv,* 10 (1967): 132-145.

Thomas, Bruno. "Die Augsburger Funeralwaffen Kaiser Karls V." *Zeitschrift für historische Waffenkunde,* 18 (1959): 28-46.

—————. "Harnischstudien. III. Stilgeschichte des deutschen Harnisches von 1530 bis 1560." *Jahrbuch der kunsthistorischen Sammlungen in Wien,* NS 12 (1938): 175-202.

—————. "Kaiser Ferdinands I. Harnisch von Kunz Lochner." *Jahrbuch der kunsthistorischen Sammlungen in Wien,* 50=NS 14 (1953): 131-136.

Thomas, Christiane. " 'Moderación del Poder': Zur Entstehung der geheimen Vollmacht für Ferdinand I. 1531." *MöSA,* 27 (1974): 101-140.

Till, Rudolf. "Glaubensspaltung in Wien." *Wiener Geschichtsblätter,* 21 (1966): 1-14.

Turba, Gustav. "Beiträge zur Geschichte der Habsburger. II: zur Reichs- und Hauspolitik der Jahre 1548 bis 1558." *AöG,* 90 (1901): 1-76.

—————. "Beiträge zur Geschichte der Habsburger. III: zur deutschen Reichs-und Hauspolitik der Jahre 1553 bis 1558." *AöG,* 90 (1901): 233-319.

—————. "Verhaftung und Gefangenschaft des Landgrafen Philipp von Hessen, 1547-1550." *AöG,* 83 (1897): 107-232.

Uellenberg, Gisela. "Augsburger Frauen. Agnes Bernauer und Philippine Welser." In *Augusta 955-1955:* 137-143.

Volf, Miloslav. "Královský důchod a úvěr v XVI století." *Ččh,* 48-49 (1947/1948): 110-171.

Voltelini, Hans. "Die Wiener Stadt-u. Stadtgerichtsordnung Ferdinands I. von 1526." *Mitteilungen des Vereins für die Geschichte der Stadt Wien,* 9-10 (1929/1930): 105-129.

Waltz, O. "Der Wiener Vertrag vom 22. November 1535." *Forschungen zur deutschen Geschichte,* 13 (1873): 375-378.

Wille, ?. "Zum Religionsartikel des Friedens von Kadan 1534." *Zeitschrift für Kirchengeschichte,* 7 (1885): 50-60.

Winckelmann, Otto. "Über die Bedeutung der Verträge von Kadan und Wien (1534-1535) für die deutschen Protestanten." *Zeitschrift für Kirchengeschichte,* 11 (1890): 212-252.

Winter, Otto Friedrich. "Das Register Ferdinands I. als Quelle zu seiner ungarischen Politik." *MöSA,* 7 (1954): 551-582.

Wolf, Gustav. "Der Passauer Vertrag und seine Bedeutung für die nächstfolgende Zeit." *Neues Archiv für sächsische Geschichte,* 15 (1894): 237-282.

Zeman, J. K. "The Rise of Religious Liberty in the Czech Reformation." *Central European History,* 6 (1973): 128-147.

Žontar, Josef. "Michael Černović, Geheimagent Ferdinands I. und Maximilians II., und seine Berichterstattung." *MöSA,* 24 (1971): 169-222.

INDEX

Albrecht Alcibiades, Margrave of Brandenburg-Kulmbach-Bayreuth, 5, 154-55, 190, 195-97, 200, 204-208, 245.

Albrecht, Archbishop and Elector of Mainz, 82.

Aleander, Jerome, 102, 110, 114

Anabaptists, 7, 22, 74-75, 111-12, 140, 143, 146

Anna, Archduchess of Austria, Duchess of Bavaria, 102-103, 109, 164, 177

Anna, Queen of Hungary and Bohemia, 2, 6, 15, 18, 54, 57-58, 70, 75, 82, 85, 98, 102, 104, 144, 153-154, 231

Anne of Brittany, 13

Archimboldo, Giuseppe, 6

Augsburg: Diets, (1530), 75, 87, 94-95, 98; (1548), 166, 188-89, 204; (1555), 9, 208-16; (1559), 229, 251, 254. Interim, 188-90, 193, 196, 199, 213, 235. Peace of, 214-17, 228, 230, 232

August, Elector of Saxony, 213

Báthory, Stephen, 58-59

Batthyány, Francis, 59-60, 62-63

Bavaria, 53, 56, 60, 88, 98, 108-10, 116, 130, 183-84, 191; Albrecht V, Duke of, 109-10, 177, 203-204, 207, 240, 242; Ludwig, Duke of, 108-109; William IV, Duke or, 87, 108

Belgrade, 40, 45, 83, 98

Blahoslav, Jan, 248

Bohemia, Kingdom of, 43-46, 53-57, 63-64, 69, 71-72, 80, 85

98, 127, 130, 133, 140-60, 165, 260

Bohemian Brethren (*Unitas Fratrum*), 7, 140, 142-43, 158, 248

Bornemisza, John, 59, 72

Bouton, Claude, 28

Brodarics, Stephen, 121

Brussels, Compact of, 19, 28, 34

Burgo, Andrea da, 42-43, 45-46, 48

Cahera, Gallus, 141

Canisius, Peter, 7, 229, 249-50

Carlos, Prince of Spain, 221-22, 245, 251

Castaldo, Marquis de, 136

Cateau-Cambrésis, Treaty of, 223, 253

Catherine of Aragon, Queen of England, 19

Catherine, Archduchess of Austria, Queen of Poland, 237

Campeggi, Lorenzo, 35

Chambord, Treaty of, 190-92

Charles, Archduke of Austria, 102-103, 222, 237-38, 241-42, 257

Charles IV, Emperor, 43, 53, 141, 145

Charles V, Emperor (Charles I of Spain) 1-2, 4, 9-10, 15-17, 43, 64, 77, 81, 120, 156, 218-26, 235, 239, 244-45, 250, 260-61; and Ferdinand in Austria, 26-30, 103-106; and Ferdinand in the Empire, 30-32, 34-36, 38-39, 75, 81, 84, 86-90, 94-99, 105, 108-110, 112, 116, 128-29, 161-77, 182-217, 254; and Ferdinand in Bohemia, 54-55, 150-60, 259;

358

EAST EUROPEAN MONOGRAPHS

The *East European Monographs* comprise scholarly books on the history and civilization of Eastern Europe. They are published by the *East European Quarterly* in the belief that these studies contribute substantially to the knowledge of the area and serve to stimulate scholarship and research.

Winter into Spring: The Czechoslovak Press and the Reform Movement 1963-1968. By Frank L. Kaplan. 1977.

The Catholic Church and the Soviet Government, 1939-1949. By Dennis J. Dunn. 1977.

The Hungarian Labor Service System, 1939-1945. By Randolph L Braham. 1977.

Consciousness and History: Nationalist Critics of Greek Society 1897-1914. By Gerasimos Augustinos. 1977.

Emigration in Polish Social and Political Thought, 1870-1914. By Benjamin P. Murdzek. 1977.

Serbian Poetry and Milutin Bojic. By Mihailo Dordevic. 1977.

The Baranya Dispute: Diplomacy in the Vortex of Ideologies, 1918-1921. By Leslie C. Tihany. 1978.

The United States in Prague, 1945-1948. By Walter Ullmann. 1978.

Rush to the Alps: The Evolution of Vacationing in Switzerland. By Paul P. Bernard. 1978.

Transportation in Eastern Europe: Empirical Findings. By Bogdan Mieczkowski. 1978.

The Polish Underground State: A Guide to the Underground, 1939-1945. By Stefan Korbonski. 1978.

The Hungarian Revolution of 1956 in Retrospect. Edited by Bela K. Kiraly and Paul Jonas. 1978.

Boleslaw Limanowski (1835-1935): A Study in Socialism and Nationalism. By Kazimiera Janina Cottam. 1978.

The Lingering Shadow of Nazism: The Austrian Independent Party Movement Since 1945. By Max E. Riedlsperger. 1978.

The Catholic Church, Dissent and Nationality in Soviet Lithuania. By V. Stanley Vardys. 1978.

The Development of Parliamentary Government in Serbia. By Alex N. Dragnich. 1978.

Divide and Conquer: German Efforts to Conclude a Separate Peace, 1914-1918. By L. L. Farrar, Jr. 1978.

The Prague Slav Congress of 1848. By Lawrence D. Orton. 1978.

The Nobility and the Making of the Hussite Revolution. By John M. Klassen. 1978.

The Cultural Limits of Revolutionary Politics: Change and Continuity in Socialist Czechoslovakia. By David W. Paul. 1979.

On the Border of War and Peace: Polish Intelligence and Diplomacy in 1937-1939 and the Origins of the Ultra Secret. By Richard A. Woytak. 1979.

Bear and Foxes: The International Relations of the East European States 1965-1969. By Ronald Haly Linden. 1979.

Czechoslovakia: The Heritage of Ages Past. Edited by Ivan Volgyes and Hans Brisch. 1979.

Prima Minister Gyula Andrassy's Influence on Habsburg Foreign Policy. By Janos Decsy. 1979.

Citizens for the Fatherland: Education, Educators, and Pedagogical Ideals in Eighteenth Century Russia. By J. L. Black. 1979.

A History of the "Proletariat": The Emergence of Marxism in the Kingdom of Poland, 1870-1887. By Norman M. Naimark. 1979.

The Slovak Autonomy Movement, 1935-1939: A Study in Unrelenting Nationalism. By Dorothea H. El Mallakh. 1979.

Diplomat in Exile: Francis Pulszky's Political Activities in England, 1849-1860. By Thomas Kabdebo. 1979.

The German Struggle Against the Yugoslav Guerrillas in World War II: German Counter-Insurgency in Yugoslavia, 1941-1943. By Paul N. Hehn. 1979.

The Emergence of the Romanian National State. By Gerald J. Bobango. 1979.

Stewards of the Land: The American Farm School and Modern Greece. By Brenda L. Marder. 1979.

Roman Dmowski: Party, Tactics, Ideology, 1895-1907. By Alvin M. Fountain, II. 1980.

International and Domestic Politics in Greece During the Crimean War. By Jon V. Kofas. 1980.

Fires on the Mountain: The Macedonian Revolutionary Movement and the Kidnapping of Ellen Stone. By Laura Beth Sherman. 1980.

The Modernization of Agriculture: Rural Transformation in Hungary, 1848-1975. Edited by Joseph Held. 1980.

Britain and the War for Yugoslavia, 1940-1943. By Mark C. Wheeler. 1980.

The Turn to the Right: The Ideological Origins and Development of Ukrainian Nationalism, 1919-1929. By Alexander J. Motyl. 1980.

The Maple Leaf and the White Eagle: Canadian-Polish Relations, 1918-1978. By Aloysius Balawyder. 1980.

Antecedents of Revolution: Alexander I and the Polish Congress Kingdom, 1815-1825. By Frank W. Thackeray. 1980.

Blood Libel at Tiszaeszlar. By Andrew Handler. 1980.

Democratic Centralism in Romania: A Study of Local Communist Politics. By Daniel N. Nelson. 1980.

Prelude to Appeasement: East European Central Diplomacy in the Early 1930's. By Lisanne Radice. 1981.

The Soviet Regime in Czechoslovakia. By Zdenek Krystufek. 1981.

School Strikes in Prussian Poland, 1901-1907: The Struggle Over Bilingual Education. By John J. Kulczycki. 1981.

Romantic Nationalism and Liberalism: Joachim Lelewel and the Polish National Idea. By Joan S. Skurnowicz. 1981.

The "Thaw" In Bulgarian Literature. By Atanas Slavov. 1981.

The Political Thought of Thomas G. Masaryk. By roman Szporluk. 1981.

Prussian Poland in the German Empire, 1871-1900. By Richard Blanke. 1981.

The Mazepists: Ukrainian Separatism in the Early Eighteenth Century. By Orest Subtelny. 1981.

The Battle for the Marchlands: The Russo-Polish Campaign of 1920. By Adam Zamoyski. 1981.

Milovan Djilas: A Revolutionary as a Writer. By Dennis Reinhartz. 1981.

The Second Republic: The Disintegration of Post-Munich Czechoslovakia, October 1938-March 1939. By Theodore Prochazka, Sr.

From Trianon to the First Vienna Arbitral Award: The Hungarian Minority in the First Czechoslovak Republic, 1918-1938. By Charles Woyatsek.

Financial Relations of Greece and the Great Powers, 1832-1862. By Jon V. Kofas. 1981.